Macromedia®
Director® 8
Shockwave Studio
Illustrated Complete

Steven M. Johnson

**COURSE
TECHNOLOGY**

THOMSON LEARNING

Australia • Canada • Mexico • Singapore • Spain • United Kingdom • United States

COURSE TECHNOLOGY

THOMSON LEARNING

Macromedia® Director® 8 Shockwave Studio—Illustrated Complete
is published by Course Technology.

Managing Editor:
Nicole Jones Pinard

Product Manager:
Rebecca Berardy

Associate Product Manager:
Emeline Elliot

Editorial Assistant:
Danielle Roy

Production Editor:
Jennifer Goguen

Developmental Editor:
Barbara Waxer

Composition House:
GEX Publishing Services

QA Manuscript Reviewer:
Jeff Schwartz, Ashlee Welz

Text Designer:
Joseph Lee, Black Fish Design

Cover Designer:
Doug Goodman, Doug Goodman Designs

Exciting New Products

Try out Illustrated's New Product Line: Multimedia Tools

Multimedia tools teach students how to create text, graphics, video, animations, and sound, all of which can be incorporated for use in printed materials, Web pages, CD-ROMs, and multimedia presentations.

New Titles

- Adobe Photoshop 6.0—Illustrated Introductory (0-619-04595-7)
- Adobe Photoshop 5.5—Illustrated Introductory (0-7600-6337-0)
- Adobe Illustrator 9.0—Illustrated Introductory (0-619-01750-3)
- Macromedia Director 8 Shockwave Studio—Illustrated Introductory (0-619-01772-4)

- Macromedia Director 8 Shockwave Studio—Illustrated Complete (0-619-05658-4)
- Multimedia Concepts—Illustrated Introductory (0-619-01765-1)
- Macromedia Shockwave 8—Illustrated Essentials (0-619-05656-8)
- Macromedia Fireworks 4—Illustrated Essentials (0-619-05657-6)

Check Out Multimedia Concepts

Multimedia Concepts—Illustrated Introductory, by James E. Shuman, is the quick and visual way to learn cutting-edge multimedia concepts. This book studies the growth of multimedia, has an Internet focus in every unit, includes coverage of computer hardware requirements, and teaches students the principles of multimedia design. This eight-unit book has two hands-on units: Incorporating Multimedia into a Web site and Creating a Multimedia Application Using Macromedia® Director® 8.

A CD-ROM and companion Web site accompany this book and bring the concepts to life! This CD also includes a time-limited trial version of Macromedia® Director® 8 to give students the tools they need to practice creating multimedia movies.

Enhance any Illustrated Text with these Exciting Prducts

Course Technology offers a continuum of solutions to meet your online learning needs. Three Distance Learning solutions enhance your classroom experience: MyCourse.com (hosted by Course Technology), Blackboard, and WebCT.

MyCourse.com is an easily customizable online syllabus and course enhancement tool. This tool adds value to your class by offering brand new content designed to reinforce what you are already teaching. MyCourse.com even allows you to add your own content, hyperlinks, and assignments.

WebCT and Blackboard are course management tools that deliver online content for eighty-five Course Technology titles. This growing list of titles enables instructors the ability to edit and add to any content made available through WebCT and Blackboard. In addition, you can choose what students access. The site is hosted on your school campus, allowing complete control over the information. WebCT and Blackboard offer their own internal communication system, including internal e-mail, Bulletin Boards, and Chat rooms. For more information please contact your Course Technology sales representative.

Create Your Ideal Course Package with CourseKits™

If one book doesn't offer all the coverage you need, create a course package that does. With Course Technology's CourseKits—our mix-and-match approach to selecting texts—you have the freedom to combine products from more than one series. When you choose any two or more Course Technology products for one course, we'll discount the price and package them together so your students can pick up one convenient bundle at the bookstore.

Preface

Welcome to *Macromedia Director 8 Shockwave Studio—Illustrated Complete.* This highly visual book offers users a hands-on introduction to Macromedia® Director® 8 Shockwave Studio and also serves as an excellent reference for future use.

This book is a member of Illustrated's **Multimedia Tools** series. These books teach students how to create text, graphics, video, animations, and sound for use in print publications, CD-ROM products, and Web-based applications. Check out books on Photoshop, Illustrator, and Multimedia Concepts for more multimedia curriculum.

▶ Organization and Coverage

This text is organized into three sections as illustrated by the brightly colored tabs on the sides of the pages. The first section, Units A–L, cover basic to advanced skills for Macromedia® Director® 8. The next section includes two introductory units on Macromedia® Fireworks® 4, which is followed by two introductory units on Macromedia® Shockwave® 8.

▶ About this Approach

What makes the Illustrated approach so effective at teaching software skills? It's quite simple. Each skill is presented on two facing pages, with the step-by-step instructions on the left page, and large screen illustrations on the right. Students can focus on a single skill without having to turn the page. This unique design makes information extremely accessible and easy to absorb, and provides a great reference for after the course is over. This hands-on approach also makes it ideal for both self-paced or instructor-led classes.

Each lesson, or "information display," contains the following elements:

Each 2-page spread focuses on a single skill.

Clear step-by-step directions explain how to complete the specific task, with what students are to type in green. When students follow the numbered steps, they quickly learn how each procedure is performed and what the results will be.

Concise text that introduces the basic principles discussed in the lesson. Procedures are easier to learn when concepts fit into a framework.

Unit J
Director 8

Changing Tweenable Sprite Properties

After you create and position all the keyframes that you will need within a sprite, you adjust the sprite's initial properties for the tween. You select the first keyframe (in most cases, the first frame) and change one or more tweenable sprite properties, such as position, size, background and foreground color, ink, blend, skew, and rotation. You can change tweenable sprite properties directly on the Stage, by using the Sprite tab in the Property Inspector, or by using the Sprite toolbar in the Score. After you adjust the tweenable sprite properties for the first keyframe, select the next keyframe within the sprite and change its tweenable properties. Director generates all the frames between this keyframe and the first one. If you need to refine tweening in a sprite, you can insert additional keyframes and change properties to create a smoother path, or add frames between keyframes to add a gradual transition. You can tween one or more sprite properties at the same time, using the Sprite Tweening dialog box. ✐ Jean changes tweenable properties of the Space sprite to create an animation.

Steps

1. Click the keyframe in **frame 1** in channel 1
   The keyframe in frame 1 of the Space sprite is selected. A sprite's first frame is a keyframe.

2. Click the **Stage window**, then click the **Sprite tab** in the Property Inspector
   The Sprite tab in the Property Inspector appears, as shown in Figure J-6.

3. Click the **Blend list arrow** ▼, then click **10**
   The blend of the transparent background for the Space sprite is changed to 10%, almost transparent.

4. Click the keyframe in **frame 7** in channel 1, click the **Blend list arrow** ▼, then click **30**
   The Space sprite transparency blend percentage is changed to 30%.

5. Click the keyframe in **frame 14** in channel 1, click the **Blend list arrow** ▼, then click **60**
   The Space sprite transparency blend percentage is changed to 60%.

6. Click the keyframe in **frame 21** in channel 1, click the **Blend list arrow** ▼, then click **80**
   The Space sprite transparency blend percentage is changed to 80%.

7. Click **Modify** on the menu bar, point to **Sprite**, then click **Tweening**
   The Sprite Tweening dialog box appears, as shown in Figure J-7. In order for tweening to work, you need to make sure the properties you want tweened are selected. In this case, the Blend check box is selected by default.

8. Click **OK**, then click the **Lock button** 🔒 in the Sprite tab of the Property Inspector
   The Space background sprite is locked to make sure it doesn't move.

Trouble?
If the movie loops, click Control on the menu bar, click Control Panel, then click Loop Playback to deselect it.

9. Click the **Rewind button** ◄◄ on the toolbar, then click the **Play button** ► on the toolbar
   The movie plays the Space animation, showing the background going from black to a star field.

▶ **DIRECTOR J-6   CREATING ANIMATION**

Hints as well as trouble-shooting advice, right where you need it – next to the step itself.

Every lesson features large-size, full-color representations of what the students' screen should look like after completing the numbered steps.

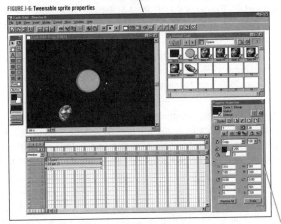

FIGURE J-6: Tweenable sprite properties

Tweenable sprite properties

FIGURE J-7: Sprite Tweening dialog box

Sprite tweenable properties

CLUES TO USE

Creating effects using tweenable properties

You can create special effects by changing the tweenable sprite properties. You can create the illusion of a sprite rotating in 3D by changing its skew angle by 90 degrees or more, or create a fade out or fade in effect by changing the blend property of a sprite from a high value to a low value (fade out), or from a low value to a high value (fade in). You can also create a zoom out or zoom in effect by changing the size of a sprite from large to small (zoom out) or from small to large (zoom in).

Director 8

CREATING ANIMATION   DIRECTOR J-7

Clues to Use boxes provide concise information that either expands on one component of the major lesson skill or describes an independent task that is in some way related to the major lesson skill.

The page numbers are designed like a road map. J indicates the tenth unit, and 7 indicates the page within the unit.

Additional Features

The two-page lesson format featured in this book provides the new user with a powerful learning experience. Additionally, this book contains the following features:

▶ **Trial Software**

At the back of this book, you will find a CD-ROM containing a trial version of Macromedia® Director® 8 Shockwave Studio and Macromedia® Fireworks® 4 for both Macintosh and Windows operating systems. Students can use this software to gain additional practice away from the classroom. *Note:* The trial software will cease operating after a limited number of days. Check the Read Me on the CD-ROM for more information.

▶ **Dual Platform**

The units in this book can be completed either on a Macintosh or on a Windows platform. The steps are written for both operating systems, with Mac and PC tips and trouble-shooting advice in the margin.

▶ **Real-World Case**

The case study used throughout the textbook, a fictitious company called SpaceWorks, is designed to be "real-world" in nature and introduces the kinds of activities that students will encounter when working with Director. With a real-world case, the process of solving problems will be more meaningful to students.

▶ **End-of-Unit Material**

Each unit concludes with a Concepts Review that tests students' understanding of what they learned in the unit. The Concepts Review is followed by a Skills Review, which provides students with additional hands-on practice of the skills. The Skills Review is followed by Independent Challenges, which pose case problems for students to solve. At least one Independent Challenge in each unit asks students to use the World Wide Web to solve the problem as indicated by a Web Work icon. The Visual Workshops that follow the Independent Challenges help students develop critical thinking skills. Students are shown completed Web pages or screens and are asked to recreate them from scratch.

Instructor's Resource Kit

The Instructor's Resource Kit is Course Technology's way of putting the resources and information needed to teach and learn effectively into your hands. With an integrated array of teaching and learning tools that offers you and your students a broad range of technology-based instructional options, we believe this kit represents the highest quality and most cutting edge resources available to instructors today. Many of these resources are available at **www.course.com**. The resources available with this book are:

Course Test Manager Designed by Course Technology, this Windows-based software helps you design, administer, and print tests and pre-tests. A full-featured program, Course Test Manager also has an online testing component that allows students to take tests at the computer and have their exams automatically graded.

Instructor's Manual Available as an electronic file, the Instructor's Manual is quality-assurance tested and includes unit overviews, detailed lecture topics for each unit with teaching tips, an Upgrader's Guide, solutions to all lessons and end-of-unit material, and extra Independent Challenges. The Instructor's Manual is available on the Instructor's Resource Kit CD-ROM or you can download it from **www.course.com**.

Course Faculty Online Companion You can browse this textbook's password-protected site to obtain the Instructor's Manual, Solution Files, Project Files, and any updates to the text. Contact your Customer Service Representative for the site address and password.

Project Files Project Files contain all of the data that students will use to complete the lessons and end-of-unit material. A Readme file includes instructions for using the files. Adopters of this text are granted the right to install the Project Files on any standalone computer or network. The Project Files are available on the Instructor's Resource Kit CD-ROM, the Review Pack, and can also be downloaded from **www.course.com**.

Solution Files Solution Files contain every file students are asked to create or modify in the lessons and end-of-unit material. A Help file on the Instructor's Resource Kit includes information for using the Solution Files.

Figure Files The figures in the text are provided on the Instructor's Resourse Kit CD to help you illustrate key topics or concepts. You can create traditional overhead transparencies by printing the figure files. Or you can create electronic slide shows by using the figures in a presentation program such as PowerPoint.

Student Online Companion This book features its own Online Companion where students can go to access Web sites that will help them complete the Web Work Independent Challenges. Because the Web is constantly changing, the Student Online Companion will provide the reader with current updates regarding links referenced in the book.

Brief Contents

Contents

Director 8

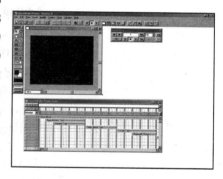

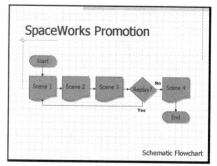

SpaceWorks Promotion

Schematic Flowchart

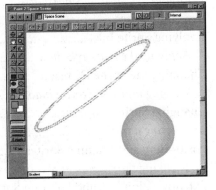

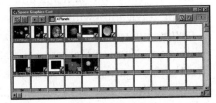

Contents

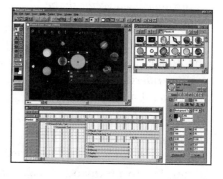

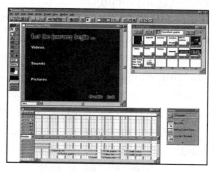

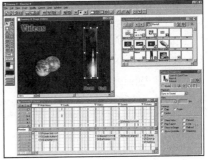

Preparing and Delivering Movies   DIRECTOR H-1

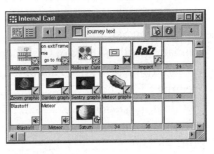

Managing Color   DIRECTOR I-1

Contents

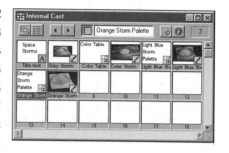

Creating Animation

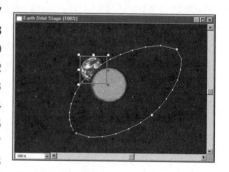

Attaching Behaviors

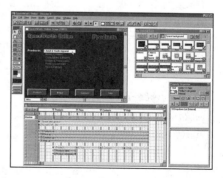

Writing Scripts with Lingo   DIRECTOR L-1

Shockwave 8

Getting Started with Shockwave 8   SHOCKWAVE A-1

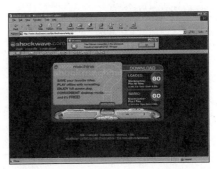

Contents

Fireworks 4

Read This Before You Begin

Project Files

To complete the lessons and end-of-unit material in this book, students need to obtain the necessary project files. Please refer to the instructions on the front inside cover for various methods of getting these files. Once obtained, the user selects where to store the files, such as to the hard disk drive, network server, or Zip disk. Depending on where you store the files, you might need to relink any external files, such as a video clip, associated with a Director project file. When you open a project file, Director will ask you the location of the external file.

Director Settings

Each time you start Director, the program remembers previous settings, such as program preferences, open or closed windows, and Control Panel options, to name a few. When you start Director, your initial screen might look different than the ones in this book. For the purposes of this book, make sure the following settings in Director are in place before you start each unit:

- Toolbar and Tool Palette on the Windows menu are turned on.

- Stage window, Score window, Cast window, and Property Inspector on the Windows menu are turned on.

- Cast window is set to Thumbnail view; click the Cast View Style button in the Cast window, if necessary.

- Loop Playback on the Control menu is turned off.

- Tempo Mode and Actual Tempo Mode on the Control Panel are set to fps (frames per second).

- Show Info on Sprite Overlay submenu on the View menu is turned off.

- Snap to Grid and Snap to Guide on the Guides and Grid tab in the Property Inspector are turned on.

- On the Guides and Grid tab in the Property Inspector—Guide: Visible is turned on, and Grid: Visible is turned off.

Director for Windows and Macintosh

This book is written for the Windows version and the Macintosh version of Macromedia Director 8 Shockwave Studio. Both versions of the software are virtually the same, but there are a few platform differences. When there are differences between the two versions of the software, steps written specifically for the Windows version end with the notation (Win) and steps for the Macintosh version end with the notation (Mac). In instances where the lessons are split between the two operating systems, a line divides the page and is accompanied by Mac and Win icons.

Free Trial Software

Included on a CD with this book is the Macromedia® Director® 8 Shockwave Studio and Macromedia® Fireworks® 4 Trial Software. The trial software is for students' use away from the classroom, and it should not be used in a classroom lab because it will expire after a limited number of days. Please check the CD for more information.

Installation instructions for the CD-ROM are included below.

Windows: Insert the CD in the CD-ROM drive, open Windows Explorer, select the CD-ROM drive, double-click director8trial.exe or fireworks4-TBYB.exe in the right pane of Windows Explorer, then follow the on-screen instructions to complete the installation.

Macintosh: Insert the CD in the CD-ROM drive, double-click the CD icon titled Director 8 Tryout, double-click the VISE™ Fireworks 4 Trial Installer icon or the StuffIt™ Install D8Trial.sea icon, then follow the on-screen instructions to complete the installation.

Getting
Started with Director 8

Objectives

- ► **Understand Director basics**
- ► **Start Director 8**
- ► **View the Director window**
- ► **Open and save a movie**
- ► **Work with Director windows**
- ► **View the score**
- ► **Play a movie**
- ► **Get Help**
- ► **Close a movie and exit Director**

Macromedia Director 8 Shockwave Studio is a multimedia program that lets you easily create animations, movies, interactive training, marketing presentations, technical simulations, and multiuser games. This unit introduces you to basic Director skills. First, you'll learn how to start Director and identify Director window elements. Then, you'll learn how to open and save a movie, how to move around the different Director windows, and how to get help. Finally, you'll learn how to play and close a movie and exit Director. ◢── Jean Young is an instructional designer at SpaceWorks Interactive, a small educational game company dedicated to teaching people about space exploration and technology. She wants to use her instructional design background and Director to create visual presentations and interactive training. As a novice multimedia developer, Jean gets started learning Director basics.

Unit A
Director 8

Understanding Director Basics

Director 8 is a software program that allows you to create your own software. It's often referred to as an **authoring tool** or a **development platform**. Director allows you to use a combination of graphics, images, digital video, sound, text, and animation, known as **multimedia**, and includes user feedback and navigation, known as **interactivity**, to develop virtually any type of software you want to deliver. Thus, the term **interactive multimedia** is often applied to the software produced with Director. With Director, you can create fully self-contained, self-running interactive multimedia software for distribution on CD-ROM or over the Internet on the World Wide Web, or Web. Since Director is available in both Macintosh and Windows versions, it's relatively easy to produce software that runs on both platforms. Jean is new to the product and the process of developing software, so she wants to learn the basic steps to developing interactive multimedia software with Director, as shown in Figure A-1, and listed below.

Step 1: Plan the project carefully
Creating a movie can take a long time; it's worth the effort to plan carefully. You need to figure out the goal of the project, the look and feel of your production, its length and size, how it will interact with the viewer, and how it will be distributed and for whom.

Step 2: Assemble the media elements in the Cast
Media elements include graphics, images, digital videos, animations, sounds, and text. You can create new media elements in Director or import ones that have already been developed and store them in the **Cast**. Director provides several tools for creating elements, including a paint tool and text creation tools. You can import elements from a variety of sources.

Step 3: Position the media elements on the Stage and sequence them in the Score
You use the Stage to create the look and feel for your production; you use the Stage and Score together to arrange the media elements from the Cast in space and time. The **Stage** is the viewing area for the visual elements of a Director movie, and the Score is the timeline you use to organize what happens when and where.

Step 4: Add interactive behaviors and scripting
If you want, you can add interactive behaviors and scripting to your production. Interactive behaviors can include buttons, arrows, or other navigation elements that move the viewer to different parts of the movie or the Internet. **Scripting** allows you to extend the functionality of your movie beyond what is possible using the Stage and Score. In Director, scripts are written in Lingo, a Director-specific programming language. To help you get started scripting and save you some time, Director comes with ready-made scripts called **behaviors**.

Step 5: Preview and test the movie with the Control Panel
After you create your movie, you use the Control Panel to preview and test the movie to make sure it runs the way you want it to. The Control Panel allows you to play, stop, rewind, and step through your movie. As needed, make refinements and adjustments in the Score.

Step 6: Package the movie as a stand-alone projector file, or save the movie as a Shockwave file for use over the Internet
When the movie runs the way you want it to, you can package your production as a stand-alone projector movie that viewers can run from a CD-ROM or hard drive. When you distribute your movie in projector form, viewers can run the movie without using Director. Viewers can't change the movies; they can only play them back. Or, you can save your production as a Shockwave movie that viewers can play back on a Web page, using a Web browser.

FIGURE A-1: Developing interactive software with Director

Step 1: Plan the project

Step 2: Assemble the media elements in the Cast

Step 6: Package or save the movie

Step 5: Preview and test the movie with the Control Panel

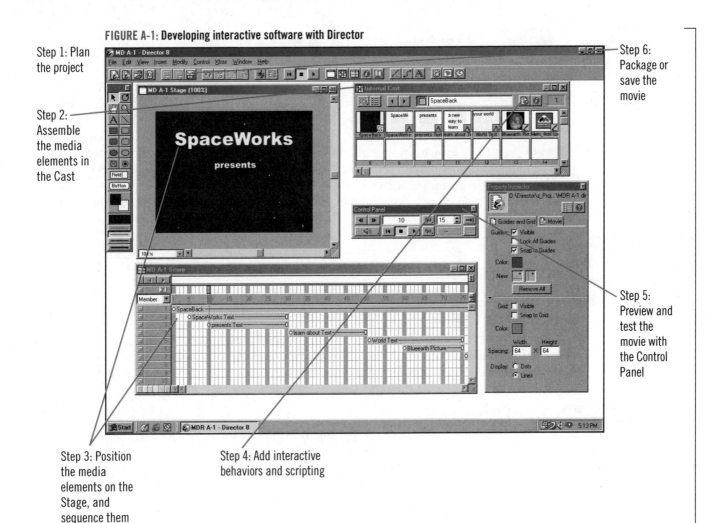

Step 3: Position the media elements on the Stage, and sequence them in the Score

Step 4: Add interactive behaviors and scripting

CLUES TO USE

Royalty-free distribution

All software created with Director can be freely sold and distributed, without having to pay Macromedia a royalty for the privilege. That may be something you take for granted, but some development platforms actually have licensing agreements stipulating that you have to pay in order to market anything created with the product. Macromedia doesn't require you to pay any fees, but they do ask that you place a special "Made with Macromedia" logo, shown in Figure A-2, on your software packaging. The logo is included with the project files that accompany this book.

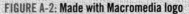

FIGURE A-2: Made with Macromedia logo

Director 8

Director 8

Starting Director

If Director is not yet installed on your computer, you must first install it according to the instructions that come with the program. After Director is installed, you can start the program in several ways, depending on the platform you are using. When you start Director, the computer displays a splash screen and then the Director window. Director displays a set of blank windows ready for you to create a new **file**, which is a collection of information stored together as an individual unit. A file in Director is called a **movie**. Jean can develop interactive multimedia software using Director on the Windows or Macintosh platform, but she will need to learn some aspects of each version in order to create final software for distribution on both Windows and Macintosh computers.

Steps

WIN

1. Click the **Start button** on the taskbar

The Start button is on the left side of the taskbar and is used to start programs on your computer.

2. Point to **Programs**, then point to **Macromedia Director 8**

The Programs menu lists all the programs, including Macromedia Director, that are installed on your computer, as shown in Figure A-3. Your Programs menu might look different, depending on the programs you have installed.

Trouble?

If Director doesn't open, check the software documentation for the required minimum configuration of hardware and operating system software.

3. Click **Director 8**

The Director program opens, displaying the work area for a new file.

MAC

1. Double-click the **hard drive icon**

The Start button is on the left side of the taskbar and is used to start programs on your computer.

2. Double-click the **Macromedia Director folder**

The Macromedia Director folder opens, displaying the program icon and associated files that come with the product, as shown in Figure A-4.

3. Double-click the **Director 8 program icon**

The Director program opens, displaying the work area for a new file.

FIGURE A-3: Starting Director (Windows)

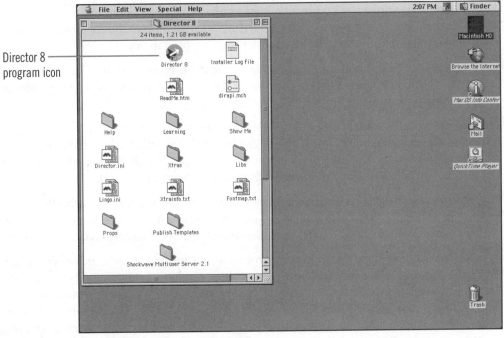

Macromedia Director 8 folder

Director 8 program

Your list of available programs might vary

FIGURE A-4: Starting Director (Macintosh)

Director 8 program icon

Starting Director and opening a movie

You can start Director and open a movie at the same time. Simply double-click the Director file icon in Windows Explorer (Win) or in a Macintosh folder (Mac). You can identify a Director movie in Windows Explorer by the .dir file extension (Win), or in a Macintosh folder by the type of file icon 🔲 (Mac). A **file extension** is a three-letter extension at the end of a filename that identifies the file type for the operating

system. You will not see a document's file extension in Windows Explorer if your system is set up to hide it. If you want to show file extensions in Windows, open My Computer, click View on the menu bar, click Folder Options, click the View tab, click the Hide file extensions for known file types check box to deselect it, then click OK. The Macintosh doesn't use file extensions.

Director 8

Viewing the Director Window

When you start Director, five main windows of varying sizes appear in the Director window: the Stage, the Score, the Cast, the Property Inspector, and the Control Panel. Depending on your installation, not all of these windows may appear, or additional ones may be visible. The windows are placed in different locations, depending on the size of your monitor. If you do not see the Control Panel, it may be behind the larger Score and Stage windows, or it may be closed. You'll do the bulk of your work in Director with these five windows. If you can't see the window you want to use, you can use the Window menu to display it. Jean takes some time to familiarize herself with the elements of the Director window. Refer to your screen and Figure A-5 as you locate the elements of the Director window described below.

Details

Trouble?
The size and location of your windows might differ.

 The program window **title bar** displays the filename of the open file (the name doesn't appear on your title bar, because the file has not been named yet) and the program name, Director 8. The title bar also contains a Close button and resizing buttons.

 A **menu** is a list of commands that you use to accomplish certain tasks. You've already used the Start menu to open Director. A **command** is a directive that accesses a feature of a program. Director has its own set of menus, which are located on the menu bar along the top of the program window.

 The **menu bar** organizes commands into groups of related operations. Each group is listed under the name of the menu, such as "File" or "Help." You can choose a menu command by clicking it. See Table A-1 for examples of items on a typical menu.

 The **toolbar** contains buttons for the most frequently used commands. Clicking a button on a toolbar is often faster than clicking a menu and then clicking a command. When you position the mouse pointer over a button, a **ScreenTip** appears.

 The **Tool palette** contains a set of tools you can use to create shapes, such as lines, rectangles, rounded rectangles, and ellipses, and to create simple buttons, such as radio, check box, and command buttons. You can fill shapes with a color, pattern, or custom tile. The shapes and buttons you create in Director are saved as media elements in the Cast.

 The **Stage window** title bar displays the movie name and the zoom factor. Notice that the default values are Untitled Stage (100%). The Stage is the visible portion of a movie, on which you determine where your media elements appear. You can define the properties of your Stage, such as its size and color.

 The **Cast window** is the storage area that contains your media elements, such as graphics, images, digital videos, sounds, animations, text, color palettes, film loops, and scripts. The media elements in the Cast window are called **cast members**. In the Cast window you can view your cast members as a list or as thumbnails. You can create your own cast members, and you can import existing media to include in your cast. You can also open or create Cast windows to organize sets of cast members. When you open Director with a new movie, the Cast window is called **Internal Cast**.

 The **Score window** organizes and controls media elements over a linear timeline, in rows called **channels** and in columns called **frames**. The Score displays a movie's timeline and monitors the playback frame by frame. A frame represents a single point in a movie. The Score includes special channels that control the movie's tempo, sound, transitions, and color palettes.

 The **Property Inspector** provides a convenient way to view and change attributes of any selected object or multiple objects in your movie. Once you select an object, relevant category tabs and associated fields for it appear on the Property Inspector.

 The **Control Panel** provides VCR-type control over the playback of your movie, including Rewind, Stop, and Play buttons. You can also modify volume, tempo, and playback settings.

FIGURE A-5: Director window

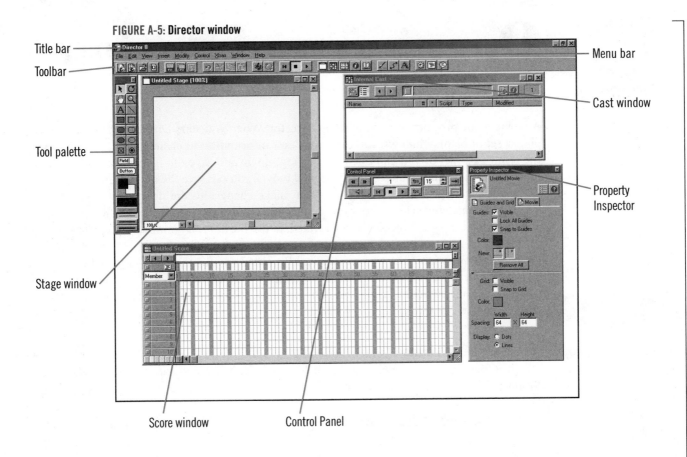

Title bar · Toolbar · Tool palette · Stage window · Score window · Control Panel · Menu bar · Cast window · Property Inspector

TABLE A-1: Typical items on a menu

item	description	example
Dimmed command	A menu command that is not currently available	Undo Ctrl+Z
Ellipsis	Indicates that this menu command opens a dialog box that allows you to select from several options	Save As...
Triangle	Indicates that this menu command opens a cascading menu containing an additional list of menu commands	Zoom ▶
Keyboard shortcut	An alternative to using the mouse for executing a menu command	Paste Ctrl+V
Underlined letter	Pressing the underlined letter while also pressing [Alt] (Win) or [Command] (Mac) executes the menu command	Print Ctrl+P

Director 8

Opening and Saving a Movie

A movie is the product you create using Director. When you start Director, the program displays a set of blank windows. You can insert new information to create a new movie and save the result as a file, or you can open an existing movie and save the file with any changes. To prevent any accidental changes to the original movie, you can save the movie with a new name. This makes a copy of the movie, so you can make changes to the new movie and leave the original file unaltered. Throughout this book, you will be instructed to open a file from a drive and folder where your Project Files are located, to use the Save As command to create a copy of the file with a new name, and then to modify the new file by following the lesson steps. Saving the files with new names keeps your original Project Files intact, in case you need to start the lesson over or wish to repeat an exercise. ✐ Jean wants to open an existing Director movie to learn more about using Director windows. She opens an existing movie and saves it with a new name before making any changes to it.

QuickTip

To open Director 5, 6, and 7 movies, click Xtras on the menu bar, click Update Movies, select one of the Action options, select one of the Backup Folder options, click OK, select the movies and casts you want to update, then click Update.

QuickTip

Use the List View 🏭 or Details View 📄 button (Win) in the Open and Save As dialog boxes to display the list of files and folders with more or less information. Details View on the Macintosh is in the operating system.

QuickTip

To open the last saved version of your current movie, click File on the menu bar, then click Revert.

1. Click the **Open button** 📄 on the toolbar
   The Open dialog box opens. In this dialog box, you locate and choose the file you wish to open. The file Jean wants to open is stored in your Project Files.

2. Click the **Look in list arrow**, then click the drive and folder where your Project Files are located
   A file appears in the file list, as shown in Figure A-6. You can select a file in the file list or type the name of the file you want in the File name text box.

3. In the file list, click **MD A-1**, then click **Open**
   The MD A-1 file opens.

4. Click **File** on the menu bar, then click **Save As**
   The Save Movie dialog box opens, as shown in Figure A-7. The Save As command allows you to save an existing document under a new name and also in a different folder or drive location.

5. Make sure that the **Save in list box** displays the folder where your Project Files are located

6. In Windows, if **MD A-1** is not already selected, click in the **File name text box**, then select the entire filename by dragging the mouse pointer over it
   In Director, as in most other Windows programs, you must select text in order to modify it. When you **select** text, the selection appears **highlighted** (white text on a dark background) to indicate that it has been selected. Any action you now take will be performed on the selected text.

7. Type **SpaceWorks Promo** as the new filename
   The text you type replaces the selected text. It's a good idea to use descriptive names for your files so you can identify their contents more easily.

8. Click **Save**
   The file is saved under the new name, SpaceWorks Promo, in the same folder and drive location as the MD A-1 file. The original MD A-1 file automatically closes, and the new filename appears in the title bar of the Director, Score, and Stage windows.

FIGURE A-6: Open dialog box

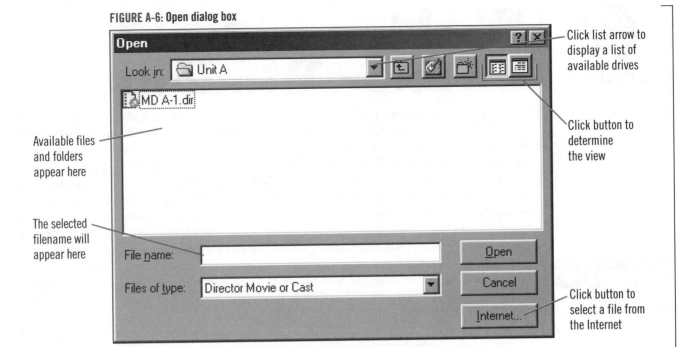

Available files and folders appear here

The selected filename will appear here

Click list arrow to display a list of available drives

Click button to determine the view

Click button to select a file from the Internet

FIGURE A-7: Save Movie dialog box

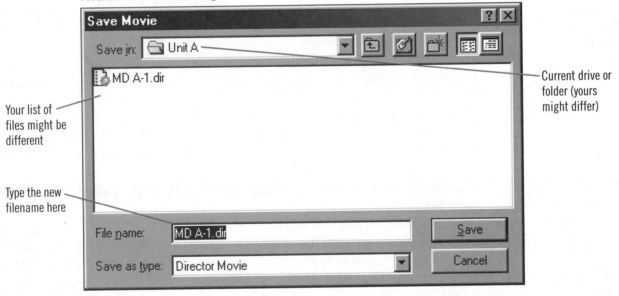

Your list of files might be different

Type the new filename here

Current drive or folder (yours might differ)

Director 8

CLUES TO USE

About saving files

Until you save them, the movies you create are stored in the computer's random access memory (RAM). **RAM** is a temporary storage space that is erased when the computer is turned off. To store a document permanently, you must save it as a file to a disk. You can save files to a **floppy disk** or other **removable media** that you insert into the disk drive of your computer (usually drive A, B, D, or E [Win] or an icon [Mac]), to

a **hard disk**, which is built into the computer (usually drive C [Win] or an icon [Mac]), or to a **server**, which is a computer on a network. This book assumes that you will save all of your files to your Project Files, which your instructor has provided to you. Windows and Macintosh let you save files using names that have up to 255 characters, including spaces.

Unit A

Director 8

Working with Director Windows

With Director you work with several windows at one time. This means that the Director window can easily become cluttered with open windows. To organize the Director window, sometimes it is necessary to change the size of a window, move it to a different location, or close it altogether. Each window, except the Control Panel, is surrounded by a standard border that you can drag to change the size of the window. The Control Panel is a **windoid**, a window that can be moved but not resized. Each window has one or more buttons in the upper-right corner that allow you to close it or change its size. In addition to using the resizing buttons, you can also drag the mouse pointer to resize a window. Table A-2 shows the different mouse pointer shapes that appear when resizing windows. To open a window, you can use the Windows menu or a shortcut key. Jean doesn't see the Control Panel in her Director window, so she opens it and moves it out of the way. She also resizes the Stage and Score windows to make more room to see other windows.

Steps 1 2 3 4

QuickTip

You can use keyboard shortcuts located on the right side of the Windows menu to quickly open and close Director windows; for the Control Panel window, press [Ctrl][2] (Win) or [Command][2] (Mac).

1. Click **Window** on the menu bar

The Window menu appears, displaying the available View commands, as shown in Figure A-8. On a menu, a **check mark** identifies a feature that is currently selected (that is, the feature is enabled or on). To disable (turn off) the feature, you click the command again to remove the check mark. A menu can contain several checkmarked features. A **bullet mark** also indicates that an option is enabled, but a menu can contain only one bullet-marked feature per menu section. To disable a command with a bullet mark next to it, you must select a different bullet option on the menu in the section.

2. On the Window menu, click **Control Panel**, if turned off (no check mark)

The Control Panel opens and appears in front of the other Director windows. The Control Panel window is active, unlike other Director windows.

3. Click the **title bar** on the Cast window

The Cast window is now **active** (the color of the title bar changes from gray to blue); this means that any actions you perform will take place in this window. At times, you may want to close a window.

QuickTip

You can use buttons on the toolbar to quickly open and close many Director windows; for the Property Inspector window, click the Property Inspector button to toggle the window open and closed.

4. Click **File** on the menu bar, click **Close**, then click the **Close button** in the Property Inspector window

The Cast and Property Inspector windows no longer appear in the Director window. When you close a window, you can open the window again at any time. When you reopen a window, it appears in the same position in which it was last closed. You'll open these windows again later.

5. Position the **mouse pointer** on the Control Panel window title bar, then click and drag the **title bar** to an empty area of the Director window

The window moves to a new location.

6. Position the mouse pointer on the lower-right corner of the **Stage window** until the pointer changes to ⬊, then drag the **border** to the right to expand the window, as shown in Figure A-9

The window is now resized equally on each side. You can also resize a window's height or width by dragging any border.

QuickTip

You can also double-click the title bar of a window to switch between maximizing and restoring the size of a window.

7. Click the **Maximize button** ▫ in the Stage window

The Stage window takes up the entire screen. Notice that the Control Panel window is still visible.

8. Click the **Restore button** ▣ in the Stage window

The **Restore button** returns a window to its previous size. The Restore button only appears when a window is maximized.

FIGURE A-8: Window menu

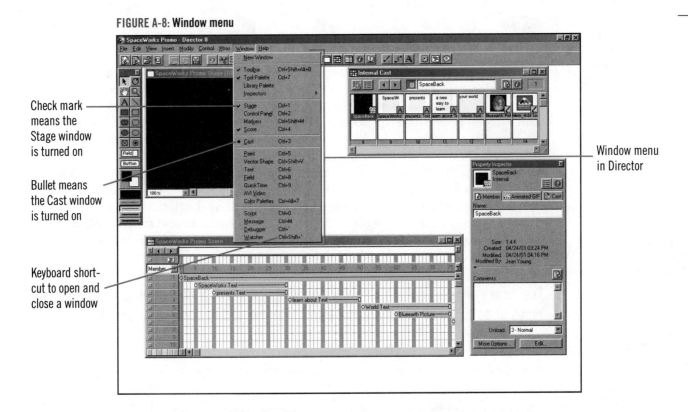

Check mark means the Stage window is turned on

Bullet means the Cast window is turned on

Keyboard short-cut to open and close a window

Window menu in Director

FIGURE A-9: Director window

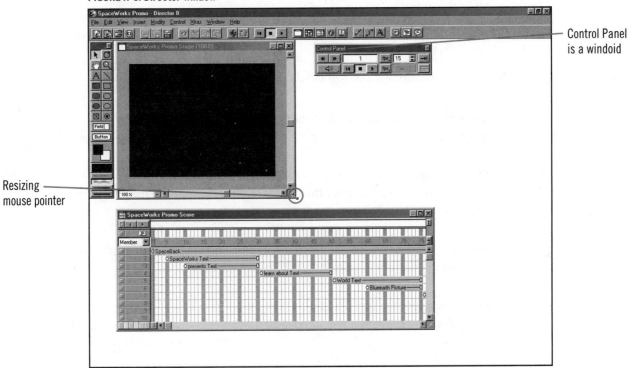

Control Panel is a windoid

Resizing mouse pointer

TABLE A-2: Mouse pointer shapes that appear when resizing windows

mouse pointer shape	use to
↔	Drag the right or left edge of a window to change its width
↕	Drag the top or bottom edge of a window to change its height
↖ or ↗	Drag any corner of a window to proportionally change its size

Director 8

Viewing the Score

While the movie is displayed in the Stage window, the Cast window stores the media elements, or cast members that play in the movie. The Score window is where you instruct the cast members where to appear on the stage, what to do, and where to exit, as shown in Figure A-10. The Score window resembles a spreadsheet with lots of individual cells divided into rows and columns. The rows are used as channels; the columns are used as frames. Each column has a number associated with it; they are marked off in shaded, five-column intervals, and each channel begins with either a number or a distinctive icon, called a **marker**. When you first view the Score window, all the channels might not be visible. The upper channels are called the **effects channels**. You can display and hide the effects channels using the Hide/Show Effects Channels arrows on the right side of the window.  Jean takes some time to familiarize herself with the elements of the Score window. Refer to your screen and Figure A-11 as you locate the elements of the Score window described below.

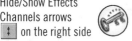

The Score window contains seven channel types, each designed to hold different types of data. These channels and other features are described below.

 The **tempo channel** is used to adjust the speed, or time, of the movie as it plays. The tempo determines how many frames per second are displayed in the movie.

 The **palette channel** sets the available colors for the movie.

 The **transition channel** allows you to set screen transitions, such as fades, wipes, dissolves, and zooms.

 The two **sound channels** are used to add music, sound effects, and voice-overs.

 The **behavior channel**, or **script channel**, provides a place to write frame scripts. **Frame scripts** provide one way to add interactivity and extended functionality to a movie.

 The **frame channel**, or **timeline**, is the shaded channel that contains the numbers 5, 10, 15, 20, and so on. These numbers identify the frame number. An individual frame represents a single point in a movie.

 The **playback head** is the object in the frame channel that moves through the Score, indicating the frame that is currently displayed on the Stage.

The **sprite channels** are the numbered channels at the bottom of the Score window. You use these channels to assemble and synchronize all the cast members in the Cast window. A **sprite** is a representation of a cast member that has been placed on the Stage or in the Score. Director provides 1000 available sprite channels.

FIGURE A-10: Cast, Score, and Stage interaction

Cast

Score

Stage

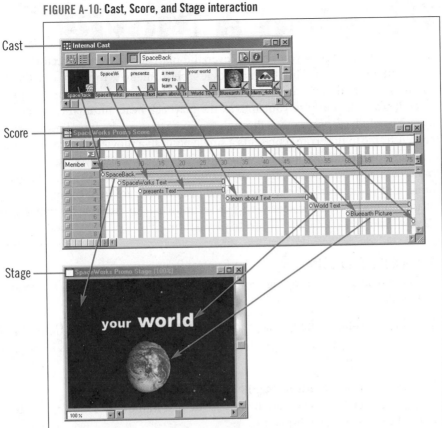

FIGURE A-11: Score window

Tempo channel

Palette channel

Transition channel

Sound channels

Behavior channel

Sprite channels

Click arrows to
hide or show
Effects channels

Playback head

Click button
to display
Zoom menu

Sprite · Cell · Frame · Frame channel (Timeline)

CLUES TO USE

Understanding the playback head and channels

As Director plays a movie, the playback head moves from left to right across the frame channel in the Score window. As the playback head enters a frame, Director draws the sprites (representations of cast members) that it finds in the sprite channels for that frame. When the playback head moves to another frame, Director redraws the stage with the sprites in the frames it enters. When sprites change or move from frame to frame, animation effects are created. When drawing each frame on the stage, Director draws the contents of each sprite channel starting with channel 1, and the remaining channels overdraw the lower-numbered channels wherever they might overlap. As a result, the highest-numbered sprite will always be visible, and the lower-numbered sprites will be visible only if no higher-numbered sprite appears at the same location. For this reason, the background image is usually kept in sprite channel 1, the lowest-numbered sprite.

Director 8

Playing a Movie

The Control Panel gives you control over the playback of your Director movie and displays important information about your movie's performance. You can use the buttons on the Control Panel, as described in Table A-3, to play a movie or to monitor the speed, or **tempo**, at which it plays. As you play your movie, the playback head automatically moves through your Score. The playback head moves through the Score to show the frame currently displayed on the Stage. A frame in the Score represents a single point in a movie; it is similar in theory to a frame in a traditional celluloid film. To go to a specific frame number, you can enter a number in the frame counter. You can also click any frame in the Score to move the playback head to that frame, and you can drag the playback head backward or forward through frames. You can also set the number of frames displayed per second (fps) to control the movie's playback speed. Jean uses the Control Panel to play a movie.

QuickTip

You can also access many of the same commands on the Control Panel using the Control menu.

1. Click the **Play button** ▶ on the Control Panel

The movie plays on the Stage, and the playback head moves from frame to frame through the Score.

2. Before the end of the movie, click the **Stop button** ■ on the Control Panel

The movie stops in the Stage window, and the playback head stops in the Score window, as shown in Figure A-12.

QuickTip

The Play, Stop, and Rewind buttons are also available on the main toolbar in Director.

3. Click the **Rewind button** ◄◄ on the Control Panel

The playback head moves all the way to the first frame of the movie, and the frame number on the Control Panel displays 1.

4. Click the **Step Forward button** ▮▶ on the Control Panel 10 times

The playback head in the Score window moves forward one frame at a time, the movie in the Stage window plays forward, and the frame number in the Control Panel increases by one each time you click the button.

5. Click the **Step Backward button** ◀▮ on the Control Panel 6 times

The playback head moves back one frame at a time, the movie in the Stage window plays backward, and the frame number in the Control Panel decreases by one each time you click the button.

6. Click **number 1** on the frame channel in the Score window

The playback head moves to frame 1. Notice that the Score and Control Panel windows also display frame 1 settings.

Controlling and monitoring tempo in the Control Panel

Tempo mode displays the playback rate that Director is currently attempting to achieve. If you have specified a tempo in the Score's tempo channel, it will be displayed here; otherwise, Director's default of 15 **frames per second (fps)** will be displayed. Click the Tempo Mode button [fps] on the Control Panel to reveal the **seconds per frame (spf)**. The spf rate is a little more accurate, since it times a frame's duration right down to the millisecond—but unless you need the accuracy, the distinction is really a matter of taste. **Actual Tempo** documents the real speed of playback.

It's often enlightening to compare and contrast the number displayed here with the set tempo above it. You can click the Actual Tempo Mode button [fps] on the Control Panel to display three additional modes: Seconds Per Frame, Running Total, and Estimated Total. Running Total calculates the total time elapsed since the beginning of your movie, and Estimated Total does the same thing, but with a little more accuracy. Director will use the last setting change you made the next time you create a new movie or open an existing movie.

FIGURE A-12: **Control Panel**

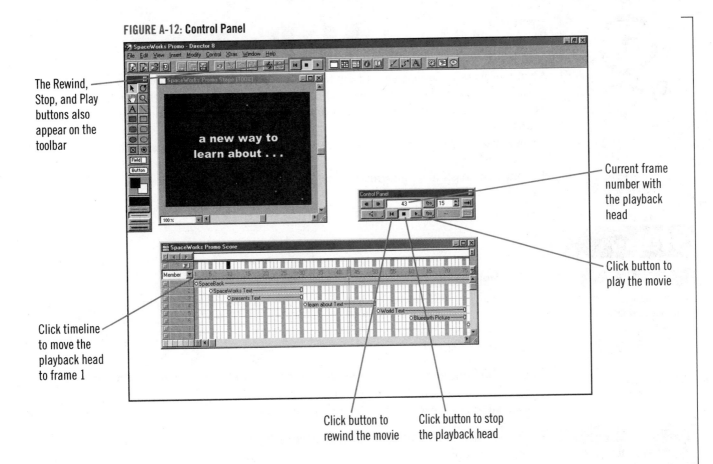

The Rewind, Stop, and Play buttons also appear on the toolbar

a new way to learn about . . .

Click timeline to move the playback head to frame 1

Current frame number with the playback head

Click button to play the movie

Click button to rewind the movie

Click button to stop the playback head

TABLE A-3: **Control Panel buttons**

button	name	function
◀▌	**Step Backward**	Moves the playback head backward one frame
▐▶	**Step Forward**	Moves the playback head forward one frame
43	**Frame**	Displays the current location of the playback head in the Score; you can jump to a specific frame number by typing that number in this box and then pressing Enter (Win) or Return (Mac)
fps	**Tempo Mode**	Displays the playback type (frames per second or seconds per frame) of the movie
15	**Tempo**	Displays the playback rate that Director is currently attempting to achieve
⟳	**Loop Playback**	Indicates whether playback stops at the end of the Score or continuously repeats until further notice (On/Off)
◀))	**Volume**	Lets you temporarily lower the volume or mute your movie while keeping your soundtracks intact; this control is useful when you continually play a movie and do not want to hear the audio
◀	**Rewind**	Moves the playback head all the way to the first frame of the movie
■	**Stop**	Stops the playback entirely
▶	**Play**	Starts the playback
fps	**Actual Tempo Mode**	Displays the actual playback type, running time total, or estimated total
15	**Actual Tempo**	Documents the real speed of playback
▭	**Selected Frames Only**	Limits playback to the frames highlighted in the Score; this control is useful when you're working on a single section of a larger movie

Getting Help

When you have a question about how to do something in Director, you can usually find the answer with a few clicks of your mouse. Director provides an extensive Help system that you can access for definitions, explanations, and useful tips. Help system information is displayed in a separate window. You can resize the Help window and set it to display on-screen so you can refer to it as you work. You can also access **context-sensitive help** that specifically relates to what you are doing; when you are working in a dialog box, you can click the Help button [?], and then click any item to get more information about the item (Win). Jean decides to use Help to find out about Director basics.

Steps 1234

QuickTip

You can also press [F1] to open the Director 8 Help dialog box.

1. Click **Help** on the menu bar, then click **Director Help**
The Help Topics: Director 8 Help dialog box opens, with the Contents tab in front. The Contents tab provides you with a list of Help categories. Each book icon has several "chapters" (topics) that you can see by clicking the book icon or the name of the Help category next to the book.

2. Click the **Contents tab** (if necessary), then double-click the **Director Basics** category
A list of Help topics underneath the Director Basics category appears, as shown in Figure A-13. To collapse a category, you double-click the open category.

QuickTip

To print a Help topic, click the Print button on the window bar.

3. Double-click the **Director basics: Overview** topic
The Director basics: Overview topic window opens, as shown in Figure A-14. Read the information on the Director basics. You can move back and forth between Help topics you have already visited by clicking the Back button and the Forward button on the Help toolbar.

QuickTip

The Find tab helps you locate the topic you need, using keywords. You can find a topic by entering a keyword in the text box, clicking List Topics, selecting a topic, and then clicking Display.

4. Click the **Index button** on the Help toolbar
The Help Topics: Director 8 Help dialog box opens, with the Index tab in front. The Index tab provides you with an alphabetical list of all the Help topics that are available, much like an index at the end of a book. You can find out about any Director feature by either entering the topic in the text box, or by scrolling down to the topic for which you want help, selecting a topic, and then clicking Display.

5. Type **stage**
As you type each letter, relevant topics scroll in the list box below the text box. Information about the Stage now appears, as shown in Figure A-15.

6. Click **Display**
The Introducing the Director workspace topic window opens.

7. Read about the Help topic, click the **Close button** in the Help window, then click the **Close button** in the Help Topics: Director 8 Help dialog box, if necessary

Keeping a Help window open while working

In Windows, you can keep any Help window open while working in Director. To keep the Help window open, click Help on the menu bar, locate and open a Help topic, click Options on the Director 8 Help window menu bar, point to Keep on Top, then click On Top. Once you change the option, you can click the Director 8 taskbar button. You will be able to work on any open window, and the Help window will remain visible. You might want to resize the Help window so that it does not obscure your view of a Director window.

FIGURE A-13: Help Topics: Director 8 Help window

Double-click topic to display Topic window

Director 8 Help Topics

Double-click category to expand or hide a Help category

Close button

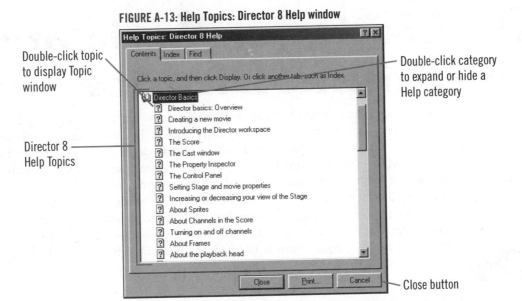

FIGURE A-14: Director basics: Overview Help topic

Help window navigation buttons

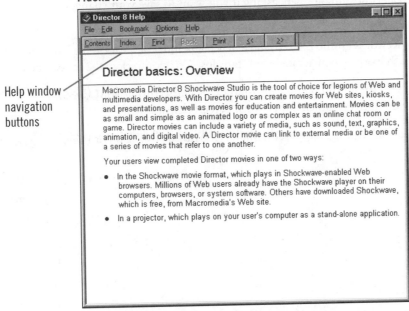

FIGURE A-15: Director 8 Help window with Index tab

Type initial characters for topic here

List of available topics

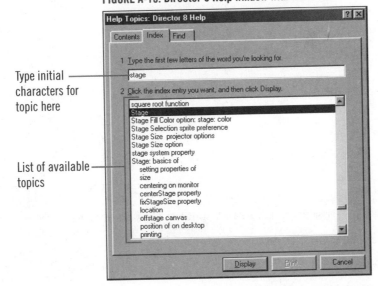

Director 8

Closing a Movie and Exiting Director

After you work on a movie, you can close the movie by saving it, by creating a new movie, by opening an existing movie, or by exiting Director. You should save the movie before closing it. Creating a new movie or opening an existing movie closes the current movie but leaves the Director window open. Exiting Director closes the current movie and the Director window. You can use the Exit command on the File menu to close a movie and exit Director, or you can use the Close button on the Director window title bar, as shown in Figure A-16. Unlike the Close command in other Windows programs, the Close command on the File menu doesn't close the movie file; it only closes the active Director window. Table A-4 describes the different methods to close a movie. ▟▓▓▓ Jean is finished reviewing Director, so she closes the Spaceworks Promo movie and exits Director.

Steps

QuickTip

If you saved your movie before opening a new one, the previous movie closes immediately and a new blank movie appears.

QuickTip

You can also close a movie and exit Director by clicking the Close button on the Director window title bar.

1. **Click the New Movie button** 🎬 **on the toolbar**
   An alert box might open, asking if you want to save your changes.

2. **If asked to save your work, click Yes (Win) or Save (Mac)**
   Spaceworks Promo is saved, and a new blank movie appears in the Director window. When you finish working with a movie, you can close Director to close the movie and exit the program.

3. **Click File on the menu bar, then click Exit (Win) or Quit (Mac)**
   If you didn't perform any actions, Director closes.

4. **If asked to save your work, click No (Win) or Don't Save (Mac)**
   Director closes.

TABLE A-4: How to close a movie

command	function
Create a new movie	Closes the current movie and creates a blank Stage, Score, and Cast in the Director window
Open an existing movie	Closes the current movie and opens a movie in the Director window
Exit Director	Closes the current movie, closes the Director window, and returns you to the desktop

FIGURE A-16: Exiting Director using the File menu

Close active
window in
Director window

Exit command

Close button

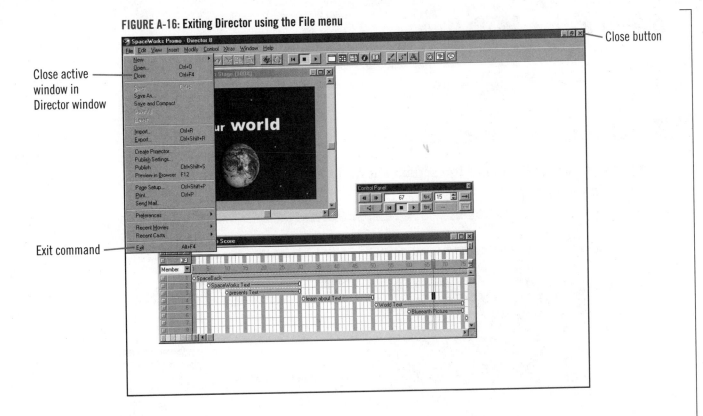

Using the Director Support Center on the Web

The Director Support Center Web site contains the latest information on Director, plus additional topics, examples, tips, and updates, explaining how to get the most out of the program. Click Help on the menu bar, click Web Links, then click the Director Support Center Web site link. Figure A-17 shows the Director Support Center Web site. Because this site is continually updated, your screen might look different. To find additional sites on the Web with Director information, you can use a search engine.

FIGURE A-17: Director Support Center Web site

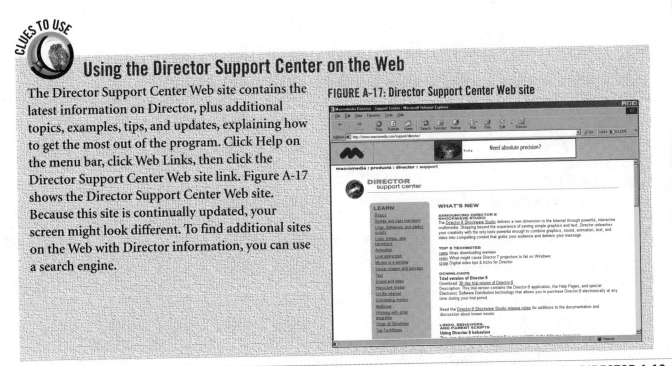

Practice

▶ Concepts Review

Label each of the elements of the screen shown in Figure A-18.

FIGURE A-18

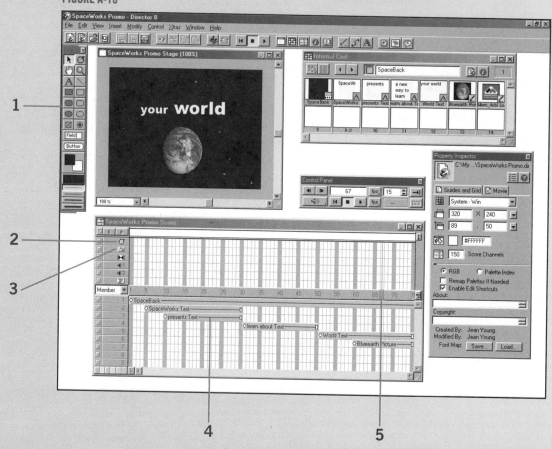

Match each of the terms with the statement that describes its function.

6. Tempo channel   a. 🕐
7. Sprite channel   b. ▦
8. Palette channel   c. ◀▮▶
9. Sound channel   d. 1
10. Script channel   e. ▤
11. Transition channel   f. ◀1

Select the best answer from the following list of choices.

12. What type of program is Director?
    a. Authoring tool
    b. Word-processing program
    c. Spreadsheet program
    d. Graphics program

13. A file is a:
    a. Collection of information stored separately.
    b. Collection of programs stored separately.
    c. Collection of information stored together.
    d. Collection of programs stored together.

14. The file extension for a Director movie in Windows is:
    a. .mov
    b. .dir
    c. .mve
    d. .dtr

15. The Tool palette in Director contains:
    a. Shapes.
    b. Buttons.
    c. All of the above.
    d. None of the above.

16. Which window is considered NOT to be a main window in Director?
    a. Property Inspector
    b. Movie Inspector
    c. Score
    d. Control Panel

17. Which window in Director can't be resized?
    a. Score
    b. Stage
    c. Control Panel
    d. Cast

18. Channels appear in which window in Director?
    a. Score
    b. Stage
    c. Control Panel
    d. Cast

19. In which window in Director can you change the tempo of a movie?
    a. Score
    b. Stage
    c. Control Panel
    d. Cast

20. Which command closes a movie?
    a. Open
    b. New
    c. Exit or Quit
    d. All of the above

▶ Skills Review

1. **Understand Director basics.**
    a. Write down the basic steps to developing interactive multimedia software with Director, without referring to the unit material.
    b. Compare your results with Figure A-1.

2. **Start Director.**
    a. Click the Start button, point to Programs, point to Macromedia Director 8, then click Director 8 (Win).
    b. Double-click the hard drive icon, double-click the Macromedia Director folder, then double-click the Director 8 program icon (Mac).

3. **View the Director window.**
    a. Identify and write down elements in the Director window, without referring to the unit material.
    b. Compare your results with Figure A-5.

4. **Open and save a movie.**
    a. Click the Open button on the toolbar.
    b. Open the Project File MD A-1 from the drive and folder where your Project Files are located.
    c. Click File on the menu bar, then click Save As.
    d. Save it as *SpaceWorks Promo2* where your Project Files are stored.

Director 8

5. Work with Director windows.

   a. Click Window on the menu bar, then click Control Panel, if turned off (no check mark).

   b. Click Window on the menu bar, then click Cast.

   c. Click Window on the menu bar, point to Inspectors, then click Property.

   d. Drag the Control Panel to an empty area of the Director window.

   e. Click the Maximize button in the Stage window.

   f. Click the Restore button in the Stage window.

6. View the Score.

   a. Identify and write down elements in the Score window, without referring to the unit material.

   b. Compare your results with Figure A-11.

7. Play a movie.

   a. Click the Play button on the Control Panel.

   b. Before the end of the movie, click the Stop button on the Control Panel.

   c. Click the Rewind button on the Control Panel.

   d. Click the number 50 on the frame channel in the Score window.

   e. Click the Step Forward button on the Control Panel 10 times.

8. Get Help.

   a. Click Help on the menu bar, then click Director Help.

   b. Click the Contents tab (if necessary), then double-click the Director Basics category.

   c. Double-click the Cast window topic.

   d. Click the Find button on the Help toolbar. (*Hint:* If the Find Setup Wizard opens, click the Maximize search capabilities option button, click Next, then click Finish.)

   e. Type **movie**, then click Movie in the text box below.

   f. Click the topic About Channels in the Score, then click Display.

   g. Click the Close button in the Director 8 Help window.

9. Close a movie and exit Director.

   a. Click the Close button on the Director window title bar.

   b. If asked to save your work, click Yes (Win) or Save (Mac).

► Independent Challenges

1. You are new to Director and want to learn how to use the product. Director 8 provides extensive online Help. At any time, you can select Director Help from the Help menu and get the assistance you need. Use the Help options to learn about the topics listed below.

To complete this independent challenge:

a. Locate and read the Help information on increasing or decreasing your view of the Stage.

b. Locate and read the Help information on sprites.

c. Locate and read the Help information on the playback head.

d. Locate and read the Help information on the Control Panel.

e. Locate and read the Help information on the Director Support Center.

f. Print one or more of the Help topics you located.

g. Close the Director Help window.

2. You have an opportunity to become the multimedia expert at your new job. First, you decide to take a Director class. The instructor asks you to open a sample file that comes with Director. The sample and instructional movies that are installed with the Director program are typically located in a subfolder inside the Director 8 folder.

To complete this independent challenge:

a. Display the Open dialog box.

b. Locate the My_Tutorial folder. For the typical Director 8 installation, the folder is located in the Programs Files folder, Macromedia folder, Director 8 folder, and Learning folder (Win) or Director 8 and Learning folder (Mac).

c. Open the chat.dir file (Win) or chat file (Mac).

d. Open the Control Panel, if turned off, and display the Stage window to play the movie.

e. Play the movie until it reaches frame 25.

f. Print the Screen. (For Windows, use the Windows Paint program. Press the Print Screen key to make a copy of the screen, start the Paint program by clicking Start, pointing to Programs, pointing to Accessories, then clicking Paint, click Edit on the menu bar, click Paste to paste the screen into Paint, then click Yes to paste the large image if necessary. Click File on the menu bar, click Print, click Print or OK in the dialog box, then exit Paint. For the Macintosh, use the SimpleText program. Hold and press the Command, Shift, and 3 keys to make a copy of the screen, double-click the document Picture 1 located on your hard drive, click File on the menu bar, click Print, then click Print in the dialog box.)(*Note*: When you create a new document with a copy of the screen and a document Picture 1 already exists, the Macintosh names the new document Picture 2.)

g. Exit Director and don't save the movie.

3. Your boss has sent your entire department to a class on Director 8. After completing the first tutorial, the instructor asks you to open the completed tutorial file that comes with Director, play the movie, and save the file so you can take it back to the office. The sample and instructional movies that are installed with the Director program are typically located in a subfolder inside the Director 8 folder.

To complete this independent challenge:

a. Display the Open dialog box.

b. Locate the Completed_Tutorials folder. For the typical Director 8 installation, the folder is located in the Programs Files folder, Macromedia folder, Director 8 folder, and Learning folder (Win) or Director 8 folder and Learning folder (Mac).

c. Open the fun.dir file (Win) or fun file (Mac).

d. Open the Control Panel, if turned off.

e. Play the movie.

f. Print the screen. (See Independent Challenge 2, Step f for screen-printing instructions.)

g. Save the movie as *Fun Tutorial* in the drive and folder where your Project Files are located.

h. Exit Director.

4. You prefer using keyboard shortcuts instead of menu commands. Director 8 provides additional Help on the Web. You want to locate a document on the Director Support Center Web site that contains Director 8 keyboard shortcuts. You need an Internet connection to complete this task.

To complete this independent challenge:

a. Open Web Links.

b. Display the Director 8 Keyboard Shortcut Web page.

c. Print the Web page.

d. If possible, download the appropriate file for keyboard shortcuts for Win or Mac, then print it out.

e. Close the Web browser.

f. Close the Director Help window.

g. Exit Director.

Director 8

▶ Visual Workshop

Recreate the screen shown in Figure A-19. Print the screen. (See Independent Challenge 2, Step f for screen-printing instructions.) Your Control Panel settings might vary.

FIGURE A-19

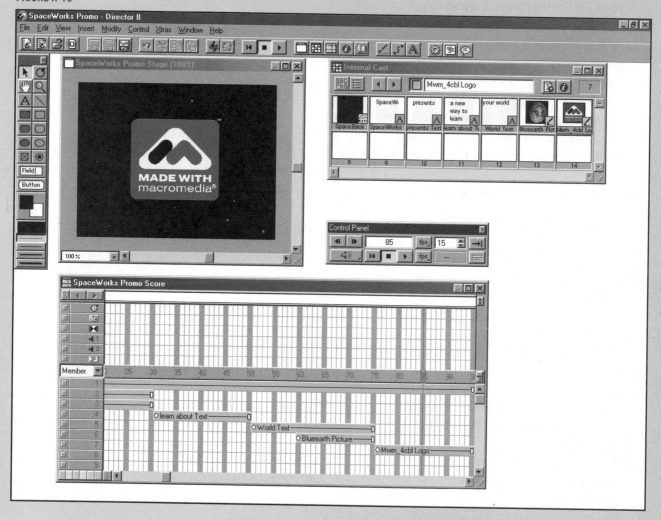

Creating
a Movie

Objectives

▶ **Plan a movie**
▶ **Set up a movie**
▶ **Import cast members**
▶ **Create and name cast members**
▶ **Create sprites**
▶ **Sequence and modify sprites**
▶ **Create animation using keyframes**
▶ **Print a movie**

Director's built-in media tools and visual production methods make it easy to create your own movie. In this unit, you'll learn how to plan a movie, and then create it step by step. To begin, you'll start Director to create a blank new movie and set movie properties, import media elements that have already been developed, and then use Director to create new ones. To create a movie, you'll position the media elements on the Stage, sequence them in the Score, and add some animation. Finally, you'll preview the results and print frames from your movie. ✎ After learning Director basics, Jean wants to create a movie that promotes the company.

Planning a Movie

Creating a movie can take a long time; it's worth the effort to plan carefully. The tendency for most first-time Director developers is to start creating a movie without carefully planning the project. Before you begin, you need to develop and follow a plan. Otherwise, you'll spend a lot of time during the project fixing or completely changing parts of the movie, which could have been avoided from the beginning. Planning a movie involves determining its purpose, identifying the audience, logically developing the content and organizing the structure of the content, developing the layout and design, and identifying the delivery computer system. Jean definitely doesn't want to spend time redoing her project, so she carefully plans the SpaceWorks Interactive promotional movie.

Details

When you want to create a movie, it's important to accomplish the following:

Determine the purpose
Is it for training? Promotion? Sales? Marketing? The consumer market? The answer will determine the types of features you may want to include or exclude in the movie. You need to make sure that what you produce is in line with the purpose of the project.

Identify the audience
How you create your movie will depend on how you classify the intended audience. If the intended audience consists of novice computer users, you will have to concentrate on making the navigational controls and layout as simple to use as possible. If the users are experienced computer users, you can include more advanced features and interactions.

QuickTip

To change a computer monitor's resolution, right-click the desktop, click Properties, click the Settings tab, drag the Screen area slider, then click OK (Win), or click the Apple menu, point to Control Panel, click Monitors & Sound, click the Monitor icon, click a resolution, then click the Close button (Mac).

Develop the content and organize the structure
The most beneficial planning tools for the multimedia developer are the script and schematic flowchart. The script tells the story of your movie production in text form, as shown in Figure B-1. Just as in the movies, a script is used to describe each section, to list audio or video, and to provide a basis for the text that will appear on-screen or will be read by a voice-over talent. Schematic flowcharts are the best way to sketch out the navigational structure of a movie and make sure that each of the sections is properly connected, as shown in Figure B-2. Once you have the script and schematic flowchart mapped out on paper, you will quickly see the correlation between what you have developed and what you will begin to set up in Director.

Develop the layout and design of the movie
The storyboard tells the story of your movie in visual form. It helps you design the layout of each screen in your movie. The storyboard follows the script and develops visual frames of the movie's main transitional points, which help you develop the Director media elements that you will use to create your movie. A storyboard can take a long time to develop, but the media elements you assemble and create in the process will shorten the overall development time.

Identify the delivery computer system to be used for playback
Some computers are more up to date than others. You need to determine the minimum computer hardware and software requirements in which your movie will be delivered. The hardware and software requirements will determine what types of media you can use and how the movie will play back. Some hardware requirements you need to consider are the CPU (central processing unit), which determines the speed with which your computer can compute data and other types of information; RAM (system memory), which determines how fast files load and how smoothly they run; sound cards, which determine whether you can use sound files; video cards, which determine the quality and speed of the graphic and video display; and monitor resolution, which determines the color display, size, and overall look of your movie. Some software requirements you need to consider are the delivery platform—Macintosh, PC, or both (cross-platform)—and operating system (Windows 95/98/2000 or Macintosh OS 7/8/9). Each platform and operating system will determine which types of image files will work on which types of systems.

FIGURE B-1: Project-planning script

Script

Project: SpaceWorks Promotion

Scene	Text	Graphics	Audio	Video	Animation	Navigation	Transition
1	SpaceWorks	SpaceWorks Background	None	None	None	None	None
1	presents	None	None	None	Text fly from bottom	None	Scene 2
2	a new way to learn about …	None	None	None	None.	None	Scene 3
3	your World	Blue Earth	None	None	None	Buttons	Scene 1 or 4
4	None	Mwm Logo	None	None	None	None	None

FIGURE B-2: Project-planning schematic flowchart

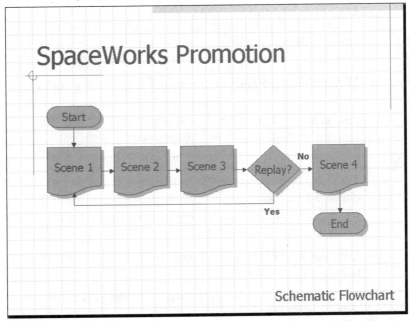

Computer requirements for developing and playing a movie

Developing a movie requires a computer with an increased level of hardware and software capabilities. The minimum requirements to develop Director movies are an Intel Pentium II 200 processor running Windows 95/98 or NT version 4.0 or later, or a Power PC 180 Macintosh running System 8.1 or later, 32 MB of installed RAM plus 100 MB of available disk space, a sound card, a color monitor, and a CD-ROM drive. The increased CPU requirements provide the necessary speed to preview and test your movie on the Stage. For the playback computer with a slower CPU (Intel Pentium 166 processor running Windows 95/98 or NT 4.0 or later[Win], or a Power PC 120 Macintosh running System 8.1 or later [Mac]), the movie is optimized to achieve the same results. The additional disk space requirements provide the necessary storage space to store large media elements, such as graphics, animation, video, and sound. For the playback computer, the movie is distributed on CD-ROM or the Web, where the available disk space exceeds the requirements.

Setting Up a Movie

When you start Director, it displays the Director window with a set of blank windows ready for you to create a new movie. Before you start, however, you need to first set up the movie properties. You set movie properties at the beginning of the project in order to make basic decisions about how your movie looks and operates. You use the Property Inspector's Movie tab to specify movie properties settings that affect the entire movie, such as how colors are defined, the size and location of the Stage, the number of channels in the Score, copyright information, and font mapping. These settings apply only to the current movie unless you set Director preferences to apply to every movie. ✒ Based on the project plans, Jean modifies the movie properties for the company's promotional movie. Before Jean makes any changes, she starts Director to create a blank work area for a new movie and saves it with an appropriate filename.

Steps 1234

QuickTip
Your initial settings in Director windows may be different.

Trouble?
If the Property Inspector is not open, click Window on the menu bar, point to Inspectors, then click Property. If necessary, click the Expander arrow ▶ to display all of the window.

QuickTip
To display a ScreenTip, point to an icon in the Property Inspector.

1. Start Director

Director opens, displaying the work area for a new movie.

2. Click File on the menu bar, click Save As, navigate to the drive and folder where your Project Files are located, type SpaceWorks Promotion in the File name text box (Win) or Saving Movie field (Mac), then click Save

3. Click the Stage window, then click the Movie tab in the Property Inspector

The Movie tab on the Property Inspector appears, as shown in Figure B-3. The Movie tab appears only if you do *not* have an object selected on the Stage or in the Score. Table B-1 describes the movie properties available in the Property Inspector. For additional information about these movie properties, click the Help button 🔘 in the Property Inspector.

4. Click the Movie Palette list arrow ▼, then click Web 216, if necessary

The Web 216 movie palette provides you with a set of Web-safe colors that will ensure that your colors will be properly displayed on the Web. This palette remains selected until Director encounters a different palette setting in the palette channel.

5. Click the Color box next to the Stage Fill Color

The Color box displays the color last selected in Director. A pop-up color palette appears, displaying the current color palette, as shown in Figure B-4. Because the RGB option is selected, the color palette is based on RGB colors. Notice that you may have to hold down the mouse button a bit longer than usual to display the color palette.

6. Click the first black color box in the first row of the pop-up color palette, as shown in Figure B-4

The Stage Fill Color changes to black, and the RGB color value in the text box to the right changes to #000000 (black).

7. Click the Save button 🖫 on the toolbar

All the changes you made to the movie since the last time you saved it are saved. This includes changes to the Property Inspector settings. It's a good idea to frequently save your work in case of power failure or other computer problems.

CLUES TO USE

Working with color palettes

Director comes with two color palette displays. One is a pop-up color palette, and the other is a color palette window. The pop-up color palette provides quick access to colors in the color palette, while the color palette window allows you to select or create a color palette, define new colors, or change foreground, background, and fill colors. To display the pop-up color palette, click the Color box. To close it, click a color or click an empty area of the screen. To open the color window, double-click the Color box or click Window on the menu bar, then click Color Palettes.

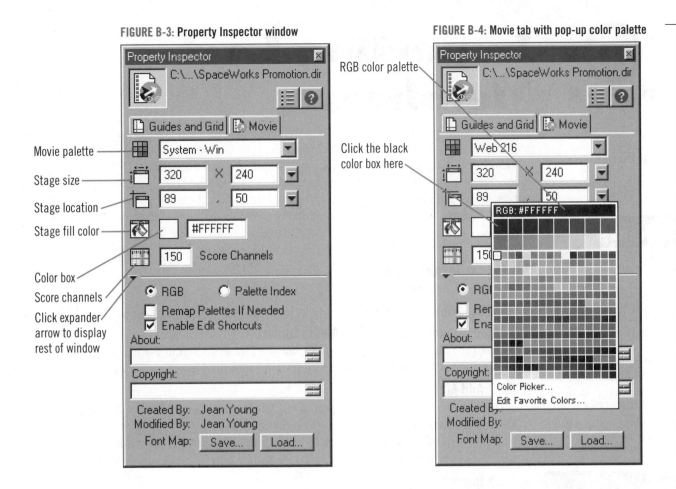

FIGURE B-3: Property Inspector window

FIGURE B-4: Movie tab with pop-up color palette

RGB color palette

Click the black color box here

Movie palette

Stage size

Stage location

Stage fill color

Color box

Score channels

Click expander arrow to display rest of window

TABLE B-1: Movie properties in the Property Inspector

movie property	allows you to
Movie Palette	Set the default color palette for your movie
Stage Size	Change the size of the Stage by choosing a monitor size from the pop-up menu, or by entering values into the Width and Heights text boxes
Stage Location	Select a stage location, either Centered, Upper Left, or Other; you enter values (in pixels) in the Left and Top text boxes to specify how far away you want the Stage to be from the top-left corner of the screen
Stage Fill Color	Select the color of the stage from a pop-up color palette
Color Box	Select the color palette for your movie, either RGB (assign all color values as absolute RGB values) or Palette Index (assign color according to its position in the current palette)
Score Channels	Set the number of channels available for sprites in the Score
Expander Arrow	Expand or collapse the Property Inspector window to display all settings
Remap Palettes If Needed	Remap different color palettes associated with cast members displayed on the Stage to a common color palette that Director creates
Enable Edit Shortcuts	Cut, copy, and paste Editable text boxes while a movie is playing
About, Copyright	Specify About and Copyright information for your movie
Save	Save current font map settings in a specific text file
Load	Load font map settings from a file

Importing Cast Members

If you have already developed animations and multimedia content, images, sounds, video, or text in other programs, you can import these media elements into the active Cast Window. Table AP-1 provides a summary of the formats and objects that you can import into Director. As Director imports images into a Cast window, the program checks that the images are compatible with the current movie property settings. If an incompatibility arises, Director prompts you on how to resolve it. Jean imports media elements provided by the art department at SpaceWorks Interactive.

1. Click the **Import button** on the toolbar

The Import Files into "Internal" dialog box opens.

2. Click the **Look in list arrow**, click the drive and folder where your Project Files are located, then double-click the **Media folder**

A list of the files and folders appears in the File List, as shown in Figure B-5. You can select files individually or as a group and import them into the active Cast window.

3. Click **Add All**

All the files in the Media folder appear in the File List. The selected files will be imported into the active Cast window according to the order of the files in the File List from top to bottom. The top file in the list will be imported into the next available location in the Cast window. You can change the import order by selecting a file and clicking Move Up or Move Down.

4. Click **Import**

The Image Options dialog box opens, as shown in Figure B-6, indicating that the graphic you are importing has a different color depth from the system into which you're importing. The number of colors that a graphic or a computer system can display is called **color depth**. Your computer monitor and the images you import into a movie can have different color depths. If your computer monitor is set to a higher color depth than 8 bits, the Stage setting in this dialog box will be a higher number, such as 16 bits.

5. In the Color Depth area, click the **Stage (8 bits) option button** or **Stage (16 bits) option button**

This value reflects the color depth set for your system, so an 8-bit or 16-bit stage setting reflects an 8-bit or 16-bit monitor setting. In most cases, you should transform images with higher color depth settings to the lower setting listed next to the Stage option button so that the color depth setting for the Stage and the image will match.

6. Click the **Same Settings for Remaining Images check box** to select it, then click **OK**

The Select Format dialog box opens, indicating that the image you are importing can be imported using multiple formats. The Animated GIF format is selected.

7. Click **OK**

All the files in the file list appear in the Cast window. In the Cast window, you can view the cast in either List view or Thumbnail view. You can click the Cast View Style button in the Cast window to switch between the two views.

8. If List view appears in the Cast window, click the **Cast View Style button** in the Cast window to change to Thumbnail view

The Cast window appears in Thumbnail view with all the files from the file list, as shown in Figure B-7. To change the default Cast window view to Thumbnail view, click File on the menu bar, point to Preferences, click Cast, click the Apply to All Casts check box, click the Thumbnail option button, click Save As Default, then click OK.

QuickTip

To import one file, click the file, then click Import. To import more than one file at once, click the file and click Add until you're done adding to the list, then click Import.

Trouble?

If your monitor is set to 32 bits, the same color depth as the graphic, the Image Options dialog box may not appear. Skip steps 5 and 6.

Trouble?

If you don't change an image to the Stage color depth when you import it, you might experience color flashes or conflicts when the image appears on the Stage.

FIGURE B-5: Import Files into "Internal" dialog box

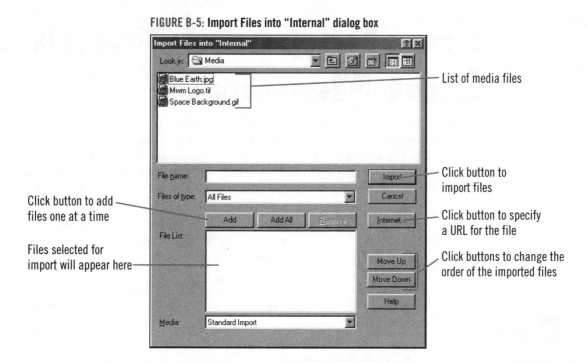

List of media files

Click button to add files one at a time

Files selected for import will appear here

Click button to import files

Click button to specify a URL for the file

Click buttons to change the order of the imported files

FIGURE B-6: Image Options dialog box

Click the Stage option button to equalize the color depth

Click check box to change all upcoming images

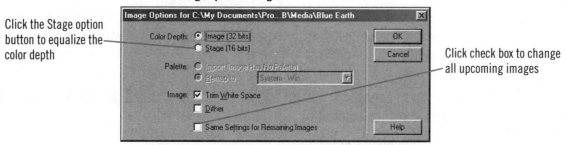

FIGURE B-7: Cast window

Click button to display cast member properties

Click button to change the view of cast members

Imported media files as cast members

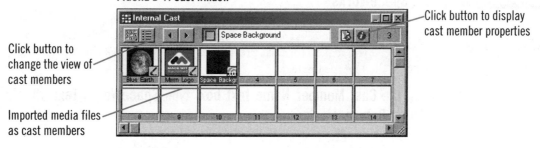

Understanding color depth

The higher the color depth value, the greater the number of colors that can be displayed, which necessitates greater system memory. An image with a 1-bit color depth appears only in black and white; similarly, a monitor with a 1-bit color depth setting displays only black-and-white images. The most common color depth display settings are: 2-bit, which displays 4 colors; 4-bit, which displays 16 colors; 8-bit, which displays 256 colors; 16-bit, which displays 32,768 colors; and 24-bit and 32-bit, both of which display 16.7 million colors.

Director 8

Creating and Naming Cast Members

You can create new media elements in Director or import ones that have already been developed. Director provides several tools for creating media elements, including a paint tool and text creation tools. The text tool provides standard text-formatting controls in a window that resembles a word-processing program. When you create or import a media element, it is stored in the Cast window. A Cast window can contain up to 32,000 cast members, each one represented by a thumbnail image and identified by its position number and an optional name. A small icon in the lower-right corner of each cast member identifies its type. Table AP-1 identifies each cast member by its icon. You can name a new cast member or rename an existing one. You can also copy, paste, delete, duplicate, relocate, and modify a cast member. Any changes you make to a cast member are reflected in its appearance on the Stage. You don't have to use every cast member in your movie; however, saving your movie with all of the unused cast members increases the file size. Jean has already imported images in the Cast window and now wants to create text cast members in Director.

Steps

QuickTip

You can also use the Text tool A on the Tool palette to create a cast member on the Stage.

QuickTip

To change the Font color, select the text, click Modify on the menu bar, click Font, click the Color box, click a color, then click OK.

Trouble?

If the text doesn't fit on one line, drag the black bar in the top-right corner of the text box until the text fits.

QuickTip

To display a text cast member not currently open in the Text window, click the Next Cast Member button ▶ or the Previous Cast Member button ◀.

1. Click the **Text Window button** A on the toolbar
   The Text window opens, displaying Text 4 on the title bar. The number 4 indicates that this cast member will be stored in location number 4 in the Cast window.

2. Position the **mouse pointer** on the bottom-right corner of the **Text window** until the pointer changes to ↘, then drag the **border** to the dimension shown in Figure B-8
   The Text window expands. The Text window provides standard text-formatting controls in a window that resembles a word-processing program.

3. Click the **Font list arrow** ▼, scroll if necessary, click **Arial Black**, click the **Size list arrow** ▼, then click **36**

4. Click the **Align Center button** ≡ in the Text Window
   The font attributes are set for the text cast member, and the insertion point (blinking cursor) appears in the Text window.

5. Type **SpaceWorks**
   The text appears in the Text window with the font attributes you set. The last set font color selected appears in the Text window; your font color might be different from the black color used here. If you make a mistake, press Backspace (Win) or Delete (Mac) to delete the incorrect text, then retype the text.

6. Click the **Cast Member Name text box**, type **SpaceWorks Text**, then press **Enter** (Win) or **Return** (Mac)
   The new name appears in the Text title bar, in the Property Inspector Name text box, and as cast member 4 in the Cast window.

7. Click the **New Cast Member button** ⊞ in the Text window
   A blank Text window entitled Text 5 appears. The Text window retains the formatting attributes from the previous Text window.

8. Click the **Size list arrow**, click **18**, type **presents**, click the **Cast Member Name text box**, type **Presents Text**, then press **Enter** (Win) or **Return** (Mac)

9. Click the **Close button** in the Text window
   The Text window closes and the new cast member, Presents Text, is stored as cast member 5 in the Cast window, as shown in Figure B-9.

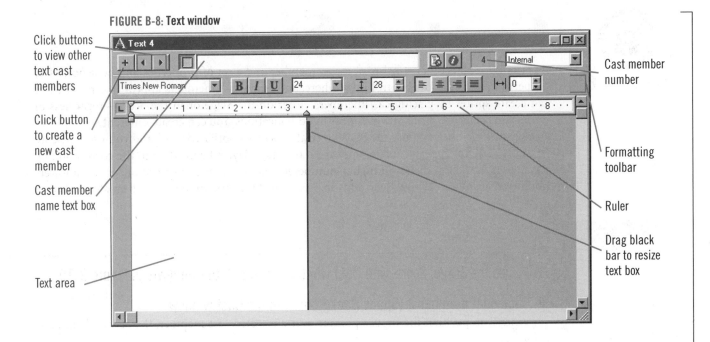

FIGURE B-8: Text window

Click buttons to view other text cast members

Click button to create a new cast member

Cast member name text box

Text area

Cast member number

Formatting toolbar

Ruler

Drag black bar to resize text box

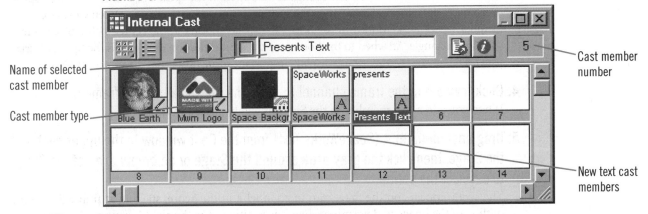

FIGURE B-9: Cast window with text cast members

Name of selected cast member

Cast member type

Cast member number

New text cast members

CLUES TO USE

Changing text alignment

In the Text window, you can change the alignment for each paragraph in a text cast member. A paragraph is a new section of text. To create a new paragraph in the Text window, press [Enter] (Win) or [Return](Mac). You can align paragraph text relative to the margins in the Text window. Although you can vary the width and placement of the margins, the right margin cannot exceed the length of the text

cast member. By default, text is left-aligned ▤, or flush with the left margin. However, you can also right-align text ▤ flush with the right margin, center text ▤ between the margins, or justify text ▤ so that both the left and right edges are evenly aligned. To align multiple paragraphs, you need to select the paragraphs, then select an alignment option.

Creating Sprites

A sprite is an object that consists of a cast member and a set of properties and behaviors. The properties and behaviors control how, where, and when cast members appear in a movie. You can create sprites by placing cast members either on the Stage or in the Score—regardless of where you create the sprite, it will appear in both locations. You can create different sprites from a single cast member. You use the Stage to control *where* a sprite appears, and you use the Score to control *when* it appears. Sprites appear on the Stage, layered according to the corresponding channel in the Score. Sprites in higher-numbered channels appear in front of sprites in lower-numbered channels. ◢ Jean adds sprites to the Stage and in the Score to create a movie.

Steps

1. Resize the Stage, Score, and Cast windows to match the windows in Figure B-10

2. Click **cast member 3** (Space Background) in the Cast window
   When you position the mouse pointer over a selected cast member, the arrow changes to a ✌.

QuickTip

You can use the playback head to locate the frame number.

3. Drag the **cast member** from the Cast window to **frame 1, channel 1** in the Score, as shown in Figure B-10
   When you drag a cast member in the Score, an outline of the sprite appears, indicating the current location of the sprite when you release the mouse. Each new sprite you create has a default duration of 28 frames, called the span duration. The range of frames in which the sprite appears is called the sprite span. You can change the duration of the sprite at any time. Placing a sprite over a range of frames indicates when the sprite appears during the movie. When you place a cast member (space background) in the Score, the sprite appears in the center of the Stage with a selection rectangle. Attached to the bottom of the sprite selection rectangle is the Sprite Overlay panel. The Sprite Overlay panel displays important sprite properties directly on the Stage.

4. Click **frame 5** in the frame channel to move the playback head to frame 5
   When you add a cast member to the Stage, it will be placed in frame 5.

5. Drag **cast member 4** (SpaceWorks Text) from the Cast window to the upper-center of the Stage, then click the **gray area around the Stage** or an **empty area of the Stage** to deselect the sprite
   The sprite appears on the Stage and in channel 2 in the Score, starting at frame 5. Use the outline of the image to determine when it is positioned in the right location; you can always adjust it again if necessary.

6. Drag **cast member 5** (Presents Text) from the Cast window to the Stage below cast member 4 (SpaceWorks Text), then click the **gray area around the Stage** or an **empty area of the Stage** to deselect the sprite
   Your screen should be similar to Figure B-11.

Trouble?

If the playback loop is turned on, click the Stop button ■ on the toolbar.

7. Click the **Rewind button** ◄ on the toolbar, then click the **Play button** ► on the toolbar
   The movie plays on the Stage and the playback head moves frame to frame through the Score until it reaches the end of the longest sprite. The movie shows the text appearing in default colors above the background, then the background disappears.

FIGURE B-10: Score window with a new sprite

New sprite on
the Stage

Sprite Overlay panel

New sprite in Score

Sprite span

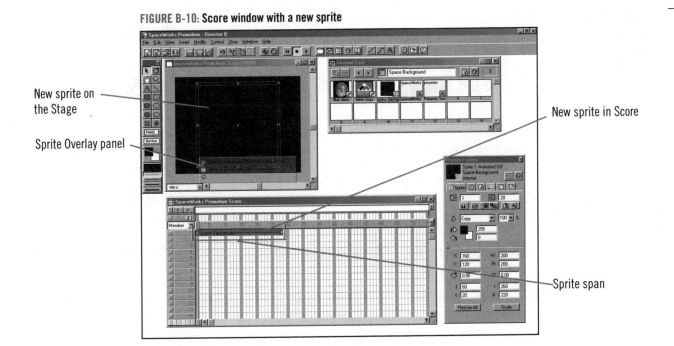

FIGURE B-11: Stage and Score windows with new sprites

New sprites

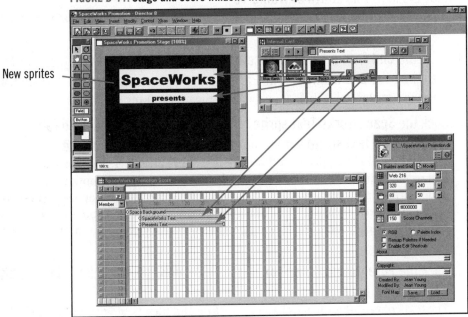

CLUES TO USE

Changing sprite preferences

You can use the Sprite Preferences dialog box to control the way sprites appear and behave in the Score and on the Stage. You can change sprite options that control Stage selection, span defaults, and span duration. To change preferences for sprites, click File on the menu bar, point to Preferences, then click Sprite. With Stage selection, you can customize how you select a sprite on the Stage; you can select the entire span of the sprite or only the current frame in the sprite. With span defaults, you can determine the appearance and behavior of sprites you'll create in the future. With span duration, you can determine the length of sprites in frames, indicating either a specified amount or the visible width of the Score window.

Director 8

Sequencing and Modifying Sprites

You can reposition sprites on the Stage and make other changes to them without affecting the original cast members. To move or edit a sprite, you must select it first. You use the Arrow tool on the Tool palette to select one or more sprites. You can also select a certain frame or range of frames within a sprite instead of the entire sprite. The first frame in a sprite is called a **keyframe** and the last frame is called an **end frame**. A keyframe is denoted in a sprite by a circle, while an end frame is denoted by a small bar. The line that connects the circle and the small bar is called the **sprite bar**.  Jean takes some time to familiarize herself with the elements of the Score window.

1. Click **anywhere** in the **Space Background sprite** in channel 1 in the Score
   The sprite is highlighted in the Score and on the Stage.

Trouble?

If the Score window is not wide enough, you can resize it or drag the playback head to the edge of the window and scroll.

2. Position the mouse pointer over the **end frame** in the Space Background sprite in channel 1, then drag the **end frame** to **frame 75**
   The sprite in channel 1 is extended to frame 75, denoting the new end of the movie. The previous end was at frame 32. Notice that the sprite outline is not visible while you drag the end frame.

3. Position the mouse pointer over the **Presents Text sprite** in channel 3 (approximately over the frame number, not over the keyframe or end frame), then drag the **sprite** so that the keyframe starts at **frame 10**
   An outline surrounds the sprite as you drag it. The sprite is repositioned in the Score, as shown in Figure B-12.

4. Drag the **end frame** for the SpaceWorks Text sprite in channel 2 back to **frame 30**, then drag the **end frame** for the Presents Text sprite in channel 3 back to **frame 30**
   Now both sprites finish their appearance in the movie at the same time.

5. Click the **SpaceWorks Text sprite** in the sprite bar, press and hold **[Shift]**, then click the **Presents Text sprite** within the sprite bar to select both sprites
   The SpaceWorks Text sprite and Presents Text sprite are selected. You can also drag a selection rectangle in the Score to select all the sprites in an area. Right now, the text color of each of the sprites on the Stage is the default color with which Director opened. These colors may not show up well against a space background. You can use tools on the Tool palette which are similar to those found in drawing programs, to change the color of the sprites, as shown in Figure B-13.

6. Click the **Foreground Color box** on the Tool palette, then click the **large white color box** at the end of the second row on the pop-up color palette
   The text color of the sprites changes to white and blends in with the white background. If the Tool palette is not open, click Window on the menu bar, then click Tool Palette.

7. Click and hold the **Background Color box** on the Tool palette, click the **large black color box** at the beginning of the first row on the pop-up color palette, then click the **gray area around the Stage** to deselect the sprites
   The background of the sprite changes to black to match the space background and the white text is visible, as shown in Figure B-14.

Trouble?

If the playback loop is turned on, click the Stop button ■ on the toolbar.

8. Click the **Rewind button** ◄◄ on the toolbar, then click the **Play button** ► on the toolbar
   The movie plays on the Stage and the playback head moves frame to frame through the Score until it reaches the end. The movie shows the text appearing in white, then disappearing.

FIGURE B-12: Sprite repositioned in the Score

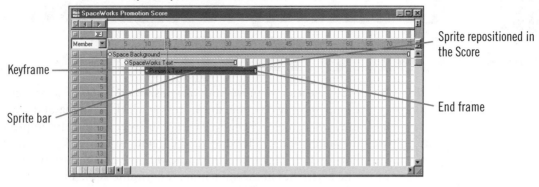

Keyframe

Sprite bar

Sprite repositioned in the Score

End frame

FIGURE B-13: Tool palette

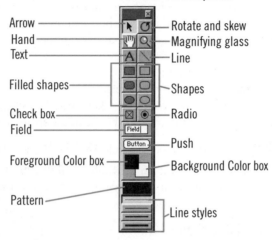

Arrow

Hand

Text

Filled shapes

Check box

Field

Foreground Color box

Pattern

Rotate and skew

Magnifying glass

Line

Shapes

Radio

Push

Background Color box

Line styles

FIGURE B-14: Stage window with new foreground and background colors

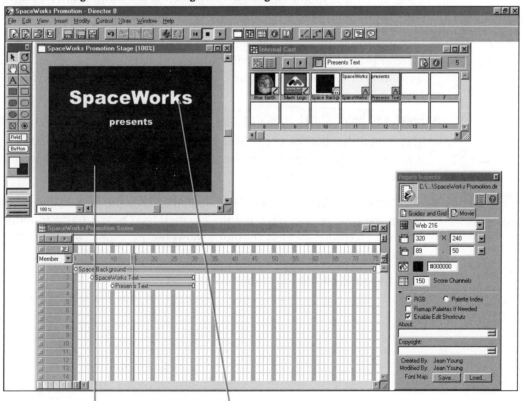

Background color of the text changes to black

Foreground color of the text changes to white

Creating Animation Using Keyframes

The simplest way to make a sprite move from one position to another is through tweening. In traditional animation, tweening describes the process in which an animator draws all the frames *in between* the frames where major changes take place in order to create the impression of movement. To tween the animation, you need to set the frames in the Score that correspond to the major change points on the Stage where the sprite will move to and from. The major change point frames are the keyframes in the animation. A keyframe is the first frame in a sprite (the starting point for the animation) and the selected frames in the Score where a sprite appears in a new location or changes appearance in some other way. As you place keyframes in the sprite, Director automatically tweens the sprites between the keyframes. You can set many keyframes in a sprite.  Jean wants to sequence a sprite in the Score to create an animation.

1. Click **frame 10** in channel 3

The first frame in the text sprite is selected in the Score to indicate the start position for the animation. A sprite's first frame is a keyframe. Selecting the keyframe of the sprite lets Director know you want to make a change to the sprite in this frame.

2. In the Stage window, press and hold **[Shift]**, then drag the **Presents Text sprite** in a straight path to the gray area at the bottom of the Stage

The text sprite is moved on the Stage to its start position for the animation, as shown in Figure B-15.

> **QuickTip**
>
> When you press and hold [Shift] as you move a sprite, the object is constrained horizontally or vertically to move in a straight line right to left or up and down, respectively.

3. Click **frame 20** in channel 3

A keyframe is selected in the Score to indicate the end point for the animation. Selecting frame 20 for a keyframe makes the animation take place in frames 10 through 20. After frame 20, the line of text will remain in place.

4. Click **Insert** on the menu bar, then click **Keyframe**

Director places a keyframe indicator in the sprite. After every keyframe, Director inserts a sprite label in the sprite so you can identify what appears after the keyframe, as shown in Figure B-16.

5. Press and hold **[Shift]**, then drag the **Presents Text sprite** in a straight path from the gray area at the bottom of the Stage to an area below the SpaceWorks text

A white vertical line appears as you move the text sprite on the Stage to its end point for the animation, as shown in Figure B-17.

> **Trouble?**
>
> If the playback loop is turned on, click the Stop button ■ on the toolbar.

6. Click the **Rewind button** ◄ on the toolbar, then click the **Play button** ► on the toolbar

The movie plays on the Stage and the playback head moves frame to frame through the Score until it reaches the end. The movie shows the text animated—"presents" moves up the screen and stops beneath Spaceworks.

7. Click the **Save button** 🖫 on the toolbar

All the changes you made to the movie since the last time you saved it are saved.

FIGURE B-15: Start position for animation

Start position for animation on the Stage

Start position for animation in Score

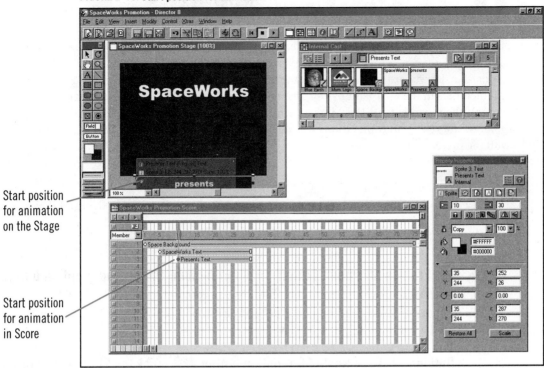

FIGURE B-16: Score window with a keyframe indicator

Keyframe indicator

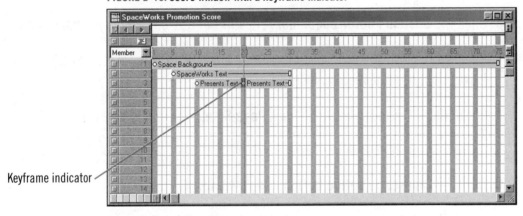

FIGURE B-17: Stage window with an animation

Animation end position

Animation path

Animation start position

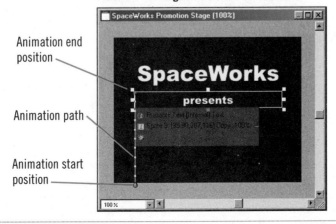

Printing a Movie

Sometimes the best way to review different parts of your movie content and mark changes is to print it out. You can print a movie in a variety of ways. You can print an image of the Stage in standard or storyboard format or print the Score, the cast member number and contents of text cast members in the Cast window, all scripts or a range of scripts (movie, cast, Score, and sprite scripts), the comments in the Markers window, the Cast window artwork, or the entire Cast window. ▰▰▰ Jean wants to print a storyboard of the Stage and the Score, and compare it with the project plan.

QuickTip

You can also press [Ctrl][P] (Win) or [Command][P] (Mac) to open the Print dialog box.

1. Click **File** on the menu bar, then click **Print**
   The Print dialog box opens. Table B-2 describes some of the options in the Print dialog box.

2. Click the **Print list arrow** ▾, then click **Stage**

3. Click the **Frames All option button**, click the **Include One in Every option button**, click the Frames text box, then type **5** in the Frames text box
   The options are set to print the Stage image one in every 5 frames for the entire movie, as shown in Figure B-18.

4. Click **Options**, click the **Scale 50% option button**, then click the **Storyboard Format check box** to select it
   The Print Options dialog box opens. The storyboard format is available only when you select 50% or 25% images to print, as shown in Figure B-19.

5. Click the **Custom Footer check box**, click in the text box, then type **your name**

Trouble?

If you have printing problems, you may need to adjust the graphics intensity and mode settings of your printer. Click File on the menu bar, click Page Setup, then click Properties.

6. Click **OK** to close the Print Options dialog box, click **Print**, then click **OK** (Win) or **Print** (Mac) to print the storyboard

7. Click **File** on the menu bar, then click **Page Setup**
   The Print Setup dialog box opens. You can specify paper size and source, and the orientation, either portrait (8½ inches × 11 inches) or landscape (11 inches × 8½ inches).

8. Click the **Landscape option button**, then click **OK**

QuickTip

The print settings stay in effect until you change them.

9. Click **File** on the menu bar, click **Print**, click the **Print list arrow** ▾, click **Score**, click **Print**, then click **OK** (Win) or **Print** (Mac)
   Director prints the entire Score window with a landscape orientation.

10. Click **File** on the menu bar, click **Exit**, then if asked to save your work, click **No** (Win) or **Don't Save** (Mac)
    Director closes.

FIGURE B-18: Print dialog box

Click arrow to select what to print

Click button to select what frames to print

Click button to select the frame interval to print

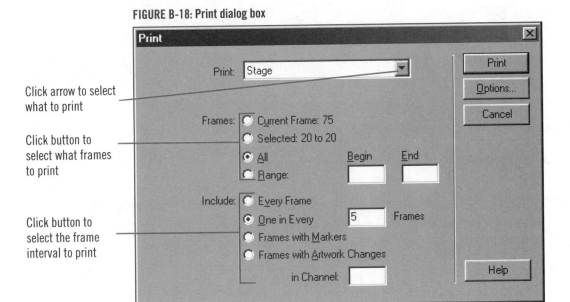

FIGURE B-19: Options dialog box

Your number of frames may be different

This option only appears when Scale is 50% or 25%

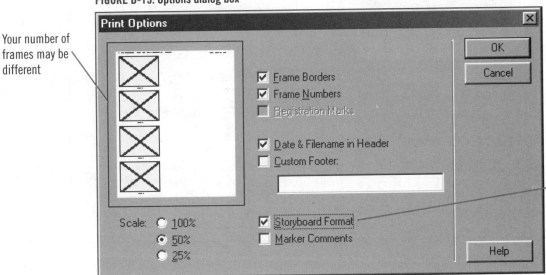

Director 8

TABLE B-2: Options in the Print dialog box

print option	use to
Print	Specify what part of the movie to print; this includes the Stage, the Score, all scripts or a range of scripts, cast text, cast art, cast thumbnails, and marker comments
Frames	Specify which frames of your movie are printed
Include	Specify which frames in the defined range to print
Options	Determine the layout of the items to print; this includes scaling frames, frame borders, frame numbers, registration marks, date and filename in the header, a custom footer, and storyboards
Help	Display the Director 8 Help topic for printing movies

Practice

▶ Concepts Review

Label each of the elements of the screen shown in Figure B-20.

FIGURE B-20

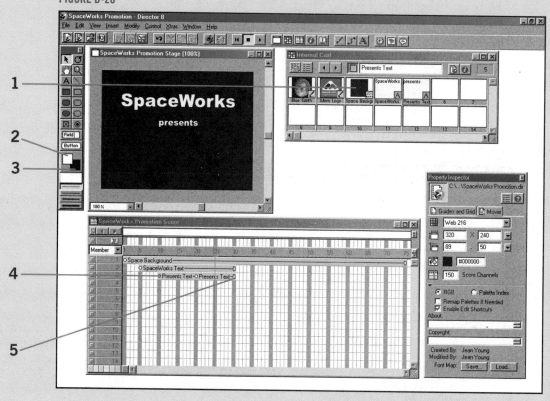

Match each of the terms with the statement that describes its function.

6. Keyframe
7. End frame
8. Keyframe indicator
9. Foreground Color box
10. Background Color box
11. Sprite Overlay panel

a. The first frame in a sprite
b. An information point for a sprite
c. An animation point in a sprite
d. The last frame in a sprite
e. The top color chip in the Tool palette
f. The bottom color chip in the Tool palette

Select the best answer from the following list of choices.

12. **What do you need to determine first when planning a movie?**
    a. Purpose
    b. Audience
    c. Content and structure
    d. Computer system requirements

13. **What planning tool is good for developing the navigational structure of a movie?**
    a. Script
    b. Schematic flowchart
    c. Storyboard
    d. Director

14. **What planning tool is good for developing the text form of a movie?**
    a. Script
    b. Schematic flowchart
    c. Storyboard
    d. Director

15. **What can you load from a file in the Property Inspector?**
    a. Color palettes
    b. Font map settings
    c. All of the above
    d. None of the above

16. **The number of colors that a graphic or a computer system can display is called the:**
    a. Color number.
    b. Color set.
    c. Color display.
    d. Color depth.

17. **How many colors does the 8-bit setting display?**
    a. 4 colors
    b. 16 colors
    c. 256 colors
    d. 32,768 colors

18. **A small icon in the lower-right corner of each cast member identifies its:**
    a. Type.
    b. Size.
    c. Name.
    d. Control.

19. **The default span duration is:**
    a. 10 frames.
    b. 20 frames.
    c. 28 frames.
    d. 36 frames.

20. **The sprite overlay panel displays the sprite:**
    a. Properties.
    b. Keyframes.
    c. End frame.
    d. Keyframe indicators.

21. **The first frame of a sprite is the:**
    a. Keyframe indicator.
    b. Keyframe.
    c. End frame.
    d. Tween.

22. **Which is not a Print option in Director?**
    a. Cast Text
    b. Cast Art
    c. Cast Window
    d. Marker Comments

Skills Review

1. **Plan a movie.**
   a. Write down the basic steps involved in planning a movie, without referring to the unit material.

2. **Set up a new movie.**
   a. Start Director.
   b. Click the Movie tab of the Property Inspector.
   c. Change the Movie Palette to Web 216, if necessary.
   d. Change the Stage Fill Color to black, if necessary.

3. **Import cast members.**
   a. Import all the media elements from the Media folder in the drive where your Project Files are located.
   b. Change the color depth to match the Stage setting and select a format for any images.

4. Create and name cast members.

a. Open the file MD B-1.dir from the drive and folder where your Project Files are located and save it as *SpaceWorks Promotion2.* Don't save the previous movie.

b. Change the foreground color to white and the background color to black.

c. Open the Text window and resize it, if necessary.

d. Drag the black bar to 3½" on the ruler, if necessary.

e. Change the font attributes to the font Arial Black, size 24, and center alignment.

f. Type **a new way to learn about ...**

g. Name the cast member Learn About Text.

h. Create a new text cast member.

i. Type **your**, press the spacebar, change the font size to 36, then type **World**

j. Name the cast member World Text.

k. Close the Text window.

5. Create sprites.

a. Position cast member 6 (Learn About Text) in the Score starting at frame 31 in channel 4, then drag the sprite to the center of the Stage, if necessary.

b. Select frame 60 in the frame channel.

c. Drag cast member 7 (World Text) from the Cast window to the top-center of the Stage.

d. Drag cast member 1 (Blue Earth) from the Cast window to the Stage below the World text.

e. Rewind and play the movie.

6. Sequence and modify sprites.

a. Adjust the Learn About Text sprite in channel 4 to start at frame 31 and end at frame 50.

b. Move the World Text sprite to channel 5, then adjust it to start at frame 51 and end at frame 75.

c. Move the Blue Earth sprite to channel 6, then adjust it to start at frame 60 and end at frame 75.

7. Create animation using keyframes.

a. Start the animation at frame 60.

b. Move the Blue Earth image to the gray area directly to the right. (*Hint*: Do not grab the dots in the center of the earth.)

c. End the animation at frame 70.

d. Insert a keyframe.

e. Move the Blue Earth image in a straight path from the gray area to the center of the Stage.

f. Rewind and play the movie.

g. Save the movie.

8. Print a movie.

a. Create a custom footer with your name in it, then print the entire storyboard at 25% scale in portrait orientation. (*Hint*: If you have printing problems, you may need to adjust the graphics intensity and mode settings of your printer.)

b. Print all the cast members as thumbnails in landscape orientation.

c. Exit Director and don't save the movie.

Director 8

▶ Independent Challenges

1. As the public relations manager for an international charity, you want to create a multimedia presentation that celebrates the 50th anniversary of the organization and promotes increased participation in charitable events. The charity wants to hire a multimedia development company to create the presentation. In order to get funds for the project, you need to create a project plan.

To complete this independent challenge:

a. Start WordPad (Win) or SimpleText (Mac) and create a project plan.

b. Save the document as Project Plan in the folder where your Project Files are located.

c. Determine the purpose.

d. Identify the audience.

e. Develop the content and organize the structure.

f. Develop the layout and design.

g. Identify the delivery computer system.

h. Type your name.

i. Print the project plan.

j. Exit WordPad (Win) or SimpleText (Mac).

2. As the lead designer for BannerAD Designs, you regularly use Director to create the designs. A new client recently approached you about creating a banner ad for a company called ABC123 Learning. You use the media creation tools in Director to create a banner ad with some animation.

To complete this independent challenge:

a. Start Director and save the new movie as *ABC123* in the location where your Project Files are stored.

b. Set up the Stage to be 468 x 60 with a blue background and Web 216 color palette.

c. Create a text sprite for the letters A, B, and C.

d. Create a text sprite for the numbers 1, 2, and 3.

e. Animate the letters and numbers.

f. Create a custom footer with your name in it.

g. Print all of the cast members and all of the Stage frames. (*Hint*: If you have printing problems, you may need to adjust the graphics intensity and mode settings of your printer.)

h. Save the movie and exit Director.

3. You're an independent multimedia producer. You just got a part time job teaching Director 8. The course materials use the tutorial included with the Director 8 package. In preparation for the first class, you want to open the completed tutorial, play the movie, and print the Stage, Score, and Cast. After reviewing the course materials, you want to print some handouts for class. The sample and instructional movies that are installed with the Director program are typically located in a subfolder inside the Director 8 folder.

To complete this independent challenge:

a. Display the Open dialog box.

b. Locate the Completed_Tutorials folder. For the typical Director 8 installation, the folder is located on the hard drive in the Programs Files folder, Macromedia folder, Director 8 folder, and Learning folder (Win) or Director 8 folder and Learning folder (Mac).

c. Open the fun.dir file.

d. Create a custom footer with your name in it.

e. Print the Stage every 20 frames, Score, and Cast.

f. Exit Director and don't save the movie.

4. You are an astronomy professor at a local college. You have been asked by a colleague to prepare a multimedia presentation on the topic of your choice for an upcoming space exploration convention.
You use media elements from the NASA Web site and the media creation tools in Director to create a self-running slide presentation.
To complete this independent challenge:

a. Connect to the Internet and go to www.course.com. Navigate to the page for this book, click the link for the Student Online Companion. Use the link for Unit B to begin your search.
b. Find and download five media elements for your movie presentation.
c. Start Director and save the new movie as *Space Pres* in the drive and folder where your Project Files are located.
d. Set up the Stage to be 468 x 60 with a black background.
e. Import the media elements into the Cast.
f. Create sprites with the cast members to create a slide show.
g. Create text sprites for titles and animate the introduction title.
h. Create a custom footer with your name in it.
i. Print all the cast members and the Score.
j. Play and save the movie presentation.
k. Exit Director.

▶ Visual Workshop

Create the movie screen shown in Figure B-21. You can import the image Mwm Logo.tif from the location where your Project Files are stored. Save it as *MWM* in the drive and folder where your Project Files are located, create a custom footer with your name in it, then print frame 18 of the Stage.

FIGURE B-21

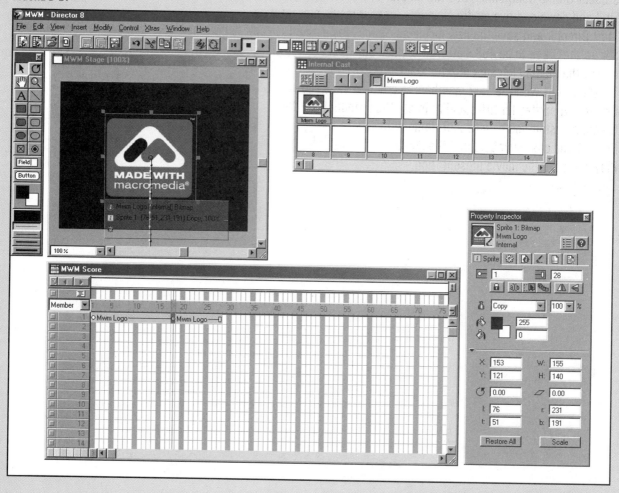

Creating
Graphic Cast Members

Objectives

► **Understand vector shapes and bitmaps**
► **Draw a vector shape**
► **Add a gradient to a vector shape**
► **Edit a vector shape**
► **Use the Paint window**
► **Flip, rotate, and apply effects**
► **Apply Ink effects**
► **Apply Paint effects**
► **Add text to a bitmap**

In Director, you can create new graphical media elements for the Cast or import ones that have already been developed. Director provides several tools for creating graphical cast members. This unit introduces you to basic Director skills for creating, editing, and enhancing graphical cast members. First, you'll learn how to draw and edit graphical elements. Then, you'll learn how to modify and enhance these elements. After creating a basic promotional movie for SpaceWorks Interactive, Jean wants to create a set of graphical cast members for use in an upcoming movie.

Understanding Vector Shapes and Bitmaps

With Director's graphical tools, you can create vector shapes or bitmaps. A **vector shape** is a mathematical description of a geometric form, which is composed of line thickness, line color, line slope, fill color, corner points, and so on, while a **bitmap** is a pixel-by-pixel representation of a graphic. A **pixel** is an individual point in a graphic with a distinct color. To understand the difference between a vector shape and a bitmap, imagine a simple line. You can draw a line pixel-by-pixel as a bitmap, as shown in Figure C-1, or you can draw a line from point A (the starting point) to point B (the ending point) as a vector shape, as shown in Figure C-2. The simple line looks the same on the screen using either method, but the vector shape is more versatile. If you need a simple shape with minimal detail, a vector shape is the best choice. If you need a more complex graphic that you can edit, a bitmap is the right choice. Jean is new to the process of creating graphics in Director, so she wants to learn the basic properties of vector shapes and bitmaps, as listed below.

Properties of a vector shape:

 A vector shape uses less drive storage and memory space than a bitmap and requires less download time from the Internet or other network.

 A vector shape can consist of only one distinct shape as a cast member. For example, a vector shape cannot contain a separate square and circle that do not connect.

 A vector shape can be resized without distortion, unlike a bitmap.

 A vector shape can be controlled with Lingo (a scripting language specific to Director) while a movie is playing.

 You can create a vector shape entirely with Lingo.

Properties of a bitmap:

 A bitmap requires more drive storage and memory space than a vector shape. The larger the bitmap, the greater the amount of storage and memory space required.

 A bitmap can consist of any arrangement of pixels, connected or disconnected.

 When you resize a bitmap, the image can become distorted. You can alleviate part of the problem by using the anti-aliasing feature. **Anti-Aliasing** blends the bitmap's colors with background colors around the edges to make the edge appear smooth instead of jagged.

 You can edit single pixels, groups of pixels, or the entire bitmap of pixels.

FIGURE C-1: A bitmap of a line

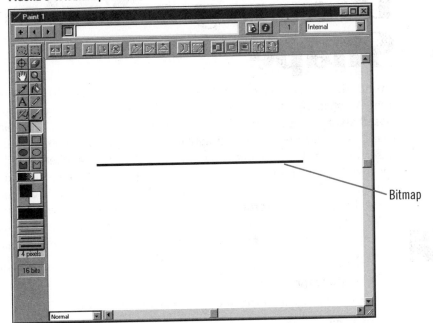

Bitmap

FIGURE C-2: A vector shape of a line

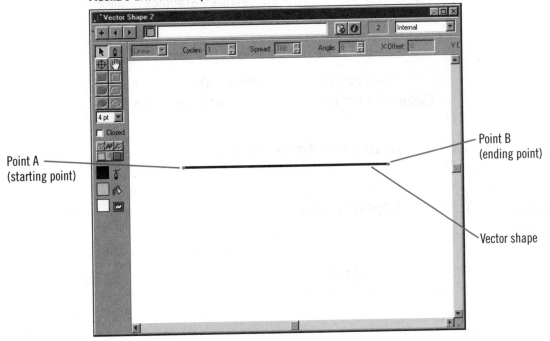

Point A
(starting point)

Point B
(ending point)

Vector shape

Understanding a PostScript graphic

Many graphic designers create graphics in a common format called **PostScript**, using programs such as Macromedia Illustrator or Adobe Illustrator. A PostScript graphic, known as an Encapsulated PostScript (EPS) file, is similar in nature to a vector shape; it is also described in mathematical terms, but is more complex. EPS files are commonly used to transfer graphics between applications and across platforms. EPS allows you to create a complex graphic with several shapes and still save storage and memory space. In Director, you cannot create or import a PostScript graphic. If you have an EPS file that you want to use in a movie, you will need another graphics program, such as Adobe Photoshop, to save it into a Picture (PICT) file, a graphic format that Director can import.

Drawing a Vector Shape

A vector shape can be a line, a curve, or an open or closed shape that you can fill with a color or gradient. An **open shape** is one in which the starting point and the ending point do not connect. A **closed shape** is one in which the points do connect. A shape can be **regular**, such as an oval, rectangle, or rounded rectangle, or **irregular**, such as a free-form object. You can fill the inside of a closed vector shape with a solid color, two-color pattern, or **gradient** blend, which is shading from one color to another color. You create a vector shape in the Vector Shape window by plotting points to define a path and by controlling the curvature of the line between the points. When you create a vector shape, you create **vertices** (also called points), which are fixed points, and **control handles**, which determine the degree of curvature between the vertices. Every vector shape you create becomes a cast member. Jean draws a vector shape for use in an upcoming movie.

Steps

1. Start **Director**

   Director opens, displaying the work area for a new movie.

2. Click **File** on the menu bar, click **Save As**, go to the drive and folder where your Project Files are located, type **SpaceWorks Graphics** in the File name text box (Win) or Saving Movie field (Mac), then click **Save**

   The initial settings in Director will vary depending on the settings last used; you can change the Stage color for better viewing.

3. Click the **Stage window**, click the **Movie tab** in the Property Inspector, click and hold the **Stage Fill color box**, then click the **white color box** at the end of the second row of the color palette

4. Click the **Vector Shape Window button** on the toolbar

   The Vector Shape window opens, displaying Vector Shape 1 on the title bar. Director will store this cast member in location number 1 in the Cast window.

QuickTip

To quickly create a vector shape, click a tool on the Tool palette, then click a blank area in the Vector Shape window.

5. Click the **Filled Ellipse tool** on the Tool palette in the Vector Shape window, then position ✛ in the drawing area

   The Filled Ellipse tool is active and the pointer changes to ✛, as shown in Figure C-3.

6. Press and hold **[Shift]**, then drag ✛ in a right downward diagonal to create the shape shown in Figure C-4

   As you drag, the vector shape draws an ellipse in perfect proportions to create a circle. When you drag the pointer, control handles appear on the vertices: round curve points for vertices with handles and square corner points for vertices without handles, as shown in Figure C-4.

QuickTip

To resize and keep the proportions of a vector shape, click the Arrow tool, press and hold [Ctrl], press [Alt] (Win), or press and hold [Command], press [Option] (Mac), point to a vertice, then drag to the size you desire.

7. Click the **Cast Member Name text box**, type **Jupiter**, then press **[Enter]** (Win) or **[Return]** (Mac)

   The new name appears in the Vector Shape window title bar.

8. Click the **Close button** on the Vector Shape Window

   The Vector Shape window closes. The new vector shape, Jupiter, appears in the Cast window as cast member 1.

FIGURE C-3: Vector Shape window

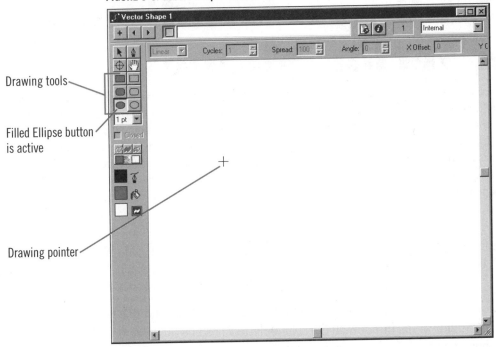

Drawing tools

Filled Ellipse button is active

Drawing pointer

FIGURE C-4: Vector shape of a circle

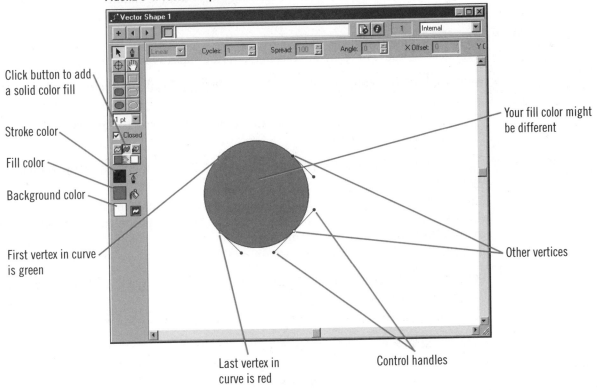

Click button to add a solid color fill

Stroke color

Fill color

Background color

First vertex in curve is green

Your fill color might be different

Other vertices

Last vertex in curve is red

Control handles

Drawing on the Stage

With Director's Tool palette, you can create text, shapes, and buttons directly on the Stage. The shapes you create with the Tool palette are called **QuickDraw graphics**. These graphics are neither vector shapes nor bitmaps. You can resize and edit the QuickDraw shapes on the Stage, but you cannot edit them in the Paint window or in the Vector Shapes window. QuickDraw graphics use a lot less memory than bitmaps, print much better to laser printers, and animate more slowly than bitmaps or vector shapes.

Adding a Gradient to a Vector Shape

Director 8

Once you create a vector shape, you can modify it by adding and changing the color, pattern, or gradient blend. A gradient can be **linear** (shading from one color on one side to another color on the other side) or it can be **radial** (shading from one color in the center to another color on the outside). Once you add a gradient, you can change how many times the gradient repeats, how it is distributed, at what angle it appears, and how offset from the vector shape's center the gradient appears. To modify a vector shape, you need to open the vector shape in the Vector Shape window. Jean modifies the vector shape to create a planet graphic.

Steps

Trouble?

To reselect control handles around a vector shape, click the Arrow tool, position in a blank area of the window, then drag until the selection box surrounds any vertices on the shape.

1. Double-click the **Jupiter vector shape** cast member in the Cast window
The Vector Shape window opens, displaying the selected vector shape. The vertices appear as colored round curve points, indicating that the vector shape is selected.

2. Click and hold the **starting Gradient Colors box**, click the **orange color box** at the beginning of the fifth row on the color palette, click and hold the **ending Gradient Colors box**, then click the **yellow color box** at the end of the third row on the color palette
The starting Gradient Colors box changes to orange, and the ending Gradient Colors box changes to yellow.

3. Click the **Gradient tool** on the Tool palette
A gradient of orange to yellow appears in the vector shape, as shown in Figure C-5.

QuickTip

To change the stroke color in a vector shape, click the Stroke Color box, then click a color. To change a fill color in a vector shape, click the Fill Color box, then click a color. To change the background color, click the Background Color box, then click a color.

4. Verify that the Gradient Type is Linear, then click the **Gradient Cycles up arrow** until it reaches **7**
The **cycle value** determines how many times the gradient repeats from start color to end color within the vector shape.

5. Double-click the **Gradient Spread text box**, type **200**, then click a **blank area** of the Vector Shape window
The **spread value** controls whether the gradient is weighted more towards the start color or end color. A value of 100 makes the gradient evenly distributed between starting and ending colors. Values greater than 100 weight the gradient toward the starting color, and values less than 100 weight it toward the ending color.

6. Double-click the **Gradient Angle text box**, type **75**, then click a **blank area** of the Vector Shape window
For a linear gradient, the **angle value** controls the slope of the gradient.

QuickTip

To remove a gradient, select the shape, then click the No Fill tool on the Tool palette.

7. Click the **Stroke Width list arrow**, then click **0 pt**
The **stroke width** determines the thickness of lines and outlines. The outline of the vector shape is removed, as shown in Figure C-6.

8. Click the **Save button** on the toolbar
The Vector Shape window remains open for the next lesson.

FIGURE C-5: Adding a gradient to a vector shape

Click button to add a gradient

Starting gradient color

Click area to display the Gradient pop-up menu

Ending gradient color

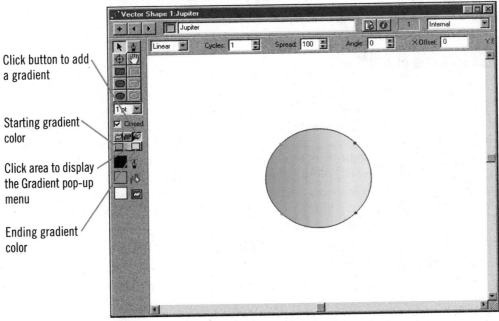

FIGURE C-6: Modifying a gradient

Click list arrow to select gradient type

Click arrows to determine gradient angle

Click list arrow to change stroke width

Click arrows to determine gradient distribution

Click arrows to determine how many times the gradient repeats

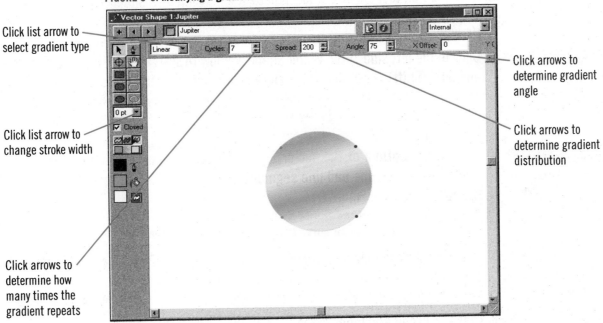

CLUES TO USE

Adjusting the registration point

When you place a vector shape on the Stage, the shape is placed relative to its registration point. You use the registration point, which is initially set to the center of the shape, to accurately position the shape, bitmap, or cast member on the Stage. Director uses the registration point to determine the position when you animate a shape. To adjust the registration point for a vector shape, open the vector shape in the Vector Shape window, then click the Registration Point tool ⊕. The default registration point appears as cross hairs at the center of the vector shape. When you move the pointer in the drawing area, it changes to ⊹. Click a new location in the window to set a new registration point. To reset the registration point to the center of the vector shape, you can double-click ⊕. To remove the cross hairs, click another button. You can change the registration point for a bitmapped cast member in the same way.

Editing a Vector Shape

Director 8

In addition to inserting a gradient, you can edit a vector shape by moving, adding, or deleting control points and by changing the way the control points affect control curves. To edit a vector shape, you use the Pen tool, also known as the selection pointer tool, to select the point you want to edit. Once you select a point on a vector shape, you can press [Delete] or [Backspace] to remove it, or you can drag the point to a different location to change a curve. When you view a vector shape in the Vector Shape window, selected points are unfilled and unselected points are filled. For curves in a vector shape, the first point is green, the last point is red, and all other points are blue. Jean decides to create a free-form vector shape and then edit it.

1. In the Vector Shape window, click the **New Cast Member button** ⊞, click the **Stroke Width list arrow** ▾, then click **4 pt**
   A blank Vector Shape window entitled Vector Shape 2 appears. The Vector Shape window retains the formatting attributes from the previous Vector Shape window. The stroke width changes to 4 points so that you can create a thick line.

2. Click the **Pen tool** ▨ on the Tool palette, then position ╶╁╴ in the Vector Shape window
   The Pen tool is active, and the pointer changes to ╶╁╴. You can use this tool to create a straight line.

> **QuickTip**
>
> You can add a new point by clicking anywhere on the line.

3. Click in the **left side** of the Vector Shape window to start the first line segment, press and hold **[Shift]**, then click in the **right side** to end the first line segment
   The line for the first segment appears, displaying two corner points: green on the left and red on the right. To constrain the control handle to vertical, horizontal, or a 45-degree angle, press and hold [Shift] as you drag the control handles.

> **Trouble?**
>
> If you release the mouse button before you drag the angle that you want, press [Delete] and redrag.

4. Click in the **bottom** of the Vector Shape window, approximately halfway down the window, even with the **end line segment**, then immediately drag to the left to create the **curve** shown in Figure C-7
   A curved segment appears. Notice that you can control the angle of the curve by pivoting a control handle. This type of curve is known as a **Bézier curve**.

> **QuickTip**
>
> If you want to close the path to create a shape that you can fill, click the Closed check box to select it.

5. Click the **Arrow tool** ▨ on the Tool palette, then position ▨ over a point or a control handle
   When you position ▨ over a point or a control handle, the pointer changes to ▨.

6. Drag the **green end point** to the top middle of the Vector Shape window
   The line segment adjusts to the new location when you release the mouse button, and the solid green point changes to an outline.

7. Click the **red end point**, then drag a **control handle** to adjust the curve, as shown in Figure C-8
   The wider you drag the control handle, the larger the curve; the closer you drag, the smaller the curve. If you drag a control handle out of the visible area, drag an edge of the Vector Shape window to resize it.

> **QuickTip**
>
> To change a corner point to a curve point, press and hold [Alt] (Win) or [Option] (Mac), then click a corner point and drag the control handle.

8. Click the **blue point** at the top of the curve, then press **[Backspace]** or **[Delete]**
   The point is removed and the vector shape is redrawn without the point.

9. Click the **Close button** on the Vector Shape Window, then press **[Backspace]** or **[Delete]**
   The Vector Shape window closes, and vector shape cast member 2 is deleted.

FIGURE C-7: Creating a free form vector shape

Start of line segment

End of line segment

End of curve segment

Bézier curve

FIGURE C-8: Adjusting the curvature of a vector shape

Drag point to adjust the position of a line

Drag control handle to adjust the curve

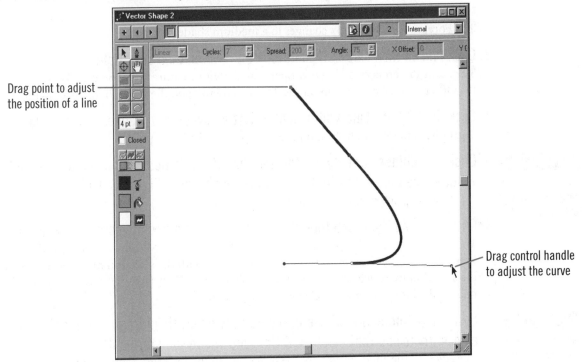

Anti-aliasing a vector shape

When you create a vector shape with thick lines, the edges can look jagged around the curves. You can anti-alias a vector shape to blur the edges, which makes the jagged edges appear smooth. To anti-alias a vector shape, click the vector shape in the Cast window, click Modify on the menu bar, point to Cast Member, click Properties, click the Vector tab in the Property Inspector window, then click the Anti-Alias check box.

Using the Paint Window

Director includes a simple paint program that allows you to create and edit bitmapped cast members without having to open another program, such as Adobe Photoshop. You create and modify a bitmapped cast member by using the tools on the Tool palette. Table AP-3 describes the Paint tools available on the Paint Tool palette. A small arrow in the lower-right corner of a tool indicates that pop-up menu options are available for that tool. To display the pop-up menu, click a tool, then press and hold the mouse button. Before you can work on a bitmap, you need to select it. Director has two main tools that you use to select all or part of a bitmap: lasso and marquee. The **lasso** selects anything that you surround with the tool, while the **marquee** selects everything within its rectangular bounds. Once you select a bitmap, you can apply effects to it using the buttons on the toolbar at the top of the Paint window. Every bitmap you create in the Paint window becomes a cast member. Jean wants to create a space scene, using the Paint window.

Steps

1. Click the **Paint Window button** on the toolbar, then verify that the Ink setting is Normal
   The Paint window opens, displaying Paint 2 on the title bar. Director will store this cast member in location number 2 in the Cast window.

2. Click and hold the **Foreground Color box**, then click the **light gray color box** in the middle of the third row of the color palette
   The Foreground Color box changes to a medium shade of gray.

3. Click **File** on the menu bar, point to **Preferences**, then click **Paint**
   The Paint Preferences dialog box opens, as shown in Figure C-9. You can also double-click the Other Line Width button on the Tool palette to open the Paint Preferences dialog box.

4. Click the **"Other" Line Width right or left arrow** until it reaches **6**, then click **OK**
   The Other Line Width button on the Tool palette displays 6 pixels.

   > **Trouble?**
   > If the shape doesn't match Figure C-10, click the Eraser tool, drag ☐ over the shape to erase it, then repeat Step 5.

5. Click the **Ellipse tool** on the Tool palette, position + on the left side of the window, then drag an **elliptical shape**, as shown in Figure C-10
   An ellipse appears in the Paint window.

6. Click and hold the **Lasso tool** until the pop-up menu appears, then click **Lasso**
   The Lasso tool provides you with three selection options: No Shrink, Lasso, and See Thru Lasso. No Shrink selects everything that you encase with the selection marquee. Lasso makes the selection marquee tighten around the shape. See Thru Lasso is similar to Lasso, but it makes all white pixels in the selection transparent.

   > **Trouble?**
   > If you did not entirely enclose the selection, Director connects its starting and ending point when you release the mouse button.

7. Position ℘ **near the ellipse** in the Paint window, then drag an **outline** around the ellipse (try to end the selection at the point where you started it)
   The edges of the shape might appear to flash with the selection tight around the shape.

8. Click a **blank area** of the Paint window to deselect the shape

9. Click the **Cast Member Name text box**, type **Space Scene**, press **Enter** (Win) or **Return** (Mac), then click the **Close button** in the Paint window
   The Paint window closes and the new cast member is stored as cast member 2 in the Cast window.

FIGURE C-9: **Paint Window Preferences dialog box**

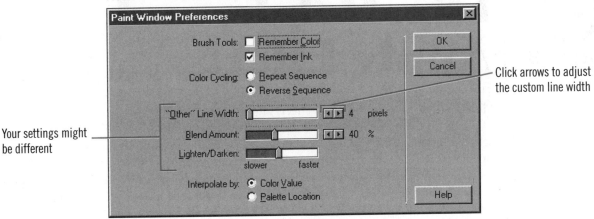

Your settings might be different

Click arrows to adjust the custom line width

FIGURE C-10: **Drawing an elliptical shape**

Start drag here

Foreground color

Other line width set to 6

Verify that the Ink setting is Normal

End drag here

Selecting with the Lasso and Marquee tools

The Lasso tool and Marquee tool allow you to select a bitmap of any size and shape in the Paint window. You use the Lasso tool to select irregular areas or polygons and the Marquee tool to select a rectangular area. To select an irregular area with the Lasso tool, click the Lasso tool, then drag to enclose the area you want to select. To select a polygon area with the Lasso tool, press and hold [Alt] (Win) or [Option] (Mac) while you click to create anchor points to enclose the shape. The Lasso tool selects only those pixels that are of a different color than the ones you select when you first drag the selection. To select a rectangular area with the Marquee tool, drag the tool to enclose the area you want to select. Once you select an area with the Marquee tool, you can press and hold [Ctrl] (Win) or [Command] (Mac), then drag a border of the selected area to resize the selection. To proportionately resize the selection, press and hold [Shift] at the same as you drag. To make a copy of the area that is selected with the Marquee tool, press and hold [Alt] (Win) or [Option] (Mac), then drag the selection. You can press and hold the Lasso tool to display a pop-up menu containing settings that control the way the selection occurs.

Director 8

Unit C
Director 8

Flip, Rotate, and Apply Effects

The toolbar at the top of the Paint window contains buttons you can use to apply effects to bitmapped cast members. These effects allow you to flip, rotate, skew, and warp the contents of a selection. You can also create a perspective effect and an outline around the edges of a selected bitmap. The Paint window also includes tools for controlling the color and pattern of cast members. You can apply color effects to soften edges, reverse colors, increase or reduce brightness, fill solid or pattern, or switch colors. Table AP-4 describes the buttons on the Paint toolbar. Before you can apply an effect, you need to select all or part of the bitmap with the Lasso tool or Marquee tool. Effects that change the shape of the selection, such as flip, rotate, skew, warp, and perspective, work only when you make the selection with the Marquee tool. Effects that change colors within the selection work with both the Marquee and the Lasso tools. Jean applies a few special effects to the space scene.

Steps

1. Double-click the **Space Scene** cast member in the Cast window
   The Paint window opens, displaying the Space Scene cast member.

2. Click and hold the **Marquee tool**, click **No Shrink**, then drag a **selection rectangle** around the ellipse
   The rectangle selection marquee surrounds the ellipse.

3. Click the **Trace Edges button** on the Paint toolbar twice
   Two sets of edges appear in place of the solid line, as shown in Figure C-11. To hide or display the Paint toolbar, click View on the menu bar, then click Paint Tools.

4. Click the **Free Rotate button** on the Paint toolbar
   The pointer changes to +.

5. Position + on a corner rotate handle, drag to rotate the ellipse approximately 45 degrees, as shown in Figure C-12, then click a blank area of the window (outside the selection)
   The shape is deselected.

6. Click and hold, click **Lasso**, then drag a selection rectangle around the shape
   The selected ellipse might flash.

7. Drag the ellipse to the upper-left corner of the visible Paint window (don't scroll), then click a blank area of the window (outside the selection)

8. Click the **Close button** in the Paint window
   The Paint window closes and the cast member is saved in the Cast window.

QuickTip

To select the entire drawing, double-click the Marquee tool.

QuickTip

To add perspective to the shape, select a shape, click the Perspective button on the Paint toolbar, then drag a corner handle.

QuickTip

To zoom in, click the Magnify Glass tool on the Tool palette, then click the artwork. Click again to increase the magnification. Press [Shift] and click to zoom out. Notice that as you gain in magnification, a shape miniature appears in the corner of the Paint window.

FIGURE C-11: A bitmap with trace edges

Arrow indicates a pop-up menu is available

No Shrink Marquee selection

Click button to trace edges

Trace edges

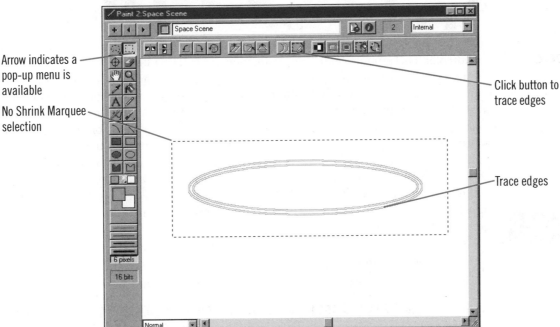

FIGURE C-12: Rotating a bitmap

Click buttons to rotate in 90-degree increments

Click button to rotate in 1-pixel increments

Drag any corner point to rotate a selection

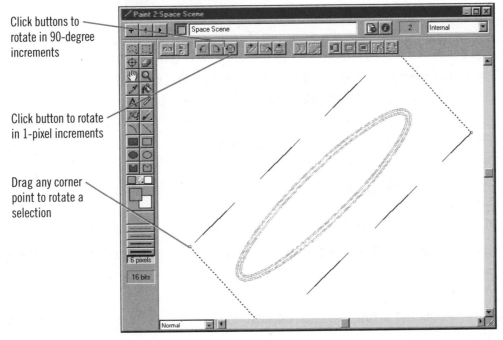

Using rulers in the Paint window

You can display vertical and horizontal rulers in the Paint window to help you align and size your bitmaps. To hide or show the rulers in the Paint window, click View on the menu bar, then click Rulers. The rulers can display measurement values in inches, centimeters, or pixels. The current unit of measurement displays in the upper-left corner. To change the display measurement value, click the upper-left corner where the unit of measurement is displayed. Instead of calculating odd measurements every time you want to align a bitmap, you can set an arbitrary zero point on the ruler to make measuring easier. To change the location of the zero point, click the ruler at the top or side of the window, then drag horizontally or vertically across the ruler until you reach the location where want the zero point to appear.

Applying Ink Effects

Color is an important element of any bitmap. You can set three colors in the Paint window: foreground color, background color, and destination color. The **foreground color** is the default color that you use with the painting tools, the fill color for solid patterns, and the primary color in multicolored patterns. The **background color** is the secondary color in multicolored patterns. The **destination color** is the ending color of gradient blends that start with the foreground color. You can use Paint window inks to create color effects for bitmap cast members. You can select an ink effect from the Ink pop-up menu at the bottom of the Paint window. The result of the ink you choose depends on whether you are working in color or black and white. In addition, some inks work better when painting with patterns, and others work better when painting with solid colors. Table AP-5 describes the different ink effects. You apply Paint ink effects, which are permanent, in the Paint window. Jean creates a bitmap with an ink effect to add to the space scene.

Steps

1. Double-click the **Space Scene** cast member in the Cast window
   The Paint window opens, displaying the Space Scene cast member.

2. Click the **starting Gradient Colors box**, click the **orange color box** at the beginning of the fifth row on the color palette, click the **ending Gradient Colors box**, then click the **yellow color box** at the end of the third row on the color palette

3. Click the **middle Gradient Colors box**, then click **Sun Burst**
   A pop-up menu appears with a list of different gradients. Notice that when you click Sun Burst, a check mark appears next to it.

   > **QuickTip**
   >
   > To create a custom gradient, click the middle Gradient Colors box, click Gradient Settings, then specify the method, direction, cycles, spread, and range for the gradient.

4. Verify that the Pattern tool ▬ is solid, click the **No Line tool** ▭ on the Tool palette, then click the **Filled Ellipse tool** ◉ on the Tool palette
   A filled shape tool must be active in order for the Gradient ink effect to appear as an Ink option.

5. Click the **Ink list arrow** ▾, then click **Gradient**
   When you draw a filled shape, the currently selected gradient settings appear.

6. Press and hold [Shift], position + beneath the ellipse, then drag a **circle**, as shown in Figure C-13
   A filled circle with the previously selected gradient settings appears.

7. Click and hold the **Marquee tool** ▣, click **Lasso,** then drag a **selection rectangle** around the circle
   A circular selection marquee might flash around the circle.

8. Click the **Ink list arrow** ▾, click **Darkest,** then drag the **circle** over the ellipse, as shown in Figure C-14
   The circle and ellipse overlap. Notice that the pointer changes to ☝ when you position the pointer in a blank area of the Paint window.

9. Click a **blank area** of the window (outside the selection), then click the **Close button** in the Paint window
   The Paint window closes and the cast member is saved in the Cast window.

FIGURE C-13: **Applying a gradient ink effect**

Gradient end color

Click middle Gradient Colors box to display pop-up menu

Gradient start color

Pattern tool

No Line tool

Gradient ink effect

FIGURE C-14: **Moving artwork**

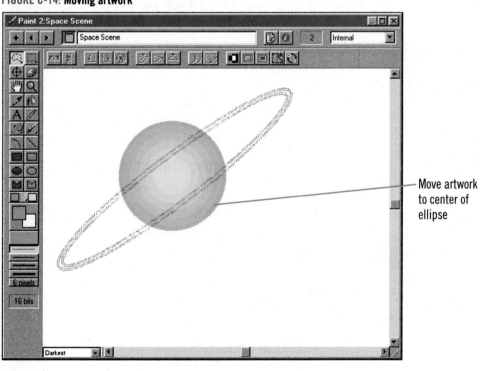

Move artwork to center of ellipse

Using patterns

Instead of using a solid fill color in a bitmap, you can use a pattern. A pattern consists of a small image that is repeated continuously to fill in a shape, such as a rectangle, ellipse, or polygon. The current foreground and background colors are the primary and secondary colors, respectively, in a multicolored pattern. To display a palette of patterns, click and hold the Pattern tool on the Tool palette. The pattern palette includes preset patterns, but you can also click Pattern Settings to add your own patterns. When you create your own pattern, the Pattern Settings dialog box displays an enlarged version of any pattern you select, then you can edit it.

Director 8

Applying Painting Effects

The Paint window includes tools for applying painting effects to your artwork. The main painting tools are the Paint Bucket, Eyedropper, Brush, and Air Brush tools. You can use the Paint Bucket tool to fill all adjacent pixels of the same color with the foreground color. The Eyedropper tool is commonly used with the Paint Bucket tool; it selects a color from the artwork, which you can then use as the foreground, background, or destination color. You use the Brush tool to brush strokes with the current foreground color, ink, and fill pattern. The Brush tool displays a pop-up menu where you can define five different brush sizes and shapes. You use the Air Brush tool to spray the current foreground color, ink, and fill pattern. The longer you spray the Air Brush tool in one spot, the more it fills in the area. You define spray settings in the Air Brush pop-up menu, just as you do in the Brush tool pop-up menu. The spray settings include flow rate, spray area, dot size, and dot options. ⟍ Jean applies some painting effects to the space scene.

Steps 1 2 3 4

1. Double-click the **Space Scene** cast member in the Cast window
   The Paint window opens, displaying the Space Scene cast member.

2. Click and hold the **Foreground Colors box**, then click the **black color box** at the beginning of the first row on the color palette

Trouble?
If the inside of the ring does not fill with black, click ⟨⟩ inside the ring in a blank area to fill the entire area black.

3. Click the **Paint Bucket tool** 🪣 on the Tool palette, then click ⟨⟩ in a **blank area** of the Paint window
   When you click the mouse button, the Paint Bucket fills all adjacent pixels of the same color in the visible portion of the Paint window with the foreground color, black, as shown in Figure C-15. Since the ring bitmap is not white (the same color of the adjacent pixels), the inside of the ring remains the original background color until you click inside the ring.

4. Click and hold the **starting Gradient Colors box**, then click the **white color box** at the end of the second row on the color palette

5. Click and hold the **Brush button** ✏ on the Tool palette, then click **Brush 1**
   The Brush 1 settings are selected.

QuickTip
To quickly open the Brush Settings dialog box, double-click the Brush tool ✏.

6. Click and hold ✏ on the Tool palette, then click **Settings**
   The Brush Settings dialog box opens, as shown in Figure C-16.

7. Click the **smallest dot** in the lower-left corner, then click **OK**
   The new Brush 1 settings are saved.

8. Click **individual brush dots** in the Paint window, as shown in Figure C-17
   When you position the pointer in the Paint window, it changes to the shape and size of the brush. When you click in the Paint window, the brush shape paints with the foreground color.

9. Click the **Close button** in the Paint window

FIGURE C-15: Applying the Paint Bucket effect

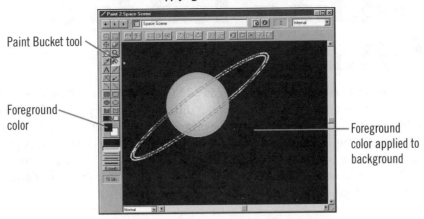

Paint Bucket tool

Foreground color

Foreground color applied to background

FIGURE C-16: Brush Settings dialog box

Current brush size (yours might differ)

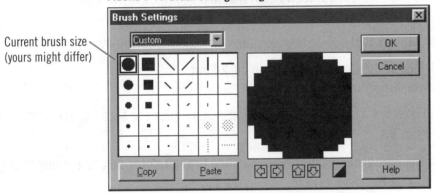

FIGURE C-17: Applying the Brush effect

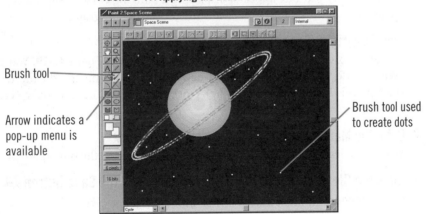

Brush tool

Arrow indicates a pop-up menu is available

Brush tool used to create dots

Selecting colors with the Eyedropper tool

If you want to match the color of one or more pixels with another set of pixels, you can use the Eyedropper tool. This tool allows you to select a color currently in the Paint window as the foreground, background, or destination color. To select a color as the foreground, click on the Tool palette, position the bottom tip of over the color you want to select, then click in the Paint window. To use to select a background color, press [Shift], then click a color. To select a color as the destination color, press [Alt] (Win) or [Option] (Mac), then click a color. You can also press [D] to temporarily activate while using other paint tools. Once you select a color, you can use the Paint Bucket tool to fill an area of pixels to match colors.

Director 8

Adding Text to a Bitmap

When the Paint window is open, you can add text to a bitmap. When you add text to a bitmap, the text becomes part of the bitmap and is difficult to edit. If you decide to change a word, font style, or text spacing, you must erase the original text and start over again. However, you can use effects in the Paint window to transform and change bitmapped text just as you would any other bitmap. You can flip, rotate, skew, and warp bitmapped text. Because bitmapped text is difficult to edit, carefully consider the text you want to include in your bitmaps. Jean adds copyright text to the space scene.

1. Double-click the **Space Scene** cast member in the Cast window
   The Paint window opens, displaying the Space Scene cast member.

2. Click the **Text tool** A on the Tool palette in the Paint window

3. Click **Modify** on the menu bar, then click **Font**
   The Font dialog box opens, as shown in Figure C-18.

4. In the Font list, click **Arial** (scroll if necessary), click the **Size list arrow** ▼, click **10**, then click **OK**

QuickTip

You can also select a color by clicking the color box in the Font dialog box.

5. Click the **Foreground Color box**, click the **orange color box** at the beginning of the fifth row on the color palette

6. Click in the **lower-left corner** of the Paint window
   A small empty text box appears, displaying a blinking cursor. You can type and edit text in the text box in the same way as in a word-processing program.

QuickTip

To move the text box, drag any edge of the text box.

7. Type **Copyright, SpaceWorks Interactive**
   The text box expands as you type the text, as shown in Figure C-19. You can press [Enter] (Win) or [Return] (Mac) to start a new line. If you want to edit the text, you can press [Backspace] (Win) or [Delete] (Mac). Once you deselect the text box, you can no longer edit the text.

8. Click the **Marquee tool** ▦ to deselect the text box
   When you deselect the text box, the text becomes part of the bitmap.

9. Click the **Close button** in the Paint window, click the **Save button** ▦, then click **File** on the menu bar, click **Exit** [Win] or **Quit** [Mac]
   The movie is saved and Director closes.

FIGURE C-18: Font dialog box

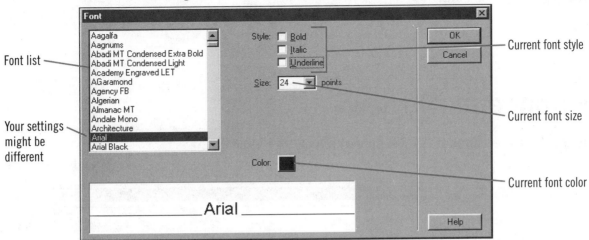

Font list

Your settings
might be
different

Current font style

Current font size

Current font color

FIGURE C-19: Adding text to a bitmap

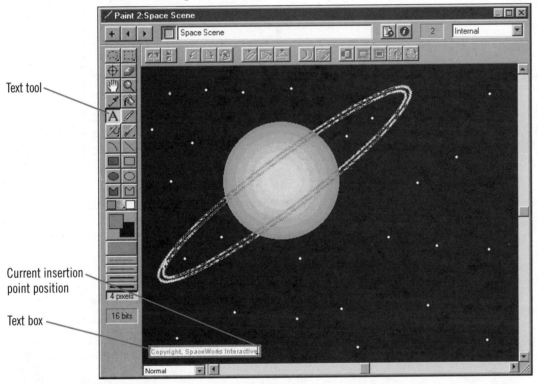

Text tool

Current insertion
point position

Text box

Creating a custom tile

A **tile** is a graphic that you can repeat in a pattern to create backgrounds, textures, or fillers. Custom tiles provide an effective way to create a background without using a lot of memory or increasing the download time for movies on the Web. A custom tile uses the same amount of memory no matter what size area it fills. You can create tiles from an existing cast member. To create a custom tile, display a bitmap cast member in the Paint window, click and hold the Pattern tool ▮▮▮, click Tile Settings, click an existing tile position to edit, click Cast Member, drag the dotted rectangle to the area of the cast member you want tiled, specify the size of the tile, then click OK. The new tile appears at the bottom of the Pattern palette. You can use the custom tile as a fill pattern. To select the custom tile as a fill pattern, click and hold ▮▮▮, then click the custom tile at the bottom of the Pattern palette. You can use one of the Filled drawing tools or the Paint Bucket tool ▮ to fill an area with the custom tile.

Director 8

Practice

► Concepts Review

Label each of the elements of the screen shown in Figure C-20.

FIGURE C-20

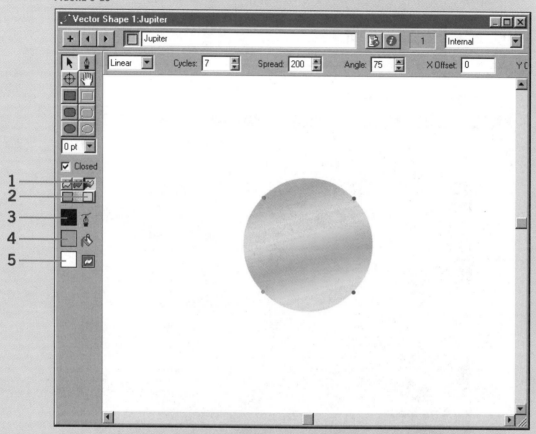

Match each of the terms with the statement that describes its function.

6. Vertices
7. Handles
8. Gradient
9. Pixel
10. Registration Point
11. Anti-Aliasing

a. The point used for animation
b. An individual point in a bitmap
c. Determine the degree of curvature between points
d. Fixed points on a vector shape
e. Shading from one color to another color
f. Blending the edges of a bitmap with background colors

Select the best answer from the following list of choices.

12. A graphic represented by pixels is called a:
   a. Bitmap.
   b. Vector shape.
   c. QuickDraw shape.
   d. PostScript shape.

13. A graphic represented by a mathematical description in Director is called a:
   a. Bitmap.
   b. Vector shape.
   c. QuickDraw shape.
   d. PostScript shape.

14. **Which is NOT a vector shape property?**
   a. Uses less memory
   b. Uses less storage space
   c. Requires less download time
   d. Resizes with distortion

15. **A shape in which the starting and ending points do not connect is called a(n):**
   a. Closed shape.
   b. Regular shape.
   c. Open shape.
   d. QuickDraw shape.

16. **Which value determines how many times a gradient repeats?**
   a. Spread
   b. Angle
   c. Cycle
   d. Range

17. **What color is the first point in a vector shape?**
   a. Red
   b. Green
   c. Blue
   d. None of the above

18. **Which selection tool allows you to change the shape of the selection?**
   a. Lasso only
   b. Marquee only
   c. Lasso and Marquee
   d. None of the above

▶ Skills Review

1. **Understand vector shapes and bitmaps.**
   a. Write down at least three properties of vector shapes and bitmaps, without referring to the unit material.

2. **Draw a vector shape.**
   a. Start Director, then open the file MD C-1 from the drive and folder where your Project Files are located, then save it as *SpaceWorks Graphics Final*.
   b. Open the Vector Shape window.
   c. Create a new cast member, if necessary.
   d. Draw a circle, then name the cast member *Sun*.
   e. Close the Vector Shape window.

3. **Add a gradient to a vector shape.**
   a. Open the Sun vector shape cast member, then add a gradient to the circle.
   b. Change the starting Gradient Colors box to a bright yellow.
   c. Change the ending Gradient Colors box to a bright red.
   d. Change the Gradient Type to Radial, then change the Gradient Cycle to 2.
   e. Change the Stroke Width to 0 pt.

4. **Edit a vector shape.**
   a. Create a new cast member.
   b. Change the Stroke Width to 4 pt.
   c. Draw a line and add a curve to it.
   d. Adjust a line to a longer length, then change the curvature of a line.
   e. Close the Vector Shape window.

5. **Use the Paint window.**
   a. Open the Paint window.
   b. Change the foreground color to brown.
   c. Change the Other Line Width to 4, then draw a long narrow ellipse.

d. Select the ellipse shape and move it to the center of the window.

e. Name the cast member *Planet Scene* and close the Paint window.

6. **Flip, rotate, and apply effects.**

   a. Open the Planet Scene in the Paint window.

   b. Change the perspective of the oval shape.

   c. Rotate the ellipse shape 45 degrees, then flip the ellipse shape horizontally.

   d. Move the ellipse shape to the lower-left corner of the window.

   e. Close the Paint window.

7. **Apply ink effects.**

   a. Open the Planet Scene in the Paint window, then change the line width to No Line.

   b. Change the ink effect to Blend.

   c. Draw a filled oval shape in a blank area of the window.

   d. Change the ink effect to Normal.

   e. Select the oval shape tightly, then move the oval shape inside the ellipse.

   f. Close the Paint window.

8. **Apply painting effects.**

   a. Open the Planet Scene in the Paint window, then change the foreground color to black.

   b. Fill the background of the Paint window with black.

   c. Change the brush setting to the second-smallest dot.

   d. Change the foreground color to white, then click individual dots in the window.

   e. Close the Paint window.

9. **Add text to a bitmap.**

   a. Open the Planet Scene in the Paint window, then select the Text tool.

   b. Verify that the font is Arial, that the font size is 10, and that the color is orange.

   c. Add your initials to the lower-right corner of the Paint window.

   d. Close the Paint window, then save the movie and close Director.

► Independent Challenges

1. You are the chief designer and owner of Unique Pools, a company that designs uniquely shaped swimming pools. The owner of Gourmet Jelly Beans asks you to design the corporate swimming pool in the form of a jelly bean. You use Director's Vector Shape tools to create the jelly bean shape and add a blue gradient to represent water.

   To complete this independent challenge:

   a. Start Director and save the movie as *Unique Pools* in the drive and folder where your Project Files are located.

   b. Open the Vector Shape window.

   c. Draw a large circle and change the curves to form a jelly bean.

   d. Add a blue gradient from left to right to represent water.

   e. Change the Stroke Width to 2 pt and the Stroke Color to dark blue.

   f. Name the cast member *Jelly Bean Pool*, and close the Vector Shape window.

   g. Create a text cast member with the text **Pool designed by Unique Pools**.

   h. Place both cast members on the Stage and add a color background.

   i. Print the Stage, save the movie, and exit Director.

2. You are a student at the State University. Your history professor gives you an assignment to create a multimedia presentation on your home state. You use Director's Vector Shape tools to create the shape of your state and add a gradient to represent the terrain.

To complete this independent challenge:

a. Start Director and save the movie as *US State* in the drive and folder where your Project Files are located.

b. Open the Vector Shape window.

c. Draw a free-form shape with lines and curves to represent any state in the U.S. (*Hint*: If you live in Colorado, Kansas, Nebraska, North Dakota, South Dakota, New Mexico, or Wyoming, try to pick another state.)

d. Modify the lines and curves to display the outline of the state.

e. Add a gradient that represents the terrain of the state.

f. Change the Stroke Width to 1 pt and the Stroke Color to black.

g. Name the cast member *US State*, and close the Vector Shape window.

h. Create a text cast member with the text **US State presentation by [Your Name]**.

i. Place both cast members on the Stage and add a color background.

j. Print the Stage, save the movie, and exit Director.

3. You are the chief designer at Borderlines, a company that designs signs and banners. The president of Garfield Graffiti Removal, Inc. asks you to design a company logo and a sign for the front of their company building. You use Director's Paint tools to create a sign with the company logo.

To complete this independent challenge:

a. Start Director and save the movie as *Borderlines* in the drive and folder where your Project Files are located.

b. Open the Paint window, then draw a large unfilled rectangle with a gray 2 pt border for the sign.

c. Add the text **Garfield Graffiti Removal, Inc.** to the sign, using the Text tool.

d. Add different color graffiti to the sign, using the Airbrush tool. (*Hint*: Do not cover the text with the Airbrush tool.)

e. Name the cast member *GGRI Logo*, and close the Paint window.

f. Create a text cast member with the text **GGRI Sign designed by Borderlines**.

g. Place both cast members on the Stage, then print the Stage, save the movie, and exit Director.

4. You are a graphics designer at Fifth Avenue Advertising & Design. The president of the New York City Olympic Committee asks you to create an Olympic logo for a multimedia presentation they are developing for the International Olympic Committee. You use Director's Paint tools to create the Olympic logo.

To complete this independent challenge:

a. Connect to the Internet and go to www.course.com. Navigate to the page for this book, click the link for the Student Online Companion, click the link for this Unit, then review past Olympic logos for ideas.

b. Start Director and save the movie as *NYC Olympics* in the drive and folder where your Project Files are located.

c. Open the Paint window, then draw the Olympic rings.

d. Add the text **New York** to the logo, using the Text tool.

e. Design the rest of the logo, using the Paint tools.

f. Name the cast member *NYCOC*, and close the Paint window.

g Create a text cast member with the text **New York Olympic Logo designed by Fifth Avenue Advertising & Design**.

h. Place both cast members on the Stage and add a color background.

i. Print the Stage, save the movie, and exit Director.

Director 8

▶ Visual Workshop

Recreate the screen shown in Figure C-21. Print the screen. Save the file as *Letters* in the drive and folder where your Project Files are located. (For Windows, use the Windows Paint program. Press the Print Screen key to make a copy of the screen. Start the Paint program by clicking Start, pointing to Programs, pointing to Accessories, then clicking Paint. Click Edit on the menu bar, click Paste to paste the screen into Paint, then click Yes to paste the large image if necessary. Click File on the menu bar, click Print or OK in the dialog box, then exit Paint. For the Macintosh, use the SimpleText program. Hold and press the Command, Shift, and 3 keys to make a copy of the screen, double-click the document Picture 1 located on your hard drive, click File on the menu bar, click Print, then click Print in the dialog box. *Note*: When you create a new document with a copy of the screen, and a document Picture 1 already exists, the Macintosh names the new document Picture 2.)

FIGURE C-21

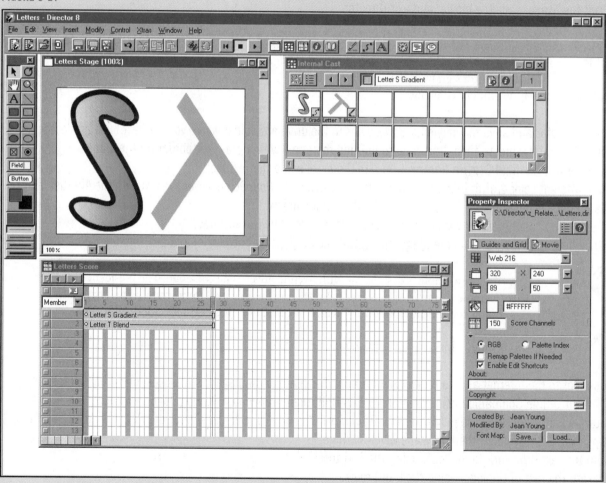

Managing
and Modifying Cast Members

- ▶ **Create a Cast**
- ▶ **Use the Cast window**
- ▶ **Organize cast members**
- ▶ **Find cast members**
- ▶ **Change cast member properties**
- ▶ **Transform a paint cast member**
- ▶ **Add and edit a text cast member**
- ▶ **Modify a text cast member**
- ▶ **Save and unlink a Cast**

A complex Director movie can often require a large number of cast members. When you assemble a large number of cast members in a Cast window, it can sometimes be difficult to locate the one you want. You can use management and organization tools in Director to help alleviate the hassle of scrolling through a long list of cast members. This unit introduces you to basic skills for managing, organizing, and modifying cast members. First, you'll learn how to create a new Cast. Then you'll learn how to change Cast preferences, organize and find cast members, change cast member properties, and modify cast members. Finally, you'll learn how to save and unlink a Cast. ✎   After creating graphical cast members in Director, Jean wants to organize them with other imported cast members in an External Cast for use in an upcoming movie.

Director 8

Creating a Cast

In Director, your movies literally can have a Cast of thousands—you can include up to 32,000 cast members in a Cast window. Before you create and assemble a large number of cast members for a movie, it is important to think about how you want to organize them. Director allows you to create and work with multiple Casts within a movie. If you notice that you use certain media elements repeatedly, you can organize them into separate Casts. Separating them saves the time and inconvenience of importing them individually for each movie. Each Cast has its own window. When you create a new Cast, you need to decide whether to create an **Internal Cast**, which is saved as part of the movie, or an **External Cast**, which is saved in a separate file outside of the movie. When you use cast members from an External Cast, it's easiest if you first link the Cast to the movie. However, even if you don't link an External Cast to the movie, you can still open the External Cast and add, remove, and modify cast members. If you plan to use cast members in one movie only, then use an Internal Cast. If you plan to share cast members in more than one movie, then use an External Cast. You can add as many Internal or External Casts as you want; each Cast is viewed in a separate Cast window. ✒️ Jean creates an external cast so she can organize and reuse cast members for several upcoming movies.

Steps

1. Start **Director**, open the file **MD D-1** from the drive and folder where your Project Files are located, then save it as **SpaceWorks Game Promo**
   Director opens, displaying the movie. Initial settings in Director can vary, depending on previous usage.

2. Position ↖ on the lower-right corner of the **Stage window**, then drag the **border** diagonally to the right to expand the window to display the gray area around the Stage

3. Click the **Close button** in the Score window, click **Window** on the menu bar, then click **Cast**, if necessary, to display the Internal Cast window

4. Click and hold the **Choose Cast button** 🎛️ in the Internal Cast window
   A pop-up menu appears, displaying a list of current Casts and the New Cast command.

> **QuickTip**
> You can also click File on the menu bar, point to New, then click Cast to open the New Cast dialog box.

5. On the pop-up menu, click **New Cast**
   The New Cast dialog box opens.

6. In the Name box, type **Space Graphics**

7. Click the **External option button**
   The Use in Current Movie option becomes available and is selected, as shown in Figure D-1. This option links the new External Cast to the current movie.

> **QuickTip**
> To open an unlinked External Cast to the current movie, click File on the menu bar, click Open, select an external cast file, then click Open.

8. Click **Create**
   The new blank Cast window opens. When you link an External Cast to the current movie, Director opens that Cast whenever you open the movie.

9. Drag the **title bar** of the Space Graphics Cast window to the blank area below the Stage
   The Space Graphics Cast window appears in the Director window, as shown in Figure D-2.

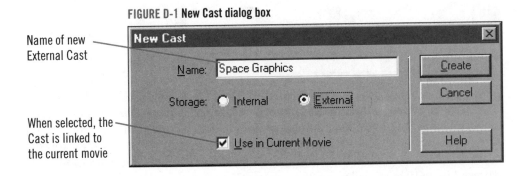

FIGURE D-1 New Cast dialog box

Name of new External Cast

When selected, the Cast is linked to the current movie

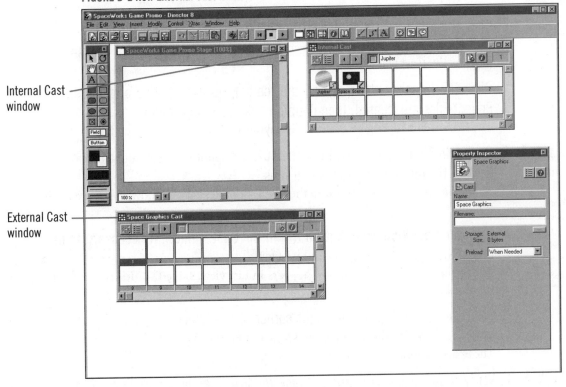

FIGURE D-2 New External Cast window

Internal Cast window

External Cast window

Techniques for organizing cast members

Organizing your cast members from the beginning will ensure that both your movie-making process and your movie will run smoothly. You can use several techniques to organize and manage cast members: (1) name each cast member with a unique identifier, (2) group similar cast members together, and (3) create multiple Casts, either Internal or External. It is important to name each cast member. Lingo, Director's programming language, identifies cast members in scripts by their name. The naming convention should identify the media element's function or purpose. Appropriate cast member names could be Help button, Space background, Blue Earth

graphic, or Welcome text, instead of simply Button, Graphic, Text, or no name at all. Another technique is to group similar cast members together. You can move cast members around to any location in the Cast window; they are not required to be in consecutive order. You can leave a few blank cast member windows in between each group, to visually separate each section of the cast. Finally, you can create multiple Cast windows that contain cast members by type, such as buttons and navigation, text, pictures, sounds, videos, transitions and effects, and behaviors and scripts.

Using the Cast Window

The Cast window allows you to view and organize all of the media elements in a movie, move one cast member or groups of cast members around in a Cast, sort cast members by type, and use paint and text tools on cast members. In the Cast window, you can view the Cast in List view or Thumbnail view. You can use the Cast View Style button in the Cast window to easily toggle between List and Thumbnail views. You can use Cast window preferences to control the appearance of the current or all Cast windows. You can also open the Property Inspector to view and modify cast member properties. ◢◣ Jean changes the Cast window view and preferences to make it easier to organize the cast members.

Steps 1234

1. **Click the title bar of the Space Graphics Cast window, if necessary**
   The Space Graphics Cast window is active. When you import graphics, Director places them in the active Cast window.

2. **Click the Import button 🔳 on the toolbar, go to the drive and folder where your Project Files are located, then double-click the Media folder**
   The Import Files dialog box opens, displaying a list of the files in the Media folder.

   Trouble?
   If the Image Options dialog box or Select Format dialog box appears, use the selected settings, click the Same Settings for Remaining Images check box (if available) to select it, then click OK as necessary.

3. **Click Add All, click Import, then click OK to accept the selected graphic settings for each of the remaining images and files**
   All the files in the file list appear in the Space Graphics Cast window, identified by their location number, name, and type.

4. **Click the Cast View Style button 🔳 in the Cast window, if necessary, to display the Space Graphics Cast window in List view**
   The Space Graphics Cast window appears in List view. Table D-1 describes the display features of List view.

5. **Position 🔾 over the bottom-right corner of the Space Graphics Cast window, then drag 🔾 to resize the window, as shown in Figure D-3**
   The Space Graphics Cast window is resized.

   QuickTip
   You can also open the Cast Window Preferences dialog box by right-clicking a cast member (Win), or pressing and holding [Option] and clicking a cast member (Mac), then clicking Cast Preferences.

6. **Verify that the Space Graphics Cast window is active, click File on the menu bar, point to Preferences, then click Cast**
   The Cast Window Preferences for "Space Graphics" dialog box opens, as shown in Figure D-4. The title bar of the dialog box displays the names of the Cast window preferences that you can change.

7. **Click the Size check box to select it, then click the Apply to All Casts check box to clear it, if necessary**
   The options you check in the List Columns area appear as new columns in List view.

8. **Click the Label list arrow 🔽, then click Number:Name**
   The number and name of the cast member appear below the thumbnail in Thumbnail view.

   QuickTip
   To make your preferences settings the default settings, click Save as Default. To apply your preferences to all Cast windows, click the Apply to All Casts check box to select it.

9. **Click OK**
   The Space Graphics Cast window appears with the Size column added to the list. These settings are only set for the Space Graphics Cast window. The Internal Cast window remains the same.

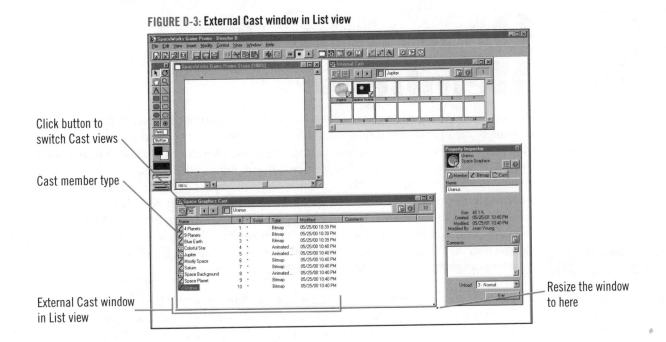

FIGURE D-3: External Cast window in List view

Click button to switch Cast views

Cast member type

External Cast window in List view

Resize the window to here

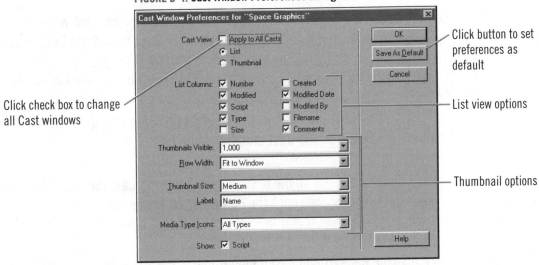

FIGURE D-4: Cast Window Preferences dialog box

Click button to set preferences as default

Click check box to change all Cast windows

List view options

Thumbnail options

TABLE D-1: List view display features

column title	description	column title	description
Name	Name of the cast member and an icon describing its type	**Comments**	Comments field in the Member tab of the Property Inspector
#	Number assigned to the cast member	**Size**	Size in bytes, kilobytes, or megabytes
×	Cast member changes need to be saved	**Created**	Date and time the cast member was created
Script	Script type: *Member* means the cast member is a script; *Movie* means the cast member is a movie script; *Behavior* means the cast member is a behavior	**Modified By**	Name of the person who modified the cast member
Type	Cast member type	**Filename**	Full path to the cast member if it is a linked asset
Modified	Date and time the cast member was changed		

Director 8

Organizing Cast Members

Director allows you to move, copy, delete, and sort cast members. However, before you perform some of these organizational functions, you need to first select the cast members in the Cast window. You can easily move or copy a cast member in the same Cast window or to another one. You might want to create copies of a cast member with minor differences, such as color or position, to create an animation effect. Sometimes you will import or create cast members but not use them in the movie. You can delete them at any time. When you delete a cast member, it is removed from the movie, even if it is being used on the Stage and in the Score. You can use the Sort command to arrange cast members by their media type, name, size, or usage in the Score. You can also use the Sort command to remove empty locations in a Cast window. ✐ Jean organizes cast members in the external Space Graphics Cast window.

Steps

QuickTip

To resize the columns in List view, position ↔ over the column title border, then drag the column to the desired size.

1. **In the Space Graphics Cast window, click the Name column title (Win)**
   List view is sorted in descending order by the name of the cast members, as shown in Figure D-5. You can click the column titles in List view to easily toggle between ascending and descending sort order. When you click a column title, List view changes the display of the cast member information, but it doesn't change their physical location in the Cast.

2. **Click the Cast View Style button ▤ on the Space Graphics Cast window to display the Cast window in Thumbnail view, then click the Cast View Style button ▤ on the Internal Cast window to display it in Thumbnail view, if necessary**
   The cast members appear in Thumbnail view, displaying the cast member number, name, and type.

3. **Click the Jupiter cast member in the Internal Cast window, press and hold [Shift], then click the Space Scene cast member to its right**
   Both cast members are selected.

4. **Click the Copy button ▤ on the toolbar, click the empty cast member 11 in the Space Graphics Cast window, then click the Paste button ▤ on the toolbar**
   The copied cast members appear in locations 11 and 12. Notice that the copied cast members retain the exact same name as the originals.

Trouble?

If you drag a cast member to a location that already contains a cast member, the selected cast member will move where you place it, and the existing one will move one location to the right.

5. **Drag the Space Background cast member in the Space Graphics Cast window to empty cast member 23, then drag the cast members to the locations shown in Figure D-6**
   When you drag a cast member in Thumbnail view, the pointer changes to ✍, and a highlight bar appears in the new location. When you move a cast member to a new location, Director assigns it a new location number and updates all references to the cast member in the Score, but it does not update references to the cast member number in Lingo scripts.

QuickTip

Make sure the cast member Name box is not highlighted when you delete the cast member.

6. **Click the orange Jupiter cast member in the Space Graphics Cast window, then press [Delete] or [Backspace]**
   The cast member is deleted.

7. **Click the 4 Planets cast member in Space Graphics Cast window, press and hold [Shift], then click the Uranus cast member to select all of the cast members in the first row**

8. **Click Modify on the menu bar, then click Sort**
   The Sort dialog box opens.

9. **Click the Name option button, then click Sort**
   The cast members in the first row of the Space Graphics Cast window are sorted by name, as shown in Figure D-7. Notice that when you sort the cast, any empty cast members are removed.

FIGURE D-5: Sorting columns in List view

Column titles ——

Click column title to sort list ——

Drag border to resize columns ——

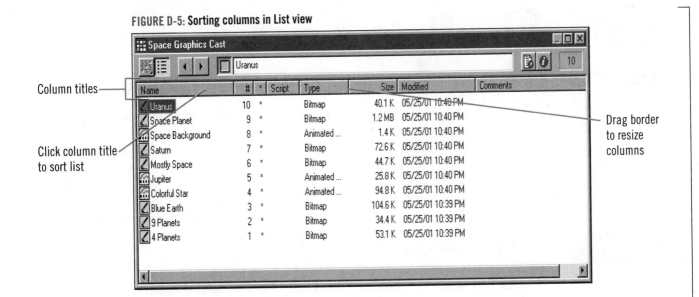

FIGURE D-6: External Cast window in Thumbnail view

Click button to switch views ——

Thumbnail view displays cast member number, name, and type ——

Selected cast member ——

Cast members copied from the Internal Cast window ——

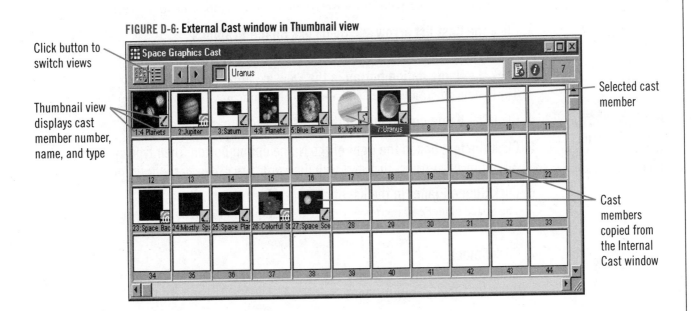

FIGURE D-7: Sorting cast members

Cast members sorted by name ——

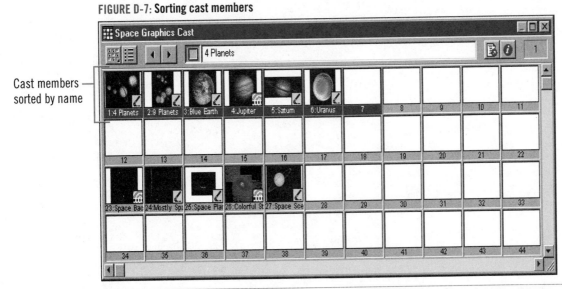

Director 8

Finding Cast Members

If your movie contains several cast members, it may be difficult to locate a particular one. You can use the Find feature to locate cast members by name, type, color palette, or usage in the Score, and then select them in the Cast window. When you name your cast members logically, you make it easy to find them. You can find multiple cast members with similar names. For example, cast members with the names Space Background and Space Scene share the common word "space". When you search, Director finds all the cast members with the common word at the beginning of the name. Once Director completes the word search, you can specify which cast members to select in the Cast window. ✐ Jean wants to find all the cast members that begin with the word "space".

Steps 1 2 3 4

1. **Click Edit on the menu bar, point to Find, then click Cast Member**
   The Find Cast Members dialog box opens, as shown in Figure D-8. The list of cast members at the bottom of the dialog box displays all the cast members in both Casts.

2. **Click the Cast list arrow ▼, then click Space Graphics**
   The search criteria are narrowed down to cast members in the Space Graphics Cast window.

3. **Click the Name option button in the View by: area**
   The cast members are sorted alphabetically by name in the list of cast members

4. **Click the Name option button that has an accompanying text box**

5. **Click the text box to the right of the Name option button, then type space**
   All cast member names that start with the word "space" appear in the list of cast members.

6. **Click Space Planet in the list of cast members**
   The Space Planet cast member is selected, as shown in Figure D-9. You can specify whether to select one or all of the cast members in the Cast window.

7. **Click Select**
   The Find Cast Member dialog box closes, and the Space Planet cast member is selected in the Space Graphics Cast window.

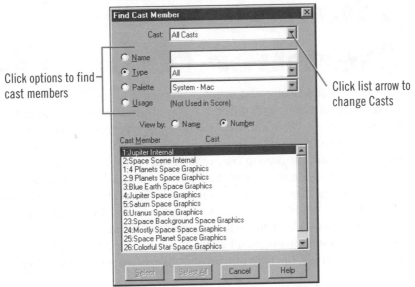

FIGURE D-8: Find Cast Member dialog box

Click options to find cast members

Click list arrow to change Casts

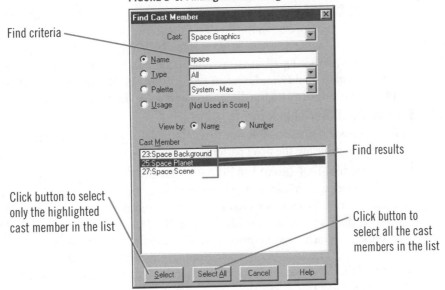

FIGURE D-9: Finding and selecting cast members

Find criteria

Find results

Click button to select only the highlighted cast member in the list

Click button to select all the cast members in the list

Finding and deleting unused cast members

Sometimes you will import or create a cast member that you don't end up using in the movie. Director makes it easy to find and delete unused cast members. When you delete unused cast members, your movie's file size becomes smaller, faster to load, and more efficient in using computer memory. Before you close your finished movie, it's important to remove unused cast members. To delete unused cast members, click Edit on the menu bar, point to Find, then click Cast Member. In the Find Cast Member dialog box, click the Cast list arrow, click a Cast with unused cast members, click the Usage option

button, click in the cast member list, then click Select All. Director finds and selects all cast members not used in the Score from the selected Cast. Before you complete the deletion, make sure that the selected cast members are not used in any Lingo scripts, which do not appear in the Score. To view a Lingo script for a selected cast member, click the Cast Member Script button 📇 in the Cast window. To delete the selected cast members, click Select or Select All in the Find Cast Member dialog box, then press [Delete] or [Backspace], or click Edit on the menu bar, then click Clear Cast Members.

Director 8

Changing Cast Member Properties

You can view and change cast member properties for one or more cast members. If you select multiple cast members with different types, the information common to all of the selected cast members appears. When you view cast member properties, a tab labeled with the cast member's type appears in the Property Inspector. For example, if you click the Blue Earth cast member in the Cast window, the Bitmap tab in the Property Inspector appears. The property information available depends on the type of the selected cast member. You can also use cast member properties to manage memory usage in a movie. If Director determines that memory is running low while you play a movie, it unloads some cast members from memory so that other ones can be loaded. If you are about to perform a memory-intensive operation, you can use the Memory Inspector to monitor usage and purge all removable items from memory. ✎ Jean views cast member properties for a bitmap and changes a memory-related setting.

1. Verify that the Space Planet cast member is selected in the Space Graphics Cast window

2. Click the **Cast Member Properties button** 🔘 in the Space Graphics Cast window

The Bitmap tab appears in the Property Inspector, as shown in Figure D-10. The Bitmap tab displays options for selecting a color palette, highlighting a bitmap, such as a button, when you click it, dithering a bitmap (color matching), trimming white space around a bitmap, setting bitmap quality, and selecting Alpha settings (the transparent area of a bitmap). The Bitmap tab also displays the dimension and color depth of the cast member.

3. Click the **Dither check box** to select it

When a color is not available due to a color palette problem, the Dither option estimates the color by combining the pixel pattern.

4. Click the **Member tab** in the Property Inspector

The Member tab appears in the Property Inspector. The Member tab displays text boxes for changing the cast member's name, adding a comment that appears in the Comments column of the Cast window in List view, and selecting an unload value. The **unload value** determines which cast members stay in memory and which ones are removed when the movie plays. The Member tab also displays the size of the cast member, the date when the cast member was created and modified, and the name of the person who modified it.

5. Click the **Cast tab** in the Property Inspector

The Cast tab appears in the Property Inspector, as shown in Figure D-11. The Cast tab displays text boxes, including boxes that change the cast member's name and link to an External Cast window, and boxes that select a preload value. The **preload value** determines when cast members are loaded into memory as the movie plays.

6. Click the **Preload list arrow** 🔽, then click **After Frame One**

The After Frame One setting loads the cast members for the first frame as quickly as possible and then loads other cast members in the order in which they are used in the Score, up to the limit of available memory. Table D-2 describes the preload values.

7. Click **Window** on the menu bar, point to **Inspectors**, then click **Memory**

The Memory Inspector opens, as shown in Figure D-12. The Memory Inspector displays information about how much memory is available to Director for your movie and indicates how much memory different parts of the current movie use and the total disk space the movie occupies. Notice how much space is allocated in the Total Used area.

8. Click **Purge**, then click the **Close button** on the title bar

The Memory Inspector purges all removable items from memory.

9. Click the **Bitmap tab** in the Property Inspector

FIGURE D-10: Cast member properties

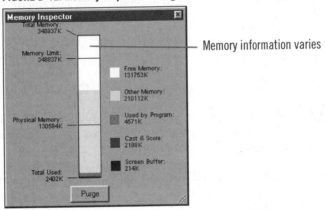

Click button to view information in a list

Click button for Help information

Cast member type

Click button to optimize bitmap in an external program

FIGURE D-11: Cast properties

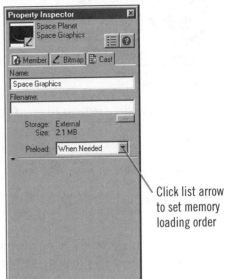

Click list arrow to set memory loading order

FIGURE D-12: Memory Inspector dialog box

Memory information varies

TABLE D-2: Preload values

preload value	description
When Needed	Loads each cast member into memory when it is needed by the movie
After Frame One	Loads all cast members, except those required for frame 1, when the movie exits frame 1
Before Frame One	Loads all cast members before the movie plays frame 1

CLUES TO USE

Setting cast member priorities in memory

Director loads and unloads cast members in order to keep the movie playing as smoothly as possible. When memory is limited on the playback computer, the priority setting for loading and unloading cast members becomes crucial to the movie's performance. You can set unload values to determine which cast members stay in memory and which ones are removed. To set a cast member's priority in memory, click a cast member in a Cast window, click Modify on the menu bar, point to Cast Member, click Properties, click the Member tab in the Property Inspector, click the Unload list arrow, then click an unload value. The unload value ranges from 0 to 3, where 0 means to never remove this cast member from memory, and 3 means to unload this cast member from memory first (before cast members that have a 2 or 1 value assigned to them). You should assign heavily used cast members, such as a background, a 0 value, moderately used cast members a 2 or 1 value, and sparingly used cast members a 3 value.

Transforming a Paint Cast Member

Sometimes, after you import a bitmap into a Cast, you may need to resize it or change its color settings to match the movie. You can use the Transform Bitmap command to change the size, color depth, and palette of selected cast members. You cannot undo the changes you make to a cast member after using the Transform Bitmap command. Make sure you have a duplicate of the original cast member before making any changes. You can change the physical dimensions of a cast member by setting the Scale value as a percentage of the cast member's current size or by entering width and height values in pixels. The color depth option allows you to reset the number of colors used in the cast member, while the palette option allows you to assign a new color palette to the cast member. When you change to a new palette, you can choose the method with which to match current colors with the ones in the new palette. You can either remap or dither the colors. **Remapping** replaces the original colors in the bitmap with the most similar solid colors in the new palette. This is the preferred option in most cases. **Dithering** blends the colors in the new palette to approximate the original colors in the bitmap. ✐ Jean wants to resize a bitmap cast member to fit on the Stage. The Stage is set to 320 × 240 pixels.

Steps 1 2 3 4

1. Verify that the Space Planet cast member is selected in the Space Graphics Cast window

2. Click **Modify** on the menu bar, then click **Transform Bitmap**

3. If a dialog box opens, asking you to launch an external editor, click **Continue**
   The Transform Bitmap dialog box opens, as shown in Figure D-13. The original size of the bitmap is 640 × 480 pixels.

4. Click the **Maintain Proportions check box** to clear it
   When you clear this option, it allows you to enter specific measurements in the Width and Height boxes.

5. Double-click the **Width box**, type **320**, press [Tab], then type **240** in the Height box

6. Click **Transform**
   A confirmation dialog box opens, asking if you want to transform the bitmap. You cannot undo the change.

7. Click **OK**
   The dimensions of the bitmap change from 640 × 480 pixels to 320 × 240 pixels in the Bitmap tab of the Property Inspector.

8. Drag the **Space Planet cast member** on the Stage, click the **cast member** on the Stage, then press the **Arrows keys** to reposition the cast member in the center of the Stage
   When you drag a cast member to the Stage, the pointer changes to ⛶.

9. Click the **gray area** around the Stage to deselect the cast member, then click the **Space Planet cast member** in the Space Graphics Cast window
   The bitmapped cast member appears on the Stage, as shown in Figure D-14.

Trouble?

If you click Launch External Editor, an imaging program, such as Fireworks opens, in which you can modify the bitmap.

FIGURE D-13: Transform Bitmap dialog box

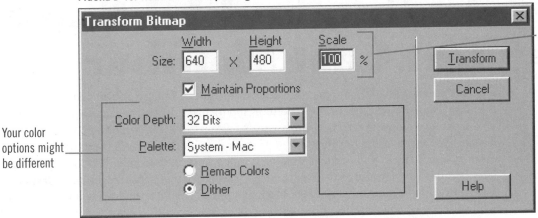

Sizing options

Your color options might be different

FIGURE D-14: Sizing a bitmapped cast member

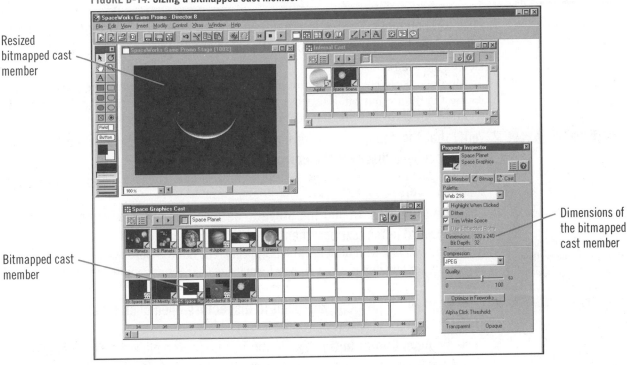

Resized bitmapped cast member

Bitmapped cast member

Dimensions of the bitmapped cast member

Converting text to a bitmap

You can use the Convert to Bitmap command to change a text or field cast member to a bitmap. This command works only with text and field cast members; you cannot convert a shape to a bitmap. To convert text to a bitmap, select the text cast member, click Modify on the menu bar, then click Convert to Bitmap. The cast member type changes from text to bitmap. Once you convert a cast

member to a bitmap, you cannot undo the change. Make sure you have a duplicate of the original cast member before making the change. You can modify the converted bitmap in the Paint window to create special effects, such as gradients, textures, and fills, and manipulate the bitmapped text with warp, flip, and rotate commands.

Director 8

Unit D

Director 8

Adding and Editing a Text Cast Member

Director provides several ways to create text cast members. You can add and edit text directly on the Stage using the Text tool or the Field tool, and format it using the Text Inspector. If you prefer a separate window in which to work, you can also use the Text window or the Field window. The text you create using the Text tool or Text window is called **regular text**, while the text you create using the Field tool or Field window is called **field text**. Regular text looks good at large sizes because you can use anti-aliasing, which smoothes the jagged edges and curves of text. Field text works best for short passages of small-sized text. Field text allows you to save space and use less memory. The Text Inspector allows you to modify both regular text and field text. You can use the Text Inspector to change text formatting on the Stage without having to move to the Cast window and open the text in the Text or Field windows. Jean adds regular and field text directly on the Stage.

Steps 1 2 3 4

1. Click **cast member 3** in the Internal Cast window, click the **Text tool** A on the Tool palette, position + in the upper-left side of the Stage, then drag + to the right side of the Stage

   As you drag + to create a text box, a sprite overlay panel appears on the Stage. When you release the mouse button, a text box appears with an insertion point, and a slanted-line selection box surrounds the text box. You can edit the text in the text box.

2. Verify that the Foreground Color box is white and that the Background Color box is black, then type **discover the universe beyond your world**

   Director might pause as it wraps the text to the next line. The text appears on the Stage, as shown in Figure D-15.

3. Click the **gray area** around the Stage to deselect the text box, position the pointer over **any word** in the text box, then click the text

   A selection text box with double borders appears. The double-border selection box indicates that the entire text box is selected. Any formatting changes are applied to all the text in the text box.

4. Click **Window** on the menu bar, point to **Inspectors**, then click **Text**

   The Text Inspector opens, as shown in Figure D-16.

5. Click the **Align Center button** on the Text Inspector, click the **Font list arrow** ▼, click **Arial Black**, click the **Size list arrow** ▼, then click **18**, if necessary

6. Drag the right-middle sizing handle and **center** the text box to match Figure D-17

   When you position ⟨ over a sizing handle, the pointer changes to black (Win) or white (Mac). The text box appears on the Stage.

7. Click the **Field tool** [Field] on the Tool palette, position + in the lower-left side of the Stage, then drag + to the right side of the Stage

   As you drag to create a field text box, a sprite overlay panel appears on the Stage. When you release the mouse button, a field text box appears with a slanted-line selection box surrounding the text box and an insertion point in the text box.

8. Click on the Text Inspector, click the **Font list arrow** ▼, click **Arial**, click the **Size list arrow** ▼, then click **12**, if necessary

9. Type **www.spaceworksgames.com**, drag the edge of the slanted-line selection box to center the text, then click the **gray area** around the Stage to deselect the field text box

   The field text appears on the Stage.

Trouble?

To select the correct Foreground and Background colors, click the Foreground Color box on the Tool palette, click the white color box in the color palette, click the Background Color box on the Tool palette, then click the black color box on the color palette.

QuickTip

To edit text in a text box, double-click the text box. A slanted-line selection box appears around the text box.

FIGURE D-15: Creating a text cast member on the Stage

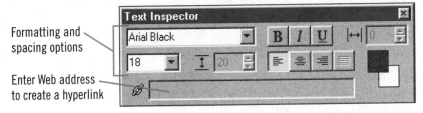

Your font attributes
might be different

Text box

Slanted-line selection box

FIGURE D-16: Text Inspector

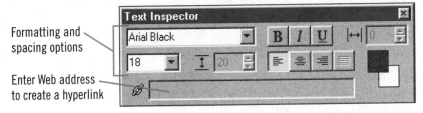

Formatting and
spacing options

Enter Web address
to create a hyperlink

FIGURE D-17: Formatting a text cast member on the Stage

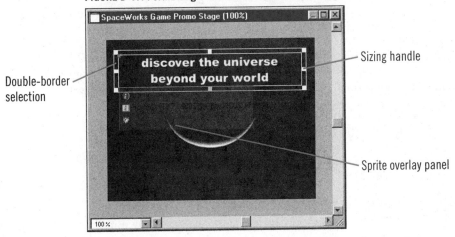

Double-border
selection

Sizing handle

Sprite overlay panel

Creating a hyperlink

You can turn any part of a text cast member into a hyperlink. Director adds standard hyperlink formatting to the selected text so that it initially appears underlined in blue and then becomes purple after a user clicks the hyperlink. To make the hyperlink actually connect to a Web site address or jump to a location, you need to write an *on hyperlinkClicked* event handler in Lingo. For more information about the Lingo event handler, see Director 8 Help. You cannot create a hyperlink bitmapped text and field text. To create a hyperlink, select the text you want to make into a link, click Window on the menu bar, point to Inspectors, then click Text. In the hyperlink box, type the Web address or other text you want to send on the *on hyperlinkClicked* handler, then press [Enter] (Win) or [Return] (Mac). Director styles the text as a hyperlink. If the text is not styled as a hyperlink, click the Text tab on the Property Inspector, then click the Use Hypertext Style check box. This makes the hyperlink appear as it does in a Web browser, initially appearing with a blue underline, and then switching to red once the link has been visited.

Modifying a Text Cast Member

In the Text window, you can change the alignment, indentation, tabs, and spacing for each paragraph in a text cast member. The ruler in the Text window contains controls for indentation and tabs. You can change the indentation from the right or left margins (or both), or you can indent just the first line of text and leave the remaining lines aligned with the left margin. **Indent markers** on the ruler show the indent settings for the paragraph that contains the insertion point in the Text window. Dragging the **Left Indent marker** indents the entire text, dragging the **First Line Indent marker** indents only the first line of the text, and dragging the **Right Indent marker** indents the text from the right margin. Since field text is limited, you can't change indentation and tabs in the Field window. Line spacing controls the vertical spacing between lines of text. **Kerning** is a specialized form of spacing between certain parts of characters. Kerning improves the appearance of text in large sizes but does very little to improve small text. You can change kerning for an entire text cast member or for individual text. When you kern individual text, you can refine letter spacing without affecting the kerning for an entire text cast member. Jean modifies the spacing and alignment of a text cast member.

Steps

1. Double-click the **"discover the universe beyond your world"** text on the Stage, then select all the text in the text box (Mac)

   A slanted-line selection box surrounds the selected text.

2. Click the **Line Spacing up arrow** or **down arrow** on the Text Inspector until it reaches **28**

   The spacing between the lines increases. If you want to use kerning, you must use regular text; it doesn't work in field text or bitmapped text.

3. Click the **Kerning up arrow** or **down arrow** on the Text Inspector until it reaches **2**

   The spacing between the letters increases, as shown in Figure D-18. You can't change margins using the Text Inspector. You need to open the text cast member in the Text window to change the margins or text alignment.

4. Click the **Close button** in the Text Inspector

5. Double-click **cast member 3** in the Internal Cast window

   The Text window opens with the text.

6. Drag the **Left Indent marker** ▢ to **1"** on the ruler

   The left margin for the text starts at 1", as shown in Figure D-19. The size of the text box doesn't change.

7. Drag the **First Line Indent marker** ▽ to **0"** on the ruler

   The first-line left margin starts at 0", while the margin for the remaining lines starts at 1". This is called a **hanging indent**.

8. Drag the **Hanging Indent marker** △ to the position on the ruler to match Figure D-20

9. Click the **Cast Member Name text box**, type **Discover Universe Text**, then click the **Close button** in the Text window

   The Text window closes and the cast member is updated on the Stage and saved in the Cast window.

QuickTip

To control kerning for a text cast member, select a text cast member, click Modify on the menu bar, point to Cast Member, click Properties, click the Kerning list arrow, then select a kerning option.

Trouble?

If the text doesn't appear as shown in Figure D-20, adjust the Hanging Indent marker to match the figure.

FIGURE D-18: Changing line spacing and kerning

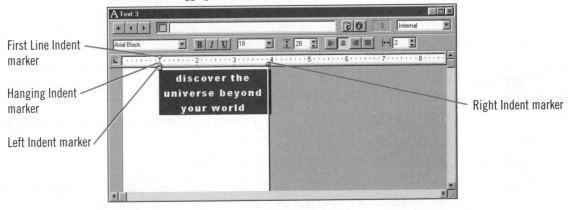

Click arrows to change line spacing

Click arrows to change kerning

FIGURE D-19: Dragging Left Indent marker

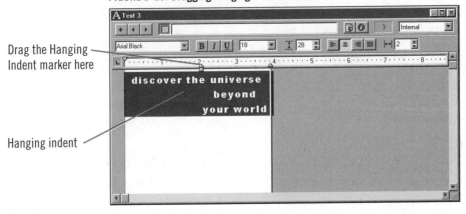

First Line Indent marker

Hanging Indent marker

Left Indent marker

Right Indent marker

FIGURE D-20: Dragging Hanging Indent marker

Drag the Hanging Indent marker here

Hanging indent

Customizing text alignment using tabs

Numerical information is often easier to read when you align the text with tabs. A **tab** is used to position text at a specific location in the Text window. You can use tabs rather than the Spacebar to vertically align your text because tabs are more accurate, faster, and easier to change. When you press [Tab], the insertion point moves to the next tab stop. A **tab stop** is a predefined position in the text to which you can align tabbed text. By default, tab stops are located every ½"

from the left margin, but you can also create and modify tab stops. You can click the tab indicator on the left side of the ruler to select the type of tab you want. The tab indicator ⌐ aligns text to the left, ⌐ aligns text to the right, ⊥ aligns text to the center, and ⊥ aligns numbers to the decimal point. After you select the type of tab you want, click the position on the ruler where you want to place the tab.

Director 8

Saving and Unlinking a Cast

You can use the Save button on the toolbar to save a movie, save an External Cast, or save both. When you select the Stage window before you save, Director saves the movie and all linked Cast windows; when you select an unlinked External Cast window, Director saves just the External Cast. Before you can use external cast members in a movie, you need to link the External Cast to the movie. After you link an External Cast to the current movie, Director opens that Cast whenever you open the movie. When you unlink an External Cast from a movie, the Cast is not available the next time you open the movie unless you open the Cast and relink it. When you make changes to an External Cast that is not linked to your movie, you need to save the External Cast. Director doesn't save changes to an External Cast when you save the movie, because the External Cast is not recognized as being part of the movie file. When you want to save an unlinked External Cast, you can select the External Cast window and use the Save button on the toolbar. Once you save an unlinked External Cast, you can use the Save All button on the toolbar to save the unlinked External Cast and the current movie. Remember to include the External Cast file when you distribute and package a movie. ✒️ Jean saves the External Cast and the movie.

Steps

QuickTip

To save an External Cast with a new name, click the Cast window, click File on the menu bar, then click Save As.

1. Click the **title bar** in the Space Graphics Cast window, then click the **Save button** 💾 on the toolbar
   The Save Cast "Space Graphics" dialog box opens.

2. Navigate to the drive and folder where your Project Files are located, then click **Save**
   The Space Graphics cast and the SpaceWorks Game Promo are saved. The External Cast file is saved with a .cst extension (Win).

3. Click **Modify** on the menu bar, point to **Movie**, then click **Casts**
   The Movie Casts dialog box opens, as shown in Figure D-21.

QuickTip

To link an External Cast to the current movie, click Modify on the menu bar, point to Movie, click Casts, click Link, double-click the External Cast file, then click OK.

4. Click **Space Graphics** in the text box, then click **Remove**

5. Click **OK**
   Since a cast member in the Space Graphics cast is used in the movie, a warning dialog box opens, asking if you want to remove the Cast and remove the cast member from the movie.

6. Click **Cancel**
   The Space Graphics Cast remains linked to the movie. Figure D-22 shows the Director window. The next time you open this movie, Director looks in the specified path in Cast Properties and opens the Cast.

QuickTip

To open a linked Cast, click Window on the menu bar, point to Cast, then click a Cast name.

7. Click the **Close button** in the Space Graphics Cast window
   The Space Graphics Cast window closes. The Cast window is still linked to the movie—it's just not open.

8. Click the **Score Window button** 🖳 on the toolbar
   The Score window opens.

9. Click **File** on the Menu bar, click **Exit** (Win) or **Quit** (Mac) then if asked to save your work, click **Yes** (Win) or **Save** (Mac)
   Director closes.

FIGURE D-21: Movie Casts dialog box

List of linked Casts —

Click button to create
a new Cast —

Internal Cast cannot
be removed

Click button to link
an External Cast

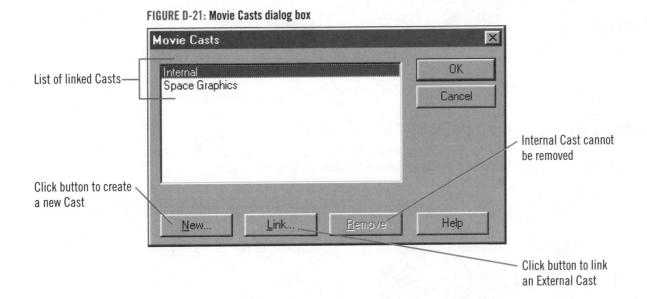

FIGURE D-22: Director window with linked External Cast

Cast member
from External
Cast

External Cast linked
to the movie

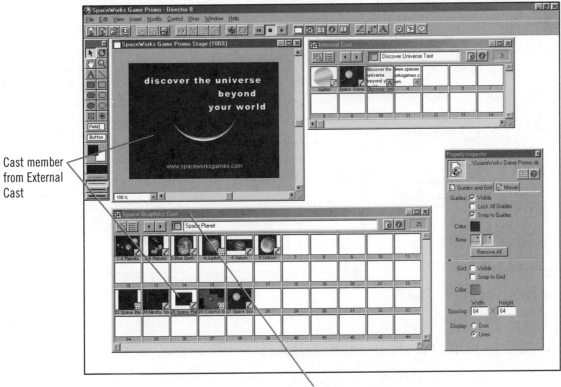

Creating a cast library

If you save an unlinked External Cast in the Libs folder in the Director folder, you create a cast library. A **cast library** is a special type of unlinked external cast. When you drag a cast member from an External Cast library to the Stage or Score, Director copies the cast member to one of the movie's Internal Casts. Libraries are useful for storing any type of commonly used cast members, especially behaviors. Unlike an External Cast, a library cannot be linked to a movie.

Director 8

Practice

► Concepts Review

Label each of the elements of the screen shown in Figure D-23.

FIGURE D-23

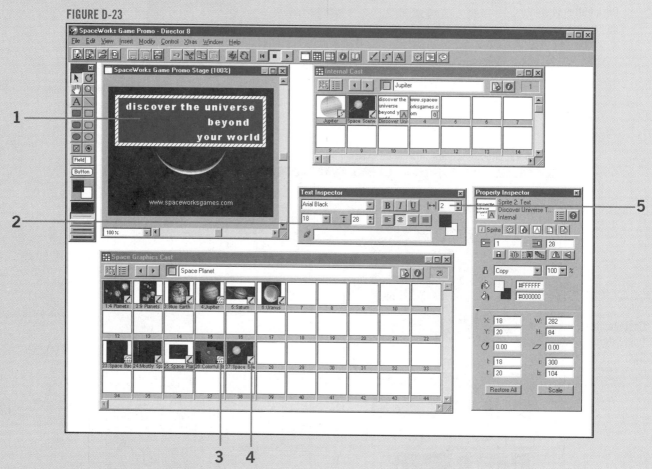

Match each of the terms with the statement that describes its function.

6. Regular   a. Determines which cast members stay in memory

7. Unload   b. A type of text that uses less memory

8. Dither   c. Replaces original color with similar colors in another palette

9. Preload   d. Determines when cast members are loaded into memory

10. Field   e. Blends colors in a palette to approximate the original colors

11. Remap   f. A type of text that uses anti-aliasing

Select the best answer from the following list of choices.

12. How many Casts can be added to a movie?
a. 32,000
b. 1,000
c. 5,000
d. Unlimited

13. An External Cast is:
a. Saved as part of the movie.
b. Saved as a separate file.
c. Always linked to a movie.
d. None of the above

14. An Internal Cast is:
a. Saved as part of the movie.
b. Saved as a separate file.
c. Always unlinked to a movie.
d. None of the above

15. Regular text allows you to:
a. Create attractive, large text.
b. Save disk space.
c. Use less memory.
d. Edit it in the Field window.

16. Field text allows you to:
a. Create attractive large text.
b. Edit it in the Text window.
c. Create a hyperlink.
d. Save disk space.

17. Which feature allows you to change the spacing between characters?
a. Line spacing
b. Kerning
c. Indent markers
d. Tabs

18. A cast library is a(n):
a. Unlinked External Cast.
b. Linked External Cast.
c. Unlinked Internal Cast.
d. Linked Internal Cast.

 ## Skills Review

1. Create a cast.
a. Start Director.
b. Save the new movie as *SpaceWorks Star* in the drive and folder where your Project Files are located.
c. Close the Score window, if necessary.
d. Create a linked External Cast as **Space Backgrounds**.
e. Move the Cast window to a blank area in the Director window.

2. Use the Cast window.
a. Import all the files in the Media folder where your Project Files are located into the Space Backgrounds Cast window (select format as Bitmap Image when requested).
b. Change the Cast view to a list.
c. Change the Cast preferences to display number, type, and size, if necessary.

3. Organize cast members.
a. Sort the list in descending order by size (Win).
b. Change the Space Backgrounds Cast window view to Thumbnail.
c. Move the cast members into two rows by planets and backgrounds.
d. Sort each row by name.
e. Select the Colorful Star and Mostly Space cast members in the Space Backgrounds Cast window.
f. Copy and paste the cast members in the Internal Cast window (locations 1 and 2).

4. Find cast members.
a. Find all cast members in the Internal Cast.
b. Select the Colorful Star cast member in the Internal Cast window.

5. View and change cast member properties.

a. Select the Colorful Star cast member in the Internal Cast window, if necessary.

b. Change the unload value to last and change the preload value to Before Frame One.

c. Purge all removable items from memory.

6. Transform a paint cast member.

a. Select the Colorful Star cast member in the Internal Cast window.

b. Change the dimensions of the cast member to 320 × 240.

c. Drag the Colorful Star cast member in the Internal Cast window on the Stage.

d. Use the Arrow keys to reposition the cast member in the center of the Stage.

7. Add and edit a text cast member.

a. Select cast member 3 in the Internal Cast window.

b. Use the Text tool to create a text box in the upper-right corner in the black area.

c. Change the Foreground color to white and the Background color to black.

d. Type **You can be a STAR!**

e. Open the Text Inspector and change the text to align right.

f. Change the text to a spacey-looking font and a large font size.

g. Close the Text Inspector.

8. Modify a text cast member.

a. Open cast member 3 in the Internal Cast window.

b. Create a hanging indent so that **You can** appears on the top line, **be a** appears on the next line, and **Star!** appears two lines down.

c. Change the line spacing and kerning to fill in the black area in the upper-right corner.

d. Name the cast member **Shining Star** and close the Text window.

9. Save and unlink a cast.

a. Save the cast as *Space Backgrounds* in the drive and folder where your Project Files are located.

b. Unlink the Space Backgrounds cast from the movie.

c. Open the Score window, save the movie, and then exit Director.

► Independent Challenges

1. You are an estate planner at Langford Financial Services, an insurance and estate planning company. After years of using the same brochure, you decide it's time to create a customizable presentation about company products and services for clients. You use Director's Text and Paint tools to create media elements and an External Cast to organize them.
  To complete this independent challenge:

a. Start Director and save the movie as *Langford Financial* in the drive and folder where your Project Files are located.

b. Create a linked External Cast and save it as *Financial Symbols* in the drive and folder where your Project Files are located.

c. Using the Text tool, create and name cast members in the Financial Symbols Cast window with numbers and financial symbols.

d. Copy cast members in the Financial Symbols Cast window and convert the text to bitmaps.

e. Create a text cast member with the text **Langford Financial Services**.

f. Organize the cast members by type (text and bitmap) in the Financial Symbols Cast window.

g. Resize a bitmap to 320 × 240 and create a background.

h. Place the background and the cast members on the Stage.

i. Print thumbnails of the Financial Symbols Cast window and the Stage.

j. Save the movie and the External Cast, then exit Director.

2. You are a software developer at the Keenen Group, a Web design and development company that was recently selected by your local Professional Web Designers Group as an industry model in Web development. You've been asked to create a multimedia demo of their development process. You use Director's Paint, Vector Shape, and Text tools to create flow-charting shapes and instructions, and an External Cast in which to organize them.

To complete this independent challenge:

a. Start Director and save the movie as *Keenen Group* in the drive and folder where your Project Files are located.

b. Create a linked External Cast and save it as *Flowchart Symbols* in the drive and folder where your Project Files are located.

c. Using the Paint and Vector Shape tools, create and name cast members in the Flowchart Symbols Cast window with flow-charting shapes and connecting lines. (*Hint:* See Figure B-2 for an example of a flowchart.)

d. Organize the cast members by type (shapes and lines) in the Flowchart Symbols Cast window.

e. Create a text cast member with the text **Keenen Group**.

f. Resize a bitmap to 320 × 240 and create a background.

g. Place the background and the cast members on the Stage.

h. Print thumbnails of the Flowchart Symbols Cast window and the Stage.

i. Save the movie and the External Cast, then exit Director.

3. You are the chief designer at Designer Flags, a custom flag company. The manager of Victory Homes asks you to design a flag for the front of their model home developments. You use Director's Paint and Text tools to create a flag with a house and the company name, and an External Cast in which to organize them.

To complete this independent challenge:

a. Start Director and save the movie as *Designer Flags* in the drive and folder where your Project Files are located.

b. Create a linked External Cast and save it as *Victory Flags* in the drive and folder where your Project Files are located.

c. Using the Paint and Text tools, create and name cast members in the Victory Flags Cast window with several different flag designs and the company name.

d. Organize the cast members by type (shapes and text) in the Victory Flags Cast window.

e. Create a text cast member with the text **Victory flag designs by Designer Flags**.

f. Place the cast members on the Stage and add a color background.

g. Print thumbnails of the Victory Flags Cast window and the Stage.

h. Save the movie and the External Cast, then exit Director.

4. You are the owner and chief baker at Only Desserts, a catering and specialty dessert company. To help promote the company, you want to create a kiosk with photos and prices of your delicious desserts. You use Director's importing feature to assemble photos, and an External Cast to organize them.

To complete this independent challenge:

a. Connect to the Internet and go to *www.course.com*. Navigate to the page for this book, click the link for the Student Online Companion, then click the link for this unit.

b. Browse the Food & Dining section for photos.

c. Download six dessert photos in the drive and folder where your Project Files are located.

d. Start Director and save the movie as *Only Desserts* in the drive and folder where your Project Files are located.

e. Create a linked External Cast and save it as *Dessert Photos* in the drive and folder where your Project Files are located.

f. Import the photos in the Dessert Photos Cast window.

g. Organize the cast members by type (photos and text) in the Dessert Photos Cast window.

h. Create text titles and prices, using the Text tool.

i. Create a text cast member with the text **Only Desserts**.

J. Place the cast members on the Stage and add a color background.

k. Print thumbnails of the Dessert Photos Cast window and the Stage.

l. Save the movie and the External Cast, then exit Director.

► Visual Workshop

Recreate the screen shown in Figure D-24. Print the screen. Save the file as *Planets* in the drive and folder where your Project Files are located. (For Windows, use the Windows Paint program. Press the Print Screen key to make a copy of the screen, start the Paint program by clicking Start, pointing to Programs, pointing to Accessories, then clicking Paint, click Edit on the menu bar, click Paste to paste the screen into Paint, then click Yes to paste the large image if necessary. Click File on the menu bar, click Print or OK in the dialog box, then exit Paint. For the Macintosh, use the SimpleText program. Hold and press the Command, Shift, and 3 keys to make a copy of the screen, double-click the document Picture 1 located on your hard drive, click File on the menu bar, click Print, then click Print. (*Note*: When you create a new document with a copy of the screen, and a document Picture 1 already exists, the Macintosh names the new document Picture 2.)

FIGURE D-24

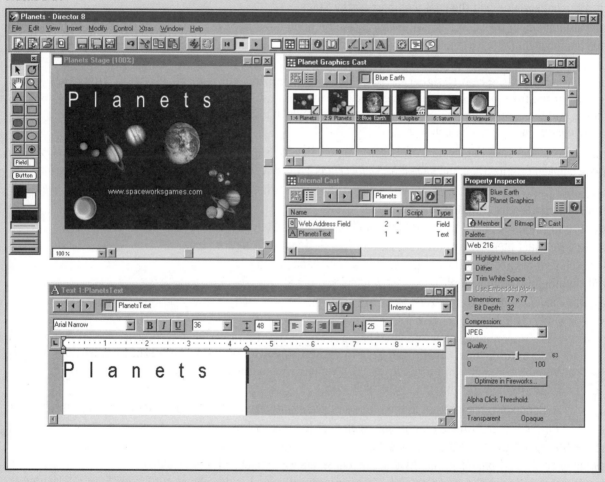

Creating
and Modifying Sprites

Objectives

► **Create and select sprites**
► **View sprite properties**
► **Layer sprites**
► **Apply sprite inks**
► **Change the sprite display**
► **Change sprite properties**
► **Position and align sprites**
► **Extend, join, and split sprites**
► **Set text for end users to change**

A sprite is an object that consists of a cast member and a set of properties and behaviors. The properties and behaviors control how, where, and when cast members appear in a movie. You use the Stage to control where a sprite appears, and you use the Score to control when it appears. This unit introduces you to basic skills for creating, selecting, moving, and modifying sprites. First, you'll learn how to create, select, and move sprites. Then you'll learn how to apply sprite inks, change the sprite display in the Score, change sprite properties, align sprites on the Stage, and modify sprite spans. Finally, you'll learn how to set text for users to change during a movie. ✐ Jean wants to create and modify sprites for a matching game about planets.

Director 8

Creating and Selecting Sprites

You can create sprites by placing cast members either on the Stage or in the Score; regardless of where you create the sprite, it will appear in both locations. Before you can edit, copy, or move a sprite, you need to select it first. You can select sprites either on the Stage or in the Score. To select a sprite, you use the Arrow tool on the Tool palette. You can select sprites in different channels, all the sprites in a single channel, or frames within sprites. If you need to select a frame within a sprite (not the keyframes, the start frame and the end frame), you can use the Edit Sprite Frames command on the Edit menu. If the option is not set, the entire sprite is selected. Jean takes some time to familiarize herself with the techniques for selecting and deselecting sprites in an existing movie and for creating a new one.

1. Start **Director**, open the file **MD E-1** from the drive and folder where your Project Files are located, then save it as **Planet Game**
   Director opens, displaying the movie. Your initial settings in Director might vary, depending on previous usage.

QuickTip

To change Stage view size, click the Zoom list arrow ▼ at the bottom-left of the Stage, then click a view percentage.

2. Position ⬉ on the lower-right corner of the **Stage window**, then drag the **border** diagonally to the right to expand the window until the gray area around the Stage is displayed

3. Click the **Play button** ▶ on the toolbar
   The movie plays on the Stage, and the playback head moves frame to frame through the Score until it reaches the end. You can see the initial development of the Planet game.

4. Click the **Stop button** ■ on the toolbar, then click **number 31** on the frame channel in the Score window
   The playback head moves to frame 31.

5. Click the **Sun cast member** on the Stage
   The selected sprite appears on the Stage with a double border, as shown in Figure E-1. Attached to the bottom of the sprite selection rectangle is the Sprite Overlay panel. The selected sprite appears in the Score with a solid thick line in the sprite bar.

6. Press and hold **[Shift]**, click a **black area** on the Stage to select both sprites (Sun and Planets Start), then click the **gray area around the Stage** to deselect the sprites
   When the background takes up the entire Stage area, the easiest way to deselect all the sprites is to click the gray area around the Stage.

QuickTip

To select a range of frames, press and hold [Shift][Alt] (Win) or [Shift][Option] (Mac), then click an end frame.

7. Click **frame 31 in channel 7**
   When you select a sprite's keyframe or its first or last frame, the sprite appears on the Stage with a single border. Selecting a frame is useful for modifying keyframes and for creating animation.

8. Click **channel number 5** at the left side of the Score
   All of the sprites in channel 5 are selected.

9. Drag the **Earth cast member** from the Cast window to **frame 31, channel 6** in the Score, as shown in Figure E-2
   The Earth sprite appears in the center of the Stage behind the Sun sprite. When you drag a cast member in the Score, an outline of the sprite appears, indicating the current location of the sprite when you release the mouse. When you place a cast member in the Score, the sprite appears in the center of the Stage surrounded by a double border.

FIGURE E-1: Selecting a sprite

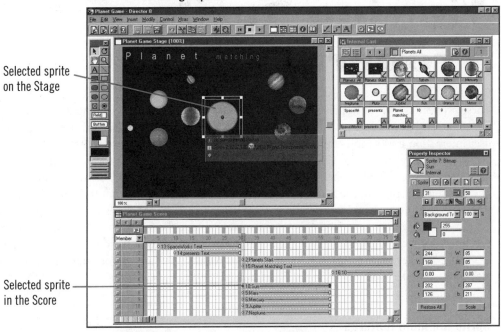

Selected sprite on the Stage

Selected sprite in the Score

FIGURE E-2: Creating a sprite

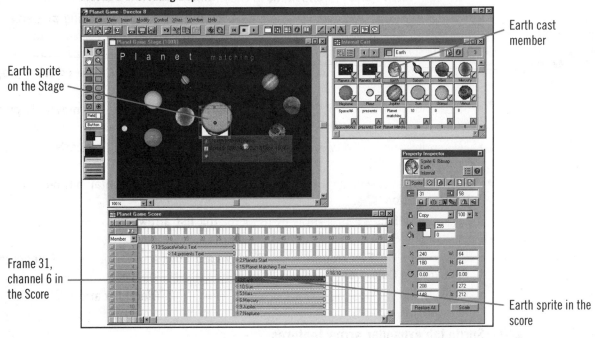

Earth cast member

Earth sprite on the Stage

Frame 31, channel 6 in the Score

Earth sprite in the score

CLUES TO USE

Editing sprite frames

At times, you might want to change how Director selects a sprite and how Director creates a keyframe. You can use the Edit Sprite Frames option for animated sprites that need to adjust frequently. It is especially useful for an animated cell where each frame contains a different cast member in a different position. When you set the Edit Sprite Frames option for a certain sprite, clicking the sprite selects a single frame (surrounded by a single border) instead of the entire sprite (surrounded by a double border). Any change you make to an animation property defines a new keyframe. To use the Edit Sprite Frames option, select the sprite, click Edit on the menu bar, then click Edit Sprite Frames. To return sprites to their normal state, select the sprite, click Edit on the menu bar, then click Edit Entire Sprite.

Director 8

Viewing Sprite Properties

Director 8

Each sprite includes a set of properties that describe how the sprite looks and behaves in a movie. These properties include a sprite's location on the Stage, its size, blend percentage, ink effect, start frame and end frame, and rotation and skew angles. You can also set sprite properties to add basic user interaction and simple animation. You can change some sprite properties, such as size and Stage location, by directly moving or resizing a sprite on the Stage. For other sprite properties, you need to use the Sprite tab in the Property Inspector, as shown in Figure E-3. To view sprite properties, you select a sprite in the Score, click Window on the menu bar, point to Inspector, then click Property. The information in the Sprite tab of the Property Inspector is also visible at the top of the Score Window, as shown in Figure E-4. To display and hide the Sprite toolbar, you click the Score window, click View on the menu bar, then click Sprite Toolbar. You can access some sprite properties using the keyboard shortcuts. Table AP-6 provides a list of the common sprite shortcuts. Jean takes some time to familiarize herself with the elements of the Sprite tab in the Property Inspector. Refer to your screen and Figure E-3 as you locate the elements described below.

Sprite tab main features

QuickTip

To get more information about sprite properties, click the Help button in the Property Inspector.

- Set a sprite's **start frame** and **end frame** by entering new values to adjust how long the sprite plays.

- Set a sprite's locking property by using the **Lock button** 🔒. The **locking property** allows you to lock a sprite on the Stage to prevent you from making any changes to the sprite. Locking sprites is not supported during playback.

- Set a text sprite's editable property by using the **Editable button** . The **editable property** allows users to enter text on the Stage while the movie is playing.

- Set a sprite's moveable property by using the **Moveable button** . The **moveable property** allows users to drag a sprite on the Stage while the movie is playing.

- Set a sprite's trail property by using the **Trails button** . The **trail property** leaves a trail of images on the Stage.

- **Flip** a sprite horizontally or vertically by using the **Flip Horizontal button** or **Flip Vertical button** .

- Set an **Ink effect** for a sprite by using the **Ink list arrow** to select an ink effect. Ink effects change the display of a sprite's colors.

- Change a sprite's **Foreground** or **Background colors** by using the **Foreground** or **Background Color box** to select a color from the palette.

- Set the **Blend**, or transparency level, of a sprite by using the **Blend list arrow** to select a percentage. A 100% blend makes a sprite completely opaque, while a 0% blend makes it transparent.

Sprite tab expander arrow features

- Change the **registration point** by entering a horizontal (X) and vertical (Y) value measured from the top-left corner of the Stage.

- **Rotate** a sprite by entering a number of degrees; a positive number rotates the sprite clockwise in degrees, and a negative number rotates it counterclockwise.

- **Restore** the height and width of the cast member by using the Restore All button.

- **Resize** a sprite by dragging a resize handle on the Stage or by entering width (W:) and height (H:) dimensions in the Sprite tab of the Property Inspector. You can also use the **Scale button** to proportionately resize a sprite.

- **Skew**, or tilt, a sprite by entering a positive value, which skews the sprite to the right, or a negative value, which skews it to the left.

FIGURE E-3: Sprite tab in the Property Inspector

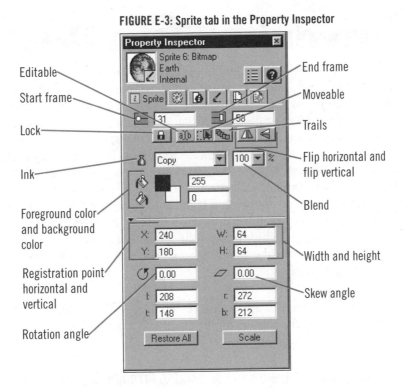

Editable
Start frame
Lock
Ink
Foreground color and background color
Registration point horizontal and vertical
Rotation angle

End frame
Moveable
Trails
Flip horizontal and flip vertical
Blend
Width and height
Skew angle

FIGURE E-4: Sprite toolbar in the Score

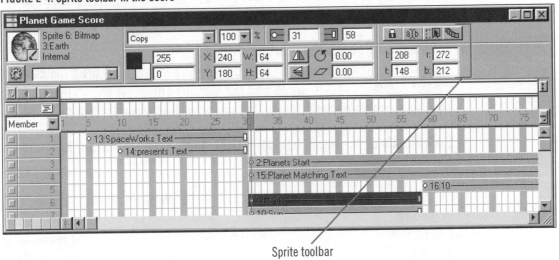

Sprite toolbar

Organizing sprites using color

When you create a sprite, it appears in the Score window in the default purple color. After you create several sprites, sometimes it is hard to distinguish them without looking intently at each sprite label. You can organize sprites in the Score window using color. For example, to help you distinguish sprites in the Score window you can set all text sprites to one color and all graphic sprites to another color. You can use the color boxes ⬚⬚⬚⬚⬚ in the bottom-left corner of the Score window to change the color of a sprite label. The color boxes only change the appearance of the sprite label in the Score window; they do not affect the sprite on the Stage or in the Cast. To change the color of a sprite in the Score window, select the sprite in the Score window, then click a color box.

Layering Sprites

A sprite is displayed on the Stage layered according to its channel in the Score. Sprites in higher-numbered channels appear in front of sprites in lower-numbered channels. For example, the Sun sprite appears in channel 7, and the Earth sprite appears in channel 6, which means that the Sun sprite appears in front of the Earth sprite. When you position the sprite that contains the background for your movie, it is important to place that sprite in a lower-numbered channel, generally channel 1, so that the background always appears on the back layer. There are several ways to change sprite layering. If there is an empty area in a higher-numbered channel, you can drag the sprite in the Score from one channel to another. If no space is available in a channel, you can use the Arrange command on the Modify menu to switch sprites in channels. When you are working with layers, it is sometimes difficult to work with sprites. You can hide the contents of any channel on the Stage. To hide or show the contents of a channel, you use the button to the left of the channel number in the Score. Jean changes the layering of a sprite to uncover it from behind another sprite.

Steps

Trouble?

If the Earth sprite is not selected, click the Earth sprite in the Score.

1. Verify that the Earth sprite is selected on the Stage and in the Score
   The selected sprite appears on the Stage with a double border and in the Score with a solid thick line or is highlighted in the sprite bar.

2. Click **Modify** on the menu bar, point to **Arrange**, then click **Move Forward**
   The sprites' positions are switched on the Stage and in the Score. The Earth sprite appears in front of the Sun sprite. Notice that the Earth sprite appears in channel 7 and that the Sun sprite appears in channel 6. The Move Forward command moves the sprite up one to the next highest channel.

Trouble?

If the Snap to Guides or Grid features are turned on, a green plus sign appears when you drag the sprite.

3. Position the Arrow pointer over the Earth sprite (not on the colored circle in the middle or on the sizing handles on the edge) on the Stage, then drag the **Earth sprite** to the left between the Sun sprite and the Mercury sprite, as shown in Figure E-5
   The Earth sprite is layered between the Sun sprite and the Mercury sprite.

4. Click **Modify** on the menu bar, point to **Arrange**, then click **Bring to Front**
   The Earth sprite moves to the top layer.

5. Click the **title bar** in the Score, then click the **scroll down arrow** to display channel 15 in the Score
   The Earth sprite is in channel 15, the highest-numbered sprite in the movie, as shown in Figure E-6.

6. Click the **gray button** ▣ in the first column of the Score window to the left of channel 15
   A dark gray button indicates that the channel is hidden, as shown in Figure E-7. The Earth sprite is no longer visible on the Stage, but it is still visible in the Score. When you hide a channel, the hide option does not affect the movie as a projector movie or Shockwave movie.

QuickTip

To view or hide a single Score channel on the Stage while performing the opposite function to all of the other channels, press and hold [Alt] (Win) or [Option] (Mac), then press ▣ or ▣ on the selected channel.

7. Click the **dark gray button** ▣ in the first column of the Score window to the left of channel 15
   The Earth sprite is visible on the Stage.

8. Position the Arrow pointer over the Earth sprite (not on the colored circle in the middle or the sizing handles on the edge) on the Stage, then drag the **Earth sprite** over the white dot on the lower-right side of the Sun sprite

FIGURE E-5: Layering sprites

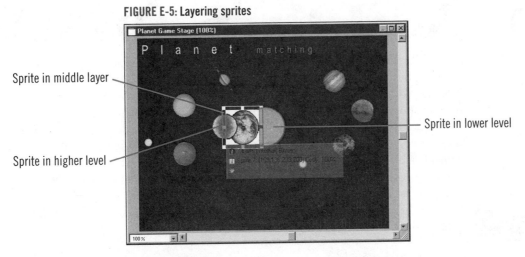

Sprite in middle layer

Sprite in higher level

Sprite in lower level

FIGURE E-6: Switching channels

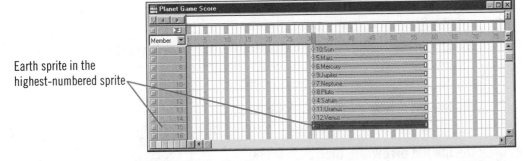

Earth sprite in the
highest-numbered sprite

FIGURE E-7: Hiding sprites on the Stage

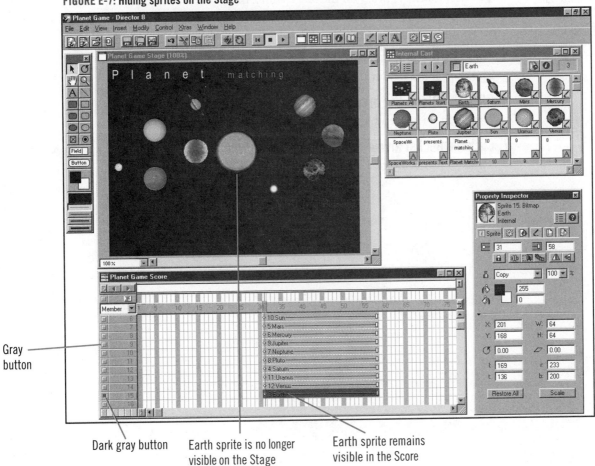

Gray
button

Dark gray button

Earth sprite is no longer
visible on the Stage

Earth sprite remains
visible in the Score

Director 8

Director 8

Applying Sprite Inks

Sprite inks change the display of a sprite's colors. Inks are most useful to hide white backgrounds, but they can also create useful and dramatic color effects. Inks can reverse and alter colors, make sprites change colors depending on the background, and create masks that obscure or reveal portions of a background. Unlike Paint ink effects, which are applied in the Paint window and are permanent, sprite ink effects are applied in the Score and can be changed at any time. Table AP-7 describes the different sprite ink effects. For many of the ink effects, you can set a blend value. The **blend value** makes a sprite more or less transparent. A blend value of 100% makes a sprite completely opaque, and a blend value of 0% makes a sprite completely transparent. You can set the end points of a sprite to different blend values, and Director will blend together the points in between. This creates a fading in or fading out effect. Jean experiments with different sprite ink effects.

Steps

1. Verify that the Earth sprite is selected on the Stage and in the Score
The selected sprite appears on the Stage with a double border and in the Score with a solid thick line or is highlighted in the sprite bar.

2. Click **Window** on the menu bar, point to **Inspectors**, then click **Property**, if not checked
The Property Inspector appears with the Sprite tab in front. The current sprite properties for the Earth sprite appear in the Property Inspector.

3. Click the **Ink list arrow** ▼, then click **Ghost**
The Earth sprite appears on the Stage with the ghost effect (washed-out color).

4. Click the **Ink list arrow** ▼, then click **Mask**
The Earth sprite appears on the Stage with a mask of the Saturn cast member, which is the cast member that follows the Earth cast member in the Cast. You can use blending to make sprites transparent.

QuickTip

The Blend percentage value affects only Copy, Background Transparent, Matte, Mask, and Blend inks.

5. Click the **Blend list arrow** ▼, then click **50%**
The mask ink effect for the Earth sprite is more transparent.

6. Click the **Blend list arrow** ▼, then click **100%**
The Earth sprite blend is restored to 100%.

7. Click the **Ink list arrow** ▼, then click **Background Transparent** (scroll up, if necessary)
The Earth sprite appears on the Stage with a transparent background, as shown in Figure E-8.

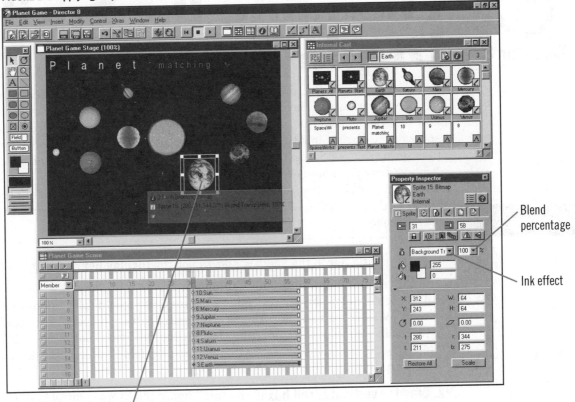

Earth sprite with the
Background Transparent
ink effect

Blend
percentage

Ink effect

Applying the mask ink effect

You can apply the mask ink to a sprite to create transparent effects. The mask ink allows you to define which parts of a sprite are transparent and which are opaque. To use the mask ink, you first create the cast member that will be masked. You can use any color depth when you create the cast member. Then, in the Cast window position immediately following the cast member to be masked, create the mask cast member with a color depth of 32 bits. The black areas of the mask cast member make the sprite completely opaque, and white areas make it completely transparent. Colors between black and white are more or less transparent. However, darker colors are more

opaque than the lighter colors. The mask ink effect is a memory-intensive feature, so use it sparingly for movies on playback machines that have limited memory. To create a mask effect, select the cast member you want to mask, copy and paste it in the next position in the same Cast, edit the mask cast member in the Paint window using black, white, or any colors in between, transform the bitmap of the mask cast member to 32 bits (if necessary), drag the cast member to the Stage or Score to create a sprite, display the Sprite tab in the Property Inspector, click the Ink list arrow, then click Mask. The parts of the sprite revealed by the mask appear on the Stage.

Director 8

Changing the Sprite Display

The text that identifies the sprite in the Score window is called a **sprite label**. To make it easier to work with sprites, you can change the display for sprite labels in the Score to show different information about the sprite, such as member name and number or ink effect. When you select a sprite on the Stage or in the Score, the sprite overlay panel appears on the Stage at the bottom of the sprite. You can determine when the sprite overlay panel appears; the panel can appear when you move the mouse over, or roll over, a sprite, when you select a sprite, or all the time. If the text in the sprite overlay is difficult to read, you can change the panel text display color or the shading of the panel. Jean changes the sprite display to view the ink effects currently used in the movie.

Steps

QuickTip

To change the Extended display in the Score, click File on the menu bar, point to Preferences, click Score, then click the Extended Display check boxes in the Score Window Preferences dialog box to select them.

1. Click the **title bar** in the Score window, click the **Display list arrow** ▼ on the left side of the Score window, then click **Extended**

   The Score window displays extended information for the display options selected in the Score Window Preferences dialog box. Extended settings include cast member number (depending on your Director settings) and name, ink blend, and location. Figure E-9 displays the Score window under the Extended setting. Table E-1 describes the display options for sprite labels.

2. Drag the **vertical scroll box** in the scroll bar of the Score window to the top, click the **Display list arrow** ▼ on the left side of the Score window, then click **Ink**

   The Score window displays the sprite labels with ink effects.

QuickTip

To show or hide keyframes in the Score, click View on the menu bar, then click Keyframes.

3. Click the **Display list arrow** ▼ on the left side of the Score window, then click **Member**

   The Score window displays the sprite labels with member names.

4. Click the **Earth sprite** on the Stage, if necessary

   The selected sprite appears on the Stage with a double border and a sprite overlay with information about the sprite.

5. Click **View** on the menu bar, point to **Sprite Overlay**, then click **Settings**

   The Sprite Overlay Settings dialog box opens. You can select sprite overlay color and display options.

6. Press and hold the **Text Color box**, then click the **white color box** at the end of the second row on the color palette

QuickTip

To open the Bitmap, Sprite, or Behavior tabs in the Property Inspector, you can click the corresponding icon in the Sprite Overlay panel.

7. Click **OK**, then click the **Planets Start sprite** (the black background)

   The sprite overlay text changes from black to white, which makes it easier to see against the black background.

8. Drag down the **slider** that appears on the right edge of the Sprite Overlay panel, as shown in Figure E-10, to change the shading of the panel

9. Click **View** on the menu bar, point to **Sprite Overlay**, then click **Show Info** to deselect

   The sprite overlay is removed from the selected sprite on the Stage.

FIGURE E-9: Score window with extended sprite display

Click list arrow to change the sprite display options

Sprite display options

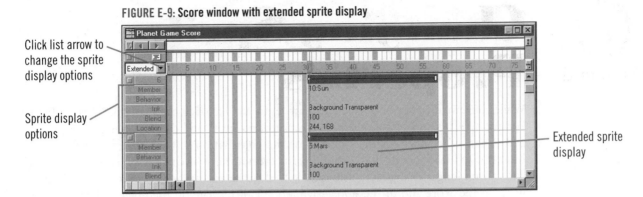

Extended sprite display

FIGURE E-10: Changing the Sprite Overlay panel

Sprite Overlay panel

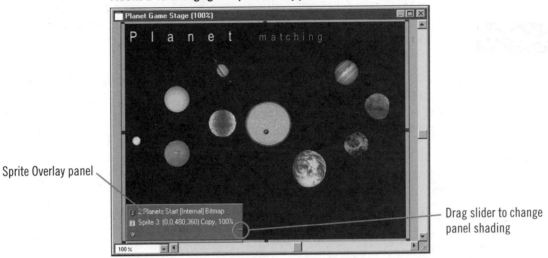

Drag slider to change panel shading

TABLE E-1: Score Window display options

format	description
Member	Identifies the number and name of the cast member (depending on your Director settings)
Behavior	Tells you which (if any) behaviors have been assigned to the sprite by number or name
Ink	Displays the ink effect that is applied to the sprite
Blend	Indicates the percentage of the sprite's blend setting
Location	Describes the sprite's registration point relative to the top-left corner of the Stage
Extended	Displays Member, Behavior, Ink, Blend, and Location information

Viewing multiple Score windows

You can display different views of the Score window to make it easier to display information or to move a sprite to a different part of the Score without scrolling. If you have a large Score window and want to move a sprite a long distance, you can open the same Score window, scroll to a different portion, then drag the sprite between the two windows. To open a copy of the Score window, click the title bar in the Score window, click Window on the menu bar, then click New Window. You can change the Score display settings for sprite labels in the new window. When you change the Score display options in one Score window, the other Score window retains its original settings, but if you alter a sprite in either window, both Score windows update the change.

Director 8

Changing Sprite Properties

While you develop a movie, you can lock sprites to avoid making unintentional changes to them. For example, if you are working with a background sprite and do not want to move it as you make changes to other sprites, you can use the Lock button in the Sprite tab of the Property Inspector to make sure the background sprite cannot move or change. When you lock a sprite, you can no longer change its settings. A locked sprite appears with a lock icon in front of its name in the Score and in the upper-right corner of a sprite on the Stage. When you use the Moveable button, you can allow end users to move sprites around while your movie is playing. This option is useful for creating educational games. If you need to resize a sprite, you can use the Scale button to set a specific height and width or a percentage. ◆ Jean locks the background sprite, resizes a sprite, and sets a group of sprites for movement in the Planet game.

Steps

1. Verify that the **Planets Start sprite** is selected on the Stage, press and hold **[Shift]**, then click the **Sun sprite** on the Stage
   The selected sprites appear on the Stage with a double border and in the Score with a solid thick line or is highlighted in each sprite bar.

2. Click the **Lock button** 🔒 in the Property Inspector
   A lock icon appears on the sprite border on the Stage and in the sprite bar in the Score, as shown in Figure E-11.

3. Click the **Earth sprite** on the Stage
   The selected sprite appears on the Stage with a double border and in the Score with a solid thick line or is highlighted in the sprite bar.

4. Click **Scale** in the Property Inspector
   The Scale dialog box opens.

5. Double-click the **Scale box** (if necessary), type **75**, then click **OK**
   The Earth sprite is scaled to 75%.

6. Click the **title bar** in the Score, click the **scroll up arrow** to display channel 6, press and hold **[Shift]**, then click the **Sun Sprite** in channel 6 to select all the planet sprites
   The planet sprites from channel 15 to channel 6 are selected on the Stage and in the Score.

7. Click the **Copy button** 📋 on the toolbar, click **frame 59** in **channel 6**, then click the **Paste button** 📋 on the toolbar
   A copied set of planet sprites is pasted in frame 59 and selected in the Score.

8. Press and hold **[Ctrl]** (Win) or **[Command]** (Mac), click the **Sun Sprite** in frame 59 of channel 6, then click the **Moveable button** 🔲 in the Property Inspector
   The Moveable property is set for the planet sprites. When you play the movie, you can move the planets.

9. Click the **Center Current Frame button** 🔲 in the bottom row of the Score window
   The frames in the Score are centered to the playback head, as shown in Figure E-12. You can view both sets of planet sprites in the Score.

QuickTip

To unlock a sprite, select the sprite, then click the Lock button 🔒 in the Sprite tab of the Property Inspector. To select a locked sprite on the Stage, press and hold [L], then click a sprite.

QuickTip

You can skew sprites with the Rotate and Skew tool on the Tool palette. To skew the sprite, click the Rotation and Skew tool 🔲, click a sprite on the Stage, then drag a border until you achieve the desired effect.

FIGURE E-11: Locking sprites

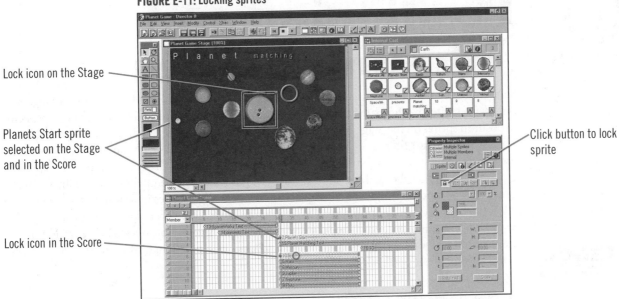

Lock icon on the Stage

Planets Start sprite
selected on the Stage
and in the Score

Lock icon in the Score

Click button to lock
sprite

FIGURE E-12: Setting sprites to move during playback

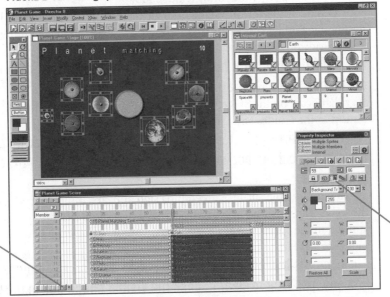

Click button to center
current frame in the Score

Click button to move
sprites during playback

CLUES TO USE

Creating a trail effect

You can set sprites to leave a trail of images as they move on the Stage. When you click the Trails button in the Property Inspector, the Stage doesn't erase previous versions of the sprite as the playback head moves through the Score. The result is an impression of a continuous string of sprites, as shown in Figure E-13. This option is useful for fine-tuning animations. When you select a sprite with an animation and set the Trails option, you can determine where motion in an animation needs to slow down, speed up, or smooth out. You cannot select or move any of the trailed images, but you can change the animation points, or keyframes, in the Score. You can also use the trail effect with the Moveable option. When you select the Moveable option and the Trails option for a cast member, the end user can drag the cast member on the Stage during playback to create a trail effect.

FIGURE E-13: Sprite with trails

Positioning and Aligning Sprites

Sometimes you need to change the position of a sprite or align a group of sprites on the Stage. You can drag a sprite, use the arrow keys, or set coordinates in the Sprite tab of the Property Inspector to position sprites on the Stage. You can align sprites on the Stage using the grid, the guides, or the Align window. The **grid** is a set of rows and columns of a specified height and width that you can use to help place sprites on the Stage. When you select the Snap to Grid option, sprites snap to the grid points, whether the grid is visible or not. The **guides** are horizontal or vertical lines you can either drag around the Stage or lock in place to help you align sprites in a straight line. When you select the Snap to Guides option, sprites snap to the guide line. When you are not using the grid or guides, you can hide them. The **Align window** moves sprites not to a specific location on the Stage, but to positions relative to one another. Jean positions and aligns the planet sprites at the bottom of the Stage, as part of the Planet game.

Steps

1. Click the **Planets Start sprite** (the black background), then click the **Guides and Grid tab** in the Property Inspector, if necessary
   Your initial settings for the Guides and Grid tab might be different. The Visible check box and the Snap to Guides check box in the Guides: area are selected, and the Snap to Grid check box in the Grid: area is selected.

2. Click the **Visible check box** in the Grid: area to select it, then click the **Snap to Grid check box** in the Grid: area to select it, if necessary
   A grid appears on the Stage. You can change the grid lines to dots by clicking the Dot option button in the Guides and Grid tab of the Property Inspector.

QuickTip

To change the height and width of the rows and columns in the grid, enter a value in the Spacing: Height or Width box in the Guides and Grid tab of the Property Inspector, then press [Enter] (Win) or [Return] (Mac).

3. Position the Arrow pointer over the bottom part of the Earth sprite, drag the pointer down to the bottom horizontal grid, as shown in Figure E-14, then click the **Planets Start sprite**
   When you drag the sprite, a green plus sign appears, indicating where the sprite will snap to the grid. The position where you drag the sprite determines where the green plus sign appears in the sprite. For example, when you drag the left side of the Earth sprite, the green plus sign appears to the left of a grid line.

4. Click the **Visible check box** in the Grid: area on the Guides and Grid tab of the Property Inspector to clear it, click the **Visible check box** in the Guides: area to select it, if necessary, then click **Remove All**
   Any guides on the Stage are removed.

QuickTip

You can add as many horizontal and vertical guide lines as you want.

5. Press and hold 🖑 over the **New Horizontal guide** 🔲 in the Guides and Grid tab of the Property Inspector, then drag the **guide** to the bottom of the Stage, as shown in Figure E-15

6. Drag the bottom part of each **planet** (don't forget Pluto on the far left) to the horizontal guide in any order, position ⧨ over the **horizontal guide** on the Stage, then drag the **horizontal guide** down off the Stage to remove it

7. Click a **planet sprite** on the Stage, press and hold **[Shift]**, then click each of the other **planet sprites** to select all the planet sprites

8. Click **Modify** on the menu bar, then click **Align**
   The Align window opens, as shown in Figure E-16.

9. Click the **Horizontal Alignment list arrow** 🔽, click **Distribute Widths**, click **Align**, then click the **Close button** in the Align window
   The sprites are evenly aligned horizontally across the bottom of the Stage.

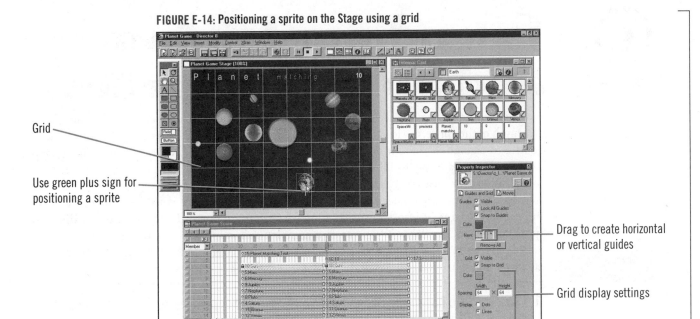

Grid

Use green plus sign for positioning a sprite

Drag to create horizontal or vertical guides

Grid display settings

FIGURE E-15: **Creating a guide**

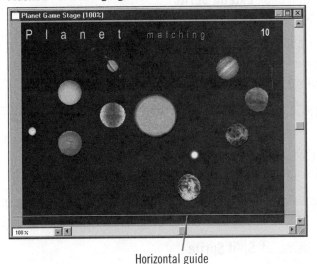

Horizontal guide

FIGURE E-16: **Aligning sprites**

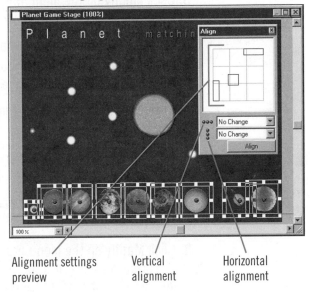

Alignment settings preview

Vertical alignment

Horizontal alignment

Tweaking the placement of a sprite

Sometimes you need to make only minor adjustments to the placement of a sprite. You can drag the sprite with the mouse, use the arrow keys, or use the Sprite tab in the Property Inspector to enter specific coordinates, but these techniques can sometimes be time-consuming or inefficient in achieving the exact placement you want. The Tweak window allows you to make an adjustment with the mouse and know the exact distances involved. To open the Tweak window, click Modify on the menu bar, then click Tweak. You can drag the alignment in the Tweak window to a line to set a specific movement and then use the horizontal and vertical arrows to make any final adjustments to the sprite's location. When you finish making adjustments, you select one or more sprites and click Tweak to apply the movement. You can apply the Tweak settings to as many sprites as you want. The Tweak settings stay in effect until you change them or close the Tweak window.

Director 8

Unit E
Director 8

Extending, Joining, and Splitting Sprites

You can change the duration of a sprite on the Stage by adjusting the length of the sprite. The longer the length of the sprite, the longer the sprite appears in the movie. You can drag the end frame of a sprite to change the length or use the Extend command on the Modify menu. The Extend command is an easy way to fill up channels with blocks of sprites. You can also use the Extend command to shorten a sprite. Sometimes you might need to split an existing sprite into two separate sprites, or join separate sprites. For example, if you create a text sprite with a long duration and need to separate it into two sprites to make changes in one of them, you can use the Split Sprite command. Similarly, if you create a complex animation as separate sprites and need to consolidate them into a single sprite, you can use the Join Sprite command. ✎ Jean extends a group of sprites, joins all the sprites in a channel, and splits a sprite in two.

Steps

1. Click the **title bar** in the Score, then verify that the copied set of 9 planets is selected (channels 7 through 15 starting at frame 59)

2. Drag the **horizontal scroll box** to frame 365, then click **365** in the timeline
   The playback head appears in frame 365.

3. Click **Modify** on the menu bar, then click **Extend Sprite**
   The selected sprites are extended to frame 365, as shown in Figure E-17.

4. Click **341** in the timeline, then click the **Center Current Frame button** 🔲 on the bottom row of the Score window
   The playback head is centered in the middle of the Score window at frame 341.

5. Click **Sprite channel 5** on the left side of the Score to select all the sprites in the channel

QuickTip

Drag the horizontal scroll box to confirm that the sprites are joined.

6. Click **Modify** on the menu bar, then click **Join Sprites**
   All the sprites in channel 5 are joined together to create one sprite, as shown in Figure E-18.

7. Click **341** in the timeline (if necessary), then click the **Planet Matching Text sprite** in channel 4

8. Click **Modify** on the menu bar, then click **Split Sprite**
   The Planet Matching Text sprite is split into two sprites at frame 341, as shown in Figure E-19. You can select the new text sprite that starts at frame 341 and modify it without affecting the Planet Matching Text sprite that ends at frame 340.

FIGURE E-17: Extending sprites

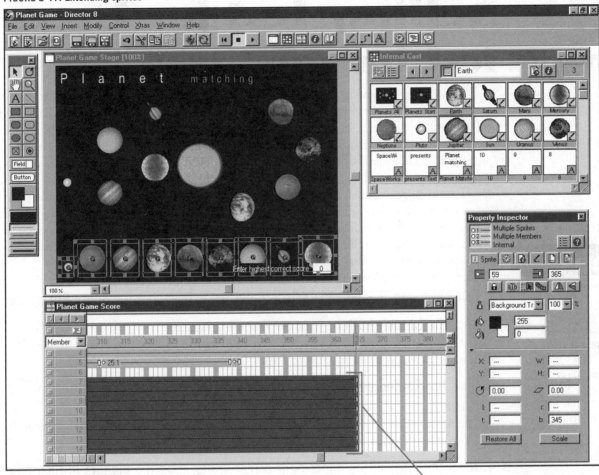

Selected sprites extended to playback head

FIGURE E-18: Joining sprites

Click sprite channel to select all sprites

Selected sprites joined together

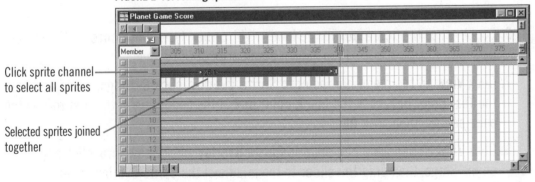

FIGURE E-19: Splitting sprites

One sprite split into two at the playback head

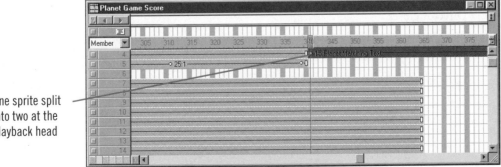

Setting Text for Users to Change

You can set regular text and field text cast members so that end users can edit the text as the movie plays. For example, if your movie calls for end users to enter their names, include an editable text or field sprite where the users can click and type. During a movie, users can click the text box to place a blinking cursor there and modify the contents of the text box. You can use the Editable button in the Sprite tab or the Editable check box in the Text tab and Field tab of the Property Inspector to make text and field sprites editable. You can also use the Editable button to make a field sprite editable in only a certain range of frames in the Score. If you choose the Edit Sprite Frames command on the Edit menu, you can select individual frames and make a text box editable in one frame but not in another. Keep in mind that any edits you make to a text or field sprite will also affect the original text or field cast member, as well as all succeeding sprites that you create. ✐ Jean changes a text sprite setting so that end users can change text as the Planet game plays.

Steps

1. Scroll to frame 365 and channel 17 in the Score, then click the **Score Box sprite**

QuickTip

You can also click the Editable check box in the Text or Field tab of the Property Inspector to edit text for an entire sprite while the movie plays.

2. Click the **Editable button** a|b in the Property Inspector

   The Editable text property is set for the Score box sprite, as shown in Figure E-20. When you play the movie, you can add text in the text box.

3. Click the **Rewind button** on the toolbar, then click the **Play button** on the toolbar

   The movie plays on the Stage, and the playback head moves frame to frame through the Score until it reaches the end. You can test the Planet match game.

Trouble?

If you need to restart the movie, click the Rewind button , then click the Play button.

4. When the timer in the upper-right corner starts, drag the **planets** to their original positions around the sun

5. When the timer reaches 0, count how many planets you placed in the correct position on the screen

Trouble?

If the movie plays again, click the Stop button on the toolbar. To turn off the playback loop, click Window on the menu bar, click Control Panel, then click Loop Playback.

6. Double-click the **score box** in the lower-right corner, type **your score** on the screen, as shown in Figure E-21, then click a **blank area** of the screen

7. Click **View** on the menu bar, point to **Sprite Overlay**, click **Settings**, press and hold the **Text Color box**, click the **black color box** at the beginning of the first row on the color palette, then click **OK**

8. Click **View** on the menu bar, point to **Sprite Overlay**, click **Show Info**, click any sprite on the Stage, then drag the **slider** to the middle of the Sprite Overlay panel

9. Click the **Save button** on the toolbar, click **File** on the menu bar, then click **Exit** (Win) or **Quit** (Mac)

   Director closes.

FIGURE E-20: Setting sprites for editing during playback

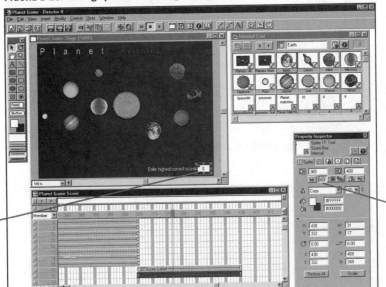

Text sprite set for editing during playback

Click button to edit text during playback

FIGURE E-21: Editing text during playback

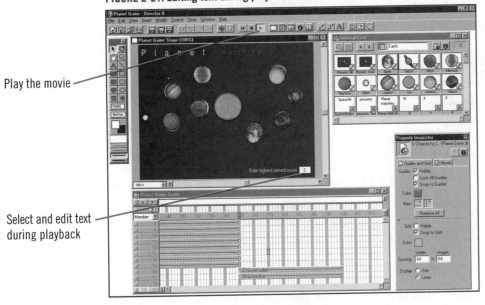

Play the movie

Select and edit text during playback

CLUES TO USE

Changing text and field properties

You can use the Text or Field tab in the Property Inspector to view and change settings for selected text sprites. You can select a framing option to determine how Director places text within the boundaries of a text box. The Framing options include Adjust to Fit, Scrolling, Fixed, and Limit to Field Size. The Adjust to Fit option expands the text box vertically when text that is entered extends beyond the current size of the box. The Scrolling option attaches a scroll bar to the right side of the text box, which is useful when there is a large amount of text. The Fixed option retains the original size of the text box. If you enter text that extends beyond the limits of the box, the text is stored but not displayed. The Limit to Field Size option for field text accepts only the amount of text that fits within the limits of the box. You can also set editing and display options in the Text or Field tab of the Property Inspector. The Editable option makes the cast member editable while the movie plays. The Wrap option increases the vertical size of the text box or field on the Stage so that all text is visible. The Tab to Next Editable Item option advances the text insertion point to the next editable sprite on the Stage when the end user presses Tab.

Practice

► Concepts Review

Label each of the elements of the screen shown in Figure E-22.

FIGURE E-22

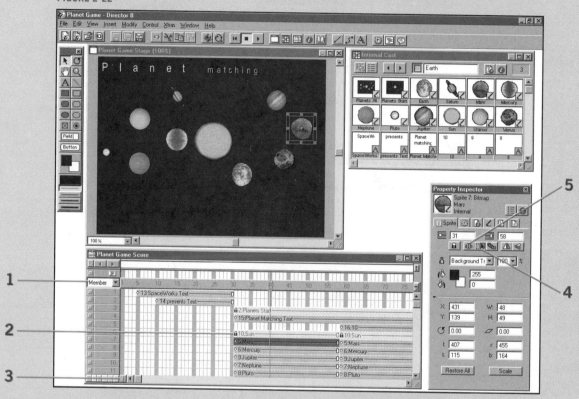

Match each of the terms with the statement that describes its function.

6. Blend
7. Trail
8. Grid
9. Ink effect
10. Label
11. Guide

a. Change the display of a sprite's colors
b. A transparency level
c. A string of continuous sprite images on the screen
d. Text that identifies a sprite
e. A set of rows and columns that you use the place sprites
f. A horizontal or vertical line that you use the place sprites

Select the best answer from the following list of choices.

12. **Which tool do you use to select a sprite?**
    a. Hand tool
    b. Magnifying Glass tool
    c. Arrow tool
    d. none of the above

13. **Which is NOT a sprite property?**
    a. Location
    b. Blend
    c. Keyframe
    d. End frame

14. What is the base point of reference for the horizontal (X) and vertical (Y) value for the registration point?
    a. Top-left corner
    b. Top-right corner
    c. Bottom-left corner
    d. Bottom-right corner

15. A 100% blend makes a sprite:
    a. Completely opaque.
    b. Partially opaque.
    c. Completely transparent.
    d. Partially transparent.

16. A sprite will appear in front in channel:
    a. 1.
    b. 5.
    c. 10.
    d. 15.

17. Which is NOT an ink effect?
    a. Copy
    b. Transparent
    c. Contrast
    d. Reverse

18. Which ink effect removes the white bounding box around a sprite?
    a. Transparent
    b. Ghost
    c. Mask
    d. Matte

19. Which ink effect defines the transparent or opaque parts of a sprite?
    a. Blend
    b. Mask
    c. Matte
    d. Copy

▶ Skills Review

1. **Create and select sprites.**
    a. Start Director, open the file **MD E-2** from the drive and folder where your Project Files are located.
    b. Save the file as *States Game* in the drive and folder where your Project Files are located.
    c. Resize the Stage to display the gray area around the Stage.
    d. Select the Title cast member on the Stage with a double border and then with a single border.

2. **View sprite properties.**
    a. View the sprite properties for the Title sprite.
    b. Write down the sprite feature name and properties in the Sprite tab for the Title sprite.

3. **Layer sprites.**
    a. Select the Name Title sprite in the Score, then move the sprite forward one channel.
    b. Drag the Name Title sprite on the Stage above the Name sprite.
    c. Drag the Name sprite on the Stage below and aligned with the Name Title sprite.
    d. Hide channel 1 to display the background, then show channel 1 to restore it.

4. **Apply sprite inks.**
    a. Select the USA Map Blank sprite.
    b. Open the Property Inspector.
    c. Change the ink to Background Transparent.
    d. Select the Title sprite, then change the ink to Matte.

5. **Change the sprite display.**
    a. Change the display in the Score window to Extended, Ink, and then Member.
    b. Open the Sprite Overlay Settings dialog box, then change the color to blue.
    c. Change the shading of the Sprite Overlay panel, then hide the Sprite Overlay panel.

6. **Change sprite properties.**
    a. Select and lock the USA Map Blank sprite.
    b. Select all the state text sprites and set them to Moveable.

7. Position and align sprites.

a. Display the Guides and Grid tab in the Property Inspector.

b. Drag a horizontal guide on the Stage.

c. Align the state text sprites in four rows at the top of the Stage.

d. Remove the guide.

e. Select each row of state text sprites individually and change the horizontal alignment to Distribute Widths.

8. Extend, split, and join sprites.

a. Select all the state text sprites.

b. Extend the state text sprites to frame 1250. (*Hint*: Depending on the speed of your computer, you might need to wait a few moments for Director to perform this task.)

c. Click 1000 in the timeline, select the Title sprite in channel 2, then split the sprite.

9. Set text for users to change.

a. Select the Name sprite and set it to Editable.

b. Rewind the movie, then play it.

c. Select the text *Your Name* (if necessary), type **Your Name**, then deselect the text box.

d. Drag the state names for the purple states in the map until the answers appear.

e. When the movie stops, show the Sprite Overlay panel.

f. Open the Sprite Overlay Settings dialog box and change the color to black.

g. Change the shading of the panel to the middle.

h. Save the movie and exit Director.

▶ Independent Challenges

1. You are a student at Benson Art College. The multimedia department is having a graphic design contest. First prize is $500.00. Recently, you have been experimenting with the ink effects in Director and want to use your newly acquired skills for the contest. You use Director's Paint tool to create two cast members and apply the Mask ink effect.

To complete this independent challenge:

a. Start Director and save the movie as *Design Contest* in the drive and folder where your Project Files are located.

b. Open the Paint window, then open the Pattern pop-up menu on the Tool palette and select a tile at the bottom.

c. Create a filled rectangle with the pattern, then close the Paint window.

d. Copy the cast member.

e. Paste the cast member in the next location to the right.

f. Open the duplicate cast member and change the tile color and pattern to black, then use the Paint tools to fill the rectangle with black.

g. Use the Airbrush tool to create white brush strokes in the black area, then close the Paint window.

h. Transform the duplicate cast member bitmap to 32 bits. (*Hint*: Use the Transform Bitmap command on the Modify menu.)

i. Drag the original cast member on the Stage, then change the ink effect for the cast member to the mask effect.

j. Create a text cast member with the text **Designs by [Your Name]**.

k. Print the Stage and the cast members, then save the movie and exit Director.

2. You are a game designer at Freeware Games, a software company that develops memory games for kids. Your boss asks you to create a simple shape matching game for ages three to four. You use Director's Paint tool to create circle, square, and triangle cast members and a background cast member with the outline of the shapes.

To complete this independent challenge:

a. Start Director and save the movie as *Shape Matching* in the drive and folder where your Project Files are located.

b. Create and name a background cast member with the outline of a circle, square, and triangle.

c. Create and name filled cast members with the circle, square, and triangle shapes.

d. Drag the background on the Stage and lock it.

e. Drag the shapes on the Stage and set them to be moveable.

f. Create a text cast member with the text **Shape Matching Game**.

g. Change the duration and modify the shape sprites to create a matching game.

h. Print the Stage and the cast members, then save the movie and exit Director.

3. You are a customer service specialist at 24-7 Answers, an online technical support company. You've been tasked with creating a data structure with the information you need from your customers, including different types of information, such as name, e-mail address, and problem. You use Director's Text tool to create text labels and empty text boxes where users can enter text.

To complete this independent challenge:

a. Start Director and save the movie as *Answers Prototype* in the drive and folder where your Project Files are located.

b. Write down on paper a list of the different types of information you might need from a person to provide online technical support.

c. Create and name text label cast members, using the Text tool.

d. Create and name empty text cast members, using the Text tool, and set them to be editable.

e. Extend the sprites in the Score for enough time to enter information in the editable text cast members.

f. Create a text cast member with the text **24-7 Answers**.

g. Place and arrange the cast members on the Stage and add a color background.

h. Play the movie and enter text in the editable text cast members.

i. Print the Stage, then save the movie and exit Director.

4. You run the Fun and Games truck, a mobile teaching unit that delivers books and software games to kids in rural areas. You want to create a new animal matching game for four to five year olds. You use Director's import capabilities to create a cast of animals, and the Paint tool to create a background for matching the animal with its name.

To complete this independent challenge:

a. Connect to the Internet and go to www.course.com. Navigate to the page for this book, click the link for the Student Online Companion, then click the link for this unit.

b. Browse the Animals section for clip art.

c. Download six different animals in the drive and folder where your Project Files are located.

d. Start Director and save the movie as *Animal Matching* in the drive and folder where your Project Files are located.

e. Create and name a background cast member with an unfilled rectangle and a text label with the name of each animal.

f. Drag the background on the Stage and lock it.

g. Drag the animal cast members on the Stage and set them to be moveable.

h. Create a text cast member with the text **Animal Matching Game**.

i. Change the duration and modify the animal sprites to create a matching game.

j. Print the Stage and the cast members, then save the movie and exit Director.

▶ Visual Workshop

Re-create the screen shown in Figure E-23. Print the screen. (For Windows, use the Windows Paint program. Press the Print Screen key to make a copy of the screen, start the Paint program by clicking Start, pointing to Programs, pointing to Accessories, then clicking Paint, click Edit on the menu bar, click Paste to paste the screen into Paint, then click Yes to paste the large image if necessary. Click File on the menu bar, click Print, click Print or OK in the dialog box, then exit Paint. For the Macintosh, use the SimpleText program. Hold and press the Command, Shift, and 3 keys to make a copy of the screen, double-click the document Picture 1 located on your hard drive, click File on the menu bar, click Print, then click Print in the dialog box. (*Note*: When you create a new document with a copy of the screen and a document Picture 1 already exists, the Macintosh names the new document Picture 2.)

FIGURE E-23

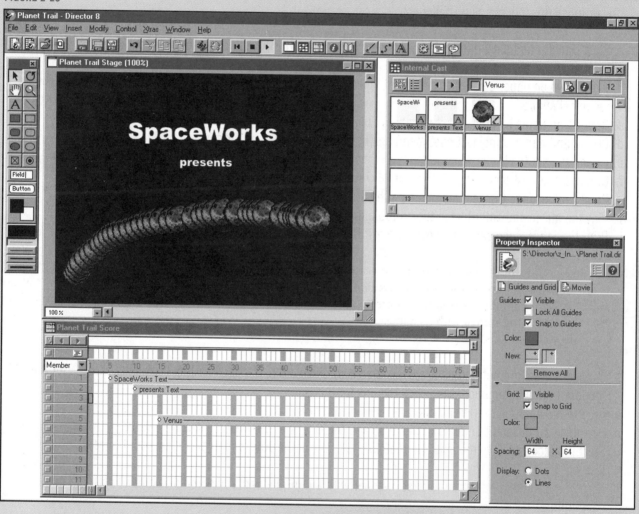

Adding
Navigation and User Interaction

Objectives

- ► Understand navigation and user interaction
- ► Change the tempo
- ► Compare tempo performance
- ► Add a wait time
- ► Create navigation with behaviors
- ► Add and name markers
- ► Create navigation with markers
- ► Add rollover effects
- ► Add a transition

Adding navigation and user interaction to your movies lets you involve your audience in the movie. You can use these features to jump to different parts of movies during authoring or in the completed movie, or to allow end users to perform functions such as clicking buttons and downloading files from the Internet. In the previous unit, you learned how to move objects and enter text on the Stage while the movie is playing. This unit introduces you to basic skills for changing the tempo, or speed, of a movie, adding a wait time, creating navigation controls and markers, and adding transitions between movie scenes. Jean wants to add navigation and user interaction for an informational multimedia movie about space exploration.

Understanding Navigation and User Interaction

Director 8

As you discovered in the planning process, the script and schematic flowchart are important planning tools for the multimedia developer. While the script tells the story of your movie production in text form, as shown in Figure F-1, the schematic flowchart sketches out the navigational structure of a movie to ensure that each of the sections is properly connected, as shown in Figure F-2. Once you have the script and schematic flowchart mapped out on paper, you can see the correlation between what you have developed and what you will begin to set up in Director. Jean develops an initial script and schematic flowchart for the Space Journey project. First, Jean takes some time to familiarize herself with some of the navigational and interactive elements available in Director.

Types of navigation and user interaction

 Moveable sprites

The moveable property allows users to drag a sprite on the Stage while the movie is playing. You can set a sprite's moveable property by clicking the Moveable button in the Sprite tab of the Property Inspector.

 Editable sprites

The editable property allows end users to enter text (in a field or text sprite) on the Stage while the movie is playing. You can set a sprite's editable property by clicking the Editable button in the Sprite tab of the Property Inspector.

 Tempo settings

The tempo settings allow you to set the speed of the movie and to pause the movie at a specific frame, such as when the end user clicks a mouse or presses a key, or when a specific cue point occurs in a sound or video. You can change tempo settings by double-clicking a frame in the Tempo channel, and then selecting the tempo options you want to change. You can use the Control Panel to compare the current tempo settings with actual tempo results.

 Library behaviors

The Library behaviors allow you to add navigation controls and interaction to a movie using a built-in behavior from the Library palette with a prewritten Lingo script. You can attach a behavior to a sprite or frame by opening the Library Palette window, selecting a behavior category, and then dragging a behavior to a frame or sprite.

 Lingo scripts

The Lingo scripts allow you to create simple scripts that you can attach to sprites or frames to navigate to a specific location in a movie. You can create a script by double-clicking a frame in the Behavior channel, and then typing one or more Lingo instructions, such as *go to frame "Menu"*.

 Transition settings

The transition settings allow you to select a transition effect that you can use to move smoothly from one scene to another, and to set the duration and smoothness of a transition. You can select a transition effect and set other related settings by double-clicking a frame in the Transition channel, and then selecting a transition and setting other options you want to apply to the frame.

FIGURE F-1: Project planning script

Script

Project: Space Journey

Scene	Text	Graphics	Audio	Video	Animation	Navigation	Transition
1	SpaceWorks	SpaceWorks Background					
1	presents						
2	a journey through space	Rocket graphic	TBD		Fly from bottom left to center		
2	click to continue					Pause: wait for click	
3		Title graphic					
3	Videos			TBD		Scene 5	
3	Sounds		TBD			Scene 6	
3	Pictures	TBD				Scene 7	
3		Credits button				Scene 4	
3		Exit button				Quit	
4		Credits graphic					Zoom Close
4	Credits list				Fly from bottom center	Pause 4 seconds, then Scene 3	

FIGURE F-2: Project planning schematic flowchart

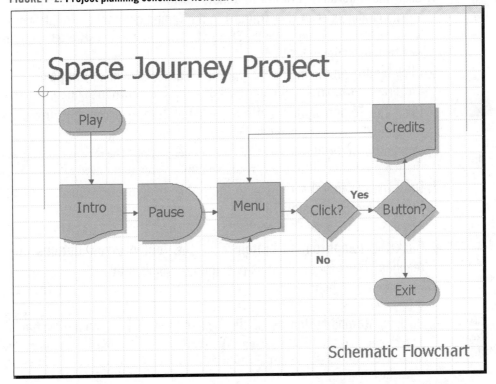

Schematic Flowchart

Changing the Tempo

Director plays a movie at a particular **tempo**, or speed. You can set the tempo rate to control the maximum speed at which the movie plays from frame to frame. The tempo rate is measured in frames per second (fps). The higher the tempo rate, the faster Director plays back animation. You can make animated sprites fly across the Stage to create a high-speed effect, or crawl across the Stage to create a slow-motion effect. You can set the tempo for the entire movie or selected frames. You use the Tempo channel in the Score window to set the tempo rate. It's a good idea to set the tempo rate for a movie in the first frame. Otherwise, the playback speed will be determined by the frame-by-frame settings in the Control Panel, which can be inconsistent. When you set the tempo rate in the Tempo channel, Director uses the tempo rate from the selected frame until it reaches the next different tempo setting. You can set the tempo rate from 1 to 999 frames per second. The tempo rate doesn't affect the playback rate of sounds and video or the duration of transitions. Jean sets the tempo rate at the beginning of a new space movie and then changes the tempo rate towards the end to slow down an animation.

Steps

1. Start **Director**, open the file **MD F-1** from the drive and folder where your Project Files are located, then save it as **Journey**
   Director opens, displaying the movie. Your initial settings in Director can vary, depending on previous usage.

2. Position ↖ (Win) or ↖ (Mac) on the lower-right corner of the **Stage window**, then drag the **border** diagonally to the right to expand the window until the gray area around the Stage is displayed
   The window is now resized on each side. You can also resize a window's height or width by dragging any border.

3. Click the **Play button** ▶ on the toolbar
   The movie plays on the Stage, and the playback head moves frame to frame through the Score until it reaches the end. You can see the initial development of the multimedia project. Now, you will change the movie tempo and add navigation and user interaction to complete the project.

4. Click the **Hide/Show Effects Channels button** in the Score window to display the effects channels, then click **frame 1** in the **Tempo channel** in the Score window
   The effects channels appear in the Score window with frame 1 selected in the Tempo channel, as shown in Figure F-3.

5. Click **Modify** on the menu bar, point to **Frame**, then click **Tempo**
   The Frame Properties: Tempo dialog box opens, as shown in Figure F-4.

6. Click the **Tempo option button**, click the **Tempo arrow buttons** until the setting reaches 25 fps (or as close as possible), then click **OK**
   The tempo for the movie is set to 25 frames per second. The tempo rate appears in frame 1 of the Tempo channel. If you can't read the number, you might need to zoom the Score window.

7. Drag the horizontal scroll box to the right in the Score window to display frame 78, then double-click **frame 78** in
   The Frames Properties: Tempo dialog box opens.

8. Click the **Tempo option button**, click the **Tempo arrow buttons** until the setting reaches 15 fps (or as close as possible), then click **OK**
   The tempo for the movie changes from 25 frames per second to 15 frames per second at frame 78.

9. Click the **Rewind button** on the toolbar, then click ▶ on the toolbar
   The movie plays on the Stage, and the playback head moves frame to frame through the Score at 25 frames per second for frames 1 to 77 then changes to 15 frames per second until it reaches the end.

Trouble?
If the movie loops, click Window on the menu bar, click Control Panel, click the Loop Playback button to deselect it, then click the Close button on the Control Panel.

QuickTip
To zoom the Score window, click the Zoom Menu button at the right edge of the Sprite channel, then click a percentage.

QuickTip
To pause the movie until a sound or video cue point passes, in the Frame Properties: Tempo dialog box, click the Wait for Cue Point option button, choose a channel and cue point, then click OK.

FIGURE F-3: Effects channels in the Score window

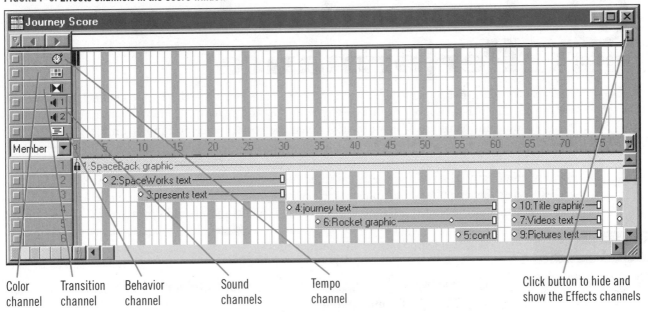

Color channel

Transition channel

Behavior channel

Sound channels

Tempo channel

Click button to hide and show the Effects channels

FIGURE F-4: Frame Properties: Tempo dialog box

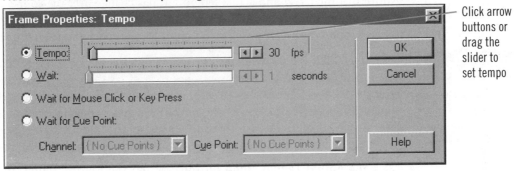

Click arrow buttons or drag the slider to set tempo

Understanding tempo rate on different computers

Director always attempts to play a movie at the specified tempo rate, but the computer running the movie might not be fast enough to play it at the desired tempo rate. If you want your movie to play on a variety of computer systems, you need to set a tempo rate that allows low-end computers (low CPU speed and small amount of RAM; see Director Help for system requirements) to play the movie at the desired tempo rate. If you have complex animations and transitions or large cast members in the movie that might cause slower playback, you might need to redesign parts of the movie to play at slower tempo rates. Otherwise, low-end computer users might be disappointed with the playback performance.

Comparing Tempo Performance

Director 8

Director tries to play the movie at the tempo rate you set in the Tempo channel. However, the actual playback speed might be different. Computer systems run at different speeds and include different hardware, which can slow down the performance of a movie on the playback computer. You can alleviate this performance problem by testing your movie on a computer similar to the ones your target audience will use. The Control Panel includes the tempo rate you set in the Tempo channel and the actual speed of the movie. While you play the movie, you can compare the tempo rate, also known as the target tempo, with the actual tempo rate. You can change tempo settings in the Tempo channel or use the Tempo up and down arrows in the Control Panel to adjust the tempo rate for specific frames. Jean compares the target tempo rate with the actual tempo rate for the Journey movie.

QuickTip

The tempo you set in the Tempo channel overrides any value you set in the Tempo box in the Control Panel.

1. Click **Window** on the menu bar, then click **Control Panel** (if necessary), then click **frame 75** in the **Frame channel**

   The Control Panel appears, displaying the target and actual tempo settings for frame 75, as shown in Figure F-5.

2. Click the **Step Forward button** ⏸ on the Control Panel until you reach the end of the movie, frame 95, and compare the tempo and actual tempo settings on the Control Panel

   Notice that the target and actual tempo settings change over the course of the movie. The target tempo value is how fast you want the computer to play back the given frame, while the actual tempo value is how fast the computer did play back the given frame.

QuickTip

If you leave Actual Tempo set to Estimated Total, the movie might play back at a reduced speed due to its more intensive calculations.

3. Click the **Actual Tempo Mode button** fps on the Control Panel, then click **Running Total**

   The Actual Tempo Mode button changes to tot, as shown in Figure F-6. Running Total indicates the total elapsed time in seconds from the start of the movie to the current frame, which in this case is the end of the movie. You can also choose Seconds Per Frame, also known as SPF, or Estimated Total; it is similar to Running Total, but is more accurate because it includes palette changes and transitions in its calculations of the frame's length.

4. Click the **Actual Tempo Mode button** tot on the Control Panel, then click **Frames Per Second**

   The Actual Tempo Mode button changes to fps.

QuickTip

If the movie jumps to other parts, make sure you play through all of these parts to record the actual speed at which to store these values in the Actual Tempo box.

5. Click the **Rewind button** ◄◄ on the Control Panel, then click the **Play button** ► on the Control Panel

   When you play back the movie from beginning to end, Director records the actual speed at which it plays each frame, and stores these values in the Actual Tempo box in the Control Panel.

6. Click **Modify** on the menu bar, point to **Movie**, then click **Playback**

   The Movie Playback Properties dialog box opens, as shown in Figure F-7.

7. Click the **Lock Frame Durations check box** to select it, then click **OK**

   Each frame is locked to play at the actual speed recorded when the movie is played back.

8. Click ◄◄ on the Control Panel, click ► on the Control Panel, then click the **Close button** on the Control Panel

   The movie plays with each frame locked to play at the actual speed recorded.

9. Click **Modify** on the menu bar, point to **Movie**, click **Playback**, click the **Lock Frame Durations check box** to clear it, then click **OK**

   The movie's playback speed is unlocked.

FIGURE F-5: Control Panel with tempo settings

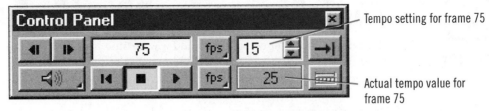

Tempo setting for frame 75

Actual tempo value for frame 75

FIGURE F-6: Control Panel with total running time

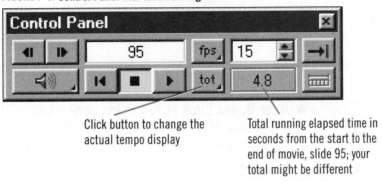

Click button to change the actual tempo display

Total running elapsed time in seconds from the start to the end of movie, slide 95; your total might be different

FIGURE F-7: Movie Playback Properties dialog box

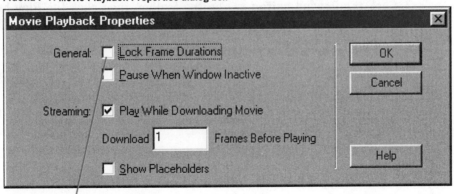

Click check box to lock the movie playback speed

Director 8

Director 8

Adding a Wait Time

You can use the Tempo channel to add a wait time in the playback of a movie. You can set a movie to wait at a frame for a specified number of seconds until a specific event occurs, such as a mouse click, key press, or a specific cue point in a sound or video. A **cue point** is a marker in a sound or video that you can use to trigger an event in Director. For example, you can use cue points to synchronize an animation with narration. A common use for cue points is to wait for the end of a sound or video to occur before Director starts the next frame in a movie. Jean adds two wait times to the Journey movie.

1. Click **frame 55** in the **Tempo channel** in the Score window
   The selected sprite appears in the Tempo channel, as shown in Figure F-8.

QuickTip

To quickly open the Frame Properties: Tempo dialog box, double-click a frame in the Tempo channel.

2. Click **Modify** on the menu bar, point to **Frame**, then click **Tempo**
   The Frame Properties: Tempo dialog box opens, as shown in Figure F-9.

3. Click the **Wait for Mouse Click or Key Press option button**, then click **OK**
   The Wait for Mouse Click or Key Press option is applied to frame 55. Director waits until the end user clicks the mouse button or presses a key before it continues.

4. Double-click **frame 95** in
   The Frame Properties: Tempo dialog opens.

5. Click the **Wait option button**, then drag the **Wait slider** or click the **Wait arrow buttons** until the number reaches 4 seconds (or as close as possible)

QuickTip

To delete a tempo, select the frame with the tempo setting, then press [Delete].

6. Click **OK**
   A four-second wait period is applied to frame 95.

7. Click the **Rewind button** on the toolbar, then click the **Play button** on the toolbar
   The movie plays on the Stage and stops at frame 55.

8. When the movie stops at frame 55, position on the Stage, then click anywhere on the **Stage** to continue playing the movie
   The movie plays on the Stage, and the playback head moves frame to frame through the Score until it reaches the end.

FIGURE F-8: Frame selected in the Tempo channel

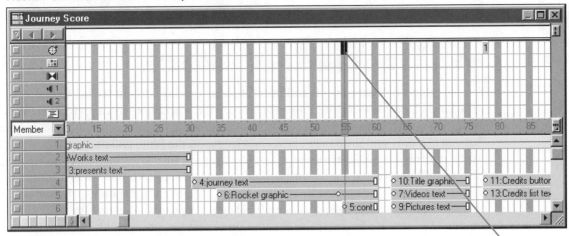

Frame 55 in the
Tempo channel

FIGURE F-9: Frame Properties: Tempo dialog box

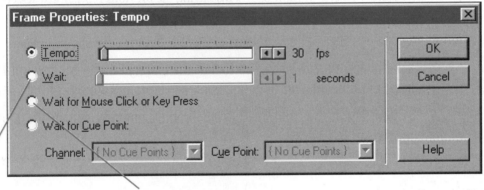

Click button to set the
frame to wait for a
specified number of
seconds

Click button to set the frame to
wait for mouse click or key press

Inserting cue points in sound and video files

To use the Wait for Cue Point option in the Frame Properties: Tempo dialog box to pause the playback head at certain points in a sound or video, you need to place cue points in the sound or video file that correspond to the times when you want to trigger an event, such as displaying text or starting an animation in Director. In Windows, use Sound Forge 4.0 or later, or Cool Edit 96 or later to insert cue points (called markers or regions within these programs). Cue points are not supported in AVI video. On the Macintosh, use Sound Edit 16 2.07 or later, or Peak LE 2 or later, to insert cue points in AIFF and Shockwave Audio sounds, and in QuickTime video. If you insert cue points into QuickTime files on the Macintosh, you can also use the QuickTime files in Director on the Macintosh and in Windows.

Director 8

Creating Navigation with Behaviors

You can add navigation controls and interaction to a movie without having to understand and write Lingo, Director's scripting language. You can use a behavior with a prewritten Lingo script to add interactivity to a movie. Director provides a Library palette of useful built-in behaviors that you can drag-and-drop onto sprites and frames in the Score and on the Stage. The Library palette of ready-to-use behaviors is grouped by category, such as animation, controls, text, navigation, and Internet, and comes with a tooltip description of each built-in behavior that makes it easier for you to find and use in a movie. You can attach the same built-in behavior to multiple sprites and frames. You can attach multiple behaviors to an individual sprite, but only one to a frame. If you want a behavior to affect the entire movie, such as Hold on Current Frame, you attach the behavior to a frame. When you attach a behavior to a sprite or frame, a Parameters dialog box might appear, asking you for specific settings. Director copies the behavior from the Library palette to the cast member in the Cast window. Jean adds a navigation control from the Library palette to the Journey movie.

1. Click **Window** on the menu bar, then click **Library Palette**
   The Library Palette window opens, displaying the previous Library List selection.

QuickTip

To hide/show the names of the behaviors in the Library Palette window, click the Library List button, then click Show Names.

2. Click the **Library List button**, then click **Navigation**
   The Library Palette window displays navigational controls, as shown in Figure F-10.

3. Click the **down arrow** at the bottom of the Library Palette window until the **Hold on Current Frame behavior icon** appears, as shown in Figure F-11

4. Position on the Hold on Current Frame behavior icon in the Library Palette window
   A brief description of the behavior appears. The Hold on Current Frame behavior prevents you from accidentally changing the original behavior.

QuickTip

To attach the same behavior to several sprites at once using the Library Palette window, select the sprites on the Stage or in the Score, then drag a behavior to any one of them. You cannot apply every behavior to every sprite.

5. Drag the **Hold on Current Frame behavior icon** in the Library Palette window to **frame 63** in the Behavior channel
   The behavior is attached to frame 63, and the behavior is copied as cast member 14 in the Cast window, as shown in Figure F-12. If you attach a behavior to a frame that already has a behavior, the new behavior replaces the old one.

6. Click the **Close button** in the Library Palette window
   The Library Palette window closes.

7. Click the **Rewind button** on the toolbar, then click the **Play button** on the toolbar
   The movie plays on the Stage and stops at frame 55.

8. When the movie stops at frame 55, position on the Stage, then click the **Stage** to continue playing the movie
   The movie plays on the Stage and stops at frame 63.

9. Click the **Stop button** on the toolbar
   The movie stops playing.

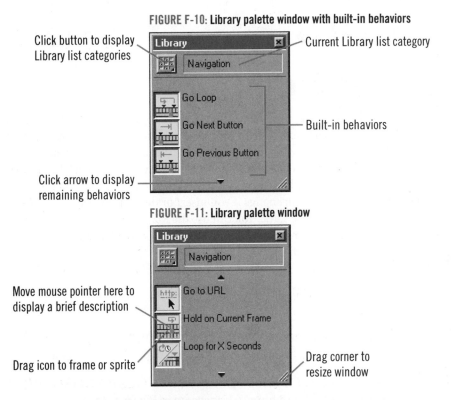

FIGURE F-10: Library palette window with built-in behaviors

Click button to display Library list categories

Current Library list category

Navigation

Go Loop

Go Next Button

Go Previous Button

Built-in behaviors

Click arrow to display remaining behaviors

FIGURE F-11: Library palette window

Navigation

Move mouse pointer here to display a brief description

Go to URL

Hold on Current Frame

Loop for X Seconds

Drag icon to frame or sprite

Drag corner to resize window

FIGURE F-12: New behavior in the Cast window

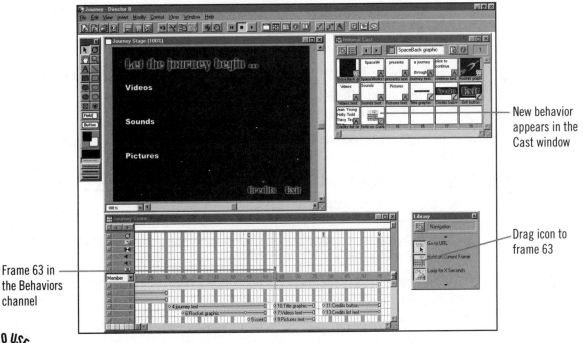

New behavior appears in the Cast window

Drag icon to frame 63

Frame 63 in the Behaviors channel

Director 8

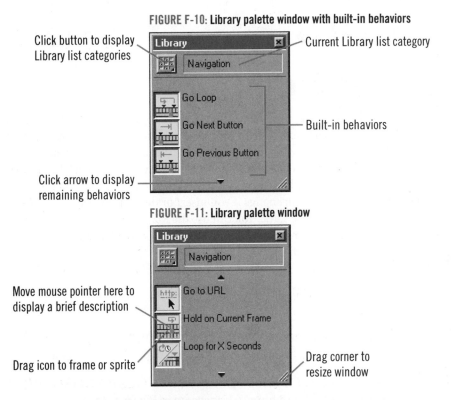

Getting information about behaviors

Behaviors included in the Library palette come with brief tooltip descriptions that appear when you position 🖑 over a behavior icon. Some behaviors have long descriptions and instructions, which you cannot read using the tooltip description in the Library palette. To read a complete description and a set of instructions provided by the behavior's author for a behavior already attached to a sprite or frame, you can use the Behavior Inspector. To display more information about a behavior in the Behavior Inspector, attach a behavior to a sprite or frame, click Window on the menu bar, point to Inspector, then click Behavior. The behavior information appears in a scrolling pane at the bottom of the Behavior Inspector.

Adding and Naming Markers

Director 8

While writing a movie, you often might want to move to a specific scene. Markers make it easy to identify and navigate to specific locations in a movie. You can use the Markers channel at the top of the Score window to add and name markers. After you add and name a marker, you can use the marker name in behaviors or scripts to move the playback head to any marker frame in the Score window. Marker names are more reliable to use during authoring than frame numbers. Frame numbers can change if you insert or delete frames in the Score, whereas, unless you move them, markers are static. You can use the Markers window to write comments for individual markers and to move the playback head to a particular marker in the Score. ✐ Jean adds and names markers in the Journey movie.

Steps

1. Click the **Markers channel** above **frame 40**
   A marker appears in the Markers channel with the title highlighted, as shown in Figure F-13.

2. Type **Menu**, then press **[Enter]** (Win) or **[Return]** (Mac)
   The marker appears in the Markers channel with the name Menu.

QuickTip

To delete a marker, drag the marker up or down out of the Markers channel.

3. Position 🖑 over the Menu marker ▽, then drag the **marker** to **frame 63**
   The marker appears in frame 63, as shown in Figure F-14.

4. Click the **Markers channel** above **frame 78**, type **Credits**, then press **[Enter]** (Win) or **[Return]** (Mac)
   The Credits marker appears in frame 78.

5. Click the **Rewind button** on the toolbar, then click the **Next Marker button** on the left side of the Markers channel
   The playback head moves to the Menu marker at frame 63.

6. Click the **Next Marker button** on the left side of the Markers channel
   The playback head moves to the Credits marker at frame 78.

QuickTip

To jump to a specific marker, click the Markers Menu button, then click a marker name in the list.

7. Click the **Markers Menu button** to the left of the Next Marker and Previous Marker buttons, then click **Markers**
   The Markers window opens, displaying all the markers in the movie, as shown in Figure F-15. The current marker is selected in the left box, its comment is selected in the right box, and its current location appears above the boxes.

8. Click **Menu** in the left box, then type **Main Menu**, then click **[Enter]** (Win)
   The marker is renamed and appears in both boxes.

9. Click the **Close button** in the Markers window
   The Markers window closes and the renamed marker, Main Menu, appears in the Markers channel.

FIGURE F-13: Creating a new marker

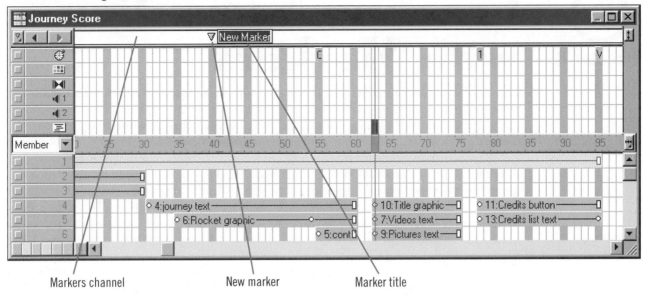

Markers channel — New marker — Marker title

FIGURE F-14: Naming and moving a marker

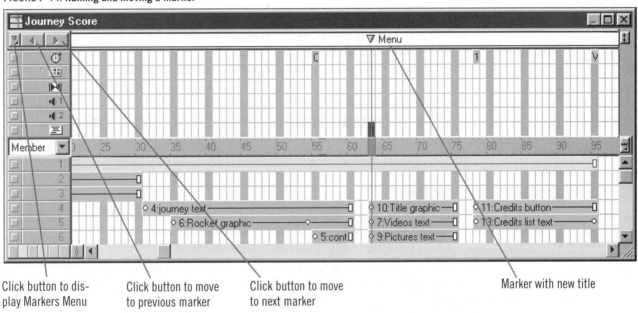

Click button to dis-play Markers Menu — Click button to move to previous marker — Click button to move to next marker — Marker with new title

FIGURE F-15: Marker window

Click button to move to next marker in the Score

Markers

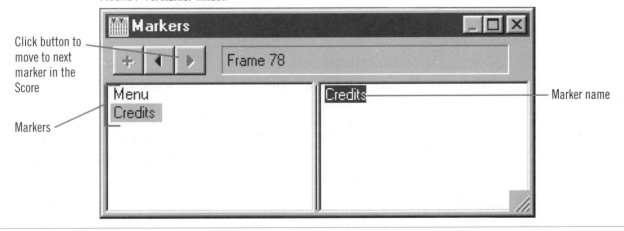

Marker name

Creating Navigation with Markers

Once you have added a marker to a frame, you can use the marker name in Lingo scripts and behaviors to navigate to a specific location in a movie. Sometimes it is easier to create a simple Lingo script in a movie than it is to find and use a built-in behavior in the Library palette. You can write a Lingo script to create simple navigation with markers. A Lingo script is a set of instructions that tells Director how to respond to specific events in a movie. A Lingo script is composed of one or more **handlers**, which respond to messages triggered by a specific event during the movie's playback. A handler starts in the Behavior Script window with the word *on* followed by the name of a trigger message, such as *mouseDown*. The handler waits for the specific movie event to occur (such as the end user pressing the mouse button), and then carries out the next Lingo instruction in the script. Table F-1 shows a partial list of movie events and Lingo trigger messages. You don't have to remember all of the Lingo instructions; Director provides a list of instructions by category in a pop-up menu. If the event associated with a handler doesn't occur in the duration of a sprite or frame, Director continues to play the movie. A handler stops when it comes to the word *end* in the script. Jean creates navigation between different points in the Journey movie, using markers and scripts.

Steps

1. Click **frame 95** in the **Behavior channel** in the Score window
   The selected frame appears in the Behavior channel.

QuickTip

To quickly open the Behavior Script window, double-click a frame in the Behavior channel.

2. Click **Modify** on the menu bar, point to **Frame**, then click **Script**
   The Behavior Script window opens, displaying the handler associated with a frame, as shown in Figure F-16. The script is color-coded to make it easier to identify different script elements.

3. Click the **Categorized Lingo button** on the toolbar, point to **Navigation**, then click **go to frame**
   The Lingo instruction *go to frame whichFrame* appears in the script with the text *whichFrame* selected.

QuickTip

To change a script's type, select the script in the Cast window or open it in the Script window, click the Script tab of the Property Inspector, click the Type down arrow, then click a script type.

4. Type **"Main Menu"**
   The Lingo instruction *go to frame "Main Menu"* appears in the script, as shown in Figure F-17. Lingo is not case-sensitive, but it does make the script easier to read when you use capital letters.

5. Click the **Close button** in the Behavior Script window
   The Behavior Script window closes, and the behavior is saved in the Cast window.

6. Click the **Credits button cast member** in the Cast window, then click the **Cast Member Script button** in the Cast window
   The Behavior Script window opens, displaying the handler, *on mouseUp*, associated with a sprite.

7. Type **go to frame "Credits"**, then click the **Close button** in the Behavior Script window
   The Cast Member Script icon appears in the Credits button cast member, as shown in Figure F-18. The cast member script is attached directly to the cast member. The cast member script is independent of the Score window, which means that the script is always available whenever the cast member is assigned to a sprite.

QuickTip

You can get help and copy Lingo examples from the Lingo Dictionary and paste them into scripts. To open the Lingo Dictionary, click Help on the menu bar, then click Lingo Dictionary.

8. Click the **Exit button cast member** in the Cast window, click the **Cast Member Script button** in the Cast window, type **quit**, then click the **Close button** in the Behavior Script window
   The Cast Member Script icon appears in the Exit button cast member.

9. Click the **Rewind button** on the toolbar, click the **Play button** on the toolbar, click the **Stage** when the movie stops at frame 55, then click the **Credits button** on the Stage when the movie stops at frame 63
   The playback head jumps to frame 78, plays the movie until it reaches frame 95, jumps quickly back to frame 63, then stops.

FIGURE F-16: Behavior Script window with a handler

Starts the handler

Ends the handler

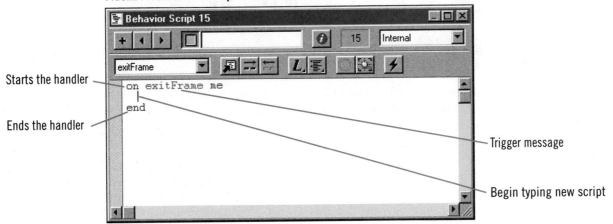

Trigger message

Begin typing new script

FIGURE F-17: Behavior Script window with Lingo instruction

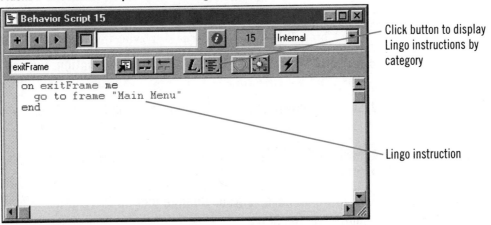

Click button to display Lingo instructions by category

Lingo instruction

FIGURE F-18: Cast members with a script

Frame script

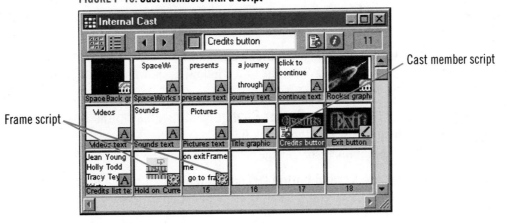

Cast member script

TABLE F-1: Movie events and Lingo messages

event	message	event	message
A window is closed	*closeWindow*	Playback head enters current frame	*enterFrame*
No event occurred	*idle*	A key is pressed	*KeyUp*
Mouse button released	*mouseUp*	Pointer enters sprite's region	*mouseEnter*
Movie starts playing	*startMovie*	A window is maximized or minimized	*zoomWindow*

Director 8

Adding Rollover Effects

Rollover effects allow you to change the appearance of sprites when the mouse pointer passes over them, even if the end user has not clicked the mouse. Rollover effects make it possible for you to give instructional help and feedback to the end user. For example, you can add a rollover effect to a graphical button that changes the appearance of the mouse pointer when it passes over the button. At this point, the end user can receive a cue where to click a button. The Library palette comes with two built-in behaviors to create rollover effects: Rollover Cursor Change and Rollover Member Change. The Rollover Cursor Change behavior allows you to modify a cursor when the mouse pointer rolls over a sprite. The Rollover Member Change behavior allows you to swap a sprite's cast member when the mouse pointer rolls over it. Jean attaches the cursor change rollover effect to a graphical button.

Steps

1. Click **Window** on the menu bar, then click **Library Palette**
   The Library Palette window opens, displaying the previous Library List selection.

2. Click the **Library List button**, point to **Animation**, then click **Interactive**
   The Library Palette window displays interactive animation controls.

3. Click the **down arrow** at the bottom of the Library Palette window until the Rollover Cursor Change behavior appears, shown in Figure F-19

4. Position ☜ on the Rollover Cursor Change behavior icon in the Library Palette window
   A brief description of the behavior appears.

QuickTip

To attach the same behavior to several sprites at once using the Library Palette window, select the sprites on the Stage or in the Score, then drag a behavior to any one of them.

5. Drag the **Rollover Cursor Change icon** in the Library Palette window to the **Credits button** on the **Stage**
   When you drag the behavior icon on a sprite on the Stage, a gray rectangle appears around the object, indicating where the behavior will be attached. The Parameters for "Rollover Cursor Change" dialog box opens, asking which cursor you want to use. The default cursor for this behavior is the Finger.

6. Click **OK**, then click the **Close button** in the Library Palette window
   The behavior is saved in the Cast window, as shown in Figure F-20, and the Library Palette window closes.

QuickTip

To delete a behavior in the Cast window, select the behavior in the Cast window, then press [Delete].

7. Drag the **Rollover Cursor Change** cast member in the Cast window to the **Exit button** on the Stage, then click **OK**
   The Rollover Cursor Change behavior with the Finger cursor is attached to the Exit button.

8. Click the **Rewind button** on the toolbar, click the **Play button** on the toolbar, then click the **Stage** when the movie stops at frame 55

9. When the movie stops at frame 63, position ☜ on the **Credits button** on the Stage, click the **Stop button** on the toolbar, then click a **gray area** of the Stage
   The cursor changes to ☜ when it moves over the Credits button.

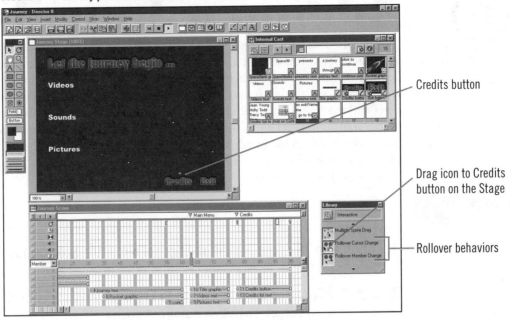

Credits button

Drag icon to Credits button on the Stage

Rollover behaviors

FIGURE F-20: Rollover effect in Cast window

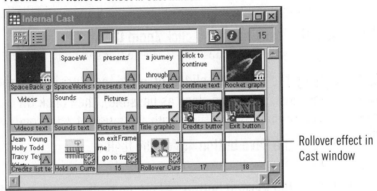

Rollover effect in Cast window

CLUES TO USE

Removing and modifying a behavior

Once you attach a behavior to a sprite or frame, you can remove it or modify parameters at any time. Before you can remove or modify a behavior, you need to select the sprite or frame to which the behavior is attached, click the Behavior tab in the Property Inspector, and select the behavior you want to remove or modify, as shown in Figure F-21. To remove a behavior, click the Clear button − in the Behavior tab, then click Remove Behavior. To change parameters for a behavior attached to a sprite or frame, use the pop-up menus or text fields in the Behavior tab to change any parameters. The Behavior tab includes the same fields for the behavior as those included in the Parameters dialog box.

FIGURE F-21: Behavior tab in the Property Inspector

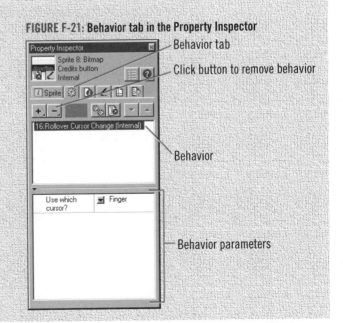

Behavior tab

Click button to remove behavior

Behavior

Behavior parameters

Director 8

Adding a Transition

Director provides special effects called transitions that you can use to move smoothly from one scene to another. You use the Transition channel in the Score window to add a transition to a frame. To create a transition between two scenes, you set the transition at the first frame of the second scene, not the last frame of the first scene. The transition begins between the frame you select and the frame that precedes it. In the Frames Properties: Transition dialog box, you can select a transition effect and adjust sliders to change the duration and smoothness of the transition as the movie plays. In addition, you can also select whether the transition will affect the entire Stage or just the area that changes in the switch between scenes. Jean adds a transition to the Journey movie.

Steps

QuickTip

To play a sound while a transition occurs, place the sound in the frame immediately before the transition.

1. Click **frame 78** in the **Transition channel** ▎◀ in the Score window
The selected frame appears in the Transition channel, as shown in Figure F-22.

2. Click **Modify** on the menu bar, point to **Frame**, then click **Transition**
The Frame Properties: Transition dialog box opens.

QuickTip

To quickly open the Frame Properties: Transition dialog box, double-click a frame in the Transitions channel.

3. In the Categories box, click **Other**
A list of transitions for the Other category appears in the Transition box.

4. In the Transitions box, click **Zoom Close**
The Zoom Close transition is selected, as shown in Figure F-23.

QuickTip

To delete a transition, select the frame with the transition effect, then press [Delete].

5. Drag the **Duration slider** or click the **Duration arrow buttons** until the number reaches 2.30 (or as close as possible), then click **OK**
The Zoom Close transition with a duration of 2.3 seconds is applied to frame 78.

6. Click the **Save button** 🖫 on the toolbar.
Director saves the program.

7. Click the **Rewind button** ◀▎ on the toolbar, click the **Play button** ▶ on the toolbar, then click the **Stage** when the movie stops at frame 55

8. When the movie stops at frame 63, click the **Credits button** on the Stage
The Zoom Close transition is displayed, the playback head jumps to frame 78, and the movie continues to play until it reaches frame 95, waits 5 seconds, and then jumps back to frame 63 and stops.

9. Click the **Exit button** on the Stage
Director closes.

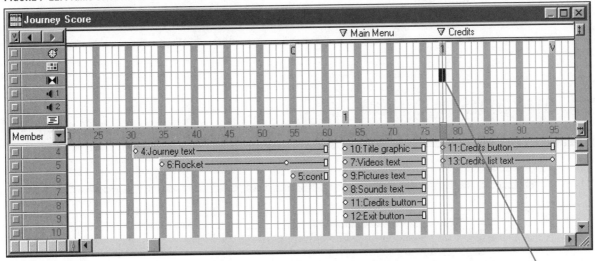

Frame 78 in the Transition channel

FIGURE F-23: Frame Properties: Transition dialog box

Click item to
select a transition
catogory

Click item to
select a transition

Drag the sliders
to set transition
duration and
smoothness

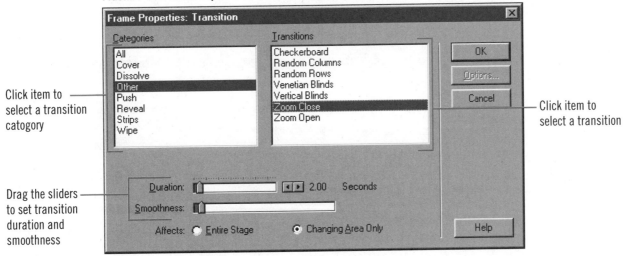

Adding Xtra transitions to Director

If you don't find exactly the transitions you want within Director, you can add new transitions by installing them as Xtras. An **Xtra** is a software module you can add to Director, which extends the capabilities of Director. To add Xtra transitions to Director, install a transition by copying the Xtra transition file into the Xtra folder within the Director program folder, exit and start Director, double-click a frame in the Transition channel for the transition, select the Xtra transition, then click OK. To see which Xtras are installed, click Modify on the menu bar, point to Movie, then click Xtras.

Director 8

Practice

► Concepts Review

Label each of the elements of the screen shown in Figure F-24.

FIGURE F-24

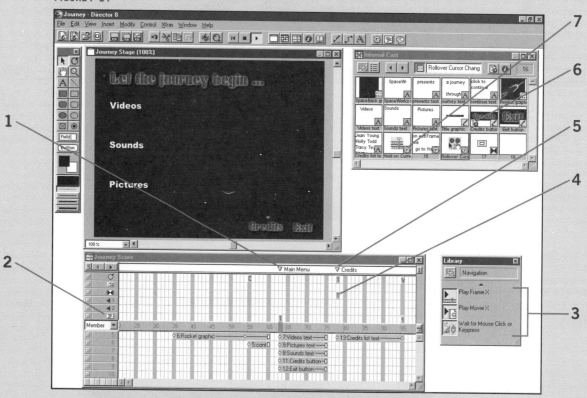

Match each of the terms with the statement that describes its function.

8. **Behavior**	**a.** Navigation points in a movie
9. **Tempo**	**b.** A marker in a sound or video
10. **Transition**	**c.** A software module that extends the capabilities of Director
11. **Cue point**	**d.** The speed of a movie
12. **Markers**	**e.** An effect that moves from one scene to another
13. **Handler**	**f.** A script that responds to messages triggered by events
14. **Xtra**	**g.** A ready-to-use script

Select the best answer from the following list of choices.

15. **Which is NOT an Actual Tempo Mode display option?**
   a. Seconds Per Frame
   b. Frames Per Minute
   c. Estimated Total
   d. Running Total

16. **Which is NOT a Tempo option?**
    a. Wait for Frame
    b. Wait for Cue Point
    c. Tempo
    d. Wait

17. **The Library palette contains:**
    a. Transitions.
    b. Markers.
    c. Behaviors.
    d. Cue points.

18. **How many behaviors can be attached to a frame?**
    a. 0
    b. 1
    c. 2
    d. Up to 999

19. **A handler starts with the word:**
    a. on.
    b. in.
    c. begin.
    d. at.

20. **In the Lingo script *go to frame "Credits"*, Credits refers to a:**
    a. Behavior.
    b. Marker.
    c. Script.
    d. Frame.

21. **A rollover effect is a:**
    a. Transition.
    b. Script.
    c. Behavior.
    d. Handler.

► Skills Review

1. **Understand navigation and user interaction.**
   a. Write down the basic types of navigation and user interaction in Director, with a description of each.
   b. Start Director, open the file **MD F-2** from the drive and folder where your Project Files are located.
   c. Save the file as *Nature's Gold* in the drive and folder where your Project Files are located.
   d. Resize the Stage to display the gray area around the Stage.

2. **Change the tempo.**
   a. Play the movie and show the Effects channel, if necessary.
   b. Change the tempo to 15 fps in frame 1.
   c. Change the tempo to 25 fps in frame 46.

3. **Compare tempo performance.**
   a. Open the Control Panel, if necessary.
   b. Rewind and play the movie.
   c. Compare the actual tempo to the tempo settings, and write down the results.
   d. Close the Control Panel.

4. Add a wait time.

   a. Add a wait until mouse click in frame 26.

   b. Add a 2-second wait time in frame 45.

5. Create navigation with behaviors.

   a. Attach the Hold on Current Frame behavior to frames 47, 66, 86, and 106.

6. Add and name markers.

   a. Add and name a marker "Main menu" at frame 46.

   b. Add and name a marker "Fruits" at frame 65.

   c. Add and name a marker "Vegetables" at frame 85.

   d. Add and name a marker "Treats" at frame 105.

7. Create navigation with markers.

   a. Attach a navigation script to *go to frame "Fruits"* to the text cast member Fruits text.

   b. Attach a navigation script to *go to frame "Vegetables"* to the text cast member Vegetables text.

   c. Attach a navigation script to *go to frame "Treats"* to the text cast member Treats text.

   d. Attach a navigation script to *quit* to the cast member Exit button.

   e. Attach a navigation script to *go to frame "Main menu"* to the cast member Menu button.

8. Add rollover effects.

   a. Add a rollover cursor change with the Finger cursor to the cast members Exit button, Menu button, Fruits text, Vegetables text, and Treats text.

9. Add a transition.

   a. Add the transition effect Dissolve, Pixels Fast with the Changing Area Only option to frame 46.

   b. Add the transition effect Wipe Right to frames 65, 85, and 105.

   c. Play the movie, then save the movie and exit Director.

▶ Independent Challenges

1. You are a multimedia Web designer at *Astronomy* magazine. In next month's issue, the feature article is about the increasing number of shooting stars. The magazine's editor asks you to create a shooting star animation for the magazine's Web site. You use Director's Paint tool to create a star and animation to move the star across a nighttime scene. You also change the tempo of the animation and compare it to the actual speed.

  To complete this independent challenge:

   a. Start Director and save the movie as *Shooting Star* in the drive and folder where your Project Files are located.

   b. Open the Paint window, then create a bright orange star.

   c. Change the background of the Stage to black.

   d. Create a text cast member with the text **Shooting Star**, and drag it to the top of the Stage.

   e. Animate the star across the Stage in frames 1 to 30.

   f. Set the tempo to 10 frames per second (fps) in the first frame.

   g. Change the tempo to 20 fps in frame 10, then change the tempo to 30 fps in frame 20.

   h. Play the entire movie to record the tempo settings.

   i. Play the movie again, compare the tempo settings to the actual speed, then write down your observations.

   j. Print the screen (see Visual Workshop for instructions), save the movie, and exit Director.

2. You work as a multimedia designer at Adventures in Reading. The company is coming out with a new line of books called *Follow the Bouncing Ball*. Your boss asks you to create a bouncing animation to promote the new series on the company's Web site. You use Director's Paint tool to create a ball, the Cast window to make copies and modify colors, and animation tools to bounce the ball three times with different colors and waiting times.

  To complete this independent challenge:

   a. Start Director and save the movie as *Bouncing Ball* in the drive and folder where your Project Files are located.

b. Create and name a Paint cast member of a ball with a filled color.

c. Make three copies of the ball cast member and change the fill color.

d. Create a text cast member with the text **Follow the Bouncing Ball**, and drag it to the top of the Stage.

e. Animate the first ball to bounce bottom-to-top on the Stage in frames 1 to 15. (*Hint:* Create a straight line angled animation from the bottom to the top.)

f. Animate the second ball to bounce bottom-to-top on the Stage in frames 15 to 30.

g. Pause the ball in frame 15 at the top of the bounce for 3 seconds.

h. Animate the third ball to bounce bottom-to-top on the Stage in frames 30 to 45.

i. Animate the fourth ball to bounce top-to-bottom on the Stage in frames 45 to 60.

j. Pause the ball in frame 45 at the top of the bounce until a mouse click.

k. Play the movie, print the screen (see Visual Workshop), save the movie, then exit Director.

3. You are a teacher at Happiness Hill Preschool. As part of a teaching lesson, you want to create an animated smiley face for the kids. You use Director's Paint tool to create a smiley face and behaviors to animate the eyes with a built-in behavior.
To complete this independent challenge:

a. Start Director and save the movie as *Smiley Face* in the drive and folder where your Project Files are located.

b. Create and name a Paint cast member of a yellow circle and a black smiling mouth.

c. Create and name a Paint cast member of a small circle with a black dot on the right side for the eye.

d. Drag the yellow circle on the Stage and the small circle in the yellow circle twice, to create two eyes.

e. Create a text cast member with the text **Smiley Face**, and drag it to the top of the Stage.

f. Open the Library palette and display the Interactive list of behaviors.

g. Drag the Turn Towards Mouse behavior onto the small circles (eyes of the smiley face) on the Stage, then set the behavior to always turn.

h. Play the movie and move the mouse around to move the eyes.

i. Print the screen (see Visual Workshop for instructions), save the movie, then exit Director.

4. You are the owner of Last Chance Nursery, a small family-operated business. You want to add a small catalog of products to your Web site. You use Director's navigation and user interaction capabilities to create a main menu with plant categories and behaviors to branch to the different plant areas.
To complete this independent challenge:

a. Connect to the Internet and go to www.course.com. Navigate to the page for this book, click the link for the Student Online Companion, then click the link for this unit.

b. Browse the Plants section for photographs.

c. Download three different flower photographs and three different food photographs in the drive and folder where your Project Files are located.

d. Start Director and save the movie as *Last Chance* in the drive and folder where your Project Files are located.

e. Change the background of the Stage to green.

f. Create a text cast member with the text **Last Chance Nursery**, and drag it to the top of the Stage.

g. Create and name separate text cast members with the text **Main menu**, **Flowers**, and **Food**, and drag them on the Stage to create a Main menu similar to the unit.

h. Set the Hold on Current Frame behavior for this frame, known as the Main menu.

i. Create separate areas for Flowers, and drag the Flowers text cast member and flower photographs on the Stage.

j. Create separate areas for Food, and drag the Food text cast member and food photographs on the Stage.

k. Set markers for Main menu, Flowers, and Food in associated areas of the Score window.

l. Set the Flowers and Food text cast members on the Main menu to a rollover cursor effect, and add scripts so that the text cast members jump to their associated markers, and return to the Main menu.

m.Play the movie and jump to the Flowers and Food areas.

n. Print the screen (see Visual Workshop for instructions), save the movie, then exit Director.

Visual Workshop

Recreate the screen shown in Figure F-25. Print the screen. (For Windows, use the Windows Paint program. Press the Print Screen key to make a copy of the screen, start the Paint program by clicking Start, pointing to Programs, pointing to Accessories, then clicking Paint, click Edit on the menu bar, click Paste to paste the screen into Paint, then click Yes to paste the large image if necessary. Click File on the menu bar, click Print, click Print or OK in the dialog box, then exit Paint. For the Macintosh, use the SimpleText program. Hold and press the Command, Shift, and 3 keys to make a copy of the screen, double-click the document Picture 1 located on your hard drive, click File on the menu bar, click Print, then click Print in the dialog box. (*Note*: When you create a new document with a copy of the screen, and a document Picture 1 already exists, the Macintosh names the new document Picture 2.)

FIGURE F-25

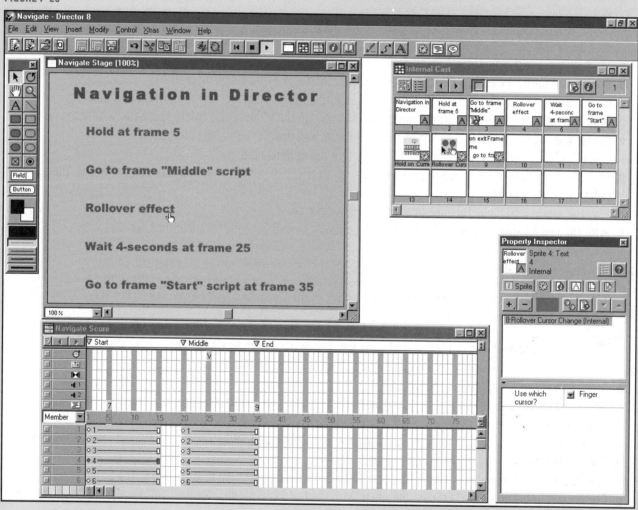

Adding
Audio, Video, and Other Media

▶ **Import audio and video media**
▶ **Control audio in the Score**
▶ **Stream Shockwave Audio**
▶ **Control video in the Score**
▶ **Play video direct to the Stage**
▶ **Crop and scale a video**
▶ **Synchronize media**
▶ **Import a Microsoft PowerPoint presentation**
▶ **Export a movie to video**

Director allows you to import audio, video, and other media into a movie and combine the cast members with text, animation, and other effects to create multimedia movies. This unit introduces you to basic skills for importing, controlling, playing, modifying, synchronizing, and exporting audio, video, and other media in Director movies. First, you'll learn how to import and play several types of media files in Director, using different options and techniques. Then, you'll learn how to control and synchronize the media to make sure everything works together smoothly. Finally, you'll learn how to import a Microsoft PowerPoint presentation into Director and export it to video. Jean wants to add audio, video, and other media to a new movie.

Director 8

Importing Audio and Video Media

If you already have created digital audio or video in other programs, you can import these media elements into the active Cast window. You can import a variety of sound formats, including AIFF (Audio Interchange File Format), WAV (either compressed or uncompressed), Shockwave Audio, AU (Sun audio), MP3, and Macintosh sounds. To create or alter a sound, you need to use another program, such as Macromedia's SoundEdit 16. You can import a sound into Director as an internal cast member, which is ideal for short sounds, or as an externally linked cast member, which is good for longer sounds, such as a voice narration. You can import QuickTime movies (Macintosh and Windows) and AVI movies as video cast members. You can also import other video formats, such as MPEG, but you need to install an Xtra to perform the function. When Director imports video, it creates and maintains a link to the external video file. If you change the video in Director or in the external video file, the corresponding external video file or video in Director changes to match. If you move the Director movie to another location on your hard disk or computer, you need to move the external sound and video files. Otherwise, the sound and video do not play. ⟍ Jean imports sound and video media into the Journey II movie.

1. Start **Director**, open the file **MD G-1** from the drive and folder where your Project Files are located, then save it as **Journey II**

   Director opens, displaying the movie. Your initial settings in Director can vary.

QuickTip

To record a simple sound in Director (Mac), attach a microphone to your computer, click Insert on the menu bar, click Media Element, click Sound, click Record to begin, then click Stop to end. When you finish, click Save, then name the sound to store it in the Cast window.

2. Click the down scroll arrow in the Cast window to display cast member 31, then click **cast member 31** (blank)

   The blank cast member is selected. The media files will be imported into the current cast member location (if blank) or the next available location in the Cast window.

3. Click the **Import button** 🔲 on the toolbar

   The Import Files into "Internal" dialog box opens.

4. Click the **Look in list arrow** ▼, click the drive and folder where your Project Files are located, then double-click the **Media folder**

   A list of files for the Media folder appears.

QuickTip

To link an external sound file to a movie, click the Import button 🔲 on the toolbar, click the Media list arrow ▼, then click Link To External File.

5. Click the **Files of type list arrow** ▼, then click **Sound**

   All the sound files in the Media folder appear in the Look in file list, as shown in Figure G-1. You can select files in the list individually or together and import them into the active Cast window.

6. Click the **Blastoff.wav file**, click **Add**, click the **Meteor.wav file**, click **Add**, then click **Import**

   The sound files appear in the file list and as new cast members in the Cast window.

7. Click the **Import button** 🔲 on the toolbar, verify that the Media folder is selected, click the **Files of Type list arrow** ▼, then click **All Files** (scroll as necessary)

   The Import Files into "Internal" dialog box opens, and all file types appear in the Look in list.

8. Click the **Blastoff.mov file**, click **Add**, click the **Earthvenus.avi file**, click **Add**, then click **Import**

   The Select Format dialog box opens (Win), indicating that Director can import the Earthvenus AVI video using multiple formats.

QuickTip

The Macintosh converts AVI files to QuickTime files. The Select Format dialog box doesn't appear (Mac).

9. Click **AVI**, then click **OK**

   The video files appear as cast members in the Cast window, as shown in Figure G-2.

FIGURE G-1: Import Files into "Internal" dialog box

Your sound icon might vary, depending on your default sound program

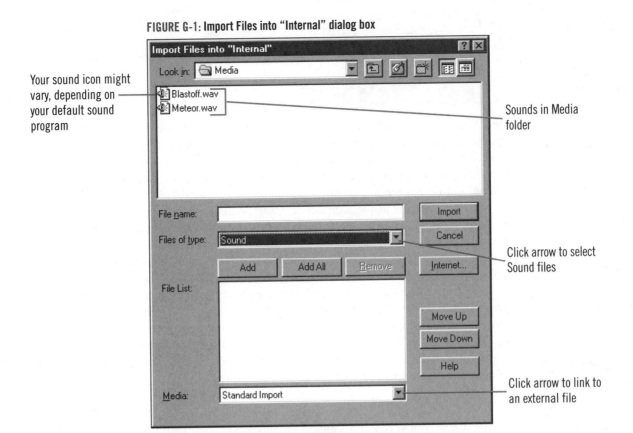

Sounds in Media folder

Click arrow to select Sound files

Click arrow to link to an external file

FIGURE G-2: Cast window with audio and video cast members

QuickTime video

Internal WAV sounds

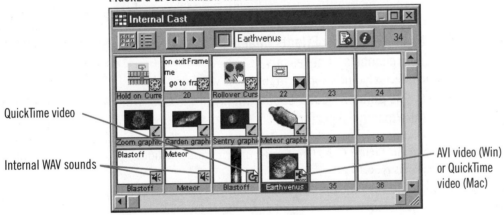

AVI video (Win) or QuickTime video (Mac)

CLUES TO USE

Understanding sound cast members

When you import a sound as an internal cast member, the sound is stored in the movie or in an External Cast window, which increases the size of the movie or Cast file. When you play a movie, Director loads all internal sounds into RAM first. This allows Director to play the movie at any time without any delays. Short sounds, such as beeps or clicks, work best as internal sound cast members. An externally linked sound cast member is stored outside of the movie or an External Cast window, which reduces the size of the movie or cast file. When the playback head reaches an externally linked sound, Director must load the sound into RAM and then start to play the sound, which can cause an initial delay. To reduce the delay, Director streams externally linked sounds. Streaming allows Director to load a small portion of the sound and then play the sound while it continuously loads the rest of the sound. Long sounds, such as a narration or instruction, work best as externally linked cast members.

Unit G
Director 8

Controlling Audio in the Score

Once you import sounds into a Cast window, you can place them in either of the two Sound channels in the Score window. A sound plays in Director at the rate and duration in which it was recorded; Director's tempo settings do not affect the sound's playback speed. Audio and video files are time-based media, which means that files play according to a timeline with a start time and an end time. Director, on the other hand, is a frame-based medium, which means that movies play according to a set number of frames. When you place an audio or video in the Score, you need to assign it a sufficient number of frames so that the file plays completely. Otherwise, the audio or video file will cut off abruptly when you play the movie. You can quickly ensure that the sound has enough frames to play completely. Simply drag the sound in the Sound channel into more frames than the sound can possibly require, then play the movie. Watch the Score to determine at which frame the sound stops, then remove the extra frames. Instead of using frames, you can also set a wait time in the Tempo channel for the length of the sound, to make sure the sound plays completely. If a sound stops prematurely, you can set the sound to loop, or repeat. If you want to match a sound with an animation, you need to place the sound in the Score to match the frame with the action. ✎ Jean places sound cast members in the Score and modifies the number of frames to control the sound's length.

Steps

QuickTip
Although you can't set a volume for a specific sound, you can set the volume in the Control Panel for the entire movie.

1. **Click the Play button** ▶ **on the toolbar, click navigation buttons to continue playing the movie, then click the Rewind button** ◄ **on the toolbar**
   The movie plays on the Stage, and the playback head moves frame to frame through the Score until it reaches the Main menu (Let the Journey Begin). The Main menu contains the elements of the multimedia project. If you click the Exit button on the Stage, save any changes, then start the Journey II movie again. Now, you will add sound and video to complete the project.

2. **Click the Hide/Show Effects Channels button** ▣ **in the Score window to display the Effects channels, if necessary**
   The Effects channels appear in the Score window.

3. **Click the Blastoff sound cast member in the Cast window, then click the Sound tab in the Property Inspector**
   The Sound tab in the Property Inspector opens, displaying information about the sound, as shown in Figure G-3. The sound information includes the sampling rate, bit depth, and channels type.

QuickTip
To repeat the sound, click the Loop check box in the Sound tab of the Property Inspector to select it, then click the Play button.

4. **Click the Play button** ▶ **in the Sound tab of the Property Inspector**
   The sound plays once.

5. **Drag the Blastoff sound cast member to frame 35 in Sound channel 1, then drag the end of the sprite to frame 60**
   The Blastoff sound cast member appears in frame 35 to frame 60, as shown in Figure G-4.

6. **Click** ◄ **on the toolbar, click** ▶ **on the toolbar, then click the Stop button** ■ **on the toolbar after the playback head stops at frame 63**
   The movie plays the sound from frame 35 to frame 60.

QuickTip
To play a sound in the Score, double-click a sound, select a sound in the Frame Properties: Sound dialog box, then click Play.

7. **Scroll in the Score to display frame 115, drag the Meteor sound cast member to frame 115 in Sound channel 2, then drag the end of the sprite to frame 127**
   The Meteor sound cast member appears in frame 115 to frame 127.

8. **Click** ◄ **on the toolbar, then click** ▶ **on the toolbar**
   The movie plays the animation and sound and stops at the Main menu.

9. **Click Sounds on the Stage, then click** ■ **on the toolbar when the playback head stops at frame 127**
   The movie plays the sound until it reaches the hold on current frame behavior in frame 127.

FIGURE G-3: Sound tab in the Property Inspector

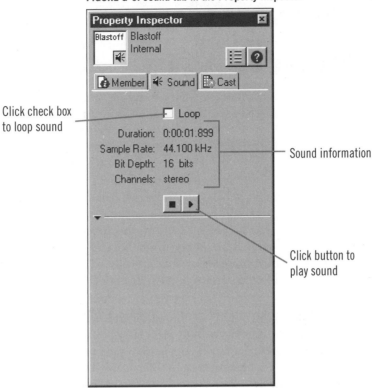

Click check box
to loop sound

Sound information

Click button to
play sound

FIGURE G-4: The Score window with a sound

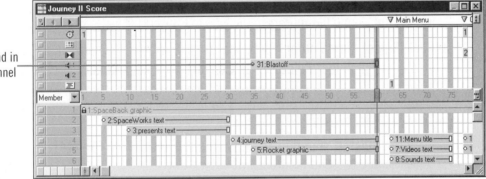

Blastoff sound in
a Sound channel

Understanding sound

When you record or modify a sound, you should consider four factors that affect the performance and quality of a sound file. The first factor is the sampling rate of the sound. The **sampling rate** (measured in kilohertz, or kHz) is the frequency with which samples are taken per second. For example, a sound sampled at 22.050 kHz saves the audio value 22,050 times per second. The higher the sampling rate, the higher the sound quality. Common sampling rates include 5.5125 kHz (standard telephone call), 11.025 kHz (broadcast television audio), 22.050 kHz (FM radio), 44.100 kHz (compact disc), and 48.000 kHz (digital audio tape). The second factor is the bit depth at which the sound is recorded. The **bit depth** is a measure of how much data space is available to store

a given moment of sound. The sounds you import into a movie can have different bit depths. The two most common are 8 bits and 16 bits. The higher the bit depth, the higher the sound quality. The third factor is the channels type, **stereo** or **mono encoding**, which are two types of sound quality. Stereo encoding produces high-quality sound, but the file size associated with a stereo file is twice the size of a mono sound. The final factor is the compression rate of the sound file. **Compression** reduces the size of a file. There are different compression standards and different compression ratios, which can produce a wide range of sound quality. The higher the compression ratio, the smaller the file size. However, the reduction in size might result in lower quality or speed.

Director 8

Unit G
Director 8

Streaming Shockwave Audio

Shockwave Audio is a technology that reduces the size of sound files and plays them faster from disk or from the Internet. You can use Shockwave Audio to compress the size of sounds by a ratio as high as 176 to 1. Compression reduces the size of a file. Director streams Shockwave Audio and MP3 sound files to reduce the delay time in playing a sound. When Director streams a sound, it doesn't have to load the entire sound file into RAM before it begins to play the sound. Director loads and plays the beginning of the sound as the rest of the sound continues to load. Before you can stream a Shockwave Audio cast member, you need to create a Shockwave Audio or MP3 sound file. You can use Peak LE 2 on the Macintosh or the Convert WAV to SWA command on Windows to convert a sound to the Shockwave Audio format. When you insert a Shockwave Audio or MP3 file, either from a local hard disk, network drive, or a URL or Web address, the sound is imported as an externally linked cast member. Jean creates a Shockwave Audio file and streams it in the Journey II movie.

Steps

QuickTip

Create or import a sound with SoundEdit 16 or Peak LE 2, then export the sound in Shockwave Audio format in the Media folder where your Project Files are located. Skip to Step 4 (Mac).

1. Click **Xtras** on the menu bar, click **Convert WAV to SWA** (Win), or skip to **Step 4** (Mac)
   The Convert .WAV Files To .SWA files dialog box opens, as shown in Figure G-5. The default **bit rate**, or degree of compression, is set to 16 kbps (kilobytes per second). The higher the bit rate, the faster a sound streams, but the quality of the sound can suffer. If you are creating movies for Internet delivery, you should use 16 kbps for the best results.

2. Click **Add Files**, click the drive and folder where your Project Files are located, double-click the **Media folder**, then double-click the **Blastoff.wav** file
   The Blastoff sound file appears in the Files to Convert file list.

3. Click **Select New Folder**, click the drive and folder where your Project Files are located, click **Select Folder**, click **Convert**, then click **Close**
   The Blastoff WAV sound file is converted to an SWA sound file. The SWA sound file size is considerably smaller than the WAV sound file. To verify, you can use Windows Explorer (Win) or Mac Operating System to compare the two file sizes.

4. Click the **Blastoff sound** in Sound channel 1, then press **[Delete]**
   The Blastoff WAV sound is deleted from the Score.

5. Click **Insert** on the menu bar, point to **Media Element**, then click **Shockwave Audio**
   The SWA Cast Member Properties dialog box opens with a default URL, as shown in Figure G-6.

QuickTip

To adjust the initial download time of an SWA sound, click the Preload Time list arrow in the SWA Cast Member Properties dialog box, then click a preload time.

6. Click **Browse**, click the drive and folder where your Project Files are located, then double-click the **Blastoff.swa file** (Win), or the **Blastoffm.swa file** (Mac)
   The SWA Cast Member Properties dialog box appears with the full path to the SWA Blastoff sound file on your hard disk or network drive.

7. Drag the **Volume Slider** to the ¾ mark on the scale, click **Play**, then click **OK**
   The volume level is adjusted, and the Blastoff sound file plays. The SWA sound cast member is stored in the Cast window with no title, a blank thumbnail, and the 🔊 icon.

QuickTip

To change SWA sound settings, click the SWA sound cast member, click the SWA tab in the Property Inspector, then modify settings.

8. Drag the **SWA cast member** with the Blastoff sound to **frame 35** in Sprite channel 7, then drag the **end of the sprite** to **frame 60**
   The SWA cast member appears in the Score from frame 35 to frame 60.

9. Click the **Rewind button** ◄ on the toolbar, click the **Play button** ► on the toolbar, then click the **Stop button** ■ on the toolbar when the playback head stops at frame 63

FIGURE G-5: Convert .WAV Files To .SWA Files dialog box

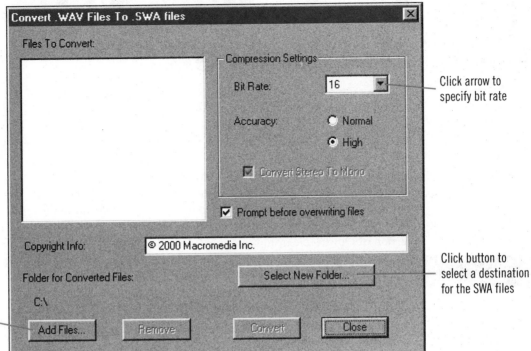

Click arrow to specify bit rate

Click button to select a destination for the SWA files

Click button to select the WAV files

FIGURE G-6: SWA Cast Member Properties dialog box

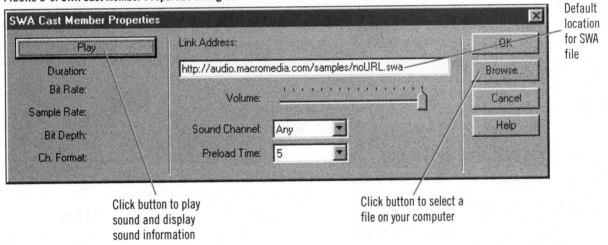

Default location for SWA file

Click button to play sound and display sound information

Click button to select a file on your computer

Compressing internal sounds with Shockwave Audio

You can store and compress a sound internally in Director, using Shockwave Audio. Compressing sounds decreases the size of the movie file, shortens the download time from the Internet, and reduces the preload time required to play a sound without a delay. You can use Shockwave Audio settings to compress internal sound cast members, but the compression takes place only when you compress the Director movie with the Create Projector, Save as Shockwave Movie, or Update Movies commands. To set the Shockwave Audio compression options for all internal sound cast members, click File on the menu bar, click Publish Settings, click the Compression tab, click the Compression Enabled check box to select it, select a bit rate setting from the kBits/seconds list (lower values produce smaller and faster files with lower quality), click the Convert Stereo to Mono check box to select it, if necessary, then click OK. You should try several different bit rates to see how the sounds change.

Controlling Video in the Score

Once you import digital videos into a Cast window, you can place them into any Frame channel in the Score window, just as you would any other sprite. Digital videos begin to play when the playback head reaches the sprite containing the video sprite. A digital video, like a sound, plays for the duration of the sprite. If you do not assign enough frames to play the video completely, it will cut off abruptly when you play the video. You can extend the video to occupy enough frames in the Score to play completely. You can use the QuickTime or AVI tab in the Property Inspector to make the video loop or pause. Director 8 supports Apple's QuickTime 4 or earlier for Macintosh and Windows. If you want to play or author Director movies that use QuickTime cast members, you must have QuickTime installed on your computer. You can download the latest version of QuickTime from the Apple Computer Web site at *www.apple.com*. In Windows, you can play AVI movies with no additional software requirements. Jean places a QuickTime and an AVI video on the Stage, adds a loop option to one of them, and plays them.

Steps

1. Click **frame 100** in **Sprite channel 8**
   The playback head appears in frame 100, and the Stage displays the Videos scene.

2. Drag the **Blastoff video cast member** to the Stage above the Menu and Exit buttons, then drag the **end of the sprite** to **frame 112** in the Score
   The Blastoff video appears on the Stage.

3. Click **frame 100** in **Sprite channel 9**, drag the **Earthvenus video cast member** to the **left side** of the Stage, then drag the **end of the sprite** to **frame 112** in the Score
   The Earthvenus video appears on the Stage along with the Blastoff video, as shown in Figure G-7.

4. Double-click the **Blastoff video sprite** on the Stage
   The QuickTime 33:Blastoff window opens, as shown in Figure G-8.

   Trouble?
   Macintosh users end lesson after Step 5.

5. Click the **Play button** at the bottom of the QuickTime window, then click the **Close button**
   The video plays once. Mac users stop here.

   QuickTip
   If the Direct to Stage check box in the QuickTime or AVI tab of the Property Inspector is not selected, you can apply ink effects to video sprites.

6. Click the **Earthvenus video sprite** in the Score, click the **AVI tab** (Win) or the **QuickTime tab** (Mac) in the Property Inspector, then click the **Loop check box** to select it, if necessary
   The AVI tab (Win) or the QuickTime tab (Mac) in the Property Inspector appears, and the Earthvenus video is set to continuously loop.

7. Double-click the **Earthvenus video sprite** on the Stage
   The AVI video window opens.

   QuickTip
   If you play an AVI video on a Macintosh, Director converts the video to QuickTime.

8. Double-click the **image** in the AVI Video window to play the video or click the **Play button** at the bottom of the QuickTime window
   The video begins to play.

9. After the video loops, click the **image** in the AVI video window to stop it, then click the **Close button**

FIGURE G-7: The Stage with digital video

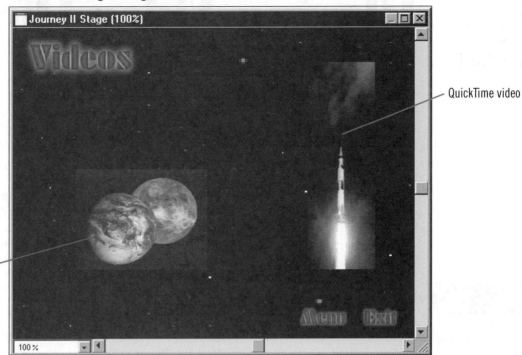

QuickTime video

AVI video (Win)
or QuickTime
video (Mac)

FIGURE G-8: QuickTime cast member window

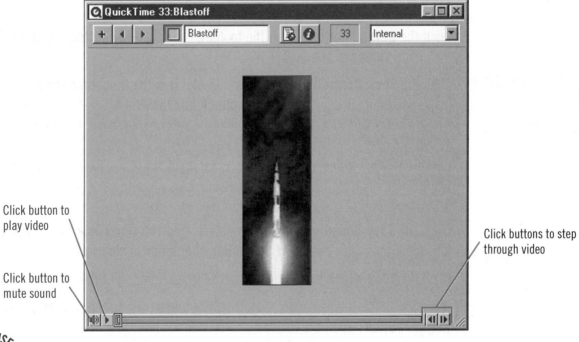

Click button to
play video

Click button to
mute sound

Click buttons to step
through video

Controlling an animated GIF

Many Web sites include animated GIF (Graphics Interchange Format) files that you can use in a Director movie. You can import an animated GIF in the same way you import a video. Director supports the GIF89a and GIF87 formats with a global color table. Once you import an animated GIF, you can set options to change the link to a file on your hard disk or a URL, play the GIF directly on the Stage at the fastest possible playback rate, or change the tempo to play the GIF at a rate consistent with the movie. To preview the GIF animation, double-click the GIF cast member in the Cast window, then click Play.

Director 8

Unit G

Director 8

Playing Video Direct to Stage

The performance of a video can vary when it plays in Director. The Direct to Stage option provides the best performance for playing QuickTime or AVI videos in a Director movie. When you select the Direct to Stage option in the QuickTime or AVI tab of the Property Inspector, Director allows QuickTime or AVI software installed on your computer to completely control the video playback. The Direct to Stage option provides optimal performance in video playback, but it also limits where you can locate the video on the Stage in relation to other sprites, and it prohibits applying ink effects to a video. When Director plays the video, it always appears in front of all other sprites on the Stage, no matter which channel contains the video sprite. When you select the Direct to Stage option, you can also choose a playback option to play the video in synchronization with a soundtrack, play every frame of the video at a normal, maximum, or fixed speed without the soundtrack, or display the controller bar to start, stop, and step through a QuickTime video on the Stage. ✐ Jean experiments with the Direct to Stage and related options to achieve the best results for the Journey II movie.

Steps

Trouble?

If the Direct to Stage check box is not selected, click the Direct to Stage check box to select it.

1. Click the **Blastoff video sprite** on the Stage, click the **QuickTime tab** 🔍 in the Property Inspector, then verify that the Direct to Stage check box is selected
   The QuickTime tab in the Property Inspector appears, as shown in Figure G-9.

2. Click the **Loop check box** to select it in the QuickTime tab of the Property Inspector
   The Blastoff video is set to continuously repeat.

3. Click the **Rewind button** ⏮ on the toolbar, click the **Play button** ▶ on the toolbar, then click **Videos** on the Stage

Trouble?

If the video delivery speed is slow, the controller bar might flicker.

4. Click the **Show Controller check box** to select it in the QuickTime tab of the Property Inspector, then click the **Play Sound check box** to clear it
   The controller bar appears at the bottom of the video on the Stage, and the sound stops, as shown in Figure G-10.

5. Click the **Show Video check box** to clear it in the QuickTime tab of the Property Inspector, then click the **Show Video check box** again to select it
   The video is hidden and stops as shown or replays.

6. Click the **Play Sound check box** to select it in the QuickTime tab of the Property Inspector, then click the **Show Controller check box** to clear it

7. Click the **Loop check box** to clear it in the QuickTime tab of the Property Inspector

8. When the Blastoff video ends, click the **Stop button** ⏹ on the toolbar, then click the **Rewind button** ⏮ on the toolbar

FIGURE G-9: QuickTime tab in the Property Inspector

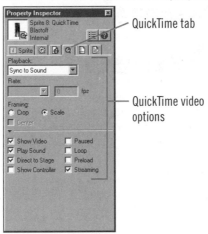

QuickTime tab

QuickTime video options

FIGURE G-10: Playing videos directly to the Stage

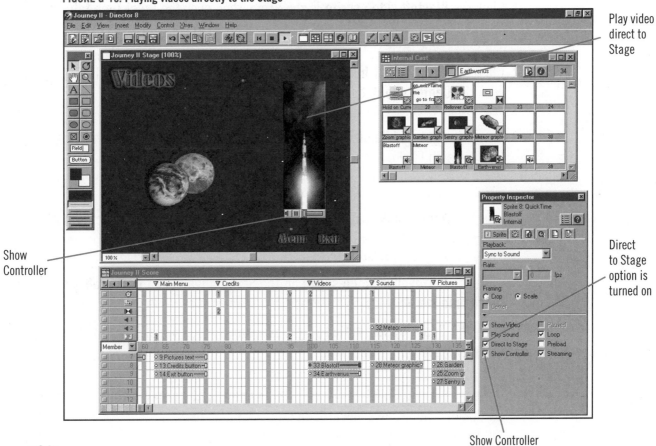

Play video direct to Stage

Direct to Stage option is turned on

Show Controller option is turned on

Show Controller

Editing a QuickTime video

Director allows you to perform simple editing tasks, such as deleting or reordering a sequence of video frames, in a QuickTime video. Before you can edit a QuickTime video, you need to first open the video in the QuickTime video window of Director. To open the video in Director, double-click the QuickTime video sprite in the Score, or the cast member in the Cast window. Once you open the QuickTime video, you can select a single video frame or a range of frames, and then use the Cut or Clear commands on the Edit menu to delete the selected video frames, or the Copy and Paste commands on the Edit menu to reorder the selected video frames. To select a range of video frames, hold down [Shift] and drag the slider until you reach the last video frame you want to select. The selected range of video frames appears in a dark shade of gray.

Unit G
Director 8

Cropping and Scaling a Video

When you place a video on the Stage, the shape and size of the video might not look the way you want. In Director, you can crop, or trim, any unwanted areas around the edge of the video, or resize the video to better fit the Stage. When you crop a video, the edges you trim are not removed from the video; they are just hidden. You can restore the cropped area of a video at any time. The Scale option allows you to change the size, or dimension, of a video. When you scale a video, hold down [Shift] to maintain a proportional playback area which ensures the best results. However, any large-scale changes can dramatically reduce the quality of the video display. ✐ Jean crops and scales a video in the Journey II movie.

Steps

1. Click the **Blastoff video sprite** in the Score, then click the **QuickTime tab** [Q] in the Property Inspector, if necessary
   The QuickTime tab in the Property Inspector appears.

2. Click the **Crop option button** in the QuickTime tab of the Property Inspector, then click the **Center check box** to clear it, if necessary
   The option to crop a video is set.

3. Drag the **right-middle sizing handle** of the Blastoff video sprite on the Stage to the **left** to match Figure G-11
   When you position the pointer over a sizing handle, the pointer changes to black (Win) or white (Mac). The Blastoff video is cropped on the Stage.

QuickTip

To undo the action you just performed, click the Undo button on the toolbar.

4. Drag the **right-middle sizing handle** of the Blastoff video sprite to the **right** until the video is restored to its original display
   The previously cropped area of the Blastoff video is redisplayed.

5. Click the **Earthvenus video sprite** on the Stage, then click the **AVI tab** [▶] (Win) or **QuickTime tab** [Q] (Mac) in the Property Inspector, if necessary

6. Click the **Scale option button** in the AVI tab (Win) or QuickTime tab (Mac) of the Property Inspector, if necessary
   The option to scale a video is selected.

7. Press and hold **[Shift]**, then drag the **upper-right-corner sizing handle** of the Earthvenus video sprite **inward** slightly to match Figure G-12
   The video is slightly reduced in size on the Stage.

8. Click the **Rewind button** [◄◄] on the toolbar, then click the **Play button** [▶] on the toolbar

9. Click **Videos** on the Stage, click the **Stop button** [■] on the toolbar when the Blastoff video ends, then click the **Rewind button** [◄◄] on the toolbar

FIGURE G-11: Cropping a video

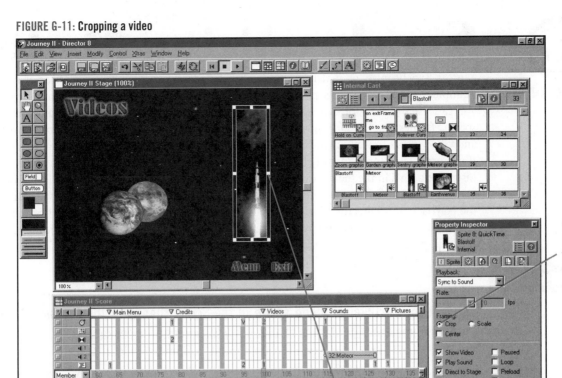

Click button to select Crop option

Drag sizing handle here to crop video

FIGURE G-12: Scaling a video

Drag sizing handle here to scale video

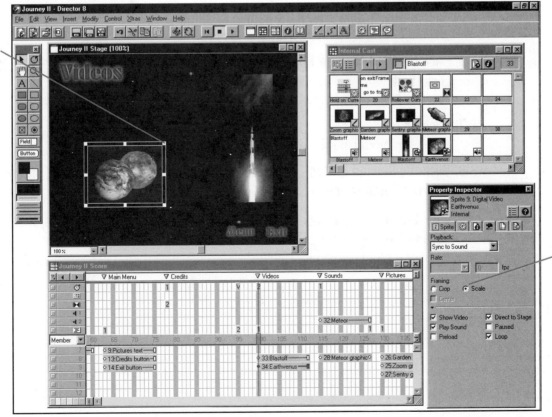

Click button to select Scale option

Unit G

Director 8

Synchronizing Media

You can synchronize, or match, sounds and videos with other actions in a Director movie. For example, you can synchronize points in a sound file to make text appear in time with the narration. You can use the Wait for Cue Points option to synchronize points in a sound or video file with specific frames in a Director movie. A common use for the Wait for Cue Point option with sound and video files is to wait for the end of the sound or video before you continue to the next frame. If you want Director to identify the cue points anywhere inside a sound or video file, you need to insert the points in the file using another program, such as SoundEdit 16 (Mac), Peak LE 2 (Mac), Sound Forge 4 (Win), or Cool Edit 96 (Win). To help eliminate delays in loading video files during the playback of a Director movie, you can preload the video into RAM at the beginning of the movie, so it's ready to play at any time, instead of playing it from disk. ✐ Jean creates navigation between different points in the Journey movie, using markers and scripts.

Steps

1. Click the **Earthvenus video sprite** in the Score, then click the **AVI tab** 🎬 (Win) or **QuickTime tab** 🍎 (Mac) in the Property Inspector, if necessary
   The AVI tab in the Property Inspector appears, as shown in Figure G-13.

2. Click the **Preload check box** to select it in the AVI tab (Win) or QuickTime tab (Mac) of the Property Inspector
   The option to preload the video is set.

3. Click the **Blastoff video sprite** on the Stage, then click the **QuickTime tab** 🍎 in the Property Inspector, if necessary
   The QuickTime tab in the Property Inspector appears.

4. Click the **Preload check box** to select it in the QuickTime tab of the Property Inspector
   The option to preload the video is set.

5. Double-click **frame 100** in the **Tempo channel**
   The Frame Properties: Tempo dialog box opens.

6. Click the **Wait for Cue Point option button**, click the **Cue Point list arrow** ▼, then click **{End}**
   The Cue Point is set to end, as shown in Figure G-14.

7. Click **OK**
   A wait for the end of the Blastoff video is applied to frame 100.

8. Click the **Rewind button** ◄ on the toolbar, click the **Play button** ► on the toolbar, then click **Videos** on the Stage

9. Click the **Stop button** ■ on the toolbar when the Blastoff video ends, then click the **Save button** 💾 on the toolbar
   Director saves the program.

FIGURE G-13: **AVI tab in the Property Inspector**

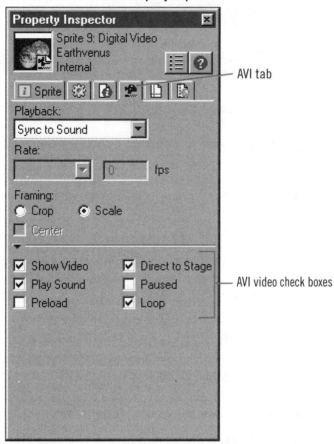

AVI tab

AVI video check boxes

FIGURE G-14: **Frame Properties: Tempo dialog box**

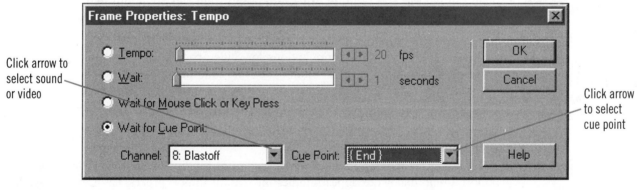

Click arrow to select sound or video

Click arrow to select cue point

CLUES TO USE

Importing Flash movies in Director

You can import Flash movies into Director movies and save them as Shockwave movies for use on the Web. Flash movies are vector-based animations and media that you can scale, rotate, and modify without losing any degree of sharpness or quality. Director can import Flash files, version 2.0 or later, and support new features in Flash 4. To import a Flash movie as a cast member, click Insert on the menu bar, point to Media Element, then click Flash Movie. In the Flash Asset Properties dialog box, click Browse to select the Flash movie (.SWF extension) you want to import. Once you select the Flash movie, you can set options to link the movie to an external file on your hard disk or network drive, or to a URL; preload the movie into memory before playing; control movie playback in Director, a projector, or a Shockwave movie; specify a quality rating for anti-aliasing; specify a scale mode for the size of the movie; and specify the tempo to play the movie at a rate consistent with the movie.

Importing a PowerPoint Presentation

If you have a PowerPoint version 4 or later presentation, you can import the presentation into a Director movie, play the presentation as a slide show, and save the movie as a stand-alone projector file or as a Shockwave movie for the Web. Director imports the graphics, transitions, and text as cast members and converts each slide into a section in the Score. In cases where there is not an exact match for a PowerPoint feature in Director, Director uses the closest matching feature. Director cannot import PowerPoint animation effects, unique fonts, or special formatting, such as shadows. See Director Help for a complete comparison of PowerPoint and Director features. ▂▂▂ Jean imports a PowerPoint presentation as the basis for a new movie.

Steps 1234

1. Click **File** on the menu bar, point to **New**, then click **Movie**
   A blank movie appears in the Director window.

2. Click the **Movie tab** in the Property Inspector, double-click the **Stage size width box**, type **720**, double-click the **Stage size height box**, type **540**, then press **[Enter]** (Win) or **[Return]** (Mac)
   The Movie tab in the Property Inspector appears with a new Stage size, 720 × 540, the size of a PowerPoint slide.

3. Click **Xtras** on the menu bar, then click **Import PowerPoint File**
   The Please select a PowerPoint to open dialog box opens.

Trouble?

If Director can't open the PowerPoint file, open the presentation in PowerPoint, click File on the menu bar, click Save As, click the Files of Type list arrow, click PowerPoint 4.0, then click Save.

4. Open the file **MD G-2** (Win) or **MD G-2m** (Mac) from the drive and folder where your Project Files are located
   The PowerPoint Import Options dialog box opens with default settings, as shown in Figure G-15. You can set import options for Slide Spacing, the number of blank lines between slides in the Score; Minimum Slide Duration, the minimum number of frames a slide takes up in the Score; Item Spacing, the number of frames used for each item in a PowerPoint build effect; and Fly Transition Item Spacing, the number of frames between keyframes in the Score.

5. Click **Import**, then click **OK**
   A progress meter appears as Director imports the presentation media. Upon completion, the Import Results dialog box appears, indicating that the import process has been successful.

6. Click the **Save button** 🖳 on the toolbar, type **PPT Pres** in the File name text box, click the drive and folder where your Project Files are located, then click **Save**

7. Click the **Score Window button** 🗐 on the toolbar, then click the **Cast Window button** 🎴 on the toolbar, if necessary
   The Score window and Cast window appear with the conversion of the PowerPoint features for Windows or Macintosh in Director, as shown in Figure G-16.

8. Click the **Stage button** 🗖 on the toolbar, click the **Play button** ▶ on the toolbar, then click the **Stop button** ■ on the toolbar at the first slide
   The first PowerPoint slide appears on the Stage, as shown in Figure G-17.

Trouble?

Director might play the movie slowly.

9. Click the **Play button** ▶ on the toolbar, then click the **Rewind button** ◄◄
   Director plays the rest of the movie.

FIGURE G-15: PowerPoint Import Options dialog box

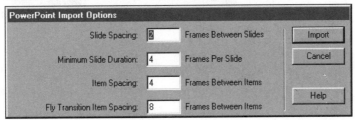

FIGURE G-16: Score window and Cast window

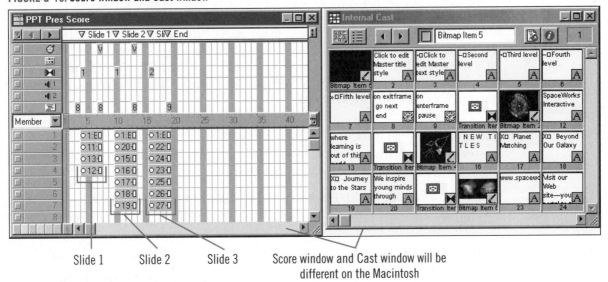

Slide 1   Slide 2   Slide 3   Score window and Cast window will be
different on the Macintosh

FIGURE G-17: Slide 1 on the Stage in Director

Exporting a Movie to Video

You can export all or part of a movie as a digital video or a series of frame-by-frame bitmaps. You can use the digital video or series of bitmaps in other applications or import it back into Director. Exporting a movie to digital video is recommended only for straightforward linear animations or presentations. When Director exports any interactivity, such as button scripts and frame scripts, the information is not included after the exporting process. When Director exports animation as a digital video, it takes snapshots of the entire Stage moment by moment and turns each snapshot into a frame in the video. Director allows you to export a movie as an AVI (Win) or QuickTime (Mac) video, or as a BMP (Win), PICT (Mac), Scrapbook (Mac), or PICS (Mac) graphic. Before you can export a movie as a QuickTime digital video, QuickTime must be installed on the computer. Jean exports the PowerPoint presentation in Director to a QuickTime digital video.

1. Click **File** on the menu bar, then click **Export**

The Export dialog box opens, as shown in Figure G-18. The options in the Export dialog box are determined by the file format you choose.

2. Click the **Format list arrow**, then click **QuickTime Movie (.MOV)**

The next step is to choose the range of frames you want to export and the method of selecting frames within that range.

3. Click the **All Frames option button**

All the frames in the presentation movie are selected for export to QuickTime.

4. Click **Options**

The QuickTime Options dialog box opens with a set of parameters specific to QuickTime, as shown in Figure G-19.

5. Click the **Tempo Settings option button**, if necessary

This option translates the tempo settings in Director to a frames-per-second rate for the export to video. The other alternative is Real Time, which records the video movie exactly as the Director movie plays on the computer.

6. Click the **Compressor list arrow**, then click **Video** (scroll as necessary)

The Video compressor setting is a standard for QuickTime video. The compressor is optimized for cross-platform use and 16-bit and 24-bit color images. The average compression ratio is about 5 to 1. See Table G-1 for a description of the Compressor options; different options appear in the list depending on the video hardware and software on your computer.

7. Click **OK**, then click **Export**

The Save File(s) as dialog box opens.

8. Click the drive and folder where your Project Files are located, click **Save**, then click **OK**

The QuickTime movie is exported to a file (PPT Pres.mov), plays on the screen, then returns to the main Director window.

9. Click **File** on the menu bar, then click **Exit** (Win) or **Quit** (Mac)

Director closes.

QuickTip

For an export to AVI, the Options dialog box only contains an option to set the export rate in frames per second. In addition, when you export to AVI, sounds in the movie are not included.

Trouble?

If a Ready to Export dialog box appears, follow the instructions.

Trouble?

If Director asks you to save the movie, click Yes (Win) or Save (Mac).

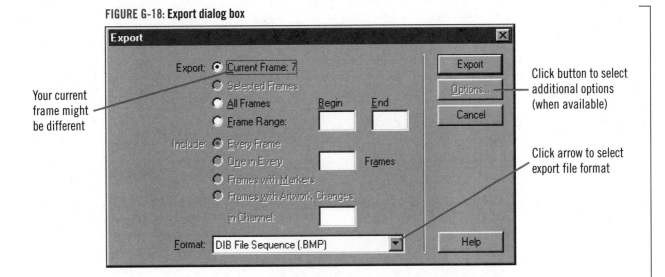

FIGURE G-18: **Export dialog box**

Your current frame might be different

Click button to select additional options (when available)

Click arrow to select export file format

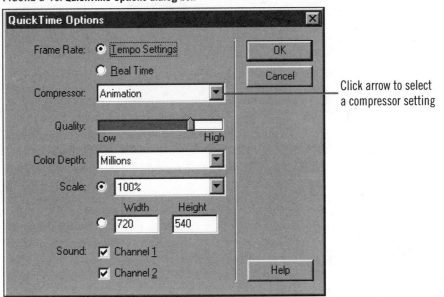

FIGURE G-19: **QuickTime Options dialog box**

Click arrow to select a compressor setting

TABLE G-1: **Compressor options**

option	description
Animation	Optimized for simple sprite motions, minimal transitions, and sound play instructions
Cinepak	A standard for high-quality video; recommended for transferring the digital video to traditional video tape; the compression ratio is 10 to 1
Component Video (Mac)	Optimized for capturing raw video footage; the compression ratio is 2 to 1
Graphics	Optimized for 8-bit color; the compression ratio is 11 to 1; files take longer to decompress
None	No compression
Photo-JPEG	A standard for digitized images, such as scanned photographs; the compression ratio is between 10 to 1 and 20 to 1
Video	A standard for QuickTime video; optimized for cross-platform use and 16-bit and 24-bit color images; the compression ratio is 5 to 1
Intel Indeo Video	Optimized for the Intel Indeo video chip

Practice

► Concepts Review

Label each of the elements of the screen shown in Figure G-20.

FIGURE G-20

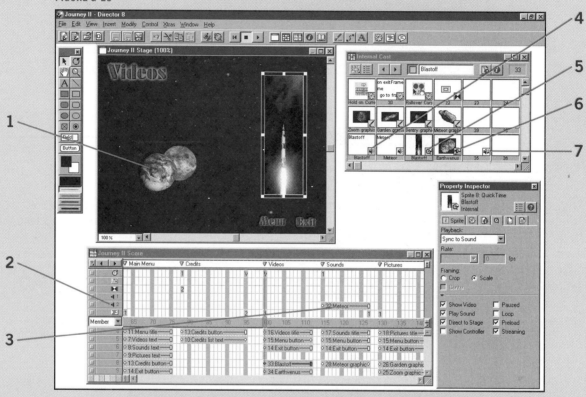

Match each of the terms with the statement that describes its function.

8. Compression	**a.** The process of continuously loading a sound or video as it plays
9. Mono	**b.** A video format common to Macintosh and Windows
10. Sampling rate	**c.** The process of reducing the size of a file
11. QuickTime	**d.** The measure of how much data space is available to store a sound
12. Streaming	**e.** A sound quality channels type
13. MP3	**f.** The frequency with which sounds are taken per second
14. Bit depth	**g.** A format that Director streams to reduce the delay time in playing

Select the best answer from the following list of choices.

15. Which is NOT an import sound format?
  a. AIFF   **b.** WAV   **c.** SWA   **d.** MP3

16. Which video format needs an Xtra installed to import a video?
  a. QuickTime   **b.** MPEG   **c.** AVI   **d.** None of the above

17. Audio and video files are:
  a. A frame-based medium.   **c.** Linked to the Cast window.
  b. A time-based medium.   **d.** None of the above

18. **Which is the common sampling size for compact discs?**
    a. 5.5125 kHz   **b.** 11.025 kHz   **c.** 22.050 kHz   **d.** 44.100 kHz

19. **A GIF is a:**
    a. Movie.   **b.** Sound.   **c.** Video.   **d.** Animation.

20. **Which is NOT a limitation of using the Direct to Stage option?**
    a. Prevents the use of ink effects   **c.** Appears in front of all sprites on Stage
    b. Plays every frame of the video   **d.** All of the above

21. **Cue points are used in Director to:**
    a. Synchronize sound or video with other actions.   **c.** Animate sound or video.
    b. Change the tempo in a sound or video.   **d.** None of the above

22. **Which QuickTime export compressor option is optimized for cross-platform use?**
    a. Animation   **b.** Cinepak   **c.** Graphics   **d.** Video

▶ Skills Review

1. **Import audio and video media.**
   a. Start Director, open the file MD G-3 from the drive and folder where your Project Files are located.
   b. Save the file as *Animal Life* in the drive and folder where your Project Files are located.
   c. Select cast member 19.
   d. Import all the sound files, except Eagle and Lion, from the Media SR folder.
   e. Select cast member 25, then import all the video files from the Media SR folder.
   f. If the Select Format dialog box appears, import AVI files in the AVI format.

2. **Control audio in the Score.**
   a. Add the Birds sound to frames 26 through 45, then loop the sound.
   b. Add the Dog sound to frames 106 through 120, and Dog video to frames 105 through 120 in channel 8.
   c. Add the Monkey sound to frames 66 through 80, and Monkey video to frames 65 through 80 in channel 8.
   d. Add the Tiger sound to frames 146 through 160, and Tiger video to frames 145 through 160 in channel 8.
   e. Add the Wolf sound to frames 126 through 140, and Wolf video to frames 125 through 140 in channel 8.
   f. Add the Zebra sound to frames 86 through 100, and Zebra video to frames 85 through 100 in channel 8.

3. **Create and stream Shockwave Audio.**
   a. Convert the Birds sound to an SWA (Win).
   b. Insert the Birds (Win) or Birdsm (Mac) SWA sound in the Cast.
   c. Add the Birds sound to frames 46 through 60 in channel 8.
   d. Play the Birds sound.

4. **Control video in the Score.**
   a. Loop the Wolf video.
   b. Play the Wolf video.

5. **Play video direct to Stage.**
   a. Verify that all the videos are set to Direct to Stage.
   b. Show the controller on the Monkey video.
   c. Play the Monkey video.

6. Crop and scale a video.
   a. Crop the edges of the Tiger video.
   b. Scale the Zebra video slightly larger.
   c. Play the Tiger video and the Zebra video.

7. Synchronize media.
   a. Select the Preload check box for all the videos.
   b. Set the wait for cue point at frame 45 for the end of the Birds sound.
   c. Save the movie.

8. Open a new movie and import a Microsoft PowerPoint presentation.
   a. Import the file MD G-4 (Win) or MD G-4m (Mac) from the drive and folder where your Project Files are located.
   b. Set minimum slide duration to 15 frames per slide, then use the default import settings.
   c. Import the sound files from the Media SR folder that correspond to the animals in the movie.
   d. Add the appropriate sound in a Sound channel to frames with the corresponding animal.
   e. Save the file as *Animal Pres* in the drive and folder where your Project Files are located.
   f. Play the movie.

9. Export a movie to video.
   a. Export the PowerPoint presentation movie to video.
   b. Export all the frames using the Real Time option and the Video compressor.
   c. Save the file as *Animal Pres*, using the Quicktime Movie format in the drive and folder where your Project Files are located.
   d. Exit Director.

► Independent Challenges

1. You are a media designer at Play It Again Media, a sound and video development company. You have developed a library of custom sounds. Your boss asks you to create a simple sound player that customers can use to play sounds. You use Director to import a variety of sounds and create a Main menu where you click the name of each sound to play it.
   To complete this independent challenge:

   a. Start Director and save the movie as *Play It Again Sounds* in the drive and folder where your Project Files are located.
   b. Create a text cast member with the text **Play It Again Sounds**, and drag it to the top of the Stage.
   c. Connect to the Internet and go to www.course.com. Navigate to the page for this book, click the link for the Student Online Companion, then click the link for this unit.
   d. Download three or four sounds, including at least one Shockwave Audio file. (*Hint*: Right-click a sound, click Save Target As, navigate to the drive and folder where your Project Files are located, then click Save.)
   e. Import the sounds into Director.
   f. Create a Main menu with the names of the sounds.
   g. Add the sounds to the Score.
   h. Add markers to the frames with each sound, and create scripts to jump to each marker from the Main menu.
   i. Play each sound, save the movie, then exit Director.

2. You are a media designer at Play It Again Media, a sound and video development company. You have developed a library of custom videos. Your boss asks you to create a simple video player with controls to start, stop, and replay the video, which customers can use to preview the material. You use Director to import a variety of videos, create a Main menu where you click the name of each video to play it, and display controls to start, stop, and replay the videos.

To complete this independent challenge:

a. Start Director and save the movie as *Play It Again Videos* in the drive and folder where your Project Files are located.

b. Create a text cast member with the text **Play It Again Videos**, and drag it to the top of the Stage.

c. Connect to the Internet and go to www.course.com. Navigate to the page for this book, click the link for the Student Online Companion, then click the link for this unit.

d. Download two or three videos. (*Hint*: Right-click a video hyperlink, click Save Target As, navigate to the drive and folder where your Project Files are located, then click Save.)

e. Import the videos into Director.

f. Create a Main menu with the names of the videos.

g. Add the videos to the Stage.

h. Add markers to the frames with each sound, and create scripts to jump to each marker from the Main menu.

i. Play the videos directly to the Stage and show controls for each video.

j. Play each video, save the movie, then exit Director.

3. You are the owner of World Travelers, Inc., an international travel tours company. You package and promote customized tours to unique destinations around the world. A client wants to book a travel tour to Israel. The client developed a promotional presentation in PowerPoint, but you need the presentation in digital video. You use Director to import the PowerPoint presentation and export the movie to a digital video.

To complete this independent challenge:

a. Start Director, then set the Stage size to 720 × 540, if necessary.

b. Import the file MD G-5 (Win) or MD G-5m (Mac) from the drive and folder where your Project Files are located.

c. Use the default import settings.

d. Save the movie as *World Travelers* in the drive and folder where your Project Files are located.

e. Export the PowerPoint presentation movie to video.

f. Export all the frames, using the Tempo Settings option and the Video compressor.

g. Save the file as *World Travelers*, using the QuickTime Movie format in the drive and folder where your Project Files are located.

h. Exit Director.

4. You are the publisher of *Animal Fun*, an online Web magazine for kids. For the anniversary issue, you want to create a fun story about an animal that includes sound and video. You use Director to insert an animal sound and video and control the playback of the media.

To complete this independent challenge:

a. Connect to the Internet and go to www.course.com. Navigate to the page for this book, click the link for the Student Online Companion, then click the link for this unit.

b. Download a sound and video for a bird. (*Hint*: Right-click a sound or video hyperlink, click Save Target As, navigate to the drive and folder where your Project Files are located, then click Save.)

c. Start Director, then save the movie as *Animal Fun* in the drive and folder where your Project Files are located.

d. Change the background of the Stage to a color appropriate to colors in the video.

e. Create a text cast member with the text **Animal Fun**, and drag it to the top of the Stage.

f. Create a text cast member with text for the story title and drag it to the top of the Stage.

g. Create a text cast member with text for the body of the story and drag it below the story title.

h. Drag the animal sound and video on the Stage.

i. Set the Hold on Current Frame behavior for the animal sound and video to the Stage at the story.

j. Set a rollover cursor effect for the story title.

k. Set the video and sound to play when you click the story title.

l. Play the movie, save the movie, then exit Director.

▶ Visual Workshop

Recreate the screen shown in Figure G-21. Your marine animal video and sound might be different. (*Hint*: Search the Web for videos, and download them to your hard drive; see Independent Challenge 4.) Print the screen. (For Windows, use the Windows Paint program. Press the Print Screen key to make a copy of the screen, start the Paint program by clicking Start, pointing to Programs, pointing to Accessories, then clicking Paint, click Edit on the menu bar, click Paste to paste the screen into Paint, then click Yes to paste the large image if necessary. Click File on the menu bar, click Print, click Print or OK in the dialog box, then exit Paint. For the Macintosh, use the SimpleText program. Hold and press the Command, Shift, and 3 keys to make a copy of the screen, double-click the document Picture 1 located on your hard drive, click File on the menu bar, click Print, then click Print in the dialog box. *Note*: When you create a new document with a copy of the screen, and a document Picture 1 already exists, the Macintosh names the new document Picture 2.)

FIGURE G-21

Preparing
and Delivering Movies

Objectives

► **Embed fonts in movies**
► **Manage Xtras for distributing movies**
► **Understand distribution methods**
► **Set movie playback options**
► **Set projector options**
► **Create a projector movie**
► **Launch the movie in a projector**
► **Create a Shockwave movie**
► **Create a protected movie**

Once you create and fine-tune a movie, you are ready to prepare and deliver it. This unit introduces you to basic skills for optimizing and preparing movie-related files, such as external sounds and movies, and a Director movie for delivery on a playback computer. First, you'll learn how to embed fonts in a movie for playback use on all computers, and how to manage Xtra files for movie distribution. Then, you'll learn about the different distribution methods for a movie in Director. Finally, you'll learn how to protect external movie files, set movie playback and projector options, and create a projector movie and a Shockwave movie for delivery. ✐ After completing the Journey movie, Jean wants to prepare and deliver the movie as a projector movie and Shockwave movie for Spaceworks Interactive management.

Embedding Fonts in Movies

If you like to use unique fonts in your movies, the fonts need to be installed on the playback computer in order for the font to display properly; otherwise, Director will use a substitute font. You can embed fonts in a Director movie so that the font will display properly even if it is not installed on the playback computer. When you embed a font in a movie, Director stores the font information in the movie file. You can only embed a font in a movie that is also installed on your computer. The embedded fonts are available only to the movie itself, so there are no legal infringements to distributing fonts in Director movies. Embedded fonts appear in a movie as cast members and work on both Windows and Macintosh computers. Once you embed a font in a movie, the font appears on all of the movie's font menus, and you can use it as you would any other font. Director compresses embedded fonts, so they usually only add 14–25K to a file. Jean embeds a font in a movie.

Steps

1. Start **Director**, open the file **MD H-1** from the drive and folder where your Project Files are located, then save it as **Journey Final**
Director opens, displaying the movie. Your initial settings in Director can vary, depending on previous usage.

2. Double-click the **Journey text** cast member in the Cast window, then select **all the text** in the Text window
The Text window opens with the Journey text cast member.

3. Click the **Font list arrow** ▼, scroll down, click **Impact**, then click the **Close button**
The font type is changed to Impact.

4. Click **Insert** on the menu bar, point to **Media Element**, then click **Font**
The Font Cast Member Properties dialog box opens.

5. Click the **Original Font list arrow** ▼, then click **Impact**
The font name appears in the Original Font box and the New Font Name box with an asterisk, as shown in Figure H-1. When you create embedded fonts using the original font name followed by an asterisk, Director uses the embedded font for all the text in the movie that uses the original font. This saves you the trouble of manually reapplying the font to all the text in existing movies.

6. Click the **Sizes option button**, click the **box to the right**, then type **9, 10, 12, 14**
Only the 9, 10, 12, and 14 point sizes are included in the movie file. If you only plan to use a few font sizes, you do not need to embed all the font sizes; you can only embed the ones you need. When you specify specific font sizes, you reduce the size of the movie file.

7. Click the **Bold check box**, then click the **Italic check box** to select them
The bold and italic versions of the font sizes are included in the movie file. The text set to Impact bold and Impact italic in the movie display properly on the screen; a substitute font is not used. When you include the bold and italic versions of a font, you increase the size of the movie file.

8. Click the **Partial Set option button**, then click the **Roman Characters check box** to select it
Only the roman characters (for example, A, a, B, b, and so on) are included with the embedded font type and sizes selected.

9. Click **OK**, then scroll down the Cast window to display the font cast member
The embedded Impact font appears in the Cast window, as shown in Figure H-2.

FIGURE H-1: Font Cast Member Properties dialog box

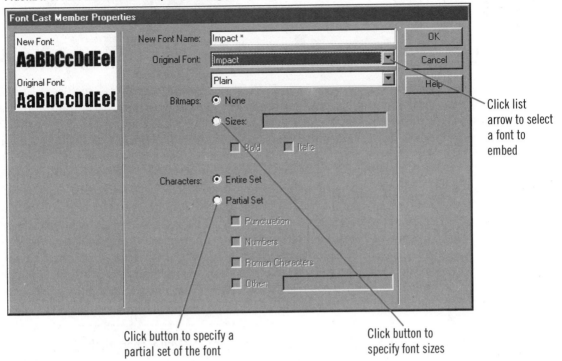

Click list arrow to select a font to embed

Click button to specify a partial set of the font

Click button to specify font sizes

FIGURE H-2: Embedded font in the Cast window

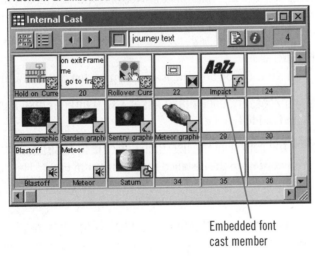

Embedded font cast member

Optimizing font embedding

For the best display at smaller sizes, include bitmap versions of a font when you embed it. For small font sizes, usually from about 7 to 12 points, bitmap fonts often look better than anti-aliased outline fonts. If you add a set of bitmap characters to the movie, you increase the size of the file. To speed up movie downloading, you can keep file size small by specifying a subset of characters to be included. You can also specify which point sizes to include as bitmaps and which characters to include in the font package. If you do not embed fonts in a movie, Director substitutes available system fonts.

Director 8

Managing Xtras for Distributing Movies

Many important features in Director are controlled by Xtras, such as creating text and vector shapes, importing different media types, or adding third-party transition effects. Like fonts, Xtras in a movie need to be installed on the playback computer so that the movie will run properly. When you distribute a movie, you either need to include the Xtras in the file or provide the end user with the opportunity to download them. You can use the Movie Xtras dialog box, which includes a list of the most commonly used Xtras, to specify the Xtras you want to include and the ones you want the end user to download. If you are not using an Xtra listed in the Movie Xtras dialog box, it is a good idea to remove it in order to reduce the file size and increase the speed of the movie. If you don't package Xtras with the movie, you need to create an Xtras folder in the folder with the projector file, copy the Xtras to the folder, select the Xtras in the Movie Xtras dialog box, and then deselect the Include in Projector check box. The Movie Xtras dialog box also includes the ability to access information about a specific Xtra on the Macromedia Web site, which requires Internet access. ✒ Jean adds an Xtra to the movie, gets more information about it from the Internet, and then decides to remove it.

QuickTip

To add the Xtras required to connect a projector to the Internet, click Add Network.

1. **Click Modify on the menu bar, point to Movie, then click Xtras**
   The Movie Xtras dialog box opens, displaying the currently installed Xtras, as shown in Figure H-3.

2. **If you have access to the Internet, click QT3Asset.x32 (Win) or QuickTime Asset (Mac), then click the Download if Needed check box to select it**
   Director accesses the Macromedia Web site and downloads the QuickTime Xtra. When you use the Download if Needed option, the movie prompts the end user to download the required Xtra.

3. **Click Add**
   The Add Xtras dialog box opens, displaying a list of commonly used Xtras.

4. **Scroll if necessary, click Flash Asset.x32 (Win) or Flash Asset PPC (Mac), then click OK**
   The Xtra is added to the list.

5. **Scroll to the bottom of the list, then click Flash Asset.x32 (Win) or Flash Asset PPC (Mac)**
   The Xtra appears in the installed list, as shown in Figure H-4. The Include in Projector check box becomes available, and the option is selected. This indicates that the Xtra is included when Director creates a projector file.

6. **If you have access to the Internet, click Info, then read the Web site information**
   Your Web browser opens, displaying the Macromedia Web site with information about the Xtra.

7. **Click File on the menu bar, then click Close (Win) or Quit (Mac)**
   Your Web browser closes. The Flash Xtra remains selected in the Movie Xtras dialog box.

QuickTip

To restore the default list of Xtras in the Movie Xtras dialog box, click Add Defaults.

8. **Click Remove**
   The Xtra is removed from the list, which reduces the size of the movie.

9. **Click OK**

FIGURE H-3: Movie Xtras dialog box

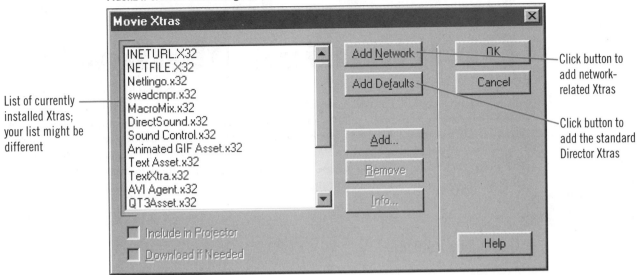

List of currently installed Xtras; your list might be different

Click button to add network-related Xtras

Click button to add the standard Director Xtras

FIGURE H-4: Adding an Xtra to a movie

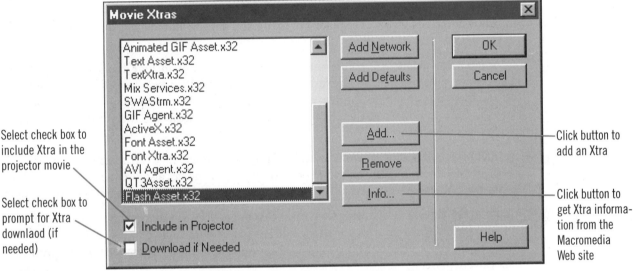

Select check box to include Xtra in the projector movie

Select check box to prompt for Xtra downlaod (if needed)

Click button to add an Xtra

Click button to get Xtra information from the Macromedia Web site

Working with third-party Xtras

You can use six types of Xtras in Director: image filters, importing, transition, cast member, Lingo or scripting, and tool, all of which are external authoring aids. Image filter Xtras allow you to modify bitmapped images in the Paint window; importing Xtras allow you to insert additional external media not standard to Director; transition Xtras allow you to add transition effects, such as a wipe left or fade right, not built into Director; cast member Xtras allow you to add new media types, such as a spreadsheet or database, to a movie; and Lingo or scripting Xtras allow you to add new Lingo language elements, such as a new command, to Lingo. Director comes with a set of third-party Xtras on the Director installation CD. You can incorporate these and many other Xtras, which you can find on the Macromedia Web site (www.macromedia.com), into your movies. To use these Xtras, you need to install them first. To install an Xtra, find the Xtras folder in the Director program folder, place the new Xtra in the Xtras folder, then restart Director. You can place the Xtra in a folder that is nested inside the Xtras folder no deeper than five folder levels. Xtras are used in Director in different ways. The transition Xtras appear in the Transition dialog box, and the cast member Xtras appear in the Cast window, while other Xtras appear as menu commands on the Xtras menu or the Media Element submenu on the Insert menu.

Director 8

Understanding Distribution Methods

Director provides several different formats to save a movie for distribution to end users. You can save your Director movie as a projector movie, a Shockwave movie, a Shockwave projector movie, a protected movie, or a Java applet. You can also distribute a movie in the Director movie format, but this method is not recommended because end users will be able to change the movie using Director. Before you save a movie in any of the distribution formats, it's important to understand how Director plays movies in each of the methods. Jean takes some time to familiarize herself with some of the distribution methods available in Director.

Distribution methods:

 A **projector movie** is a stand-alone program that end users can play on their computers without having Director installed. A projector movie can include one or more movies, the standard player, Xtras, multiple casts, and linked media in a single file. The standard player is a self-contained Director movie player that the projector uses to play the Director movie. A projector movie is intended for play in a window or on the full screen without a Web browser, as shown in Figure H-5.

 A **Shockwave movie** is a compressed movie that does not include the standard player. A Shockwave movie is intended for play over the Internet in a Web browser, as shown in Figure H-6. End users must have the Shockwave player installed on their computers in order to play the movie. You can download the Shockwave player for free from the Macromedia Web site at www.macromedia.com.

 A **Shockwave projector movie** is another compressed movie that end users can play on their computers without a Web browser. Shockwave projector movies also use the Shockwave player instead of the standard player, and are much smaller versions of an equivalent projector movie.

 A **protected movie** is an uncompressed Director movie that end users cannot open and modify in Director. Protected movies do not include any player software to play the movie. They can be played only by a projector, as a movie in a window (a Lingo operation), or by using the Shockwave player.

 A **Java applet** created in Director is a movie converted to Java, a programming language. Java applets created in Director provide extended functionality to play simple movies in a Web browser where plug-ins, such as the Shockwave player, are not allowed. When you convert a movie to Java, not all Director features are available, so you need to be aware of the authoring issues involved in the process.

FIGURE H-5: Projector movie in a window

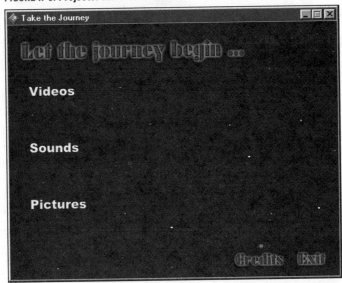

FIGURE H-6: Shockwave movie in a Web browser

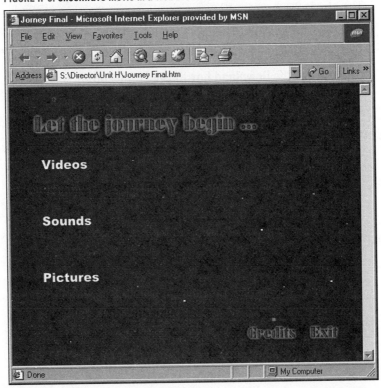

CLUES TO USE

Distributing a movie on a disk, to a local network, or to the Internet

When you distribute a movie on a disk, local network, or the Internet, all linked media, such as bitmaps, sounds, and videos, need to be in the same relative location as they were when you created the movie. To make sure you don't forget any linked media, it is a good idea to place linked files in the same folder as the projector or in a folder inside the projector folder. If you plan to place a movie on the Internet for playback in a Web browser, the linked media need to be at the specified URL when the movie plays. If you plan to link media

on a local disk only to a Shockwave movie, you need to place the media in a folder named dswmedia. To test movies in a Web browser, place the movie, linked casts, and linked media in folders within a dswmedia folder, and use relative links instead to refer to them. If you plan to place a movie on a local network, all files must be set to read-only, so that other users cannot change the movie file, and end users must have read/write access to their system folder, so that the movie player can access system files.

Setting Movie Playback Options

You can use the Movie Playback Properties dialog box to set General and Streaming playback options for the movie. In the General area, you can select options to lock the movie to its current tempo settings and make the movie pause when its window is deactivated. In the Streaming area, you can set the movie to stream, and then specify the number of frames downloaded before the movie begins to play. If you have an introductory scene that plays while other media are downloading, you need to set the download value so that all of the required media for the introductory scene are loaded before the movie begins to play. To help you determine when media elements appear in a movie, you can make the movie display placeholders (a rectangle with diagonal lines) for media elements that have not downloaded yet. The playback option can be set or changed at any time before you create the projector or Shockwave movie. ✎ Jean sets movie playback options for the projector and Shockwave movies.

Steps

1. Click **Modify** on the menu bar, point to **Movie**, then click **Playback**
   The Movie Playback Properties dialog box appears, as shown in Figure H-7.

2. Click the **Pause When Window Inactive check box** to select it
   This option makes the movie pause when its window is deactivated.

3. Double-click the **Download box** to select the current value
   The Download box allows you to specify the number of frames downloaded before the movie begins to play.

QuickTip

Setting a higher download value is useful for streaming movies that were not created for streaming.

4. Type **30**
   The download value is set to 30 frames.

5. Click the **Show Placeholders check box** to select it
   This option displays placeholders for media elements that did not completely download in time to display in the movie.

6. Click **OK**
   The options set in the Movie Playback Properties dialog box take effect when you create a projector or Shockwave movie, or preview the movie in a Web browser.

Movie Playback Properties ☒

General: ☐ Lock Frame Durations

☐ Pause When Window Inactive

Streaming: ☑ Play While Downloading Movie

Download [1] Frames Before Playing

☐ Show Placeholders

OK

Cancel

Help

Select check box to
stream the movie

Setting up a movie to stream

A streaming movie starts to play as soon as Director downloads the Score information and the cast members for the first frame. After the movie starts to play, Director continues to download cast members and any linked media in the background as they appear in the Score. When you create a movie to stream, you need to make sure all cast members have been downloaded by the time the movie needs them; otherwise, the cast member will not appear in the frame. To set up a movie to stream, you use the Movie Playback Properties dialog box. To turn on the streaming option, click Modify on the menu bar, point to Movie, click Playback, click the Play While Downloading Movie check box to select it, then click OK. If the streaming option is deselected, Director downloads all cast members before the movie starts to play.

Director 8

Setting Projector Options

Before you create a projector movie, it's important to set the options that will affect the Director movie. Some of the options are specific to the computer on which you create the projector. You can set projector options to play back one or more movies in the foreground or the background, determine the screen size and Stage size for one or more movies, compress the projector file, and select the player to use. Director retains the options settings once you define them, so you don't have to set them each time. You can include only Director 8 movies in projectors. You can use the Update Movies command on the Xtras menu to convert older movies to the latest version of Director. Jean sets options for the projector movie.

1. Click **File** on the menu bar, then click **Save and Compact**
The movie is saved and compressed to create a faster projector file.

2. Click **File** on the menu bar, then click **Create Projector**
The Create Projector dialog box appears.

QuickTip

If you want to include more than one movie in the projector, click the Play Every Movie check box to select it.

3. Click **Options**
The Projector Options dialog box appears, as shown in Figure H-8.

4. In the Playback area, click the **Animate in Background check box** to select it
This option plays the movie even when the end user switches to another program. If you clear this option, the projector pauses when the end user switches to another program and resumes playing when the end user selects the projector. Notice that it is similar to selecting the Pause When Window Inactive check box in the Movie Playback Properties dialog box.

QuickTip

To automatically switch the color depth of your monitor to the color depth of each movie in the projector play list, click the Reset Monitor to Match Movie's Color Depth check box to select it (Mac).

5. In the Options area, click the **Full Screen option button** (Win) or click the **Full Screen check box** to select it, if necessary (Mac)
The movie is set to fill the entire screen when playing. This option hides the computer's desktop. If a menu bar is used in the movie, it appears at the top of the Stage.

6. In the Stage Size area, click the **Center check box** to select it
This option plays the movie in the center of the screen, which is convenient when the Stage is smaller than the full screen size. In Windows, projectors are always centered.

7. In the Media area, click the **Compress (Shockwave Format) check box** to select it
This option compresses the movie in the Shockwave format, which reduces the projector file size but increases the time needed to load the movie. It is important to note that this option does not create a Shockwave movie; it only uses Shockwave technology to compress the projector movie.

QuickTip

To make Director use available system memory when its own partition is full, click the Use System Temporary Memory check box to select it (Mac).

8. In the Player area, click the **Compressed option button**
This option includes a compressed version of the standard player in the projector file. See Table H-1 for a description of the player options.

9. Click **OK**, then click **Cancel**
The projector options are set, even though you did not create a projector movie. These settings remain in effect until you change them.

Click option to select
player type in projector

TABLE H-1: Player options in the Options dialog box

player option	description
Standard	Includes the uncompressed player in the projector file. This option starts the movie faster than other options but creates the largest projector file.
Compressed	Includes a compressed version of the standard player in the projector file. The compressed version significantly reduces the projector file size, but decompressing the player adds a few seconds to the startup time of a movie.
Shockwave	Makes the projector use the Shockwave player installed on the end user's computer instead of including the standard player in the projector file. If the Shockwave player is not available when the movie plays, the movie prompts the end user to download it.

Director 8

Unit H
Director 8

Creating a Projector Movie

A projector is a stand-alone play-only version of your movie. You can include as many movies as you want in a projector. When you create a projector, Director embeds all files (such as Internal and External Casts and Xtras), except linked media, into a single program file. If you have linked media, you need to place the files in the same folder as the projector to make sure the movie plays properly. To create a projector for Windows or on the Macintosh, you need to use Director for Windows or Macintosh, respectively. In other words, you cannot create a projector for Windows using Director for Macintosh, or vice versa. If you want to create a cross-platform movie using either Director for Windows or Director for Macintosh, you must create a Shockwave movie. The end user can play the movie created in either platform in their Web browser. Once you create a projector movie, you cannot modify it; you need to change the original movie in Director, and then create a new projector file. Jean creates a projector of the Journey movie.

1. Click **File** on the menu bar, then click **Create Projector**

The Create Projector dialog box appears.

2. Click the **Look in list arrow** ▼, then click the drive and folder where your Project Files are located

A list of the files and folders appears, as shown in Figure H-9 (Win) or Figure H-10 (Mac). You can select files individually or together in the file list to add into the projector.

QuickTip

You can click Move Up or Move Down to change the order of multiple movies in the projector.

3. In the list of files and folders, click **Journey Final**, then click **Add**

The movie file appears in the File List.

4. Click the **Files of type list arrow** ▼, then click **Movie Cast Xtra**, if necessary (Win)

This option includes the movie, cast, and Xtra files in the projector file.

5. Click **Create**

The Save projector as dialog box appears.

6. In the File name box, type **Take the Journey**

QuickTip

To avoid problems with linked media, create the projector file in the same folder as the linked media.

7. Click the **Save in list arrow** ▼, then click the drive and folder where your Project Files are located, if necessary

8. Click **Save**

A progress meter appears as Director saves the movie, cast, and included Xtras into a single projector file.

FIGURE H-9: Create Projector dialog box (Windows)

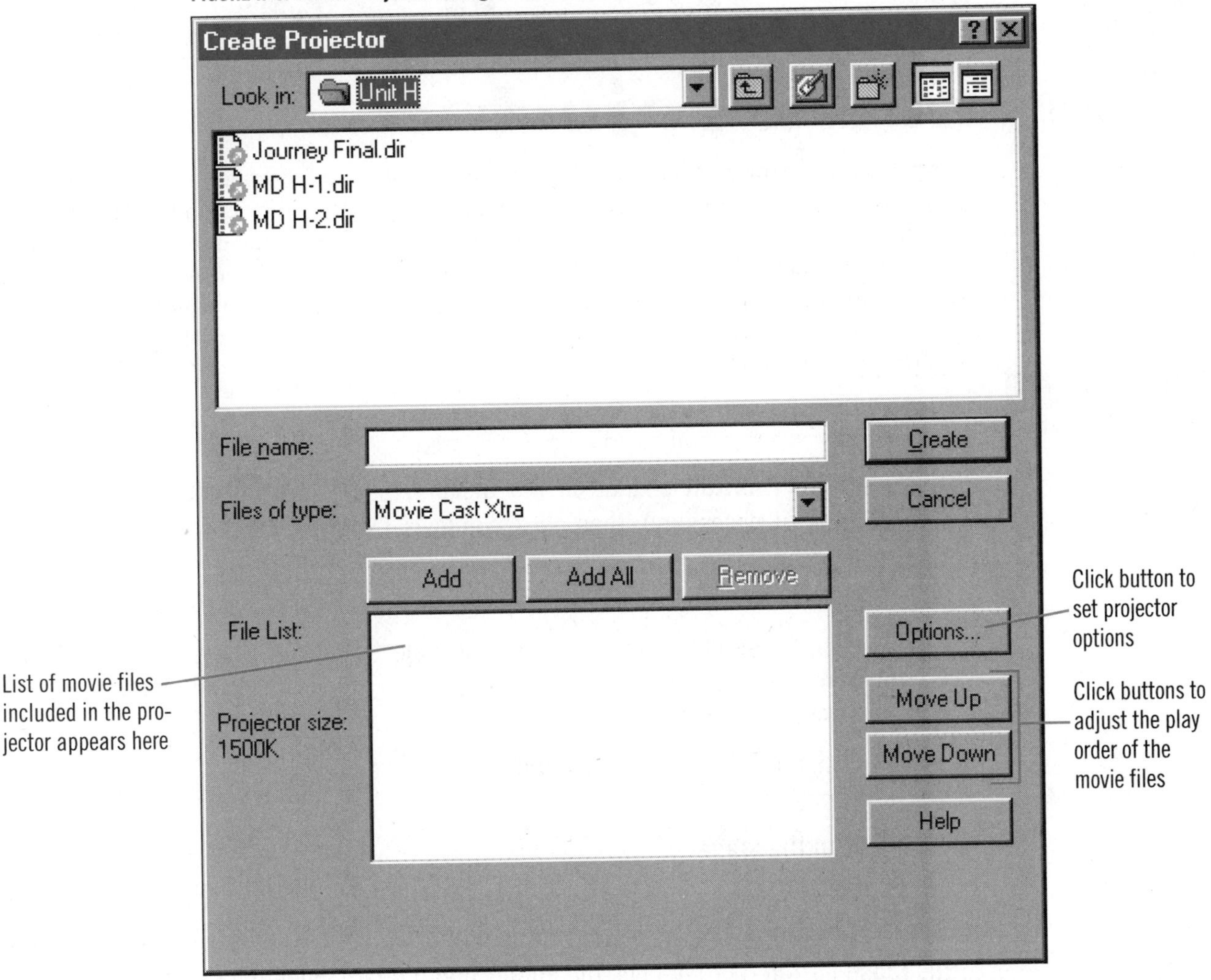

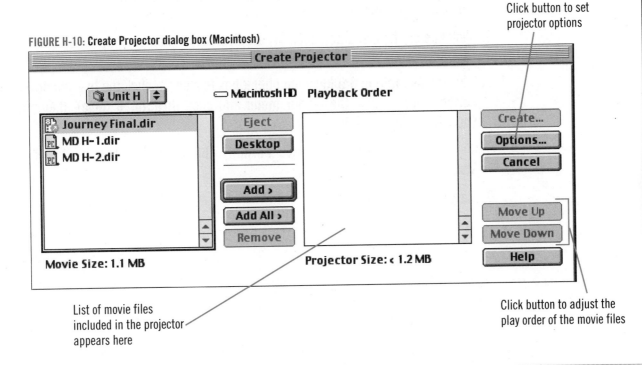

Create Projector
Look in:
Unit H
Journey Final.dir
MD H-1.dir
MD H-2.dir
File name:
Files of type:
Movie Cast Xtra
Create
Cancel
Add
Add All
Remove
File List:
Projector size:
1500K
Options...
Move Up
Move Down
Help
Click button to set projector options
Click buttons to adjust the play order of the movie files
List of movie files included in the projector appears here

FIGURE H-10: Create Projector dialog box (Macintosh)

Click button to set projector options
Create Projector
Unit H
Macintosh HD
Playback Order
Journey Final.dir
MD H-1.dir
MD H-2.dir
Eject
Desktop
Add >
Add All >
Remove
Create...
Options...
Cancel
Move Up
Move Down
Help
Movie Size: 1.1 MB
Projector Size: < 1.2 MB
List of movie files included in the projector appears here
Click button to adjust the play order of the movie files

Director 8

Director 8

Launching the Movie in a Projector

After you create a projector movie, it's a good idea to test the projector, especially if it includes linked media, to make sure the movie plays properly. A projector movie can be identified by a distinctive icon. Unless you linked files to the projector, everything the movie needs to play is included in the stand-alone program. As long as the end user's computer meets the minimum hardware requirements, the system can play the projector movie. If you include a player in the projector movie, the end user doesn't need to install Director or any other player. Jean launches the projector movie.

Steps

1. Click the **Start button** ![Start] on the taskbar, point to **Programs**, then point to **Accessories** (if necessary), then click **Windows Explorer** (Win) or double-click the **hard drive icon** (Mac)
   The Windows Explorer window (Win) or the hard drive window (Mac) appears.

2. Double-click the drive and folder where your Project Files are located
   The projector file appears in Windows Explorer, as shown in Figure H-11, or on the Macintosh, as shown in Figure H-12.

3. Double-click the **Take the Journey icon**
   The movie plays.

4. Click **Exit** on the Stage
   The projector closes.

5. Click the **Windows Explorer program icon** on the taskbar (if necessary), then click the **Close button** (Win) or click the **Finder menu** (Mac), click the **Close button** in the Windows Explorer window (Win), then click the **Director 8 program icon** on the taskbar (Win) or click the **Finder menu**, then click **Director 8** (Mac) (if necessary)
   Windows Explorer closes (Win) and the Director program window appears.

6. Click **File** on the menu bar, click **Create Projector**, then click **Options**
   The projector options remain in effect until you change them. It's a good idea to restore them.

7. Click the **Animate in Background check box** to clear it, click the **In a Window option button** (Win) or click the **Finder menu** and click **Director 8** (Mac), then click the **Show Title Bar check box** to select it

8. Click the **Compress (Shockwave Format) check box** to clear it, then click the **Standard option button**

9. Click **OK**, then click **Cancel**

FIGURE H-11: Projector icon in Windows Explorer (Windows)

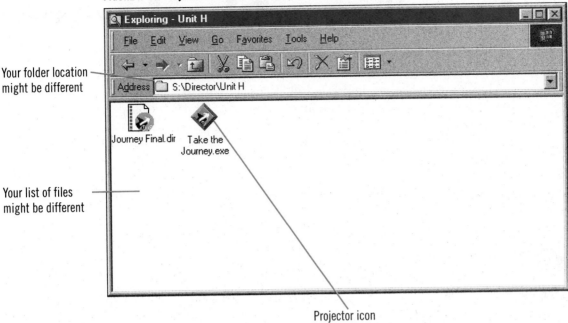

Your folder location might be different

Your list of files might be different

Projector icon

FIGURE H-12: Projector icon in a window (Macintosh)

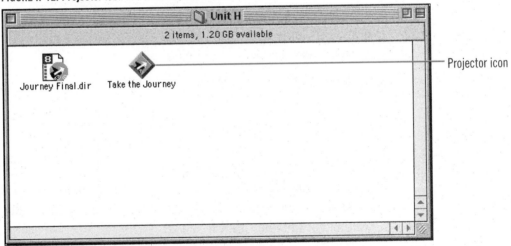

Projector icon

Testing a movie

Before you release your movie, it's important to test the final product on a variety of computer systems to make sure it plays properly in different conditions. During the testing process, check to make sure that all linked media and fonts appear correctly on the screen, and that the movie plays properly on all computers (such as Windows 95, 98, NT, 2000, Me, or later and Mac OS 8.x, 9.x, or later) and monitor display settings (8-, 16-, and 32-bit color) that end users are likely to use. If you plan to play the movie over the Internet, you need to check to make sure the movie plays fast enough over a slow Internet connection.

Director 8

Unit H
Director 8

Creating a Shockwave Movie

You can convert a Director movie and all its linked media to a Shockwave movie that you can play back in a Web browser on the Internet or on an intranet. Unlike a projector movie, a Shockwave movie cannot include the player in the file. The end user needs to have the Shockwave player installed on his or her computer to play the Shockwave movie. Before you create a Shockwave movie, you can preview and test it in your Web browser. When you create a Shockwave movie, you also need to create an HTML file (a standard Web page format) so that a Web browser can play it. After you create the HTML file, you can use other Web page editing programs, such as Macromedia Dreamweaver, to further customize the HTML file. Once you create a Shockwave movie, you cannot modify it; you need to change the original movie in Director, and then create a new Shockwave file. ✐ Jean previews the Journey movie in a Web browser, then creates a Shockwave movie.

Steps 1 2 3 4

Trouble?
If a warning dialog box about missing an Xtra appears, click OK, then see the "Managing Xtras for Distributing Movies" lesson earlier in this unit to install the missing Xtras.

1. Click **File** on the menu bar, click **Preview in Browser**, then click **Yes**, if necessary, to save the movie

Your Web browser appears, loads the movie, and plays it, as shown in Figure H-13. Director creates a temporary Shockwave file and HTML file to preview the movie in the Web browser. Notice that some Director functions and commands, such as Exit, do not function in a Web browser.

2. Click **Videos** on the Stage to play the Saturn QuickTime movie, then click **Menu** on the Stage

The movie plays properly in a Web browser.

3. Click **File** on the menu bar, then click **Close**

The Web browser closes. Now you are ready to save your Director movie as a Shockwave movie.

4. Click **File** on the menu bar, then click **Publish Settings**

The Publish Settings dialog box appears, displaying the Formats tab, as shown in Figure H-14.

5. Click the **HTML File button** ▭, click the **Look in list arrow** ▾, click the drive and folder where your Project Files are located (if necessary), then click **Select Folder** (Win) or click **Folder "Unit H"** (Mac)

6. Click the **Shockwave File button** ▭, click the **Look in list arrow** ▾, click the drive and folder where your Project Files are located, then click **Select Folder** (Win) or click **Folder "Unit H"** (Mac)

7. Click **OK**

The file locations for the HTML and Shockwave files are set to the folder where your Project Files are located.

8. Click **File** on the menu bar, click **Publish**, then click **Yes** (Win) or **Save** (Mac), if necessary, to save the movie

Director publishes the Shockwave file with the .dcr extension (Win) and the HTML file with the .htm extension (Win) in the folder where your Project Files are located, and then the movie plays in a Web browser.

9. Click **File** on the menu bar, then click **Close**

The Web browser closes.

FIGURE H-13: Previewing the movie in a Web browser

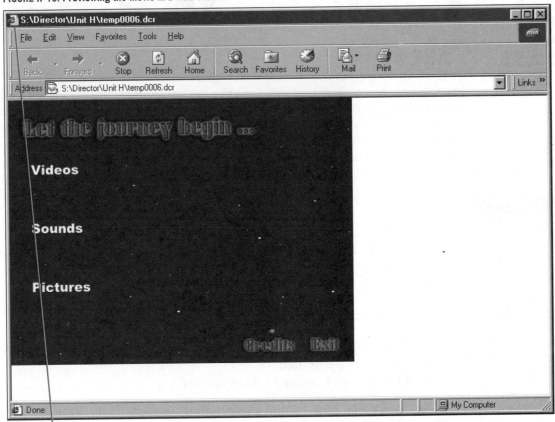

Your browser might
be different

FIGURE H-14: Publish Settings dialog box

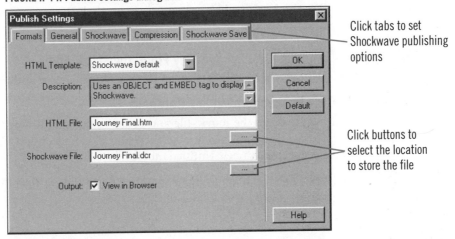

Click tabs to set
Shockwave publishing
options

Click buttons to
select the location
to store the file

Playing a Shockwave movie

If you don't have the latest version of Shockwave player installed on your computer, you can download it from the Macromedia Web site and install it. The Shockwave player works with Netscape Navigator 3.0 and later versions on Windows and Macintosh, and with Internet Explorer 3.0 and later versions on Windows and 4.01 and later on the Macintosh. It also works with browsers that are compatible with

Netscape Navigator 3.0 plug-in architecture. To play a Shockwave movie on your computer system, start your Web browser, click File on the menu bar, click Open, click Browse (if necessary), select the HTML file (.htm extension on Windows) that plays the Shockwave movie, then click Open. The HTML file should be in the same location as the Shockwave movie and any External Casts or linked media that is used.

Director 8

Creating a Protected Movie

When you create a projector file that uses other movie files or External Casts, you might want to protect those external files from being modified. When you protect external files, Director sets a flag that prevents end users from opening and editing the files in Director. Before you create a protected movie, make sure you have backup copies of the original. Once you create a protected movie, no one will be able to open it in Director. While it is important to protect your external files, there is one disadvantage: Director does not compress the movie into a smaller size. Jean creates a protected movie of the Journey movie for internal office review.

1. Click **Xtras** on the menu bar, click **Update Movies**, then click **Yes**, if necessary, to save the movie
   The Update Movies Options dialog box opens, as shown in Figure H-15.

2. Click the **Protect option button**

3. Click **Browse**, click the **Look in list arrow** , then click the drive and folder where your Project Files are located
   A list of files for your Project Files folder appears.

4. Click the **Create New Folder button** (Win), or **New** (Mac), type **Originals**, press **[Enter]** (Win) or **[Return]** (Mac), then double-click the **Originals folder** (Win)

5. Click **Select Folder** (Win) or **Folder Originals** (Mac), then click **OK**
   The Choose Files dialog box opens.

6. Click the **Look in list arrow** , then click the drive and folder where your Project Files are located

7. In the file list, click **Journey Final**, then click **Add**
   The protected file appears in the File List at the bottom of the dialog box.

8. Click **Proceed**, then click **Continue**
   Director closes the movie file and creates a protected movie and adds the .dxr extension (Win) to the protected movie files, and a .cxt extension (Win) to any protected casts. Director creates a new Untitled movie file.

9. Click **File** on the menu bar, then click **Exit** (Win) or **Quit** (Mac)
   Director closes.

QuickTip

To overwrite the originals with the new protected files, click the Delete option button. Make sure you have backup copies.

QuickTip

To include folders in addition to files, click the "Add All" Includes Folders check box to select it.

QuickTip

To play a protected movie, right-click the protected movie file, click Open with, click your Web browser (for example, iexplore), then click OK (Win).

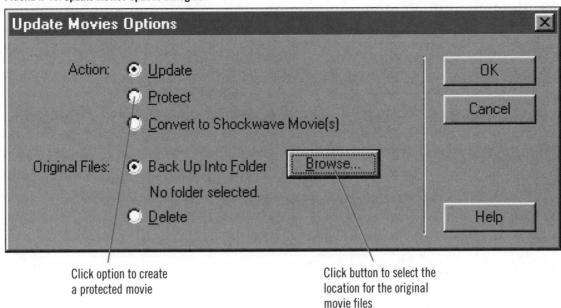

Click option to create
a protected movie

Click button to select the
location for the original
movie files

Converting multiple movies to Shockwave files

You can use the Convert to Shockwave Movie option in the Update Movies dialog box to create compressed Shockwave movies. Once a movie is compressed into the Shockwave format, you cannot edit it. You need to change the original Director movie and then reconvert the movie to Shockwave. The conversion creates a movie file with the .dcr extension and a cast with the .cxt extension, which the end user cannot modify (Win). If you have multiple Director movies and casts, you can convert them to Shockwave files all at once, instead of converting each one individually. You can convert the files while preserving the original files or convert the files and delete the original files. To convert multiple movies to Shockwave files, click Xtras on the menu bar, click Update Movies, click the Convert to Shockwave Movie option button, click the Backup into Folder option button, click Browse, select the folder where you want to put the original files, click Open, click OK, select the movie(s) you want to convert, click Add for each individual file or Add All, then click Proceed. Director does not automatically save linked External Casts; you need to add each External Cast that you want to convert.

Practice

▶ Concepts Review

Label each of the elements of the screen shown in Figure H-16.

FIGURE H-16

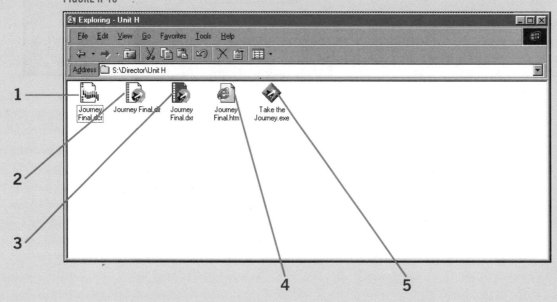

Match each of the terms with the statement that describes its function.

6. Projector movie   **a.** An uncompressed movie that end users cannot open and modify

7. Java applet   **b.** A stand-alone program that end users can play without Director installed

8. Protected movie   **c.** A compressed movie that end users play in a Web browser

9. Shockwave projector movie   **d.** A movie that end users can play in a Web browser without a plug-in

10. Shockwave movie   **e.** A compressed movie that end users can play independently of a Web browser

Select the best answer from the following list of choices.

11. Embedded fonts appear in a movie as a(n):
- **a.** Xtra.
- **b.** Cast member.
- **c.** Sprite.
- **d.** Behavior.

12. Which is NOT an Xtra type?
- **a.** Importing
- **b.** Transition
- **c.** Cast member
- **d.** Sprite

13. Which distribution method includes a player in the file?
- **a.** Shockwave movie
- **b.** Projector movie
- **c.** Protected movie
- **d.** Java applet

14. **Which is NOT a projector player option?**
    a. Shockwave
    b. Compressed
    c. Protected
    d. Standard

15. **Which extension (Win) identifies a Shockwave movie file?**
    a. .exe
    b. .dir
    c. .dcr
    d. .dxr

16. **Which extension (Win) identifies a protected movie file?**
    a. .exe
    b. .dir
    c. .dcr
    d. .dxr

17. **When Director creates a Shockwave file, it also creates a(n):**
    a. HTML file.
    b. Java file.
    c. External Cast file.
    d. Xtra file.

18. **Which menu command creates a protected movie file?**
    a. Publish
    b. Update Movie
    c. Protected
    d. Create Projector

▶ Skills Review

1. **Embed fonts in movies.**
   a. Start Director, open the file MD H-2 from the drive and folder where your Project Files are located.
   b. Save the file as Animal Life Final in the drive and folder where your Project Files are located.
   c. Change the font for the Welcome text and to text cast members to Lucida Bright or one available on your computer, and add bold to the text.
   d. Embed the Lucida Bright font or the one you selected for the 22- and 36-point sizes and Bold.

2. **Manage Xtras for distributing movies.**
   a. Add the SWAStrm.x32 (Win) or SWA Streaming PPC Xtra (Mac) Xtra to the movie. If the Xtra is not available, then add SwaCmpr.x32 (Win) or SWA Compression Xtra (Mac).
   b. Read the Web site information about the Xtra.
   c. Remove the SWAStrm.x32 (Win) or SWA Streaming PPC Xtra (Mac) Xtra.

3. **Explain distribution methods.**
   a. List and describe the differences among the five types of distribution methods.

4. **Set movie playback options.**
   a. Change the number of frames downloaded before the movie plays to 15.
   b. Select the option to pause the movie when the window is inactive.
   c. Select the option to show placeholders.

5. **Set projector options.**
   a. Save and compact the movie.
   b. Select the projector option to play in a window (Win) and show the title bar (if necessary).
   c. Select the projector option to play the movie in the center of the Stage.
   d. Select the projector option to compress the movie with the Shockwave format.
   e. Select the projector option for the compressed player.

6. **Create a projector movie.**
   a. Create a projector movie for the Animal Life Final movie.
   b. Name the projector file Wild Animal Life.
   c. Save the projector file in the drive and folder where your Project Files are located.

7. Launch the movie in a projector.

   a. Display the folder where your Project Files are located in Windows Explorer (Win) or Finder (Mac).

   b. Start the Wild Animal Life projector movie.

   c. Switch back to Director.

   d. Clear the projector option to compress the movie with the Shockwave format.

   e. Select the projector option for the standard player.

8. Create a Shockwave movie.

   a. Save the movie.

   b. Preview the Animal Life Final movie in a browser.

   c. Select the folder location for the HTML and Shockwave files to the drive and folder where your Project Files are located. Close the Web browser.

   d. Publish the Shockwave movie file and save the movie, if necessary.

9. Create a protected movie.

   a. Protect the Animal Life Final movie.

   b. Back up the original movie file in the Originals folder located in the drive and folder where your Project Files are located.

   c. Exit Director.

▶ Independent Challenges

1. You are the marketing manager at Font Mania, a font development company. You have developed two new fonts for a client. You want to create a simple font viewer for the client to review the fonts. You use Director to display two fonts, embed them in a movie, and create a projector.

To complete this independent challenge:

   a. Start Director and save the movie as *Font Catalog* in the drive and folder where your Project Files are located.

   b. Create a text cast member with the text **Font Mania**, and drag it to the top of the Stage.

   c. Create a text cast member with the entire alphabet and numbers 0 to 10, using a font, and drag it to the left side of the Stage. (*Hint*: Select a unique font on your computer.)

   d. Create a text cast member with the entire alphabet and numbers 0 to 10, using another font, and drag it to the right side of the Stage.

   e. Embed the fonts in the movie.

   f. Create a compressed projector file as *Font Mania Catalog,* with the movie centered in a window.

   g. Save the movie, then exit Director.

2. You are a multimedia instructor at a local college. You are teaching a class on Macromedia Director and want to explain and demonstrate Director's movie distribution method. You use Director to create a movie with definitions of each distribution method and save the movie in each format.

To complete this independent challenge:

   a. Start Director and save the movie as *Movie Delivery* in the drive and folder where your Project Files are located.

   b. Create a text cast member with the text **Director Movie Distribution Methods**, and drag it to the top of the Stage.

   c. Create a text cast member with the text **Projector** and its definition, then drag it on the Stage.

   d. Create a text cast member with the text **Shockwave** and its definition, then drag it on the Stage.

   e. Create a text cast member with the text **Protected** and its definition, then drag it on the Stage.

   f. Create a text cast member with the text **Java applet** and its definition, then drag it on the Stage.

   g. Create a projector movie as *Movie Delivery,* Shockwave movie, and protected movie.

   h. Play the projector movie and the Shockwave movie.

   i. Save the movie, then exit Director.

3. You are the campaign manager of a candidate for a local state senate race. You want to create a movie to promote the candidate for distribution through e-mail. Use Director to create a movie about a fictitious candidate and save the file as a Shockwave projector movie to reduce the file size and provide Web browser independence.

To complete this independent challenge:

a. Start Director and save the movie as *Senate Race* in the drive and folder where your Project Files are located.

b. Create a text cast member with the name of the candidate and drag it to the top of the Stage.

c. Create a text cast member with brief biographical information about the candidate, then drag it on the Stage.

d. Create a Shockwave projector movie as *Senate Race*.

e. Play the Shockwave projector movie with the Shockwave player, not in a Web browser.

f. Save the movie, then exit Director.

4. You are the publicist for a space documentary, *Earth Unveiled*. The producer of the documentary has given you a clip of the movie in the MPEG format. You want to create a Director movie with the documentary movie clip and package it for audiences to view on the Web. You use Director to install an Xtra, called DirectMedia Xtra, to import the MPEG movie, then create a Shockwave movie. *Note*: For Macintosh, skip Steps a through c. The Macintosh does not need an Xtra to import an MPEG movie.

To complete this independent challenge:

a. Connect to the Internet and go to www.course.com. Navigate to the page for this book, click the link for the Student Online Companion, then click the link for this unit.

b. Download the free DirectMedia Xtra from the Web site, or use the DirectMedia Xtra in the drive and folder where your Project Files are located. (*Hint*: For instructions on downloading and installing the DirectMedia Xtra, see the "Installing an Xtra" in the Appendix.)

c. Install the DirectMedia Xtra.

d. Start Director, then save the movie as *Earth Unveiled* in the drive and folder where your Project Files are located.

e. Change the background of the Stage to black.

f. Create a text cast member with the text **Earth Unveiled**, and drag it to the top of the Stage.

g. Import the Earth.mpeg movie from the drive and folder where your Project Files are located. (*Hint*: Use the DirectMedia Xtra command on the Tabuleiro Xtras submenu on the Insert menu (Win) or the Import command on the File menu (Mac) to import an MPEG movie.)

h. Preview the movie in a browser.

i. Create a Shockwave movie.

j. Save the movie and exit Director.

Director 8

▶ Visual Workshop

Recreate the projector shown in Figure H-17. Your animal video and sound might differ. Print the screen. (For Windows, use the Windows Paint program. Press the Print Screen key to make a copy of the screen, start the Paint program by clicking Start, pointing to Programs, pointing to Accessories, then clicking Paint, click Edit on the menu bar, click Paste to paste the screen into Paint, then click Yes to paste the large image, if necessary. Click File on the menu bar, click Print, click Print or OK in the dialog box, then exit Paint. For the Macintosh, use the SimpleText program. Hold and press the Command, Shift, and 3 keys to make a copy of the screen, double-click the document Picture 1 located on your hard drive, click File on the menu bar, click Print, then click Print in the dialog box. Note: When you create a new document with a copy of the screen, and a document Picture 1 already exists, the Macintosh names the new document Picture 2.)

FIGURE H-17

Managing

Color

► **Understand color in Director**

► **Change movie color depth**

► **View and change a color palette**

► **Import a color palette**

► **Edit favorite colors in a color palette**

► **Change color palettes during a movie**

► **Create a custom color palette**

► **Create an optimal color palette**

► **Cycle colors in a color palette**

Managing color in Director is an important part of creating a good-looking movie. Managing color is a balance between achieving the best color display and minimizing the amount of memory and disk space, and the time images take to load. First, you'll learn about the different aspects of using color in Director and how to change movie color depth on Windows and Macintosh computers. Then, you'll learn how to change and import a color palette, edit favorite colors, and create a custom color palette. Finally, you'll learn how to change color palettes during a movie, cycle colors from a color palette in a cast member, and create an optimal color palette. Jean creates a Space Storms movie to demonstrate the use of color in Director.

Director 8

Understanding Color in Director

Color is a resource in Director. Like any resource, color needs to be managed to balance the best look of the movie (color effects) against optimal functioning (such as memory usage, file size, download time). Director manages colors as sets of colors, or palettes. A **color palette** is a set of colors used by a movie or cast members, as shown in Figure I-1. The movie can use one color palette, while a cast member can use another palette. Director allows you to use multiple color palettes and switch between them to display each image in the color detail you want. However, you need to plan the use of each palette, because you can only use one palette at a time. You need to take into consideration all the colors on the Stage and in the cast members, and use colors that are available in the current color palette. The colors that can appear in any single frame of a movie must be in the current color palette. Because the palette you choose affects everything that is displayed on the screen, including the interface, you might find it difficult to see what you're doing in Director after you select a palette other than the system palette. Jean takes some time to familiarize herself with the use of color in Director.

 Color depth, or bit depth, is the measure of the number of colors that an image can contain. The maximum number of colors is limited by the number of bits a computer can store for each dot, or pixel, on the screen. For 8-bit color depth, a computer stores 8 bits of color information for each pixel on the screen, which can yield 256 possible color combinations; for 16-bit color depth, a computer stores 16 bits for each pixel. The higher the number of bits a computer stores for each pixel, the greater the number of different colors that can be displayed on the screen, which necessitates greater system memory. See Table I-1 for a list of color depths and memory information. For computer displays and Web browsers, typically a color depth of 8 bits per pixel, or 256 colors, offers the best balance between high-quality color and the time it takes to download a file. For computer display only (no Web browser), a color depth of 16 or 32 bits offers high-quality color because there is no need for any downloading.

 Director offers a choice of two basic **color modes**: RGB (Red, Green, Blue) and palette index, as shown in Figure I-2. The RGB color mode identifies a color by a set of hexadecimal numbers, an internal computer numbering scheme, that specify the amounts of red, green, and blue needed to create the color. The RGB color mode works best with 16-bit or 32-bit color depth and offers the most accurate way of specifying colors. For 8-bit color depth, Director uses the color in the color palette that is closest to the RGB color. The palette index color mode identifies a color by the number (0 through 255) of its position in a color palette and works best with 8-bit or less color depth. If you switch color palettes within a movie, the colors of an image in one palette need to match the colors of the other palette, by position number, to ensure that the colors of the image display correctly.

 Color is managed differently on the Macintosh than it is in Windows. If you are creating movies for both platforms, you need to be aware of the differences. The Macintosh displays 8-bit color using a constant set of 256 colors, unless a program uses a custom palette. These colors are the Macintosh system color palette. For movies created on the Macintosh, you can use Director's System - Mac color palette. Windows, in contrast, lets the program define all but 16 colors, which Windows reserves for its interface elements, in the 256-color palette. This use of a changeable color palette is called **dynamic color management**. Most Windows programs use a 256-color system palette that includes a sampling of RGB colors and a broad range of colors designed for optimum display of computer graphics and text on Windows computers. For movies created in Windows, you can use Director's System - Win color palette. For cross-platform movies, you need to create a color palette that includes the colors reserved for the Windows system palette, in addition to the common colors used in the movie from the System Mac, System Win, or custom palettes. The colors reserved for the Windows system palette are the first 10 colors and the last 10 colors (positions 1 through 10 and 246 through 255) in the Windows system palette. Including these colors ensures that the colors of your Windows interface elements will have the correct operating system colors.

FIGURE I-1: Color Palettes window

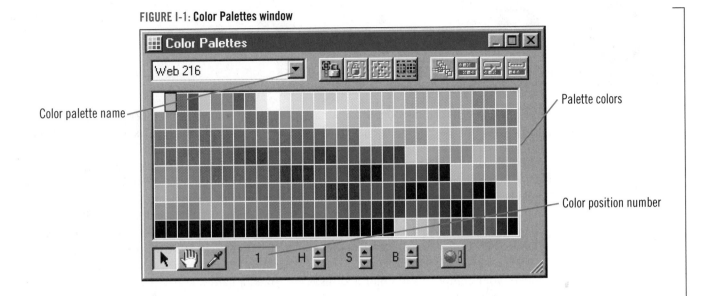

Color palette name

Palette colors

Color position number

FIGURE I-2: RGB and palette index modes

RGB mode

Hexadecimal number for black

Index number for black

Palette index mode

Black color

TABLE I-1: **Color depth**

bits	number of colors	cast member size
1	2 colors (black and white)	12 KB
2	4 colors	24 KB
4	16 colors	48 KB
8	256 colors	96 KB
16	32,768 colors	192 KB
32	16.7 million colors	384 KB

Director 8

Changing Movie Color Depth

When you specify the color depth for a movie, you set the maximum number of colors for all the images it contains. For example, a movie set to 8-bit color depth displays all 16-bit or 32-bit graphic cast members in 8-bit color, substituting the closest colors available out of the 256 colors. The color depth for a cast member can differ from the movie color depth. However, the movie color depth setting must be at least as high as the cast member color depth to display the cast member's full range of colors. The greater a cast member's color depth, the more memory it requires and the more time it takes to load. Changing the movie color depth during the development of the movie may not produce the results you want, so it is a good idea to decide the maximum color depth at the start of the project, and import graphics at a consistent color depth. The maximum color depth for a movie is the color depth of the computer on which you create your movie. Your computer's monitor and display adapter, a hardware device that processes signals from the monitor to the computer, determine the maximum color depth of the computer. Director uses the maximum color depth of the monitor and display adapter for the current movie. Jean sets the color depth for the Space Storms movie.

WIN

1. **Click the Start button** ⊞ Start **on the taskbar**
   The Start button is on the left side of the taskbar and is used to start programs on your computer. Use the set of steps designed for the platform you are using.

2. **Point to Settings, then click Control Panel**
   The Control Panel appears.

3. **Double-click the Display icon** 🖥️ **, then click the Settings tab**
   The Windows Display Properties dialog box appears, as shown in Figure I-3. Remember the current color palette setting so you can restore it at the end of the unit.

4. **Click the Colors palette list arrow** ▼ **, then click High Color (16 bit)**
   Sixteen colors is 4 bit; 256 colors is 8 bit; 32,768 colors is 16 bit; and 16.7 million colors is 32 bit.

5. **Click OK**
   If you change the color palette setting, the Compatibility Warning dialog box might appear.

6. **Click the Apply the new color settings without restarting? option button, then click OK, if necessary**
   The monitor and display adapter are set to the new color depth.

7. **Click the Close button in the Control Panel**

MAC

1. **Click Apple on the menu bar, point to Control Panels, then click Monitors**
   The Display control panel appears, displaying monitor settings, as shown in Figure I-4. Use the set of steps designed for the platform you are using.

2. **Click the Colors option button**

3. **Click Thousands, if available; otherwise click 256**
   The monitor and display adapter are set to the new color depth.

4. **Click the Close button**
   The Display control panel closes.

QuickTip

To change the monitor's color depth setting to match the current movie, click File on the menu bar, point to Preferences, click General, click the Reset Monitor to Movie's Color Depth check box to select it, then click OK.

FIGURE I-3: Changing movie color depth for Windows

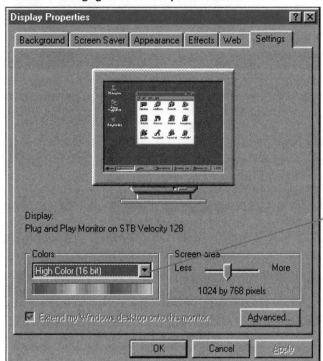

Click arrow to select color depth; your settings might be different

FIGURE I-4: Changing movie color depth for Macintosh

Click option to select a color palette

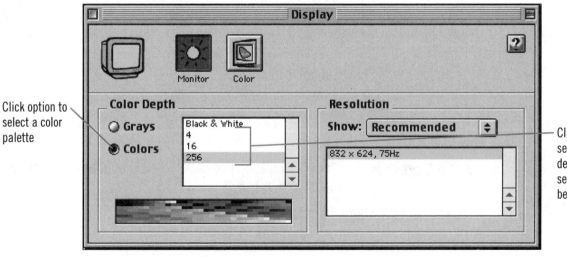

Click list to select color depth; your settings might be different

Checking the movie color depth

Once you set the movie color depth in Windows or Macintosh, you can check to make sure the color depth is set correctly in Director. To check the movie color depth in Director, click the Paint Window button [⬜] in the toolbar, click the New Cast Member button [+] in the top-left corner of the Paint window, then look at the bottom of the Tool palette in the lower-left corner of the Paint window for the movie's current color depth.

Director 8

Viewing and Changing a Color Palette

Director comes with two color palette displays: the Color Palettes window and a pop-up color palette. The Color Palettes window provides you with the ability to switch, organize, or create a color palette, define new colors, or change foreground, background, and fill colors, while the pop-up color palette provides quick access to colors in the color palette. You can find the pop-up color palette on any tools with foreground or background color boxes. When you open the pop-up color palette, you can find out the current color mode, either palette index or RGB, at the top of the menu. Director comes with several color palettes from which you can choose, or you can create your own color palettes. You can set the color palette for the entire movie or individual cast members. When you set the color palette for the movie, the color palette is used in all frames until you change it to a different one in the Palette channel, which is one of the Effects channels in the Score window. The Windows and Macintosh system palettes are the default selections. ✎ Jean views and changes the color palette for the entire movie and for a cast member.

1. Start **Director**, open the file **MD I-1** from the drive and folder where your Project Files are located, then save it as **Space Storms**

   Director opens, displaying the movie. Your initial settings in Director can vary, depending on previous usage.

2. Click the **Stage window**, then click the **Movie tab** in the Property Inspector

   The Movie tab on the Property Inspector appears. The Movie tab appears only if you do *not* have an object selected on the Stage or in the Score.

3. Click the **Movie Palette list arrow** ▼, then click **Web 216**

   The Web 216 movie palette provides you with a set of Web-safe colors that will ensure that your colors will properly display on the Web. This palette remains selected until Director encounters a different palette setting in the palette channel.

4. Click and hold the **Stage fill color box**

   The color box displays the color last selected in Director. A pop-up color palette appears, displaying the current color palette, as shown in Figure I-5. Because the RGB option is selected, the color palette is based on RGB colors. The RGB color value is set to #000000, the hexadecimal value for black.

5. Click the **Stage** to deselect the color palette, then click the **Palette Index option button**

   The color palette changes from RGB to Palette Index.

6. Click and hold the **Stage fill color box**

   A pop-up color palette appears, displaying the Palette Index color palette. The Palette Index color value is set to 255, the position number for black.

7. Click the **Stage** to deselect the color palette

8. Click the **Gray Storm cast member** in the Cast window, then click the **Bitmap tab** in the Property Inspector

   The Bitmap tab on the Property Inspector appears, displaying a color palette for a grayscale bitmap.

9. Click the **Palette list arrow** ▼, then click **Grayscale**

   The cast member color palette is changed to match the graphic on the Stage, as shown in Figure I-6. Because the palette you choose affects everything that is displayed on the screen, including the interface, you might find it difficult to see what you're doing in Director after you select a palette other than the system palette.

Trouble?

If the Property Inspector is not open, click Window on the menu bar, point to Inspectors, then click Property. If necessary, click the Expander arrow ▶ to display the entire window.

QuickTip

To open the pop-up color palette in the opposite mode, hold down [Alt] (Win) or [Option] (Mac), then click the color box.

FIGURE I-5: Movie tab in the Property Inspector

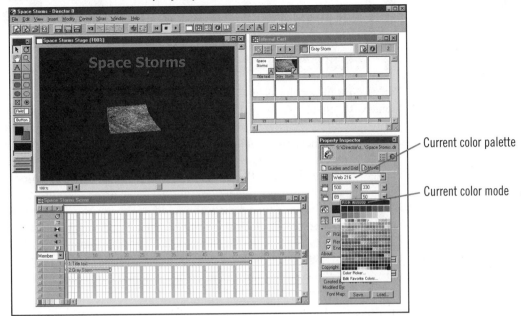

Current color palette

Current color mode

FIGURE I-6: Bitmap tab in the Property Inspector

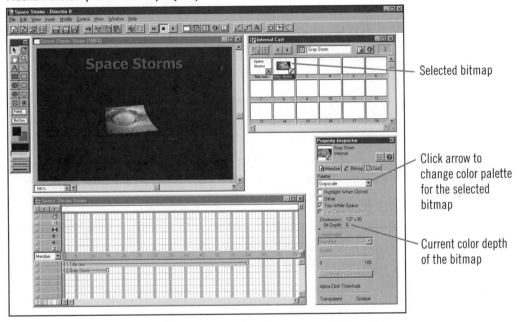

Selected bitmap

Click arrow to change color palette for the selected bitmap

Current color depth of the bitmap

Choosing a color palette for the Web

If you are developing movies for the Web, you should use the Web 216 color palette for the entire movie and all cast members. The Web 216 color palette contains the set of colors used by both Netscape Navigator and Internet Explorer on Windows and Macintosh. When you select this color palette, the Web browser, not the Director movie, controls the palette. The settings in the palette channel have no effect on a movie playing in a Web browser. To avoid color problems for bitmaps displayed on the Web, you should remap the colors in all bitmaps in your movie to the Web 216 color palette. When you remap colors, Director examines the bitmap's original colors and then remaps the colors to positions in the new color palette that contain colors that best match the original colors. For instructions to remap a bitmap, see the Clues "Remapping a cast member to a different color palette," later in this unit.

Director 8

Importing a Color Palette

You can import a color palette as a file from another program, or you can import a color palette along with an image. If you create custom images in a graphics program, such as Adobe PhotoShop or Corel Draw, with a custom set of colors for a company logo, you can export the color palette from the graphics program, and import it into Director. When you import an image, you also import the color palette that the image uses. During the importing process, you can change the color depth of the image and remap the image to a different color palette. If you change the color depth and remap the color palette of an image, Director examines the cast member's original colors and then remaps the colors to the positions in the new color palette that contain colors that best match the original colors. Remember that the look of the image could change slightly or dramatically, depending on the color depth and colors in the color palette. The original image does not change, just the copy you imported into Director. Jean imports a color palette from another program and imports a color palette with an image.

1. Click the **Import button** 🗇 on the toolbar
   The Import Files into "Internal" dialog box opens.

2. Click the **Look in list arrow** ▼, click the drive and folder where your Project Files are located, then double-click the **Media folder**
   A list of files for the Media folder appears.

3. Click the **Files of type list arrow** ▼, then click **Palette**
   The palette file in the Media folder appears in the Look in file list.

Trouble?

If you have problems importing a color palette, it may have several instances of black or white wrongly positioned in the palette. Any palette you import must have white in the first position of the palette, and black in the last position.

4. Click the file **Color Table.act** (Win) or **Color Tablem** (Mac), click **Add**, then click **Import**
   The palette file from PhotoShop appears in the file list and as a new cast member in the Cast window, as shown in Figure I-7.

5. Click the **Import button** 🗇 on the toolbar, verify that the Media folder is selected, click the **Files of Type list arrow** ▼, then click **All Files** (scroll as necessary)
   The Import Files into "Internal" dialog box opens, and all file types appear in the Look in list.

6. Click the **Color Storm.gif** file, click **Add**, click the **Light Blue Storm.gif** file, click **Add**, click the **Orange Storm.gif** file, click **Add**, then click **Import**
   The Select Format dialog box opens.

7. Click **Bitmap Image**, click the **Same Format for Remaining Files check box** to select it, then click **OK**
   The Image Options dialog box opens, indicating that the color palette you are importing with the Color Storm image has a different color palette than the currently active color palette. The color depth is set to 8 bit for the image and 16 bit for the Stage.

QuickTip

To change a cast member's color depth, click the cast member in the Cast window, click Modify on the menu bar, click Transform Bitmap, select a bit depth, then click Transform.

8. In the Palette area, click the **Remap to option button**, click the **Palette list arrow** ▼, click **Color Table Internal** if necessary, then click **OK**
   The color palette for the image is changed to match the color palette of the movie. The Image Options dialog box opens again for the Light Blue Storm image.

9. In the Palette area, click the **Import option button**, click the **Same Settings for Remaining Images check box** to select it, then click **OK**
   The images along with their color palettes appear as cast members in the Cast window, as shown in Figure I-8.

FIGURE I-7: Cast window with imported color palette

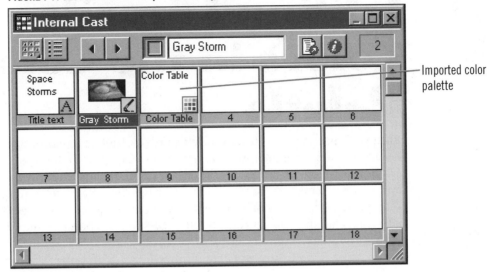

Imported color palette

FIGURE I-8: Imported color palette and images

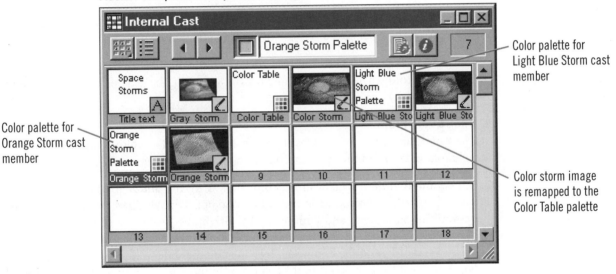

Color palette for Orange Storm cast member

Color palette for Light Blue Storm cast member

Color storm image is remapped to the Color Table palette

Remapping a cast member to a different color palette

After you have imported or created a cast member, you can remap a cast member to a different color palette. You can permanently remap a color palette to a cast member or temporarily remap a color palette to a sprite. Before you permanently remap the colors of a cast member, it is a good idea to make a copy of the cast member. Once you remap the colors of a cast member, you cannot reverse the action. To permanently remap a cast member to a different color palette, select a cast member, click Modify on the menu bar, click Transform Bitmap, click Continue, if necessary, to change a cast member, click the Palette list arrow, click a color palette, click the Remap Colors option button, then click

Transform. If you have a cast member on the Stage that uses a color palette different from the current palette, you can remap or dither the colors in the sprite to the current color palette without transforming it, which only affects the sprite appearance on the Stage, not the cast member itself. Dithering simulates a color not available in the color palette by blending pixels from two available colors. Dithering is often used when a high-quality image (16 bits) is converted to a lower-quality image (8 bits). To remap a sprite on the Stage to the current color palette, select the sprite, then click the Remap Palettes When Needed check box in the Movie tab of the Property Inspector.

Director 8

Director 8

Editing Favorite Colors in the Color Palette

When you open the pop-up color palette, the color mode indicator appears at the top of the menu. Underneath the color mode indicator are 16 larger color box spots reserved to store your favorite colors. You can edit one of the default favorite colors to specify a new favorite color. The favorite colors remain the same even if you change the color palette. You can use any of the 16 color spots to store colors of a corporate logo or a favorite color scheme. The 16 favorite colors only appear on the pop-up color palette; they do not appear in the Color Palettes window.

 Jean edits a favorite color.

1. Click and hold the **Foreground** or **Background color box** on the Tool palette

A pop-up color palette appears, displaying the current color palette. You can select a color, or you can click a command at the bottom of the pop-up color palette to change a color or edit favorite colors.

2. Click **Edit Favorite Colors** at the bottom of the pop-up color palette

The Edit Favorite Colors dialog box appears, as shown in Figure I-9.

3. Click the **first color box** in the first row, if necessary

The Setting color changes to black, and the color value in the text box to the right changes to #000000 (black).

4. Click **Color Picker**

The Color dialog box appears, as shown in Figure I-10. The color matrix box displays the full range of colors in the color spectrum.

5. Click a **color** from the color matrix box, then drag the **slider** to adjust it

The color you select is shown in the Color|Solid box. For Windows, you can enter RGB values or Hue, Saturation, and Luminosity (or Brightness) values to specify a color. You can also change the hue by moving the pointer horizontally, the saturation by moving the pointer vertically, and the luminosity by adjusting the slider at the right of the color matrix box. For Macintosh, click one of the color modes and select a color, using its controls.

You can select RGB values by selecting the RGB Picker at the left of the window, then dragging Red, Green, and Blue sliders, or by entering values to select a color. You can select Hue, Saturation, and Luminosity (or Lightness) values by selecting the HLS Picker, then entering values. The Macintosh also has numerous other choices for selecting a color, including a box of crayons.

6. Click **OK**

The Color dialog box closes.

7. Click **OK**

The Edit Favorite Colors dialog box closes and stores the new favorite color in the first color box on the color palette.

8. Click and hold the **Foreground** or **Background color box** on the Tool palette

A pop-up color palette appears with the new favorite color in the first color box.

9. Click the **Stage** to deselect the color palette

FIGURE I-9: Edit Favorite Colors dialog box

Color identification number

Color box

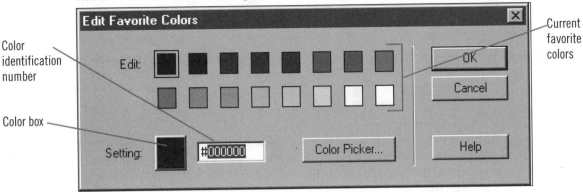

Current favorite colors

FIGURE I-10: Color dialog box

Pointer

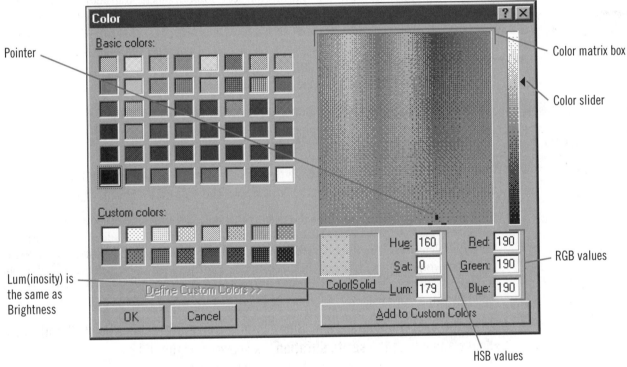

Color matrix box

Color slider

RGB values

Lum(inosity) is the same as Brightness

HSB values

CLUES TO USE

Understanding Hue, Saturation, and Brightness

Like RGB, Hue, Saturation, and Brightness (HSB) is a way to define a color in a color palette. **Hue** is the color created by mixing primary colors (Red, Blue, and Yellow). **Saturation** is a measure of how much white is mixed in with the color. A fully saturated color is vivid; a less saturated color is washed-out pastel. For example, a less saturated black is a shade of gray. **Brightness**, also known as **Luminosity**, is a measure of how much black is mixed with the color. A very bright color contains little or no black. As more black is added, the brightness is reduced, and the color gets darker. If brightness is reduced to zero, then the color remains black, no matter what the values are for Hue or Saturation.

Director 8

Changing Color Palettes During a Movie

When you play a movie in Director, you can change color palettes to display a sequence of cast members using their original color palettes. The color palette is initially set in the Movie tab of the Property Inspector, but the Palette channel in the Score determines which palette is active for a particular frame in a movie. The Palette channel settings in the Score override the palette selection in the Color Palettes window. The Palette channel works similarly to the Tempo channel. Director uses the current color palette set in the Palette channel until a new color palette is set. When you change from one color palette to another in the Palette channel, the change can be abrupt. To smooth the transition between the two color palettes, Director provides a color palette transition to add a fade transition and to control the speed at which the colors change. You can set a smooth palette transition in one frame or make a gradual transition over a series of frames. ✐ Jean changes color palettes in the Palette channel and sets a color palette transition over a frame.

1. Click **frame 1** in the Palette channel in the Score window
   Frame 1 appears selected in the Palette channel.

> **QuickTip**
>
> You can double-click a frame in the Palette channel to open the Frame Properties: Palette dialog box.

2. Click **Modify** on the menu bar, point to **Frame**, then click **Palette**
   The Frame Properties: Palette dialog box appears.

3. Click the **Palette list arrow** ▼, then click **Grayscale**
   The Grayscale color palette appears in the dialog box, as shown in Figure I-11.

4. Click **OK**
   The color palette change is set in the Palette channel. The grayscale palette changes all the colors on the Stage. The Title text cast member color changes to a shade of gray. The shade of gray is determined by the color position on the index palette—in this cast, position 91. To verify the color change, you can click a color box to display the index palette, then drag the mouse to color position 91, as indicated at the top of the pop-up color palette. Release the mouse off the color palette.

5. Drag the **cast members** (Light Blue Storm, Orange Storm, and Color Storm) to the **Score** and adjust the **sprite duration**, as shown in Figure I-12
   When you drag a cast member to the Score, the color palette associated with the cast member is automatically placed in the Palette channel.

6. Double-click **frame 16** in the Palette channel in the Score window
   The Frame Properties: Palette dialog box appears with the Palette Transition option button selected.

7. Click the **Fade to Black option button**, drag the **Rate slider** to **20 fps**, then click **OK**
   The Fade to Black option hides a palette change within a fade transition.

8. Double-click **frame 31** in the Palette channel, click the **Fade to Black option button**, drag the **Rate slider** to **20 fps**, then click **OK**

9. Click the **Rewind button** ◄ on the toolbar, then click the **Play button** ► on the toolbar
   The color palettes change for each storm image. The Space Storms title text is set to an index color. When the color palettes change, the color at the index position number changes, so the title text color changes. The fade to black transition in frame 16 and frame 31 doesn't appear in 16-bit or higher color depth. You'll change the color depth later to view the palette transition.

FIGURE I-11: Frame Properties: Palette dialog box

Color position 91

Drag to change palette transition speed

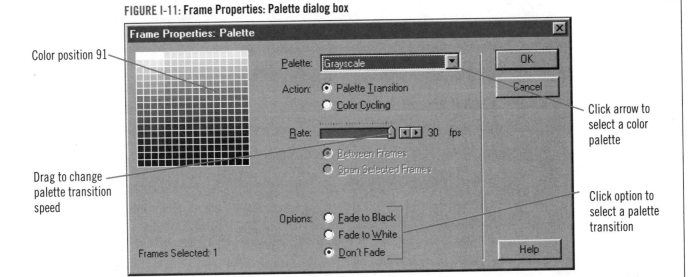

Click arrow to select a color palette

Click option to select a palette transition

FIGURE I-12: Score window with color palettes

Palette channel

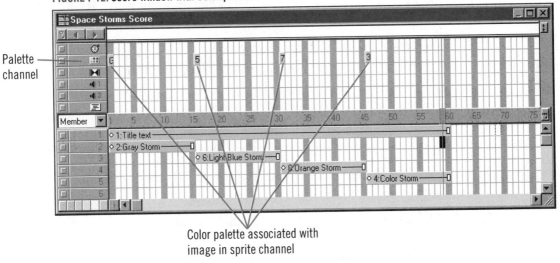

Color palette associated with image in sprite channel

Copying colors to another palette

You can use the Copy and Paste commands in Director to move colors from one palette to another palette or to rearrange colors within the same palette. To move colors from one palette to another palette, double-click a color box to open the Color Palettes window, click the Palettes list arrow, select the color palette you want to use, and select the colors you want to move. You can hold down [Ctrl] (Win) or [Command] (Mac) and click color boxes to select multiple colors not next to each other, or hold down [Shift] and click a start color box and an end color box to select a range of colors. Click Edit on the menu bar, then click Copy Colors. In the Color Palettes window, click the Palettes list arrow, then click a different destination color palette. Click a color box in the palette as the destination for pasting the copied colors. Click Edit on the menu bar, then click Paste into Palette. The moved colors replace the destination color box.

Director 8

Creating a Custom Color Palette

A custom color palette is a set of colors that you create, select, and arrange to meet the color requirements of your movie. You can create a custom color palette by duplicating one of Director's standard color palettes or by selecting an imported color palette and editing, blending, and sorting the colors in the palette. To create a duplicate color palette or select an imported one, you need to open the Color Palettes window. When you select a palette in the Color Palettes window, it does not change the palette for the movie or any frame in the movie. In the Color Palettes window, you can duplicate a color palette, move colors from one palette to another, blend colors to create a gradient, match colors in sprites, reverse the order of colors in a palette, and sort colors in a palette. When you modify a color palette, all the cast members that use the palette change, too. Remember that changing the position of colors in a movie using the indexed palette and 8-bit color depth or less may change the coloring of cast members that are based on that particular palette. ✐ Jean creates a custom palette for the Space Storms movie.

1. Click **Window** on the menu bar, then click **Color Palettes**
   The Color Palettes window opens, as shown in Figure I-13.

QuickTip

To duplicate a color palette in the Color Palettes window, click Edit on the menu bar, click Duplicate, type a palette name, then click OK.

2. Click the **Palette list arrow** ▾, then click **Color Table Internal**, if necessary
   The Color Table Internal color palette becomes the current color palette.

3. Click the **Arrow Tool button** ▶, click **color box 64** (first color box in row 3), hold down [Shift], then click **color box 159** (last color box in row 5)
   A range of colors is selected. You can hold down [Ctrl] (Win) or [Command] (Mac) and click individual colors (not in a contiguous range).

4. Click the **Blend button** ▦ in the Color Palettes window
   The palette blends from the first selected color to the destination color, as shown in Figure I-14.

QuickTip

To quickly open the Color Palettes window, double-click a color box on the Tool palette or in the Property Inspector.

5. Click the **Reverse Sequence button** ▦ in the Color Palettes window
   The selected range of colors is reversed.

6. Click the **Sort button** ▦ in the Color Palettes window
   The Sort Colors dialog box appears with options to sort the selected range of colors by hue, saturation, or brightness. The default option is hue.

7. Click the **Brightness option button**, then click **Sort**
   The selected range of colors is sorted by brightness.

8. Click the **Close button** in the Color Palettes window
   The Color Palettes window closes.

FIGURE I-13: Color Palettes window

Click arrow to select
a color palette

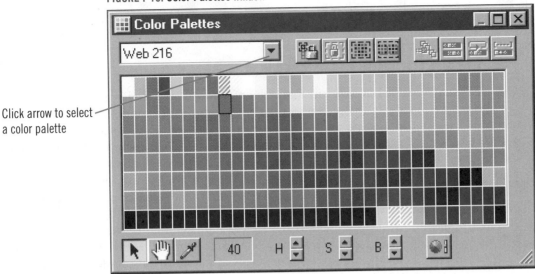

FIGURE I-14: Color Palettes with blended colors

Click button to
blend colors

Blended colors

Click button to
sort colors

Click button to
reverse color
sequence

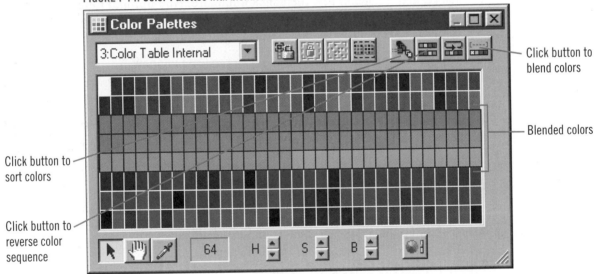

Matching colors in sprites

You can use the Eyedropper tool in the Color Palettes window to find a color box to match any color in any cast member on the Stage. To match colors in sprites, display the sprite on the Stage with the color you want to match, double-click a color box to open the Color Palettes window, click the Eyedropper tool button ✐, drag any palette color box to the color on the Stage (the arrow pointer changes to ✐) that you want to pick up. When you release the mouse button, Director selects the color in the color palette that is closest to the one you selected with ✐.

Director 8

Creating an Optimal Color Palette

You can create an optimal color palette that includes all the colors found in each cast member in the movie. An optimal color palette allows you to play a movie with consistent color in a projector or over the Web, using one common color palette. To create an optimal color palette, you need to create a new palette, find the colors used in each cast member in the movie, and copy the used colors to the new palette. There are several stages in creating an optimal palette. In the first stage, you select a cast member that uses only a small number of colors in its palette, open the Color Palettes window, and make a duplicate color palette. In the second stage, you use the Select Used Colors button and the Invert Selection button to find the colors used in the selected cast member. In the third stage, you use the Copy Colors and Paste Into Palette commands on the Edit menu to add the used colors to the new palette. You repeat the second and third stages for each cast member in the movie. To complete the process, you use the Transform Bitmap command on the Modify menu to remap each cast member to the new optimal palette. ✐ Jean completes the first three stages of the process to create an optimal color palette.

Steps 1 2 3 4

QuickTip

QuickTip

To delete a color palette, click the palette in the Cast window, then press [Delete].

1. **Double-click** the **Orange Storm Palette cast member** in the Cast window
   The Color Palettes window opens, displaying the Orange Storm Palette.

2. **Click Edit** on the menu bar, then click **Duplicate**, type **Optimal Palette**, then click **OK**
   The Orange Storm Palette is copied, and the new palette name appears in the Palette list, and the Optimal Palette cast member appears in the Cast window.

3. **Click** the **Orange Storm cast member** in the Cast window
   The Orange Storm cast member (the one associated with the Orange Storm Palette) is selected in the Cast window.

4. **Click** the **Color Palettes window title bar** to activate the window, click the **Select Used Colors button** ▦, then click **Select** in the Select Colors Used in Bitmap dialog box
   The colors used in the cast member are selected in the color palette.

5. **Click** the **Invert Selection button** ▦
   The colors used in the cast member are displayed in the color palette, as shown in Figure I-15.

QuickTip

To move one or more colors in the Color Palettes window, click the Hand tool button 🖐, then drag a color to a new location in the color palette. All selected colors are rearranged in continuous order.

6. **Click Edit** on the menu bar, then click **Copy Colors**
   Director copies the selected colors to the Clipboard.

7. **Click** the **second color box** in the first row of the Color Palettes window, click **Edit** on the menu bar, then click **Paste into Palette**
   The colors used in the cast member are pasted into the beginning of the color palette, as shown in Figure I-16. If you wanted to complete the process, you would select each color palette in the Color Palettes window and its associated cast member in the Cast window, find and copy the used colors, select the optimal palette, and paste in the used colors to complete the optimal color palette for this movie.

8. **Click** the **Close button** in the Color Palettes window
   The Color Palettes window closes.

FIGURE I-15: Color Palettes window with used colors selected

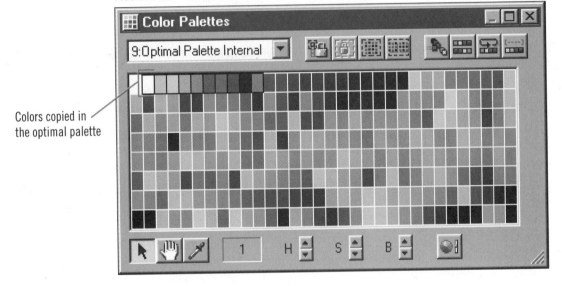

Optimal color palette

A color used in the image

FIGURE I-16: Color Palettes window with colors copied

Colors copied in the optimal palette

Reserving colors in a color palette

Sometimes you want to make sure a certain color stays in a color palette. You can reserve one or more colors in a color palette to make sure the colors remain the same after you remap them. To reserve one or more colors in a color palette, double-click a color box to open the Color Palettes window, click the Palettes list arrow, select a color palette, press and hold [Ctrl] (Win) or [Option] (Mac), click the colors you want to reserve, click the Reserve Selected Colors button ▣, click the Selected Colors option button, then click Reserve. The reserved colors appear with diagonal lines on top of them. To unreserve colors, select the reserved colors in a color palette, click the Reserve Selected Colors button ▣, click the No Colors option button, then click Reserve. To select all the reserved colors in a color palette, you can click the Select Reserved Colors button ▣.

Director 8

Cycling Colors in a Color Palette

Color cycling is a special color palette effect that changes the appearance of a display by rapidly showing each color from a range of colors in a sequence. Color cycling achieves an animation-style effect by rotating a selected range of colors in a palette over time. Color cycling is handy for effects such as fire and explosions, in which the color pulses through a series of reds, yellows, and oranges. You can set color cycling to repeat, to stop after going through all the colors, or to cycle in reverse once it completes a cycle. You apply color cycling to a selected range of colors in a single frame or over a series of frames. Within those frames, the selected colors cycle in any cast member that has colors. Color cycling presently works only when your computer's color depth is set to 8 bit, or 256 colors. Applying color effects to greater quantities of color requires computer processing that would slow the computer down to a crawl. If your monitor isn't set to 8 bit, the color effects are ignored during movie playback. ⬛︎ Jean creates a cycle animation effect to simulate a storm.

1. Double-click **frame 46** in the Palette channel in the Score window
   The Frame Properties: Palette dialog box appears.

2. Click the **Color Cycling option button**
   Additional color cycling options appear at the bottom of the dialog box. The Loop option is selected by default. This option loops through the cycled colors. You also have the option to loop the cycled colors in reverse with the Auto Reverse option.

QuickTip

To change the order of the colors in the cycle, double-click a color box to open the Color Palettes window, select the colors in the color cycle, then click the Cycle button 🔳 to move the colors one at a time.

3. Select the **range of colors** to cycle (the first color box in row 5 to the last color box in row 10), shown in Figure I-17
   The selected colors are cycled in the image when the movie is played.

4. Select the **current value** in the Cycles box, type **3**, then click **OK**
   This option cycles through the selected colors the number of times set in the Cycles box. The color cycling is applied to the selected frames that are associated with the colors, as shown in Figure I-18.

5. Click the **Stage**, click the **Movie tab** of the Property Inspector, change the **color palette** to System – Win (Win) or **System – Mac** (Mac), then click the **Save button** 💾 on the toolbar
   Director saves the movie. If you play the movie now, the color cycling and palette transitions will not display. You need to set your computer to 256 colors (8 bit) to view color cycling and palette transitions.

Trouble?

If the Office Shortcut Bar begins to close and attempts to reopen, click the Office Shortcut Bar menu, then click Exit to close it until the next computer session (Win).

6. Open the **Control Panel**, open the **Settings tab** of the **Display Properties dialog box** (Win) or **Monitors** (Mac), and change the **Colors Palette** settings to **256 colors**
   For specific steps, see the topic "Changing Movie Color Depth," earlier in this lesson.

7. Switch back to Director, click the **Rewind button** ⏮ on the toolbar, then click the **Play button** ▶ on the toolbar
   The change to 256 colors may cause the Director program window to change to a two-color display (black and white). The palette you choose might affect everything that is displayed on the screen, including the interface, so you might find it difficult to see what you're doing in Director.

8. Click **File** on the menu bar, then click **Exit** (Win) or **Quit** (Mac)
   Director closes.

9. Open the Control Panel, open the Settings tab of the Display Properties dialog box (Win) or Monitors (Mac), and change the Color palette settings to its original state

FIGURE I-17: Color cycling in the Frame Properties dialog box

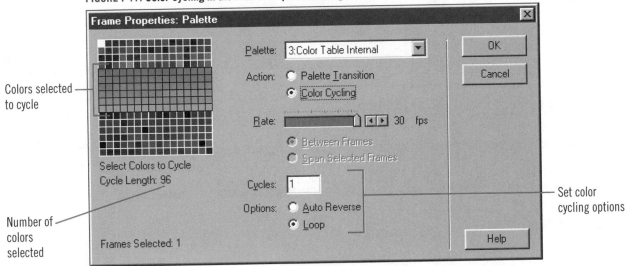

Colors selected to cycle

Select Colors to Cycle
Cycle Length: 96

Number of colors selected

Frames Selected: 1

Set color cycling options

FIGURE I-18: The Stage and Score with color cycling

Color cycling plays here

Color cycling over a series of frames

You can specify the frames in which you want to add color cycling. The Between Frames option and the Span Selected Frames option allow you to control how the color cycling takes place in the selected frames. The Between Frames option cycles through the selected colors once for each of the selected frames. The Span Selected Frames option cycles through the selected colors only once, stretching the single color cycle throughout the selected frames. To use these options, you drag to select the frames (four or more) in the Palette channel in which you want to apply color cycling, click Modify on the menu bar, point to Frame, then click Palette.

Practice

► Concepts Review

Label each of the elements of the screen shown in Figure I-19.

FIGURE I-19

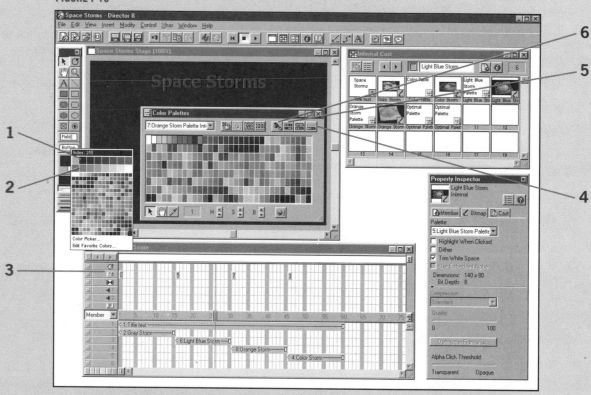

Match each of the terms with the statement that describes its function.

7. Color depth	a. The measure of the number of colors that an image can contain
8. Hue	b. The color created by mixing primary colors
9. Color mode	c. A way to identify a set of colors
10. Saturation	d. A set of colors
11. Brightness	e. The result of mixing black with a color
12. Color palette	f. The result of mixing white with a color

Select the best answer from the following list of choices.

13. What color mode works best in 8 bit or less?
   a. HSB
   c. Palette index
   b. RGB
   d. None of the above

14. Which bit depth contains 256 colors?
   a. 4
   c. 16
   b. 8
   d. 32

15. **Which color mode identifies color by a hexadecimal value?**
    a. RGB
    b. Palette index
    c. HSB
    d. None of the above
16. **Which color characteristic is created by mixing in white?**
    a. Hue
    b. Saturation
    c. Brightness
    d. Luminosity
17. **Which color characteristic is created by mixing primary colors?**
    a. Hue
    b. Saturation
    c. Brightness
    d. Luminosity
18. **Which is NOT a button in the Color Palettes window?**
    a. Blend
    b. Copy Colors
    c. Reverse Sequence
    d. Sort
19. **Which is NOT a color palette transition option?**
    a. Fade to Black
    b. Fade to White
    c. Fade to Color
    d. Don't Fade
20. **Which computer bit depth is necessary to display color cycling?**
    a. 8
    b. 16
    c. 32
    d. None of the above

▶ Skills Review

1. **Understand color in Director.**
   a. Define and describe color depth.
   b. List and describe the two basic color modes.
   c. List and describe the color differences between Macintosh and Windows.
2. **Change movie color depth.**
   a. Open the Control Panel on the computer.
   b. Change the color setting to High Color (16-bit) (Win) or Thousands (Mac).
   c. Close the Control Panel.
3. **View and change a color palette.**
   a. Start Director, open the file **MD I-2** from the drive and folder where your Project Files are located.
   b. Save the file as *Color Meters* in the drive and folder where your Project Files are located.
   c. Change the color palette for the movie to Web 216 in the Movie tab of the Property Inspector.
   d. Change the color mode to Palette Index.
4. **Import a color palette.**
   a. Import the Color Meter Table.act (Win) or Color Meter Tablem (Mac) color palette file from the Media SR folder in the drive and folder where your Project Files are located.
   b. Import the Color Meter.gif image file with the Bitmap Image format and the Remap option with the Color Meter Table from the Media SR folder in the drive and folder where your Project Files are located.
   c. Make three copies of the Color Meter cast member and paste them in positions 4 through 6 in the Cast window. (*Hint*: Use the Copy Cast Members and Paste Cast Members commands on the Edit menu.)
   d. Move cast member 3 to channel 2 in frames 1 to 15; move cast member 4 to channel 3 in frames 16 to 30; move cast member 5 to channel 4 in frames 31 to 45; and move cast member 6 to channel 5 in frames 46 to 60.
   e. Change the color palette for cast member 4 to Rainbow; change the color palette for cast member 5 to Vivid; and change the color palette for cast member 6 to Web 216. (*Hint*: Use the Property Inspector to make the color change.)

5. Edit favorite colors in a color palette.

  a. Open the Edit Favorite Colors dialog box and select the second color position.

  b. Select a new color from the Color Picker.

6. Change color palettes during a movie.

  a. Add the Rainbow color palette to frame 16; add the Vivid color palette to frame 31; and add the Web 216 color palette to frame 46.

  b. Add the palette transition duration of 20 frames per second to each color palette (except the one in frame 1).

  c. Add the Fade to Black palette transition to each color palette (except the one in frame 1).

7. Create a custom color palette.

  a. Open the Color Palettes window, then select the Color Meter Table color palette.

  b. Select the color boxes in the first two rows.

  c. Blend the selected colors, then reverse the selected colors.

  d. Cycle the selected colors 5 positions. (*Hint*: Use the Cycle button 5 times.)

  e. Close the Color Palettes window.

8. Create an optimal color palette.

  a. Open the Color Palettes window and select the Web 216 color palette.

  b. Duplicate the color palette as Optimal Palette.

  c. Select cast member 6 in the Cast window.

  d. Activate the Color Palettes window.

  e. Select the used colors in the palette and invert the selection.

  f. Copy and paste the selected colors in color box 2.

  g. Close the Color Palettes window.

9. Cycle colors in a color palette.

  a. Double-click frame 46 in the Palette channel and select the color cycling option.

  b. Select the first three rows of colors to cycle and set the number of cycles to 2.

  c. Select the option to automatically reverse the color cycling.

  d. Open the Control Panel and set the color setting to 256 colors.

  e. Play the movie to display the color cycling and the palette transitions.

  f. Change the movie color palette in the Movie tab of the Property Inspector to System – Win or System – Mac.

  g. Save the movie and exit Director.

  h. Open the Control Panel and restore the color settings to its original state.

▶ Independent Challenges

1. You are an art dealer in New York City at SoHo Art Studios. You have discovered a talented contemporary artist. The studio is holding an open house and you want to create a presentation of the artist's work to promote the event. You use Director to create a slide show of paintings, using the color palettes associated with the paintings.

  To complete this independent challenge:

  a. Connect to the Internet and go to www.course.com. Navigate to the page for this book, click the link for the Student Online Companion, then click the link for this unit.

  b. Search for two or three photographs of art and download them to the drive and folder where your Project Files are located.

  c. Start Director and save the movie as *SoHo Art Studio* in the drive and folder where your Project Files are located.

  d. Create a text cast member with the text **SoHo Art Studios**, and drag it to the top of the Stage.

  e. Create a text cast member with *your name*, and drag it below the SoHo Art Studio text on the Stage.

  f. Import the art photographs and their associated color palettes into Director.

  g. Add the art cast members to the Stage to display them one at a time.

  h. Play and save the movie, then exit Director.

2. You have found a box of old black and white photographs in the attic. Your family is planning a reunion next year, and you want to create a movie with the photographs for the event. You use Director to create a slide show of black and white photographs, using a grayscale color palette and transitions.

To complete this independent challenge:

a. Connect to the Internet and go to www.course.com. Navigate to the page for this book, click the link for the Student Online Companion, then click the link for this unit.

b. Search for two or three black and white photographs and download them to the drive and folder where your Project Files are located.

c. Start Director and save the movie as *Family Reunion* in the drive and folder where your Project Files are located.

d. Create a text cast member with the text **Family Reunion**, and drag it to the top of the Stage.

e. Import the black and white photographs and remap the color palettes to Grayscale into Director.

f. Add the black and white cast members to the Stage to display them one at a time.

g. Add Fade to Black transitions between each photograph and the next.

h. Play and save the movie, then exit Director.

3. You are an instructional designer and trainer for the Broken Ridge Regional Fire Department. You want to create a fire animation for a training movie on fighting fires in the wild. You use Director to create a fire animation using color cycling.

To complete this independent challenge:

a. Change the computer color depth to 8 bit. (*Hint*: Write down the original color depth setting.)

b. Connect to the Internet and go to www.course.com. Navigate to the page for this book, click the link for the Student Online Companion, then click the link for this unit.

c. Search for a photograph of fire and download it to the drive and folder where your Project Files are located.

d. Start Director and save the movie as *Fire Training* in the drive and folder where your Project Files are located.

e. Create a text cast member with the text **Broken Ridge Regional Fire Department**, and drag it to the top of the Stage.

f. Import the photograph of fire into Director in 8 bit.

g. Add the fire cast member to the Stage.

h. Create a color cycle that loops twice, using the colors for the flame.

i. Play and save the movie, then exit Director.

j. Set the computer color depth to its original settings.

4. You are the owner of Built to Last, a custom furniture company. You have been building custom furniture for over 25 years and want to create a furniture catalog with examples of your work. You use Director to create a slide show of furniture, using the color palettes associated with the furniture images, and then create an optimal color palette for the movie.

To complete this independent challenge:

a. Connect to the Internet and go to www.course.com. Navigate to the page for this book, click the link for the Student Online Companion, then click the link for this unit.

b. Search for two or three photographs of furniture and download them to the drive and folder where your Project Files are located.

c. Start Director and save the movie as *Furniture* in the drive and folder where your Project Files are located.

d. Create a text cast member with the text **Built to Last Furniture**, and drag it to the top of the Stage.

e. Import the furniture photographs and their associated color palettes into Director.

f. Add the art cast members to the Stage to display them one at a time.

g. Create an optimal color palette for the movie (the first three stages, as shown in the unit).

h. Play and save the movie, then exit Director.

▶ Visual Workshop

Recreate the screen shown in Figure I-20. Print the screen. (For Windows, use the Windows Paint program. Press the Print Screen key to make a copy of the screen, start the Paint program by clicking Start, pointing to Programs, pointing to Accessories, then clicking Paint; click Edit on the menu bar, click Paste to paste the screen into Paint, then click Yes to paste the large image if necessary. Click File on the menu bar, click Print, click Print or OK in the dialog box, then exit Paint. For the Macintosh, use the SimpleText program. Hold and press the Command, Shift, and 3 keys to make a copy of the screen, double-click the document Picture 1 located on your hard drive, click File on the menu bar, click Print, then click Print in the dialog box. *Note*: When you create a new document with a copy of the screen, and a document Picture 1 already exists, the Macintosh names the new document Picture 2.)

FIGURE I-20

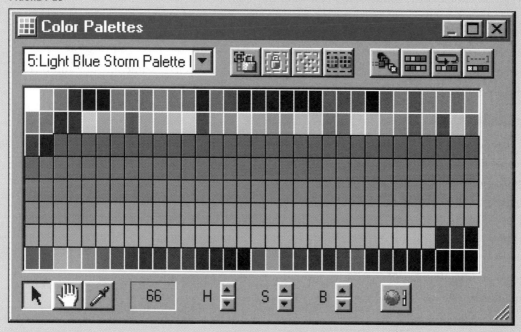

Creating
Animation

Objectives

► **Understand animation**
► **Create animation using tweening**
► **Change tweenable sprite properties**
► **Create a circular animation**
► **Create animation using step recording**
► **Create animation using real-time recording**
► **Use onion skinning**
► **Animate with a series of cast members**
► **Create a film loop**

Creating animation in Director is the process of creating movement. Director provides several ways to create animation: tweening, step recording, real-time recording, and sequencing cast members. First, you'll learn about the different ways to create animation in Director. Then, you'll learn how to create animation using tweening, step recording, and real-time recording. Finally, you'll learn how to create and animate a series of cast members, and create a film loop. Jean creates an animation of the earth orbiting around the sun.

Understanding Animation

Animation is the process of creating movement in Director. You can create animation by moving an object across the Stage, as shown in Figure J-1, or by changing its attributes, such as its size, color, or angle, over a series of frames, as shown in Figure J-2. You can create animation in Director using one of four main techniques: tweening, real-time recording, step recording, and frame animation. An important part of animation in Director involves the use of keyframes. A keyframe contains specific information about a sprite, such as its position on the Stage, size, background or foreground color, or rotation or skew angle. To create an animation effect in Director, you use one of the four main animation techniques to change the keyframe information about a sprite over a series of frames. The animation occurs when the playback head moves between the keyframes in the Score, displaying the attribute changes in the sprite. ✐ Jean takes some time to familiarize herself with the use of animation in Director.

Understanding animation techniques:

 Tweening is a quick way to animate a sprite. The process involves two or more keyframes. These keyframes define a sprite in two different locations on the Stage, or with different sets of attributes in the two keyframes. The sprite attributes can include size, color, rotation, and other effects applied to change the appearance of the cast member or its location on the Stage. Director fills in the difference between the two frames to create animation over the length of the sprite in the Score.

 Step Recording is real-time recording of one frame at a time. The process involves setting up the recording attributes, moving the playback head forward one frame, changing the sprite attributes, and moving the playback head forward again one frame.

 Real-Time Recording records the movement of a cast member on the Stage. The process involves setting up the recording attributes and manually dragging a cast member around the Stage. Director records the motions and saves them as keyframes within the sprite in the Score.

 Frame-by-Frame Animation is a series of cast members placed in the Score one frame at a time. The process involves altering cast members slightly from frame to frame to build an animated sequence, as shown in Figure J-3. When the series of frames is played back, it looks like movement. As the playback head moves through each frame, a slightly different cast member is displayed on the Stage. This technique has been used for years by Walt Disney Studios to create animation for cartoons.

FIGURE J-1: Animating by sprite position

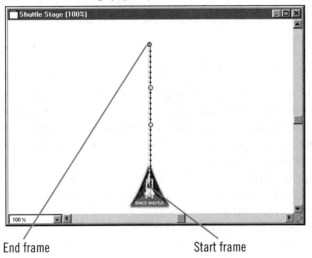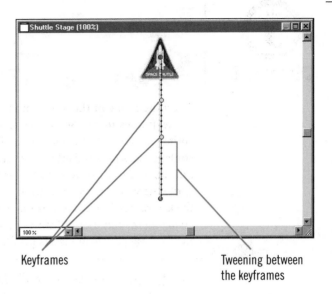

End frame   Start frame   Keyframes   Tweening between the keyframes

FIGURE J-2: Animating by sprite properties

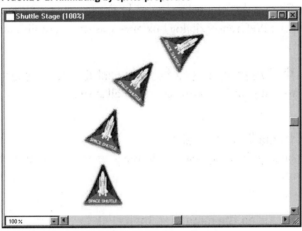

FIGURE J-3: Animating with a series of cast members

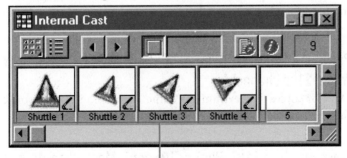

Series of cast members

Creating Animation Using Tweening

Tweening is one of the most common types of animation. To tween the animation, you need to set keyframes in the Score that correspond to the major change points where you want the sprite's movement to begin and end on the Stage. Tweening occurs between two keyframes that contain the before and after property settings of a sprite. The first frame of a sprite is a keyframe, but the end of a sprite is not a keyframe. However, you can place a keyframe at the end of a sprite. As you place keyframes in the sprite, Director automatically tweens the sprites between the keyframes. You can set as many keyframes within a sprite as there are frames in its span. By changing the number of frames between keyframes, you can control the smoothness of the animation. ✐ Jean inserts keyframes in the Score to create an animation.

Steps 1234

1. Start **Director**, open the file **MD J-1** from the drive and folder where your Project Files are located, then save it as **Earth Orbit**
Director opens, displaying the movie. Your initial settings in Director can vary, depending on previous usage.

2. Click **File** on the menu bar, point to **Preferences**, then click **Sprite**
The Sprite Preferences dialog box opens, as shown in Figure J-4.

3. Click the **Tweening check box** to select it, if necesssary, then click **OK**
The Tweening option is turned on for all sprites in Director.

4. Click **frame 7** in channel 1
The playback head appears at frame 7 of the Score and the Space sprite in channel 1 is selected.

5. Click **Insert** on the menu bar, then click **Keyframe**
Director places a keyframe indicator in the sprite. A keyframe is represented by a circle within a sprite in the Score. Selecting the keyframe of the sprite tells Director you want to make a change to the sprite in this frame.

6. Click **frame 14** in channel 1, click **Insert** on the menu bar, then click **Keyframe**
A keyframe is selected in the Score to indicate the endpoint for the animation. Selecting frame 14 for a keyframe makes the animation take place in frames 1 through 14.

7. Press and hold **[Alt]** (Win) or **[Option]** (Mac), then drag **frame 14** in channel 1 to **frame 21** in channel 1
Director copies the keyframe in frame 14 to frame 21. The sprite properties associated with the keyframe in 14 are also copied to frame 21.

8. Press and hold **[Alt]** (Win) or **[Option]** (Mac), then drag **frame 21** in channel 1 to **frame 28** in channel 1
Director copies the keyframe in frame 21 to frame 28. The keyframe indicators in the sprite appear, as shown in Figure J-5.

FIGURE J-4: Sprite Preferences dialog box

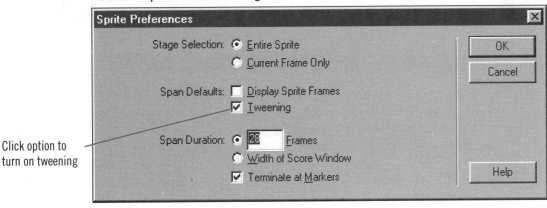

Click option to
turn on tweening

FIGURE J-5: Keyframes in a sprite

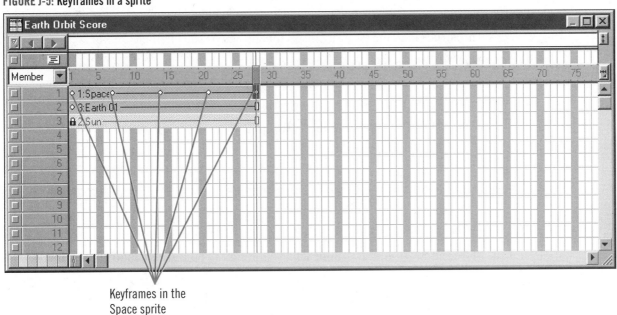

Keyframes in the
Space sprite

Repositioning keyframes in the Score

Once you insert a keyframe in the Score, you can reposition it at any time. You can reposition a keyframe in the Score by dragging it to another frame in the channel. When you reposition a keyframe, it changes the number of frames between the keyframes and modifies the animation. When you drag the start or end keyframe of a sprite to shorten or lengthen its span, all keyframes within the sprite move proportionately closer or farther apart. If you want to extend the span of a sprite without moving the keyframes, you can hold down [Ctrl] (Win) or [Command] (Mac) while you drag the start or end frame of a sprite.

Changing Tweenable Sprite Properties

After you create and position all the keyframes that you will need within a sprite, you adjust the sprite's initial properties for the tween. You select the first keyframe (in most cases, the first frame) and change one or more tweenable sprite properties, such as position, size, background and foreground color, ink, blend, skew, and rotation. You can change tweenable sprite properties directly on the Stage, by using the Sprite tab in the Property Inspector, or by using the Sprite toolbar in the Score. After you adjust the tweenable sprite properties for the first keyframe, select the next keyframe within the sprite and change its tweenable properties. Director generates all the frames between this keyframe and the first one. If you need to refine tweening in a sprite, you can insert additional keyframes and change properties to create a smoother path, or add frames between keyframes to add a gradual transition. You can tween one or more sprite properties at the same time, using the Sprite Tweening dialog box. ✒ Jean changes tweenable properties of the Space sprite to create an animation.

Steps

1. **Click the keyframe in frame 1 in channel 1**
   The keyframe in frame 1 of the Space sprite is selected. A sprite's first frame is a keyframe.

2. **Click the Stage window, then click the Sprite tab in the Property Inspector**
   The Sprite tab in the Property Inspector appears, as shown in Figure J-6.

3. **Click the Blend list arrow ▾, then click 10**
   The blend of the transparent background for the Space sprite is changed to 10%, almost transparent.

4. **Click the keyframe in frame 7 in channel 1, click the Blend list arrow ▾, then click 30**
   The Space sprite transparency blend percentage is changed to 30%.

5. **Click the keyframe in frame 14 in channel 1, click the Blend list arrow ▾, then click 60**
   The Space sprite transparency blend percentage is changed to 60%.

6. **Click the keyframe in frame 21 in channel 1, click the Blend list arrow ▾, then click 80**
   The Space sprite transparency blend percentage is changed to 80%.

7. **Click Modify on the menu bar, point to Sprite, then click Tweening**
   The Sprite Tweening dialog box appears, as shown in Figure J-7. In order for tweening to work, you need to make sure the properties you want tweened are selected. In this case, the Blend check box is selected by default.

8. **Click OK, then click the Lock button 🔒 in the Sprite tab of the Property Inspector**
   The Space background sprite is locked to make sure it doesn't move.

Trouble?

If the movie loops, click Control on the menu bar, click Control Panel, then click Loop Playback to deselect it.

9. **Click the Rewind button ⏮ on the toolbar, then click the Play button ▶ on the toolbar**
   The movie plays the Space animation, showing the background going from black to a star field.

FIGURE J-6: Tweenable sprite properties

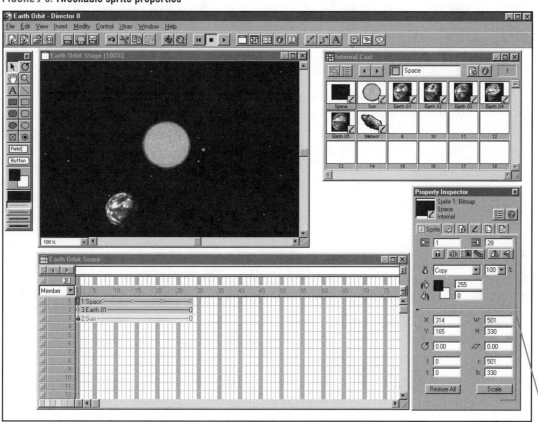

Tweenable sprite properties

FIGURE J-7: Sprite Tweening dialog box

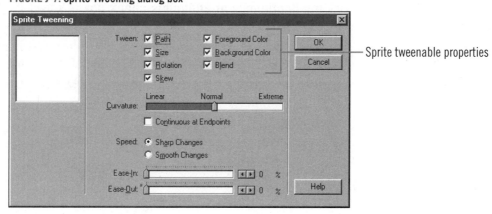

Sprite tweenable properties

Creating effects using tweenable properties

You can create special effects by changing the tweenable sprite properties. You can create the illusion of a sprite rotating in 3D by changing its skew angle by 90 degrees or more, or create a fade out or fade in effect by changing the blend property of a sprite from a high value to a low value (fade out), or from a low value to a high value (fade in). You can also create a zoom out or zoom in effect by changing the size of a sprite from large to small (zoom out) or from small to large (zoom in).

Director 8

Director 8

Creating a Circular Animation

When a sprite uses three or more keyframes, you can make the path between them follow a curve rather than a straight line. You can adjust the path by dragging any keyframe in the path or by using the Curvature slider in the Sprite Tweening dialog box. When you tween a sprite along any path, you can add a touch of realism by using the Ease-In and Ease-Out sliders in the Sprite Tweening dialog box to control the speed of a sprite at the beginning or end. A high ease-in percentage increases the time it takes for a sprite to speed up, whereas a high Ease-Out percentage increases the time it takes to slow down. The Ease-In slider controls the beginning speed, while the Ease-Out slider controls the ending speed. If the speed changes in a path are too abrupt, you can insert more frames between the keyframes and select the Smooth Changes option in the Sprite Tweening dialog box. Jean creates an elliptical animation to orbit the earth around the sun.

Trouble?

If the path is not displayed, click View on the menu bar, point to Sprite Overlay, then click Show Paths.

1. Click **frame 7** in channel 2, click **Insert** on the menu bar, click **Keyframe**, then drag the **Earth 01 sprite** to **point A** on the Stage, as shown in Figure J-8

   Director places a keyframe indicator in the sprite. A keyframe is represented by a circle within a sprite in the Score.

2. Click **frame 14** in channel 2, click **Insert** on the menu bar, click **Keyframe**, then drag the **Earth 01 sprite** to **point B** on the Stage, as shown in Figure J-8

3. Click **frame 21** in channel 2, click **Insert** on the menu bar, click **Keyframe**, then drag the **Earth 01 sprite** to **point C** on the Stage shown in Figure J-8

4. Click **Modify** on the menu bar, point to **Sprite**, then click **Tweening**

   The Sprite Tweening dialog box appears.

QuickTip

To make the sprite's path curve between more points, hold down [Alt] (Win) or [Option] (Mac) and drag a keyframe on the Stage.

5. Click the **Continuous at Endpoints check box** to select it, then drag the **Curvature slider** a little to the right of "Normal" (approximately ¼")

   The Continuous at Endpoints option causes the sprite in the animation to begin and end at the same point. The slider changes the curvature of the animation path. A preview of the curvature change appears in the preview box in the upper-left corner of the dialog box, as shown in Figure J-9.

6. Drag the **Ease-Out slider** to **50%**

   A 50% Ease-Out setting makes the sprite take a little time to slow down, to add the illusion of perspective to an orbit.

7. Click **OK**

   The Earth 01 sprite appears on the Stage with the path in a more elliptical shape. If the animation path is still not smooth, you can adjust individual keyframes on the Stage to adjust the path.

Trouble?

If you click or drag a tweening point (the smaller circles) in the path instead of a keyframe, the sprite is deselected. Click the sprite again in the Score.

8. Drag the **keyframes** (the larger circles) within the sprite on the Stage to fine-tune the elliptical path, as shown in Figure J-10

   When you position the arrow pointer over a keyframe, it changes to an alternate color to indicate that you can adjust the point in the animation path. The path becomes more elliptical.

9. Click the **Rewind button** on the toolbar, then click the **Play button** on the toolbar

   The movie plays the animation on the Stage.

FIGURE J-8: **Creating elliptical animation**

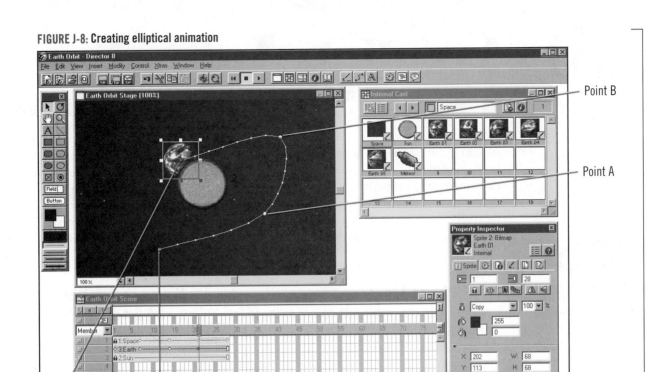

Point B

Point A

Point C; red is
the end frame

Green is the
start frame

FIGURE J-9: **Sprite Tweening dialog box with curvature preview**

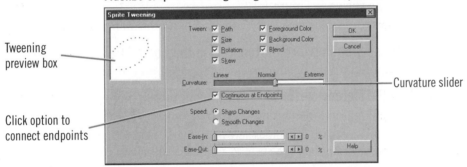

Tweening
preview box

Curvature slider

Click option to
connect endpoints

FIGURE J-10: **Elliptical animation path**

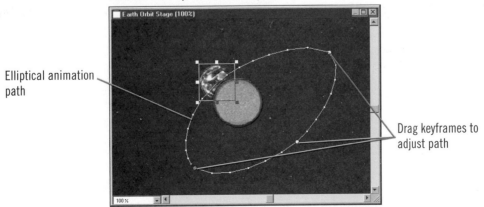

Elliptical animation
path

Drag keyframes to
adjust path

Director 8

Creating Animation Using Step Recording

Unlike tweening, in which Director creates animation frames for you, step recording is an animation technique in which you manually animate a sprite one frame at a time. You record the position of a sprite in a frame, step forward to the next frame, move the sprite to its new position or change sprite properties, step forward to the next frame, and so on, until you've completed the animation. Step recording is especially useful for creating complex animation in which you need precise, frame-by-frame control of the sprite animation. You can also use step recording to redefine a tweened sprite animation. ✐ Jean creates an animation using step recording.

Steps

QuickTip

You can select more than one sprite for step recording. When you do, the sprites animate together.

1. Click **frame 1** in channel 4 in the Score, drag the **Meteor cast member** in the Cast window to the upper-left corner of the Stage, click the **Ink list arrow** ▼ on the Sprite tab in the Property Inspector, then click **Background Transparent**
   The Meteor cast member appears on the Stage with a transparent background.

2. Click **Window** on the menu bar, then click **Control Panel**
   The Control Panel appears.

3. Click **Control** on the menu bar, then click **Step Recording**
   An indicator appears next to the selected sprite in the Score, as shown in Figure J-11.

4. Click the **Step Forward button** ⏭ in the Control Panel
   Director records the previous frame in the Score and advances to the next frame. The Earth 01 sprite also moves step by step along its elliptical path.

5. Drag the **Meteor sprite** (not the colored dot in the center) slightly down and to the right, as shown in Figure J-12
   The animation path appears from the sprite starting point to the new point.

QuickTip

To delete a step recording point, click the keyframe in the Score, then press [Delete].

6. Click the **Step Forward button** ⏭ in the Control Panel
   Director records the previous frame in the Score and advances to the next frame.

7. Drag the **Meteor sprite** to the next point on the Stage, then continue step recording until you match the positions shown in Figure J-13
   The animation path continues across the Stage. The last step is at frame 9. If necessary, you can drag keyframes on the Stage to adjust the animation path.

QuickTip

To move the entire animation path, drag the cast member on the Stage associated with the sprite animation.

8. Click **Control** on the menu bar, then click **Step Recording**
   Step Recording is turned off.

9. Click the **Rewind button** ⏮ on the toolbar, then click the **Play button** ▶ on the toolbar
   The movie plays the animation on the Stage. You will complete the path of the Meteor sprite in the next lesson.

FIGURE J-11: **Step recording an animation**

Step recording selection

Step recording indicator

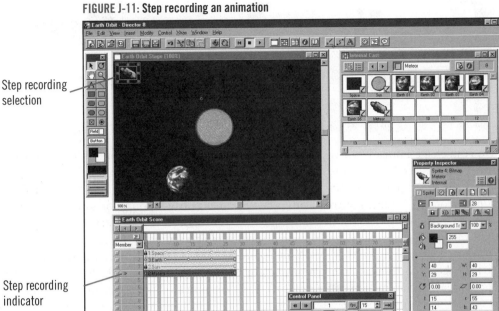

FIGURE J-12: **First step recording**

Starting point

First step recording

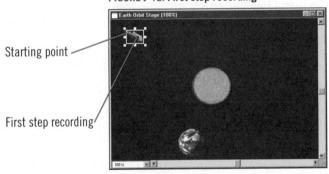

FIGURE J-13: **Completed step recording**

Continue to record steps to this point

Complete the last step at frame 9

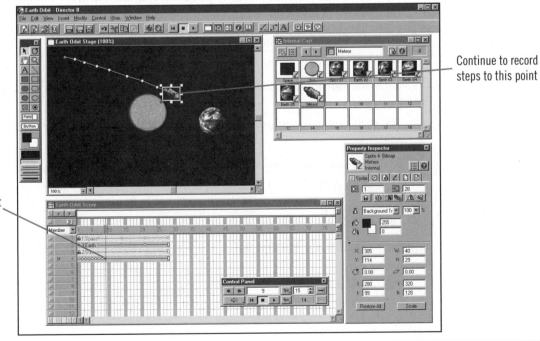

Director 8

Unit J
Director 8

Creating Animation Using Real-Time Recording

You can create animation by recording the movement of a sprite in real time as you drag it across the Stage. The real-time recording technique is especially useful for simulating the movement of a pointer, or for quickly creating a complex motion for later refinement. The disadvantage of real-time recording is difficulty controlling the movement of the mouse for intricate animation. If real-time recording seems to be too sensitive for your mouse, you can slow the recording tempo to fix the problem. In the Control Panel, select the tempo setting in the Tempo display, then type a slower tempo rate. Start the real-time recording, drag selected sprites around the Stage, then release the mouse button to stop recording. In the Control Panel, reset the tempo to a higher rate to play back the animation.  Jean creates an animation using real-time recording.

Steps

1. **Click frame 10 in the Meteor sprite in the Score**
   The Meteor sprite is selected in the Score and on the Stage.

2. **Click the Selected Frames Only button 🔲 in the Control Panel**
   The Selected Frames Only option prevents the real-time recording from extending beyond the selected sprite. A green dotted line appears in the Score at the bottom of the Frame channel to indicate the selected frames.

3. **Click Control on the menu bar, then click Real-Time Recording**
   An indicator appears next to the selected sprite in the Score, and a red selection box appears on the Stage, as shown in Figure J-14.

   > **QuickTip**
   > If the speed is too fast, adjust the tempo in the Control Panel.

4. **Drag the Meteor sprite to the point on the Stage shown in Figure J-15, then release the mouse to stop recording**
   The animation path appears on the Stage. The real-time recording stops at the end of the sprite.

   > **QuickTip**
   > If you record beyond the last frame of a sprite, Director extends the sprite through the Score until you stop recording or until the sprite reaches another sprite.

5. **Click the Selected Frames Only button 🔲 in the Control Panel to deselect it**
   The Selected Frames Only option is turned off.

6. **Click the Close button in the Control Panel**
   The Control Panel closes.

7. **Click the Rewind button 🔘 on the toolbar, then click the Play button 🔘 on the toolbar**
   The movie plays the animation on the Stage. If the animation path is not smooth, you can adjust individual keyframes on the Stage to adjust the path.

   > **Trouble?**
   > If you have problems adjusting keyframes, make sure the Snap to Grid and Snap to Guide check boxes on the Grid and Guides tab in the Property Inspector are cleared.

8. **Drag any keyframe (the larger circles) on the Stage that is not in a line, to refine the animation path**
   When you position the arrow pointer over a keyframe, it changes to an alternate color to indicate that you can adjust the point in the animation path.

9. **Click the Rewind button 🔘 on the toolbar, then click the Play button 🔘 on the toolbar**
   The movie plays the animation on the Stage.

FIGURE J-14: Real-time recording an animation

Real-time recording selection

Real-time recording indicator

Start the real-time recording in frame 10

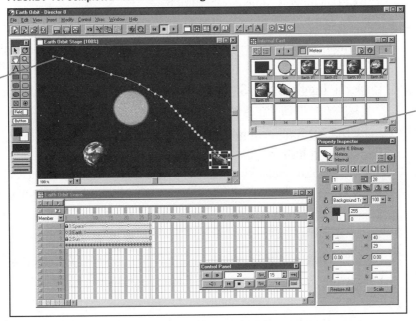

Green line indicates selected frames

FIGURE J-15: Completed real-time recording

Your path might look different

Drag the cast member here

Extending an animation using Paste Relative

If you want to extend the length of an existing animation, you can use the different animation techniques to add to the animation, but Director provides an easier way to accomplish the same task. The Paste Relative command aligns the start position of one sprite on the Stage with the end position of the preceding sprite. The Paste Relative command treats the end of the preceding sprite as a keyframe for the start position of the next sprite. To extend an animation using Paste Relative, select the animated sprite in the Score, click Edit on the menu bar, click Copy Sprites, click the frame immediately after the last frame of the selected sprite, click Edit on the menu bar, point to Paste Special, then click Relative. Director copies the animation on the Stage beginning where the previous animation ends. If you use Paste instead of Paste Relative, the pasted sprite will not synchronize with the preceding sprite.

Using Onion Skinning

Onion skinning allows you to create a new cast member in the Paint window while viewing one or more existing cast members as reference images. The reference images appear dimmed in the background with decreasing levels of brightness, as though you had tracing paper over them. You can draw on top of the reference images, tracing the parts of their features that you need for the new cast member. The cast members used as references are not altered in the process. Onion skinning is especially useful for creating a series of cast members that you can use to create animated sequences. Onion skinning uses registration points to align the current cast member with the previous reference images. Be careful not to move registration points for cast members after onion skinning. ✐ Jean uses onion skinning to create a series of meteor images for the Earth Orbit movie.

Trouble?
If the Meteor image is not centered in the Paint window, scroll to center the image.

1. **Double-click** the **Meteor cast member** in the Cast window
   The Paint window opens with the cast member.

2. Click the **Marquee button** 🔲 in the Paint window, click **No Shrink**, select the cast member in the Paint window, then click the **Copy button** 📋 on the toolbar
   The cast member is copied to the clipboard.

3. Click **View** on the menu bar, then click **Onion Skin**
   The Onion Skin toolbar appears. See Table J-1 for a description of Onion Skin toolbar buttons and options.

Trouble?
If the Preceding Cast Members box and the Following Cast Members box on the Onion Skin toolbar are not set to zero, then click the up or down arrows to set the boxes to zero.

4. Click the **Toggle Onion Skinning button** 🗙 on the Onion Skin toolbar, if necessary
   The Onion Skin feature is turned on, as shown in Figure J-16.

5. Click the **Set Background button** 🗺 on the Onion Skin toolbar, then click the **Show Background button** 〰 on the Onion Skin toolbar
   The image in the Paint window is set as a background, or reference, image. The image does not appear in the background until you create one or more new images in the series.

6. Click the **New Cast Member button** ➕ in the Paint window
   The reference image (cast member 8) appears in the Paint window.

7. Click the **Paste button** 📋 on the toolbar, click the **Rotate Right button** 🔄 in the Paint window, then click the **Set Background button** 🗺 on the Onion Skin toolbar
   An altered version of the Meteor cast member appears as a new cast member.

8. Click the **New Cast Member button** ➕ in the Paint window, then click the **Preceding Cast Members up arrow** twice on the Onion Skin toolbar
   Two reference images (cast members 8 and 9) appear in the Paint window, as shown in Figure J-17.

9. Click the **Toggle Onion Skinning button** 🗙 on the Onion Skin toolbar, click the **Close button** on the Onion Skin toolbar, then click the **Close button** in the Paint window
   The Onion Skin toolbar and the Paint window close, and a new cast member with the rotated meteor appears in the Cast window.

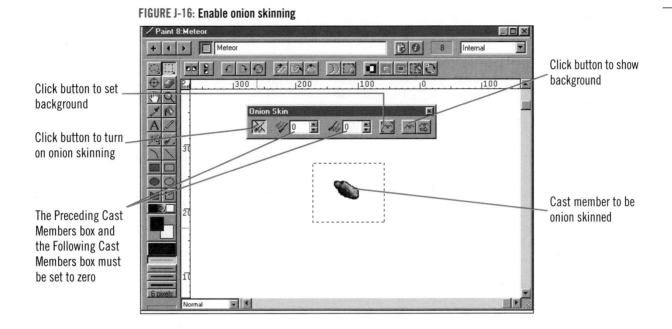

FIGURE J-16: Enable onion skinning

Click button to set background

Click button to turn on onion skinning

The Preceding Cast Members box and the Following Cast Members box must be set to zero

Click button to show background

Cast member to be onion skinned

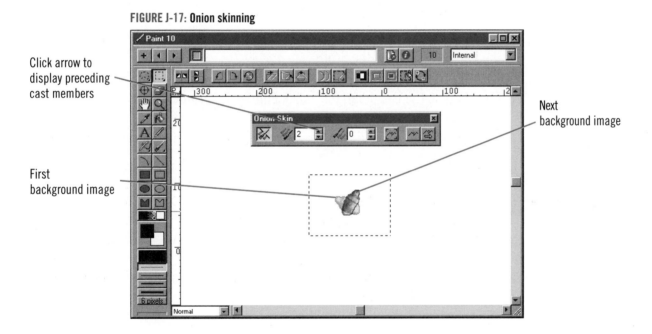

FIGURE J-17: Onion skinning

Click arrow to display preceding cast members

First background image

Next background image

TABLE J-1: Onion Skin toolbar

button or option	button name	description
	Toggle Onion Skinning	Toggles the onion skinning overlay display on or off
	Preceding Cast Members	Overlays the number of cast members in preceding positions in the Cast window
	Following Cast Members	Overlays the number of cast members in subsequent positions in the Cast window
	Set Background	Sets the image to appear in the background as an overlay
	Show Background	Displays the cast members with the background set as an overlay
	Track Background	Creates a chain of overlaid images

Animating with a Series of Cast Members

If you want more control over the images in an animation, frame animation is the most effective technique, but it also takes the longest to complete. You can use frame animation to create an animated sequence that consists of a series of cast members. Until now, you have worked with sprites that display only one cast member, but Director allows you to create a sprite that displays multiple cast members. You can change cast members in a sprite throughout its span to create an animation. For example, you can display one cast member for the first 5 frames of a sprite, exchange it for another cast member, display the exchanged cast member for the next 10 frames, and continue in the same way to create an animation using a series of cast members. If you want cast members to be displayed with different durations, the most effective way to create an animation sequence is to use the Exchange Cast Members command. If you want a consistent duration, an easy way to create an animated sequence is to use the Cast to Time command.  Jean uses a series of cast members to create an animation, using both methods.

Steps

1. Drag the **Earth 01 cast member** into the Score at **frame 30** in channel 6, then click the **Earth 01 sprite** in the Score
   The entire Earth 01 sprite in channel 6 is selected.

2. Click **Edit** on the menu bar, then click **Edit Sprite Frames**
   Individual frames appear in the Earth 01 sprite.

3. Click **frame 45** in the Earth 01 sprite in channel 6, hold down **[Shift]**, then click **frame 57** in the Earth 01 sprite
   Frames 45 through 57 are selected in the Earth 01 sprite.

4. Click the **Earth 02 cast member** in the Cast window, click **Edit** on the menu bar, then click **Exchange Cast Members**
   The Earth 02 cast member is exchanged with the Earth 01 cast member in frames 45 through 57.

5. Click the combined **Earth 01 and Earth 02 sprite** in channel 6, click **Edit** on the menu bar, then click **Edit Entire Sprite**
   The entire sprite with Earth 01 at the beginning and Earth 02 at the end appears in the Score, as shown in Figure J-18.

6. Drag the end of the combined **Earth 01 and Earth 02 sprite** to **frame 40**, then click **frame 41** in channel 6
   The duration of the sprite is changed to 10 frames (start at frame 30 and end at frame 40).

7. Click the **Earth 03 cast member** in the Cast window, hold down **[Shift]**, click the **Earth 04 cast member**, then click the **Earth 05 cast member**
   Cast members 03–05 are selected.

8. Click **Modify** on the menu bar, then click **Cast to Time**
   The cast members are combined into one sprite as an animated sequence.

9. Drag the end of the newly combined sprite in channel 6 to **frame 55**, click **frame 30**, ensure that the Playback head is set to **30**, then click the **Play button** ▶ on the toolbar
   The two sprites play an animated sequence using a series of cast members, as shown in Figure J-19.

FIGURE J-18: Exchanging cast members

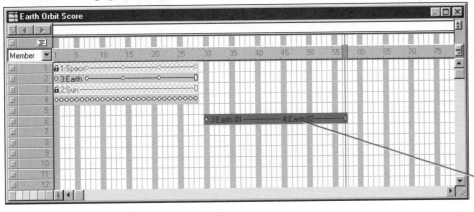

Exchanging
Earth 01 with
Earth 02 at
the end of the
sprite

FIGURE J-19: Animating cast members

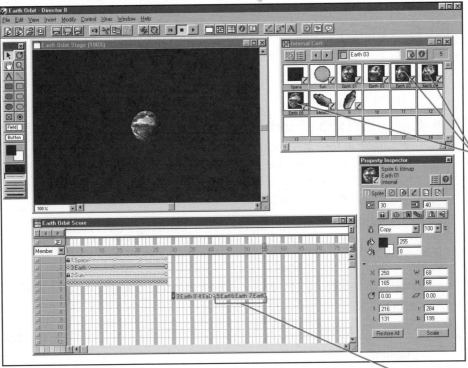

Animated
cast members

Animation with a series
of cast members

CLUES TO USE

Converting sprites to an animated sequence

When you create an animated sequence, sometimes it is helpful to place all the cast members in one frame in sequential channels in the Score, to view them all at the same time and check positioning. You can use the Space to Time command to convert all the individual sprites in one frame to a single sprite, to form an animated sequence. To convert individual sprites in one frame to an animated sequence, you select a frame in a channel in the Score as the start location. Drag the cast members to the Stage in the correct order.

Director places the cast members in sequential channels in the Score. Arrange the sprites on the Stage as you want them to appear in the animated sequence. Select the sprites and change the duration to one frame. Click Modify on the menu bar, click Space to Time, type a Separation value in the Space to Time dialog box to indicate how many frames you want to use to separate the sprites within the combined sprite animation, then click OK.

Creating a Film Loop

A **film loop** combines many sprites and effects over a range of frames into a single cast member. Film loops make it easier to develop and work with large and complex animations. You can also create a film loop using other film loops. After you create a film loop, a new cast member appears in the Cast window. Film loop cast members work a little differently than other cast members. When you create a film loop, don't delete or modify the cast members from which you created the film loop, because Director needs them to play the film loop. Film loops animate only when you play the movie. You don't see the animation if you step through the frames or drag the playback head across the frames. Resizing a film loop changes the number of cycles through the film loop, instead of changing the speed of the loop. If you want to apply ink effects to a film loop, you need to apply the ink effects to the individual sprites before they become part of the film loop. ✒️ Jean creates a film loop of the Earth sprites.

Steps

1. Click the **Earth 01 sprite** starting at **frame 30** in the Score, hold down **[Shift]**, then click the **Earth 03 sprite** starting at **frame 41** in the Score

   Two animated sprites in channel 6 are selected.

   QuickTip

   To quickly create a film loop, drag the selected sprites from the Score to a Cast window.

2. Click **Insert** on the menu bar, then click **Film Loop**

   The Film Loop dialog box opens.

3. Type **Earth Loop**, then click **OK**

   The film loop with the two animated sprites appears in the Cast window as a cast member.

   QuickTip

   To change film loop settings, click the film loop sprite, then click the Film Loop tab in the Property Inspector.

4. Click the **Earth 01 sprite** in channel 2 to select it, then click the **Earth Loop cast member** in the Cast window

   The Earth 01 sprite in channel 2 is selected in the Score, and the film loop is selected in the Cast window, as shown in Figure J-20. You can exchange the Earth 01 sprite with the film loop to animate it as it orbits the sun.

5. Click **Edit** on the menu bar, then click **Exchange Cast Members**

   The Earth 01 sprite in channel 2 that orbits the sun is exchanged with a film loop of a spinning earth.

6. Click the **gray button** to the left of channel 6 in the Score to hide the channel for playback

   Trouble?

   If the animation plays too fast, double-click frame 1 in the Tempo channel, then reduce the tempo setting in fps.

7. Click the **Rewind button** 🔘 on the toolbar, then click the **Play button** 🔘 on the toolbar

   The movie plays.

8. Click the **Save button** 🔘 on the toolbar

   Director saves the movie.

9. Click **File** on the menu bar, then click **Exit** (Win) or **Quit** (Mac)

   Director closes.

FIGURE J-20: Creating a film loop

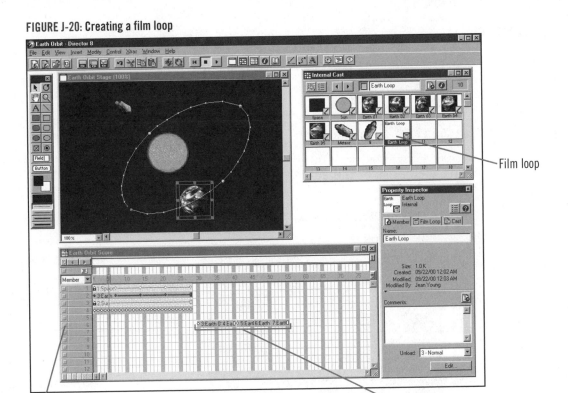

Film loop

Click gray button to
hide the channel

Sprites that make
up the film loop

Animating cursors

You can create an animated cursor to make your movies more interesting. An animated cursor is simply an animated sequence of bitmapped cast members. You can use an animated cursor during a mouse rollover effect or a long task, to communicate to your users that an action is available or in progress. Before you create an animated cursor, make sure the cast members you want to animate are 8-bit color bitmapped images, the standard color depth for cursors. To create an animated cursor, click Insert on the menu bar, point to Media Element, then click Cursor. In the Cursor Properties Editor dialog box, click the

Cast list arrow, click a Cast window, click the arrows to browse the 8-bit cast members, then click Add to include cast members in the animation. In the Interval box, enter a value (in milliseconds) to set the time delay between frames of the cursor. In the Hotspot position box, type x and y values to define the cursor position that will activate the sequence when the user clicks there (0,0 marks the top-left corner). Click the size option to select the maximum size of the cursor, click the Automask option to make white pixels in the cursor transparent, click Preview to see the cursor animation, then click OK.

▶ Concepts Review

Label each of the elements of the screen shown in Figure J-21.

FIGURE J-21

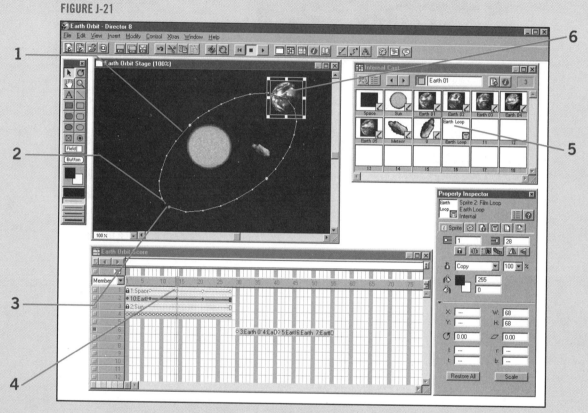

Match each of the terms with the statement that describes its function.

7. **Tweening**
8. **Real-time recording**
9. **Step recording**
10. **Frame animation**
11. **Keyframe**
12. **Onion skinning**
13. **Film loop**

a. An animation sequence of cast members
b. A part of a sprite that contains animation properties
c. The recording of cast member movement on the Stage
d. A way to create a series of cast members
e. A way to combine sprites and effects into a cast member
f. When Director fills in animation between keyframes
g. The recording of cast member movement on the Stage one frame at a time

Select the best answer from the following list of choices.

14. **Which animation technique uses a series of cast members?**
   a. Tweening   b. Real-time recording   c. Step recording   d. Frame animation

15. **Which animation technique records movement one frame at a time?**
   a. Tweening   b. Real-time recording   c. Step recording   d. Frame animation

16. **Which animation technique uses keyframes?**
   a. Tweening   b. Real-time recording   c. Step recording   d. All of the above

17. **Which is NOT a tweenable sprite property?**
   a. Blend   b. Background color   c. Ink   d. Size

18. Which option do you adjust to avoid problems recording in real time?

    a. Tempo   **b.** Size   **c.** Scripts   **d.** Registration point

19. What does onion skinning use to align cast members?

    a. Grid   **b.** Registration points   **c.** Guides   **d.** Rulers

20. Which is a feature of a film loop?

    a. Create a film loop using other film loops   **c.** Apply an ink effect directly to a film loop

    b. Animate a film loop at any time   **d.** Delete the cast members in the film loop

▶ Skills Review

1. Understand animation.

    a. List and describe the four animation techniques.

2. Create animation using tweening.

    a. Start Director, open the file **MD J-2** from the drive and folder where your Project Files are located.

    b. Save the file as *Sports* in the drive and folder where your Project Files are located.

    c. Open sprite preferences and make sure Tweening is turned on.

    d. Select the Football sprite on the Stage, then drag the red handle in the middle to the right under the Baseball sprite on the Stage.

    e. Insert keyframes at frames 10, 20, 30, and 40 in channel 2.

3. Change tweenable sprite properties.

    a. Display the Sprite tab in the Property Inspector for the Football sprite.

    b. Change the rotation angle to 60 degrees at frame 10 in channel 2; 120 degrees at frame 20 in channel 2; 180 degrees at frame 30 in channel 2; and 240 degrees at frame 40 in channel 2.

    c. Rewind and play the animation.

4. Create a circular animation.

    a. Insert a keyframe at frame 15 in channel 3, then drag the Basketball sprite down slightly to the left to the bottom of the Stage.

    b. Insert a keyframe at frame 25 in channel 3, then drag the Basketball sprite up to the left almost to the middle of the Stage.

    c. Insert a keyframe at frame 35 in channel 3, then drag the Basketball sprite down slightly to the left to the bottom of the Stage.

    d. Insert a keyframe at frame 40 in channel 3, then drag the Basketball sprite straight left along the bottom of the Stage.

    e. Adjust the curvature of the animation to be more linear (less curved at the keyframes).

    f. Change the Ease-Out setting to 100%.

    g. Rewind and play the animation.

    h. Adjust the animation path on the Stage as necessary, then rewind and play the animation again.

5. Create animation using step recording.

    a. Open the Control Panel, then select the Baseball sprite.

    b. Start step recording, then step forward in the Control Panel.

    c. Drag the Baseball sprite on the Stage to the right and down a bit.

    d. Continue to step forward and drag the Baseball sprite until you reach the bottom of the Stage at frame 15. (*Hint*: Avoid hitting the other balls as you move the sprite across the Stage.)

    e. End step recording, then rewind and play the animation.

6. Create animation using real-time recording.

    a. Click frame 16 in the Baseball sprite in the Score.

    b. Turn on Selected Frames Only, then start real-time recording.

    c. Drag the Baseball sprite to create small bounces at the bottom of the Stage.

    d. Turn off Selected Frames Only, then adjust the animation path to fine-tune it.

    e. Close the Control Panel, then rewind and play the animation.

7. Use onion skinning.

    a. Open the Basketball cast member.

    b. Select the basketball image with no shrink, then copy the image.

    c. View the Onion Skin toolbar, then turn on onion skinning.

    d. Set the background, then show the background.

    e. Create a new cast member, then paste a copy of the basketball image in the Paint window.

    f. Rotate the image to the right, then set the background.

    g. Repeat Steps e and f two more times to create two more versions of the basketball. (*Hint*: For Step f, rotate one image right twice and rotate the other image left.)

    h. Set the Preceding Cast Members box to display the preceding four cast members.

    i. Toggle Onion Skinning off, then close the Onion Skin toolbar and the Paint window.

8. Animate with a series of cast members.

    a. Click frame 45 in channel 6.

    b. Select the four versions of the Basketball sprite in the Cast window.

    c. Create an animation with a series of cast members, using Cast to Time.

    d. Extend the sprite to frame 90 in channel 6.

9. Create a film loop.

    a. Select the sprite starting in frame 45 in channel 6.

    b. Create a film loop as *Sports Loop*.

    c. Select the Basketball sprite in channel 3, then select the Sports Loop cast member in the Cast window.

    d. Exchange the cast members.

    e. Hide channel 6, then rewind and play the animation.

    f. Save the movie and exit Director.

▶ Independent Challenges

1. You are the marketing manager for On Target Enterprises, a health and fitness company. The company produces a line of natural health products that includes energy bars and drinks, protein powders, and daily supplements. You want to create an animation for a marketing presentation that depicts hitting a target. You use Director to create an animation of an arrow hitting a target.

  To complete this independent challenge:

    a. Connect to the Internet and go to www.course.com. Navigate to the page for this book, click the link for the Student Online Companion, then click the link for this unit.

    b. Search for clip art of an arrow and a target, and download it to the drive and folder where your Project Files are located.

    c. Start Director and save the movie as *On Target* in the drive and folder where your Project Files are located.

    d. Create a text cast member with the text **On Target Health and Fitness**, and drag it to the top of the Stage.

    e. Import the clip art into Director, then add the arrow and target cast members to the Stage.

    f. Animate the arrow to hit the target.

    g. Play and save the movie, then exit Director.

2. You are the director of Coin Collectors, Inc., an international coin collecting and appraisal company. Coin Collectors is the leading provider of grading and authentication services, in-depth price guides, news, and information, offering more expertise than any other collectibles company. You want to create a presentation for an upcoming coin collecting convention. You use Director to create an animation of coins rolling across the Stage.

To complete this independent challenge:

a. Connect to the Internet and go to www.course.com. Navigate to the page for this book, click the link for the Student Online Companion, then click the link for this unit.

b. Search for a photograph of a coin and download it to the drive and folder where your Project Files are located.

c. Start Director and save the movie as *Coin Collectors* in the drive and folder where your Project Files are located.

d. Create a text cast member with the text **Coin Collectors, Inc.** and drag it to the top of the Stage.

e. Import the photograph into Director, then add the coin cast member to the Stage.

f. Animate the coin across the Stage.

g. Change the position of the coin as it moves across the Stage. (*Hint*: Change the rotation value in the Sprite tab of the Property Inspector in small increments for each keyframe.)

h. Play and save the movie, then exit Director.

3. You are the Web site designer for Bug Be Gone, a termite and pest control company. Bug Be Gone employs the most technologically advanced methods for securing buildings against pests such as termites, mice, roaches, ants, and fleas. You want to create an animation of different pests for the Web site. You use Director to create an animation of different pests appearing on the page.

To complete this independent challenge:

a. Connect to the Internet and go to www.course.com. Navigate to the page for this book, click the link for the Student Online Companion, then click the link for this unit.

b. Search for photographs of two pests and download them to the drive and folder where your Project Files are located.

c. Start Director and save the movie as *Bug Be Gone* in the drive and folder where your Project Files are located.

d. Create a text cast member with the text **Bug Be Gone, We Guarantee It!** and drag it to the top of the Stage.

e. Import the photographs of pests into Director.

f. Add the pest cast members to the Stage.

g. Create a step recording across the Stage with one pest cast member.

h. Create a real-time recording across the Stage with the other pest cast member.

i. Select the two animations, then create a film loop as *Bug Loop*.

j. Play and save the movie, then exit Director.

4. You are the director of All Butterflies, a habitat for exotic butterflies. The habitat performs research on all species of butterflies and provides tours of the facilities for schools and the public. You want to create a butterfly presentation for the tour. You use Director to create an animation of a butterfly moving across the sky.

To complete this independent challenge:

a. Connect to the Internet and go to www.course.com. Navigate to the page for this book, click the link for the Student Online Companion, then click the link for this unit.

b. Search for clip art of a butterfly and download it to the drive and folder where your Project Files are located.

c. Start Director and save the movie as *All Butterflies* in the drive and folder where your Project Files are located.

d. Create a text cast member with the text **All Butterflies Tour** and drag it to the top of the Stage, then change the Stage background to light blue.

e. Import the clip art into Director.

f. Open the butterfly cast member, then view and toggle on onion skinning.

g. Copy the butterfly, set the background, then show the background.

h. Create a new cast member, paste the butterfly, rotate it right, set the background, then show the background.

i. Toggle off onion skinning, then close the Onion Skin toolbar and the Paint window.

j. Select the series of two butterfly cast members, then create an animation sequence. (*Hint*: Use the Cast to Time command.)

k. Create a real-time recording across the Stage with the animation sequence.

l. Play and save the movie, then exit Director.

▶ Visual Workshop

Recreate the screen shown in Figure J-22. Use the Shuttle.jpg file from the drive and folder where your Project Files are located. Print the screen. (For Windows, use the Windows Paint program. Press the Print Screen key to make a copy of the screen, start the Paint program by clicking Start, pointing to Programs, pointing to Accessories, then clicking Paint; click Edit on the menu bar, click Paste to paste the screen into Paint, then click Yes to paste the large image if necessary. Click File on the menu bar, click Print, click Print or OK in the dialog box, then exit Paint. For the Macintosh, use the SimpleText program. Hold and press the Command, Shift, and 3 keys to make a copy of the screen, double-click the document Picture 1 located on your hard drive, click File on the menu bar, click Print, then click Print in the dialog box. *Note*: When you create a new document with a copy of the screen, and a document Picture 1 already exists, the Macintosh names the new document Picture 2.)

FIGURE J-22

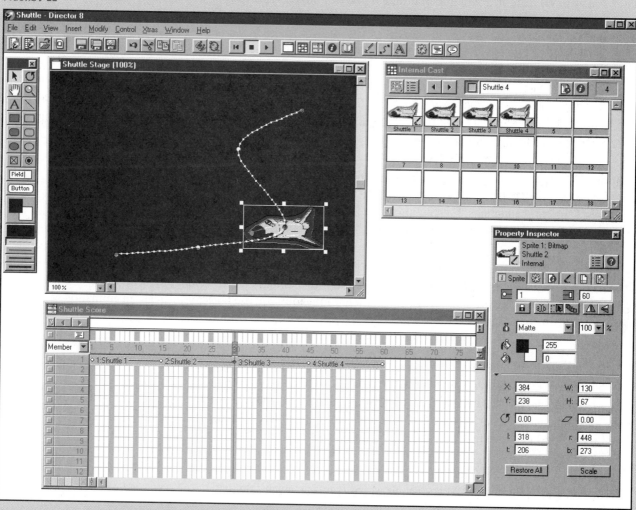

Unit K

Attaching
Behaviors

Objectives

► **Understand behaviors**
► **Attach built-in behaviors**
► **View and change behavior parameters**
► **Create a behavior**
► **Add a behavior**
► **Modify a behavior**
► **View behavior scripts**
► **Open a movie with a behavior**
► **Create a dropdown list with a behavior**

You can use built-in behaviors that come with Director, or create your own to add interactive functionality to movies without having to write or understand Lingo, Director's scripting language. First, you'll learn about the built-in behaviors available in Director, and how to attach a built-in behavior to a sprite and change its parameters. Then, you'll learn how to create and modify a behavior. Finally, you'll learn how to create behaviors to open a movie and create a drop-down menu. Jean uses behaviors to add interactive features to the SpaceWorks online store.

Understanding Behaviors

A behavior is a prewritten Lingo script that makes it easy to add interactivity to a movie. Director provides a Library palette with over 100 built-in behaviors that you can drag and drop onto sprites and frames in the Score window and on the Stage. The Library palette of built-in behaviors, as shown in Figure K-1, is grouped by category, such as animation, controls, Internet, media, navigation, paintbox, and text. If you are not sure where to find a behavior to perform a certain type of action, see Table K-1 for a list of actions you can perform with the behavior categories. You can also point to the built-in behaviors on the Library palette to quickly display a tooltip description of each ready-to-use behavior that makes it easier for you to find and use in a movie. For a complete description of each built-in behavior, visit the Director Support Center Web site. To access the Director Support Center Web site, click Help on the menu bar, click Web Links, then click Using Director 8 behaviors or Working with Multiuser behaviors. Director Help jumps to the behavior information at the Macromedia Director Support Center Web site. Jean takes some time to familiarize herself with the different types of behaviors in Director.

Details

Animation

The behaviors in the Animation library make sprites move in ways that would be difficult or impossible to achieve using conventional Score-based animation. The Animation library has three categories: Automatic, Interactive, and Sprite Transitions. The Automatic behaviors perform animation without user input, such as Rotation (Frame or Time-Based), Sway, or Waft. The Interactive behaviors require input from the user to perform the animation, such as Avoid Mouse, Draggable, or Move, Rotate, and Scale. The Sprite Transition behaviors, such as Barn Door or Wipe, allow you to control how a sprite transitions on and off the Stage.

Controls

The behaviors in the Controls library allow you to create and control user interface elements, such as push, toggle, and radio buttons, check boxes, pop-up menus, and tooltips.

Internet

The behaviors in the Internet library control activities on the Web. The Internet library has three categories: Forms, Multiuser, and Streaming. The Forms behaviors allow you to send information from a form to a Web server. The Multiuser behaviors allow two or more users to chat with each other and use a shared whiteboard to view and modify a bitmap image at the same time. The Streaming behaviors allow you to control how a movie plays while Shockwave media are downloading from a server.

Media

The behaviors in the Media library control Flash, QuickTime, and Sound media. The Media library has three categories: Flash, QuickTime, and Sound. The Flash behaviors allow you to control playback quality, and determine the scale, origin, and view for Flash and vector shape sprites. The QuickTime behaviors allow you to control playback for QuickTime movies. The Sound behaviors allow you to control how and when a sound file plays.

Navigation

The behaviors in the Navigation library allow you to control the movement and location of the playback head.

Paintbox

The behaviors in the Paintbox library allow you to create and modify bitmap images, using Director's built-in drawing tools. You can draw shapes, change colors, erase contents, and undo actions.

Text

The behaviors in the Text library allow you to format numbers, force uppercase or lowercase characters, and create hypertext. You can also create a calendar, countdown timer, custom scroll bar, or tickertape text.

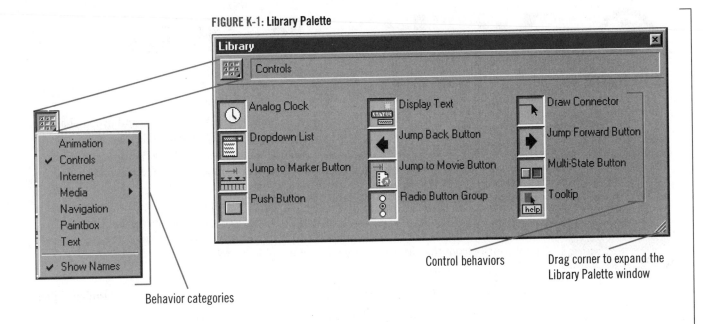

FIGURE K-1: Library Palette

Behavior categories

Control behaviors

Drag corner to expand the Library Palette window

TABLE K-1: Choosing behaviors

if you want to	use
Make sprites move, change color, and change size	Animation
Add user interface elements or provide tooltips that appear when the pointer rolls over a sprite	Controls
Control Internet forms, let two or more users simultaneously chat and modify a bitmap image, and control a movie for optimal streaming	Internet
Control Flash, QuickTime, and Sound media	Media
Move the playback head, open new movies, pause the movie, and make the playback head return to previous locations	Jump behaviors under Controls and Navigation
Let the user create and modify bitmap images, using Director's built-in drawing tools	Paintbox
Control and format text, such as clock timers and calendars	Text

Attaching Built-in Behaviors

With the Library Palette of built-in behaviors, you can quickly and easily drag and drop behaviors onto sprites and frames in the Score window and on the Stage. You can attach the same built-in behavior to multiple sprites and frames. If you want a behavior, such as Push Button, to affect a cast member, you attach the behavior to the associated sprite. If you want a behavior, such as Hold on Current Frame, to affect the entire movie, you attach the behavior to a frame. When you attach a behavior to a sprite or frame, a Parameters dialog box might appear, asking you for specific settings. Director copies the behavior from the Library Palette to the cast member in the Cast window. You cannot modify the original behaviors stored in the Library Palette. ✐ Jean adds a push button control from the Library Palette to a cast member button.

Steps 1 2 3 4

1. Start **Director**, open the file **MD K-1** from the drive and folder where your Project Files are located, then save it as **SpaceWorks Online**
   Director opens, displaying the movie.

2. Click **Window** on the menu bar, then click **Library Palette**
   The Library Palette window opens, displaying the previous Library List selection.

3. Click the **Library List button** ▦, then click **Controls**
   The Library Palette window displays interactive animation controls.

4. Click the **down arrow** ▽ at the bottom of the Library Palette window until the **Push Button behavior** appears, shown in Figure K-2, then position the pointer on the **Push Button icon** ▢
   A brief description of the behavior appears. The Push Button behavior replaces the cast member of the sprite according to the state of the mouse, either mouse elsewhere, mouse within, mouse down, or mouse up, to provide visual feedback or initiate actions in other sprites.

5. Drag the **Push Button icon** ▢ in the Library Palette window to the **Products up sprite** (the Products button) on the Stage
   When you drag the behavior icon onto a sprite on the Stage, a gray rectangle appears around the object, indicating where the behavior will be attached. The Parameters for "Push Button" dialog box opens, as shown in Figure K-3. The dialog box displays default parameter settings in three areas: Graphics, Sounds, and Interaction. If the cast members associated with the Products up sprite (the Products button) are placed consecutively in the Cast window, the cast members (Products up for Standard member, Products roll for Rollover member, and Products down for MouseDown member) appear as the default values in the dialog box. See Table K-2 for a description of the parameter settings for the Push Button behavior.

6. Click **OK**, then click the **Close button** in the Library Palette window
   The Library Palette window closes, and a new cast member appears in the Cast window with the Push Button behavior attached to it, as shown in Figure K-4.

7. Drag the **Push Button** cast member in the Cast window to the **Price up sprite**, **Contacts up sprite**, and **Help up sprite** (the Price, Contacts, and the Help buttons) on the Stage and accept the default settings for each button

8. Click the **Rewind button** ◄◄ on the toolbar, then click the **Play button** ▶ on the toolbar
   The movie plays, awaiting mouse interaction from the end user.

9. Click the **Price button** on the Stage, click the **Contacts button** on the Stage, then click the **Stop button** ■ on the toolbar
   When you click the buttons on the Stage, each button changes appearance to resemble a pushed button. As Director executes the behavior, it swaps the cast member with the behavior.

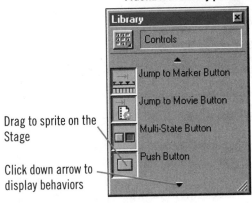

Drag to sprite on the Stage

Click down arrow to display behaviors

FIGURE K-3: Parameters for "Push Button" dialog box

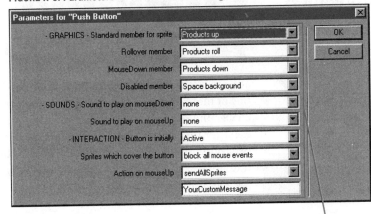

Parameters for the Push Button behavior

FIGURE K-4: Behavior in the Cast window

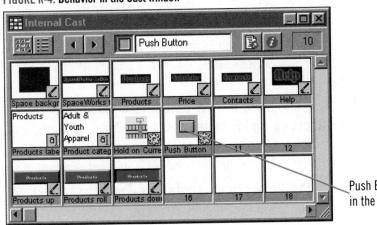

Push Button behavior in the Cast window

TABLE K-2: Parameters for "Push Button" dialog box

parameter	description
Standard member for sprite	displays the cast member when the mouse is elsewhere (not on the standard cast member)
Rollover member	displays the cast member when the mouse is within the standard cast member
mouseDown member	displays the cast member when the mouse is down on the standard cast member
Disabled member	indicates the cast member when the standard cast member is unclickable
Sound to play on mouseDown	plays a brief sound when the mouse is down on the standard cast member
Sound to play on mouseUp	plays a brief sound when the mouse is released up on the standard cast member
Button is initially	sets the initial state of the push button
Sprites which cover the button	indicates mouse functionality for sprites that cover the push button
Action on mouseUp	triggers actions to other sprites
Text box with no label	sends out a custom message on mouse up to a Lingo script

Director 8

Viewing and Changing Behavior Parameters

You can attach multiple behaviors to an individual sprite, but only one to a frame. After you attach one or more behaviors to a sprite or frame, you may need to change the parameters of a behavior, change the order of the behaviors, or remove one or more attached behaviors. You can use the Behavior Inspector or the Behavior tab in the Property Inspector to view, add, modify, and remove behaviors attached to a sprite or frame. In the Behavior tab, you can quickly change parameter settings for a selected behavior.  Jean adds multiple behaviors to a sprite and then modifies the behavior order and parameters.

Steps

1. Click **Window** on the menu bar, click **Library Palette**, click the **down arrow** ▼, then drag the **Jump to Marker Button icon** 🔳 in the Control library of the Library Palette window to the **Products up sprite** (the Products button) on the Stage
   The Parameters for "Jump to Marker Button" dialog box opens, asking which marker you want to be the target of On mouseUp (jump to marker), as shown in Figure K-5.

   QuickTip

   To create a loop with a marker, click the On mouseUp, jump to marker list arrow, then click Loop in the Parameters for "Jump to Marker Button" dialog box.

2. Click the **On mouseUp, jump to marker list arrow** ▼, click **Products**, click **OK**, then click the **Close button** in the Library Palette window
   The Library Palette window closes, and a new cast member appears in the Cast window with the Jump to Marker Button behavior attached to it.

3. Drag the **Jump to Marker Button cast member** in the Cast window to the **Price up**, **Contacts up**, and **Help up sprites** (the Price, Contacts, and Help buttons) on the Stage and select the corresponding **jump to marker**
   The Jump to Marker Button behavior is attached to the other sprites.

4. Click the **Products up sprite** (the Products button) on the Stage, then click the **Behavior tab** in the Property Inspector
   The Products up cast sprite is selected on the Stage and in the Score. The Behavior tab appears, displaying the behaviors attached to the Products up sprite.

   QuickTip

   To delete a behavior, click the behavior in the Behavior tab, click the Clear Behavior ▬ button, then click Remove Behavior or Remove All Behaviors.

5. Double-click the **Push Button (Internal) behavior** in the Behavior tab of the Property Inspector to select it
   The Parameters for "Push Button" dialog box appears.

6. Click the **Sound to play on mouseUp list arrow** ▼, click **Space**, then click **OK**
   The Space sound is attached to the Products button sprite on the Stage and plays when you release the mouse on the Products button. The Push Button behavior parameters (including the Space sound) appear at the bottom of the Behavior tab, as shown in Figure K-6.

   QuickTip

   To change behavior parameters in a dialog box, click a behavior in the Behavior tab to select it, then change a parameter at the bottom.

7. Select the **Price up**, **Contacts up**, and **Help up sprites** (the Price, Contacts, and Help buttons) on the Stage, and change the **Sound to play on mouseUp** parameter to **Space**

8. Click the **Rewind button** ⏮ on the toolbar, then click the **Play button** ▶ on the toolbar

9. Click the **Products button** on the Stage, click the **Contacts button** on the Stage, then click the **Stop button** ⏹ on the toolbar
   When you click the buttons on the Stage, Director executes the behaviors attached to each sprite: push button, the text box sprite that appears when the playback head jumps to the corresponding marker in the Score, and the Space sound.

FIGURE K-5: Parameters for "Jump to Marker Button" dialog box

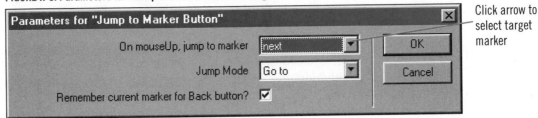

Click arrow to select target marker

FIGURE K-6: Behavior tab with a selected behavior

Sprite with behavior attached

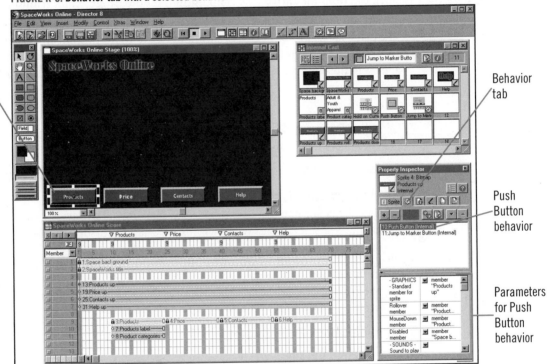

Behavior tab

Push Button behavior

Parameters for Push Button behavior

Changing the order of behaviors

When you attach more than one behavior to a sprite, the behaviors are carried out in the order in which they appear from top to bottom. You can use the Shuffle buttons in the Behavior Inspector or the Behavior tab in the Property Inspector to modify the order of behaviors so that actions occur in the proper order. In some cases the order makes a significant difference, and in other cases it doesn't matter. To change the order of the behaviors attached to a sprite, click the sprite in the Score or on the Stage, click the Behavior tab in the Property Inspector or open the Behavior Inspector, select a behavior from the list, then click the Shuffle Up button ▲ or Shuffle Down ▼ button to move the behavior up or down in the list.

Director 8

Creating a Behavior

When a built-in behavior doesn't perform the type of action you want, you can create your own behavior. For basic operations, you can use the Behavior Inspector to create simple behaviors. To create complex behaviors, you need to understand and write Lingo scripts. A behavior performs two main functions. The first function is to detect a specified event, such as a Mouse Up or End Frame, associated with a sprite or frame, and the second function is to perform one or more actions, such as Go to Frame or Wait on Current Frame, in response. The Behavior Inspector lists the most common events and actions used in behaviors. For many of the built-in behaviors, the Behavior Inspector also includes a description and a set of instructions provided by the behavior's author for a behavior already attached to a sprite or frame. The behavior information appears in a scrolling pane at the bottom of the Behavior Inspector. Jean creates a behavior to change the cursor to an hourglass when you click the Help button.

Steps

Trouble?

If the middle or bottom panes don't appear, click the expander arrow ▼ to display the panes.

1. Click the **Help up sprite** (the Help button) on the Stage, click **Window** on the menu bar, point to **Inspectors**, then click **Behavior**
   The Behavior Inspector opens, as shown in Figure K-7. The built-in behaviors attached to the Help up sprite appear at the top. The events and actions associated with the selected behavior appear in the editing pane in the middle of the Behavior Inspector. Information and instructions for using the selected behavior appear in the description pane at the bottom of the Behavior Inspector.

2. Click the **Behavior Popup button** ✚ (at the top of the dialog box) in the Behavior Inspector, then click **New Behavior**
   The New Behavior dialog box appears, asking you to enter a name for the new behavior.

3. Type **Change Cursor**, then click **OK**
   The new behavior appears in the Behavior pane of the Behavior Inspector, and a new cast member appears in the Cast window with the Change Cursor behavior attached to it.

4. Click the **Event Popup button** ✚ in the Events editing pane, then click **Mouse Down**
   The mouseDown event appears in the Events editing pane and in the Change Cursor cast member in the Cast window. Table AP-8 in the Appendix describes the available events in Director.

5. Click the **Action Popup button** ✚ in the Actions editing pane, point to **Cursor**, then click **Change Cursor**
   The Specify Cursor dialog box appears, displaying the Watch cursor in the Change Cursor to list, as shown in Figure K-8. See Table AP-9 in the Appendix for a description of the available actions in Director.

QuickTip

To lock the current selection, to prevent changes in the Behavior Inspector when new sprites are selected, click the Lock Selection button 🔒 at the bottom of the Behavior Inspector.

6. Click **OK**
   The Change Cursor to 4 action appears in the Actions editing pane, as shown in Figure K-9. The number 4 is an internal identification number for the Watch cursor. Each cursor has a different ID number.

7. Click the **Close button** in the Behavior Inspector
   The Behavior Inspector closes.

8. Click the **Rewind button** ◄◄ on the toolbar, then click the **Play button** ► on the toolbar

9. Click the **Help button** on the Stage, move the mouse around the Stage, then click the **Stop button** ■ on the toolbar
   When you move the mouse around the Stage, the cursor remains an hourglass (Win) or watch (Mac). In the next lesson, you'll restore the system cursor.

FIGURE K-7: Behavior Inspector

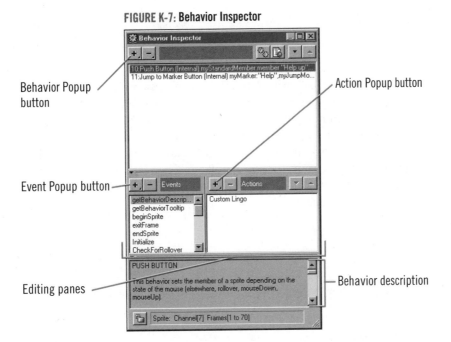

Behavior Popup button

Action Popup button

Event Popup button

Editing panes

Behavior description

FIGURE K-8: Specify Cursor dialog box

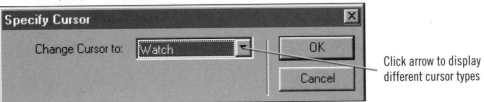

Click arrow to display different cursor types

FIGURE K-9: Behavior Inspector with a new behavior

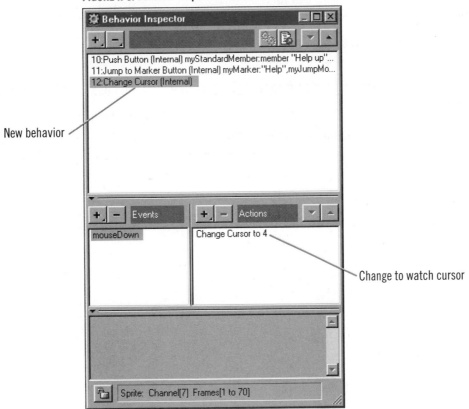

New behavior

Change to watch cursor

Director 8

Adding a Behavior

When you create a behavior, you need to consider how Director executes it along with the other behaviors attached to a sprite or frame. In many instances, you need to create a set of behaviors to complete a single operation. For example, the Change Cursor behavior and the Restore Cursor behavior are commonly used together to temporarily change a cursor when an event takes place and then restore the default cursor when the event is complete. In the previous lesson, you created a behavior to change the cursor to an hourglass when you click the Help button on the Stage. Until you change it again, the cursor will remain an hourglass (Win) or watch (Mac). You need to add another behavior to restore the default system cursor. ✐ Jean creates a behavior to restore the system cursor.

Steps 1 2 3 4

1. Click the **Help up sprite** (the Help button) on the Stage (if necessary), click **Window** on the menu bar, point to **Inspectors**, then click **Behavior**

2. Click the **Behavior Popup button** ⊞ in the Behavior Inspector, then click **New Behavior**
   The New Behavior dialog box appears.

3. Type **Restore Cursor**, then click **OK**
   The new behavior appears in the Behavior pane of the Behavior Inspector, and a new cast member appears in the Cast window with the Restore Cursor behavior attached to it.

4. Click the **Event Popup button** ⊞ in the Events editing pane, then click **Mouse Leave**
   The mouseLeave event appears in the Events editing pane and in the Restore Cursor cast member.

5. Click the **Action Popup button** ⊞ in the Actions editing pane, point to **Cursor**, then click **Restore Cursor**
   The Restore Cursor action appears in the Actions editing pane, as shown in Figure K-10.

6. Click the **Close button** in the Behavior Inspector
   The Behavior Inspector closes.

7. Click the **Rewind button** ◄ on the toolbar, then click the **Play button** ► on the toolbar

8. Click the **Help button** on the Stage, slowly move the mouse off the button, then click the **Stop button** ■ on the toolbar
   When the mouse moves off the button, the cursor reverts to the system cursor.

FIGURE K-10: Restore Cursor behavior

Restore Cursor behavior

Behavior event

Behavior action

Sprite: Channel[7] Frames[1 to 70]

CLUES TO USE

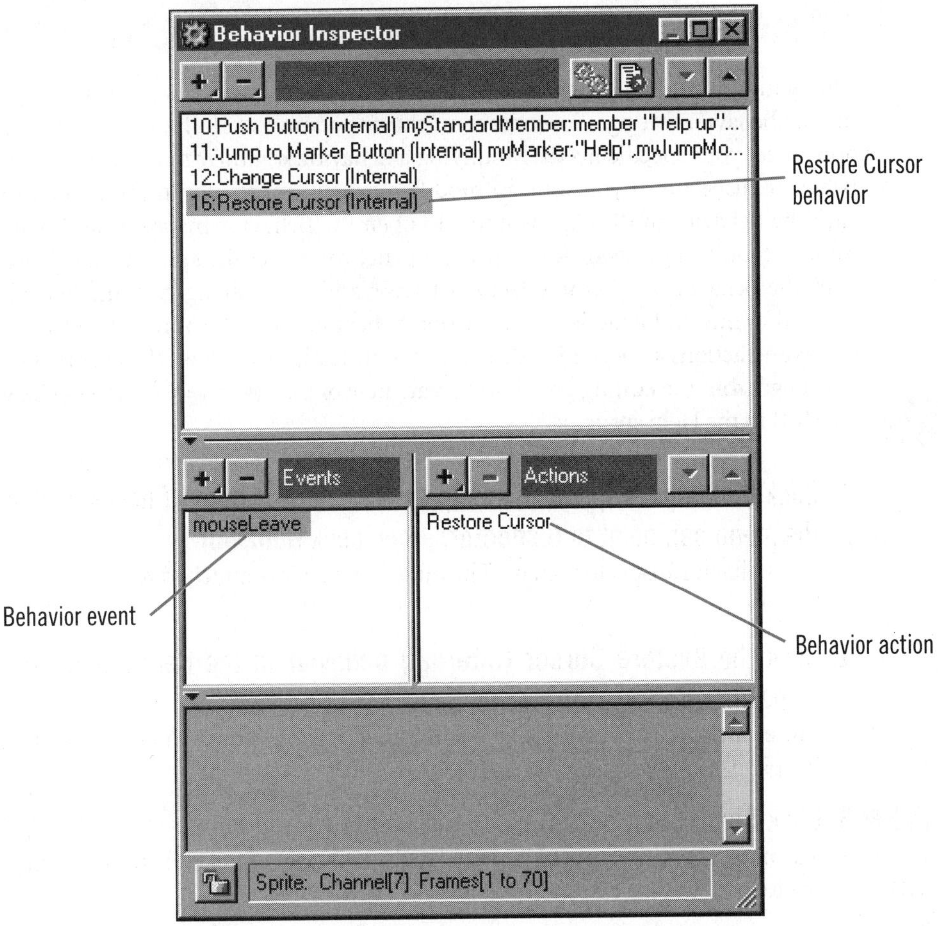

Creating a sound behavior

You can add sound behaviors to a movie to give users feedback about an operation or provide an interesting effect. You can play a simple beep or a sound from a cast member or external file in response to a specific event, such as the clicking of a button. To create a sound behavior, open the Behavior Inspector, click the Behavior Popup button [+], click New Behavior, type a name, click the Event Popup button [+], select an event, click the Action Popup button [+], point to Sound, then click Play Cast Member, Play External File, Beep, or Set Volume. Close the Behavior Inspector, drag the sound behavior from the Cast window to a sprite in the Score or on the Stage, then play the movie to test the sound.

Director 8

Modifying a Behavior

After you create a behavior and play back the movie to check its performance, you may need to modify behavior settings. Sometimes a behavior doesn't work the way you thought, or the results don't meet your specific needs. Modifying a behavior is similar to creating a behavior; you use the Behavior Inspector. If you want to modify a behavior throughout the entire movie, you double-click the behavior in the Cast window to open the Behavior Inspector and make changes. If you want to modify a behavior for a specific sprite, you select the sprite in the Score or on the Stage, open the Behavior Inspector, select a behavior, and make changes. In the Behavior Inspector, you can add events and actions to an existing behavior, but you cannot directly modify the existing events and actions associated with a behavior. Instead, you remove the events and actions you want to change from the editing panes and create new ones.  Jean makes changes to a behavior attached to the Help sprite.

Steps

1. Click the **Help up sprite** (the Help button) on the Stage (if necessary), click **Window** on the menu bar, point to **Inspectors**, then click **Behavior**

   The Behavior Inspector opens. The built-in behaviors attached to the Help up sprite appear at the top.

2. Click the **Restore Cursor (Internal) behavior** in the Behavior pane of the Behavior Inspector

   The events and actions associated with the selected Restore Cursor behavior appear in the editing pane, as shown in Figure K-11.

QuickTip

To remove an event or action from a behavior, you can also select the event or action, then press [Delete].

3. Click **Clear Event button** ▬ in the Events editing pane

   The mouseLeave event and its associated action are removed from the editing panes and from the Restore Cursor cast member in the Cast window.

4. Click the **Event Popup button** ⊞ in the Events editing pane, then click **Mouse Enter**

   The mouseEnter event appears in the Events editing pane and in the Restore Cursor cast member in the Cast window.

5. Click the **Action Popup button** ⊞ in the Actions editing pane, point to **Cursor**, then click **Restore Cursor**

   The Restore Cursor action appears in the Actions editing pane, as shown in Figure K-12.

6. Click the **Close button** in the Behavior Inspector

   The Behavior Inspector closes.

7. Drag the **Restore Cursor cast member** in the Cast window to the **Products**, **Price**, and **Contacts button sprites** on the Stage

   The Restore Cursor behavior is attached to the other sprites.

8. Click the **Rewind button** ◄ on the toolbar, then click the **Play button** ► on the toolbar

9. Click the **Help button** on the Stage, move the mouse around the screen, point to a button, then click the **Stop button** ■ on the toolbar

   When you move the mouse inside a button, the cursor reverts to the system cursor.

FIGURE K-11: Remove Restore Cursor behavior

Click Clear Event button to remove event and associated action

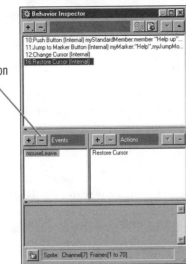

FIGURE K-12: Modify Restore Cursor behavior

Click Event Popup button to modify behavior or add new event

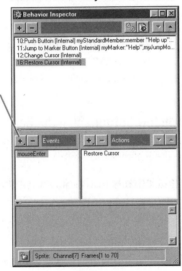

CLUES TO USE

Creating a hyperlink with a behavior

You can create hyperlinks in a movie to access Web sites on the Internet. You create a hyperlink in two steps. The first step is to create a text cast member and add hyperlink formatting, and the second is to attach the Hyperlink behavior. You use the Text window to create a text cast member, and the Text Inspector to add hyperlink formatting. In the Text Inspector, you turn any selected range of text into a hyperlink that links to a URL or initiates other actions. Director automatically adds standard hyperlink formatting to the selected text so that it initially appears with hyperlink underlining. You can enter any string in the hyperlink box; it does not have to be a URL. The string cannot contain a double quotation mark or the Lingo continuation character (\), which wraps a Lingo statement onto two lines. To complete the first step, select the text you want to define as a hyperlink, click Window on the menu bar, point to Inspectors, then click Text to open the Text Inspector. In the Hyperlink Data box, enter the complete URL to which you want to link, then press Enter (Win) or Return (Mac) to create a text cast member with hyperlink formatting. The following URL schemes are supported by this behavior: http://, https://, mailto:, and ftp://. To complete the second step, click Window on the menu bar, click Library Palette, click the Library List button 🔲, click Text, then drag the Hypertext – General icon 🔲 onto the sprite of the text cast member. When you play the movie and click the hyperlink, Lingo will perform a command (gotoNetPage) to jump to the URL.

Director 8

Viewing Behavior Scripts

Director 8

When you create a behavior, Director creates a Lingo script, which performs the action. You can use the Behavior tab in the Property Inspector or Behavior Inspector to view Lingo scripts and learn how Lingo works. If you are familiar with Lingo, you can edit a behavior's script directly. In some cases, the script associated with a behavior contains notes that explain how to use the behavior. If you want to edit a behavior's Lingo script for all sprites and frames to which the behavior is attached, select the behavior in the Cast window, then click the Script Window button to open the Script window. If you want to edit a behavior's Lingo script for an individual sprite or frame, select the individual sprite or frame, open the Behavior Inspector, select the behavior, then click the Script Window button to open the Script window. ✐ Jean views a behavior script.

1. Click the **Help up sprite** (the Help button) on the Stage (if necessary), click **Window** on the menu bar, point to **Inspectors**, then click **Behavior**

   The Behavior Inspector opens. The built-in behaviors attached to the Help up sprite appear in the Behavior pane.

2. Click the **Push Button (Internal) behavior** in the Behavior pane of the Behavior Inspector to select it, if necessary

   The events and actions associated with the selected Push Button behavior appear in the editing panes.

QuickTip

You can also select the behavior in the Behavior tab on the Property Inspector, then click the Script Window button 📑.

3. Click the **Script window button** 📑 in the Behavior Inspector

   The Script window for the Push Button behavior appears, as shown in Figure K-13. It may take a few moments for the Script window to appear.

4. Drag the **lower-right corner** of the Script window to enlarge the window, if necessary

   The gray text within the script corresponds to the text displayed in the description pane at the bottom of the Behavior Inspector and to the text displayed in the tooltip for the Push Button behavior in the Library Palette.

5. Scroll down the **Script window** to view the Push Button behavior script

   The red text in the script is comments and instructions for the user from the developer of the behavior, as shown in Figure K-14. You'll learn more about modifying a script in the next unit.

6. Click the **Close button** in the Script window

   The Script window closes.

7. Click the **Close button** in the Behavior Inspector

   The Behavior Inspector closes.

FIGURE K-13: Push Button Behavior Script window

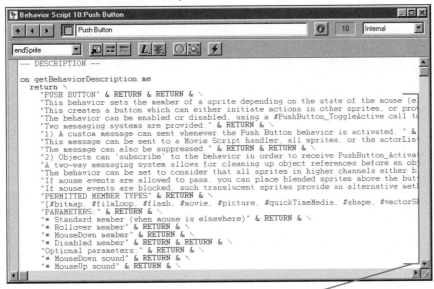

Gray text corresponds to text in the
description pane of the Behavior Inspector

FIGURE K-14: Behavior Script window with comments

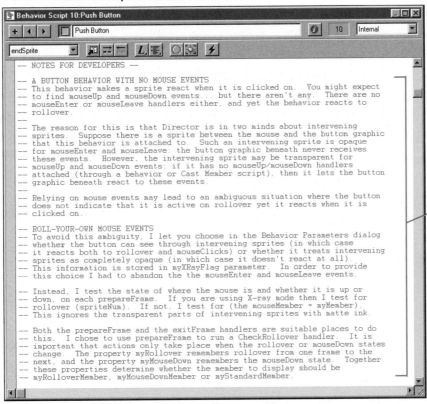

Red text indicates
comments by the
behavior developer

Director 8

Opening a Movie with a Behavior

When you create or modify a large movie, it's more difficult to organize and manage all the pieces of the production, and it occupies more RAM when loaded into memory. To help alleviate these problems, Director allows you to open a movie from within a movie. When you use this technique, you actually close the current movie and open another. This allows you to organize large sections of a movie into smaller separate movies, which require less RAM. With a multiple-movie structure, you can create independent movie modules simultaneously to save time and maximize the production effort. When you use a multiple-movie structure, you need to make sure to store the movie modules in the same location in order to play and package the movie. The best place to store movie modules is in the same location as the main movie or in a folder within it. You can quickly and easily use a behavior in the Library palette to open a movie.  Jean opens a movie with Help information for SpaceWorks online.

Steps

1. Click **Window** on the menu bar, then click **Library Palette**
   The Library Palette window opens, displaying the Controls library, the previous Library List selection.

2. Click the **down arrow** ▼, then drag the **Jump to Movie Button icon** 🔳 in the Control library to the **Help up sprite** (the Help button) on the Stage
   When you drag the behavior icon on a sprite on the Stage, a gray rectangle appears around the object, indicating where the behavior will be attached. The Parameters for "Jump to Movie Button" dialog box opens, asking the location of the movie, as shown in Figure K-15.

> **Trouble?**
> If the Help movie file isn't located in the Project Files folder with the SpaceWorks Online movie file, a Where is "Help?" dialog box appears, asking for the location of the file.

3. In the top box, type **Help**, then click **OK**
   The Help movie file is located in the same folder as your Project Files, so you don't need to specify the entire path to the movie file.

4. Click the **Jump to Movie Button (Internal) behavior** in the Behavior tab on the Property Inspector to select it, then click the **Shuffle Up button** ▲ until the **Jump to Movie Button (Internal)** behavior is above the Jump to Marker (Internal) behavior
   The Jump to Movie Button behavior appears before the Jump to Marker behavior in the list, which means the Jump to Movie Button behavior executes first. If you don't move the Jump to Movie button behavior above the Jump to Marker behavior, it will not execute. The Jump to Marker behavior will take priority.

5. Click the **Close button** in the Library Palette window, then click the **Save button** 🔳 on the toolbar
   The Library Palette window closes, and Director saves the movie.

> **Trouble?**
> If the Save dialog box appears, click Yes to save changes before Director opens the Help movie file.

6. Click the **Rewind button** ◄ on the toolbar, click the **Play button** ► on the toolbar, then click the **Help button** on the Stage
   The SpaceWorks online movie closes, and the Help movie opens. You can quickly return to the previous movie with the Jump Back Button behavior.

7. Click the **Stop button** ■ on the toolbar, then click the **Return up sprite** (the Return button) on the Stage
   The sprite is selected on the Stage.

8. Click the **Behavior tab** on the Property Inspector, if necessary
   The Jump Back Button behavior is attached to the sprite, as shown in Figure K-16.

9. Click the **Rewind button** ◄ on the toolbar, click the **Play button** ► on the toolbar, click the **Return button** on the Stage, then click the **Stop button** ■ on the toolbar
   The Help movie closes and the SpaceWorks online movie opens.

FIGURE K-15: Parameters for "Jump to Movie Button" dialog box

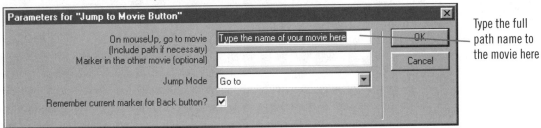

Type the full path name to the movie here

FIGURE K-16: Help movie with Jump Back Button behavior

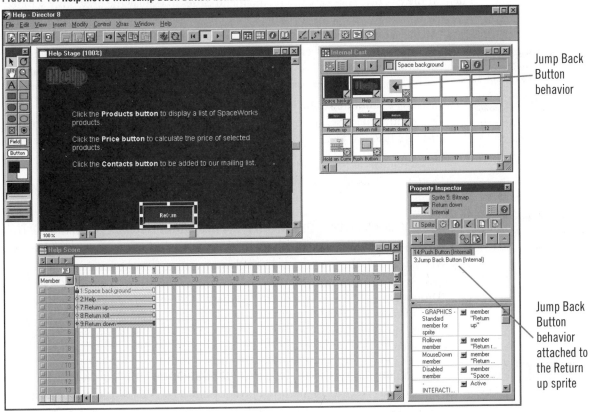

Jump Back Button behavior

Jump Back Button behavior attached to the Return up sprite

Understanding file path locations

When you open movies that reside in different locations, you need to refer to them by their full names, (in the Parameters for "Jump to Movie Button" dialog box, for example), in order to make sure the main movie can find them. The name that appears on the desktop is only part of a file's full name, according to the computer. The full name, or **path name**, includes specific information about the file's location on a floppy disk, CD-ROM, hard disk, or network. For example, the path name of the Help movie on a network drive is N:\Project Files\Unit K\Help.dir (Win) or DD Network:Project Files:Unit K:Help.dir (Mac). The N is the drive letter of the network for Windows, and Network is the name of the network drive for Macintosh. The path name for Windows separates all the elements by a backslash (\) without spaces. The backslash is a special character to the Windows operating system, which indicates another level down in the file hierarchy. For Macintosh, the colon (:) serves the same purpose.

Director 8

Creating a Dropdown List with a Behavior

The Library Palette comes with a behavior to create a dropdown list from a field text box. This behavior comes in handy when you want to select an item in a list. To create a dropdown list, you create a field sprite on the Stage, enter text for each line item, then drag the Dropdown List behavior from the Library Palette onto the field sprite. When the end user clicks the sprite, the dropdown list opens to reveal all its items. If the user immediately releases the mouse, the menu remains open until the next click. When the end user selects a menu item, the menu closes to display the selected item. If the end user clicks elsewhere, the menu closes to display the previously selected item. You can use the dropdown list to allow the user to make a selection or execute a simple command. If you use the dropdown list to execute a simple command, you can execute Lingo commands to open a movie, jump to a marker, or perform a task. The type of command executed depends on the contents of the list. Jean creates a dropdown menu for SpaceWorks online.

QuickTip
Place the dropdown list sprite in a high channel where it will not be covered by any other sprites.

1. Click the Product categories sprite in the Score
The Product categories sprite is selected in the Score and on the Stage. The Product categories sprite is a field text box.

2. Click Window on the menu bar, then click Library Palette
The Library Palette window opens, displaying the Controls library, the previous Library list selection.

QuickTip
To change the appearance of a dropdown list frame, select the field, click the Field tab in the Property Inspector, then change the frame setting at the bottom.

3. Click the down arrow , then drag the Dropdown List icon in the Control library to the Product categories sprite on the Stage
When you drag the Dropdown List behavior icon to a sprite on the Stage, a gray rectangle appears around the object, indicating where the behavior will be attached. The Parameters for "Dropdown List" dialog box opens, asking you to enter a name for the dropdown list and select other settings relevant to dropdown lists, as shown in Figure K-17. See Table K-3 for a description of the parameter settings for the Dropdown List behavior. These values can be used to create the push button.

QuickTip
You can choose any character to act as a check mark to indicate the previous selection when the dropdown list is open. Depending on the font you use, you may wish to use a check mark followed by a space.

4. In the Name of this list box, type Product Categories, then click OK
The field text box changes to a dropdown list, and a new cast member appears in the Cast window with the Dropdown List behavior attached to it.

5. Click the Close button in the Library Palette window
The Library Palette window closes.

6. Click the Rewind button on the toolbar, then click the Play button on the toolbar

7. Click the Products up sprite (the Products button) on the Stage, click the Product categories sprite on the Stage to display the dropdown list shown in Figure K-18, then click Prints & Calendars
The Prints & Calendars selection appears in the Product categories sprite.

8. Click the Save button on the toolbar
Director saves the movie.

9. Click File on the menu bar, then click Exit (Win) or Quit (Mac)
Director closes.

FIGURE K-17: Parameters for "Dropdown List" dialog box

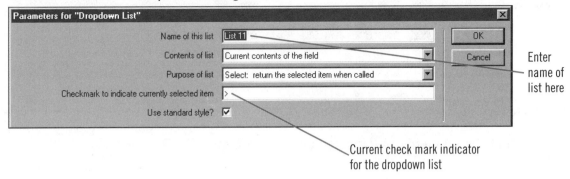

Enter name of list here

Current check mark indicator for the dropdown list

FIGURE K-18: Dropdown List behavior

Dropdown list on the Stage

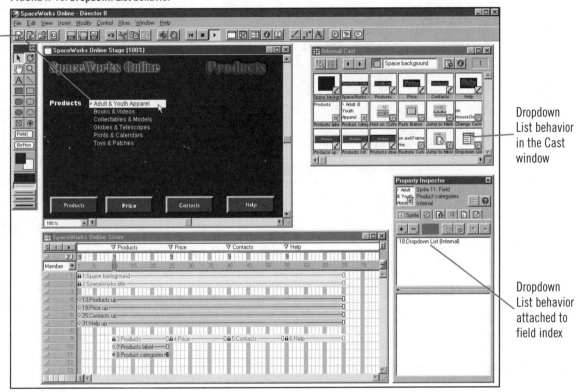

Dropdown List behavior in the Cast window

Dropdown List behavior attached to field index

TABLE K-3: Parameters for "Dropdown List" dialog box

parameter	description
Name of this list	name of the dropdown list; the name is used to identify the dropdown list in scripts
Contents of list	*Current contents of the field*: uses the current contents of the field; *Markers in this movie*: creates a list of markers in current movie; *Movie with the same path name*: creates a list of movies with the same path name
Purpose of list	*Select: return the selected item if called to do so*: displays the selected item in the list; *Execute: go movie I go marker I do selectedLine*: executes the item indicated in the Contents of list
Check mark to indicate currently selected item	character to act as a check mark to indicate the previous selection when the dropdown list is open
Use standard style	deselect this option if you want to give the field member a particular border, margin, or shadow

Director 8

Practice

▶ Concepts Review

Label each of the elements of the screen shown in Figure K-19.

FIGURE K-19

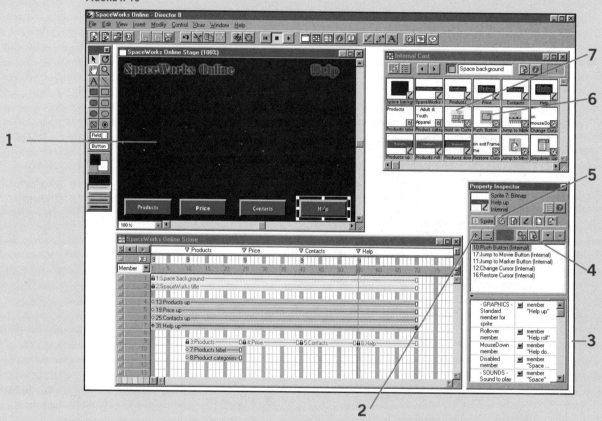

Match each of the terms with the statement that describes its function.

8. Internet library
9. Animation library
10. Controls library
11. Navigation library
12. Behavior
13. Event
14. Action

a. Contains three behavior categories: Automatic, Interactive, and Sprite Transition
b. A script that adds interactivity to a movie
c. The second function of a behavior
d. Contains behaviors that control the movement and location of the playback head
e. Contains behaviors that control interface elements
f. Contains behaviors that control activities on the Web
g. The first function of a behavior

Select the best answer from the following list of choices.

15. Which Library palette category contains the Draggable built-in behavior?
  a. Animation   **c.** Text
  b. Controls   **d.** Navigation

16. Which Library palette category contains the Jump Back Button built-in behavior?
  a. Animation   **c.** Text
  b. Controls   **d.** Navigation

17. **Which Library palette category contains the Countdown Timer built-in behavior?**
    a. Animation
    b. Controls
    c. Text
    d. Navigation
18. **Multiple behaviors are executed:**
    a. At the same time.
    b. From top to bottom.
    c. From bottom to top.
    d. In groups.
19. **Which is NOT an event?**
    a. Mouse Leave
    b. End Sprite
    c. Until Click or Key Press
    d. Exit Frame
20. **Which is NOT an action?**
    a. Exit
    b. Beep
    c. On Current Frame
    d. Prepare Frame
21. **Which button allows you to examine a behavior's Lingo commands?**
    a. Behavior Popup
    b. Script Window
    c. Event Popup
    d. Action Popup
22. **The path name for Windows separates all the elements by a:**
    a. Colon (:).
    b. Semicolon (;).
    c. Forwardslash (/).
    d. Backslash (\).

▶ Skills Review

1. **Understand behaviors.**
   a. List and briefly describe the seven types of built-in behaviors.
2. **Attach built-in behaviors.**
   a. Start Director, open the file **MD K-2** from the drive and folder where your Project Files are located.
   b. Save the file as *Nova* in the drive and folder where your Project Files are located.
   c. Open the Library Palette and the Controls library.
   d. Drag the Push Button behavior to the Loan up sprite on the Stage and accept the default parameter settings.
   e. Drag the Push Button cast member to the Calculator up, Contacts up, and Guide up sprites and accept the default parameter settings.
   f. Rewind and play the movie, click the buttons on the Stage, then stop the movie.
3. **View and change behavior parameters.**
   a. Attach the Jump to Marker Button behavior to the button sprites on the Stage, and select the corresponding jump to marker.
   b. Close the Library Palette, select the Loan up sprite, then display the Behavior tab in the Property Inspector.
   c. Double-click the Push Button behavior in the Behavior tab, then change the mouseUp sound to Chimes.
   d. Select the Calculator up, Contacts up, and Guide up sprites on the Stage, and change the Sound to play on mouseUp parameter to Chimes.
   e. Rewind and play the movie, click the buttons on the Stage, then stop the movie.
4. **Create a behavior.**
   a. Select the Guide up sprite, then open the Behavior Inspector.
   b. Create a behavior as *Change Cursor* to change the cursor to the Closed Hand on Mouse Down.
   c. Close the Behavior Inspector.
   d. Rewind and play the movie, click the Guide button on the Stage, move the mouse around, then stop the movie.
5. **Add a behavior.**
   a. Select the Guide up sprite (if necessary), then open the Behavior Inspector.
   b. Create another behavior as *Restore Cursor* to restore the cursor to the default on Mouse Leave.
   c. Close the Behavior Inspector.
   d. Rewind and play the movie, click the Guide button on the Stage, slowly move the mouse around, then stop the movie.

6. Modify a behavior.

a. Select the Guide up sprite (if necessary), then open the Behavior Inspector.

b. Select the Restore Cursor behavior.

c. Clear the event.

d. Create a new event to restore the cursor to the default on Mouse Enter.

e. Close the Behavior Inspector.

f. Drag the Restore Cursor cast member to the Loan up, Calculator up, and Contacts up sprites.

g. Rewind and play the movie, click the Guide button on the Stage, move the mouse around, point to a button, then stop the movie.

7. View behavior scripts.

a. Select the Loan button sprite, then open the Behavior Inspector.

b. Select the Jump to Marker Button behavior.

c. Open the Script window.

d. Scroll down the Lingo script.

e. Close the Script window and the Behavior Inspector.

8. Open a movie with a behavior.

a. Open the Library Palette and the Controls library.

b. Drag the Jump to Movie Button behavior to the Guide up sprite on the Stage, and type **Guide** for the movie name in the top box.

c. Select the Jump to Movie Button behavior in the Behavior tab, then shuffle it up the list, above the Jump to Marker behavior.

d. Close the Library Palette and save the movie.

e. Rewind and play the movie, then click the Guide button on the Stage.

f. Play the movie, then click the Return button on the Stage.

9. Create a dropdown list with a behavior.

a. Select the Loan up sprite, if necessary.

b. Open the Library Palette and the Controls library.

c. Drag the Dropdown List behavior to the Loan Amount list sprite on the Stage.

d. Type **Loan Amounts** and accept the default settings.

e. Close the Library Palette.

f. Rewind and play the movie, then click the Loan button.

g. Click the Loan Amount list sprite on the Stage, then click $500,000.

h. Save the movie and exit Director.

▶ Independent Challenges

1. You work in the marketing department at Toy Think, an educational toy company. You are developing a sales and promotion plan for the next six months and want to find out current customer buying trends. You want to create a survey for your company Web site to gather the customer information. You use Director to create dropdown lists from which customers can make recommendations.

To complete this independent challenge:

a. Start Director and save the movie as *Toy Think* in the drive and folder where your Project Files are located.

b. Create a text cast member with the text **Toy Think Survey** and drag it to the top of the Stage.

c. Create four field text boxes on the Stage, and name them Boys 3-5, Girls 3-5, Boys 6-10, and Girls 6-10.

d. Create a text cast member with the text **Boys 3 to 5 years**, and drag it to the left of a field text box (as a label) on the Stage.

e. Enter five toy items related to boys 3 to 5 years old in the field text box for Boys 3 to 5 years.

f. Repeat Steps d and e for **Girls 3 to 5 years**, **Boys 6 to 10 years**, and **Girls 6 to 10 years**.

g. Attach the Dropdown List behavior to the four field text boxes you created in Step c, and use the default parameter dialog box settings.

h. Play the movie, then select an item from each dropdown list.

i. Save the movie, then exit Director.

2. You are a freelance computer programmer and want to create a game in Director that allows the end user to zoom in and zoom out of the current scene. You are at the beginning stages of development and want to test the Change Cursor behavior with the two different zoom cursors. You use Director to change the cursor to the Zoom In or Zoom Out cursor.

To complete this independent challenge:

a. Start Director and save the movie as *Zoom* in the drive and folder where your Project Files are located.

b. Create a text cast member with the text **Zoom Cursor Test** and drag it to the top of the Stage.

c. Using the Filled Rectangle tool on the Tool Palette, draw a filled rectangle the size of the Stage.

d. In the Paint window, create a button cast member with the text **Zoom In**, then add the cast member to the Stage.

e. In the Paint window, create a button cast member with the text **Zoom Out**, then add the cast member to the Stage.

f. Attach a behavior to the Zoom In button on the Stage that changes the cursor to the Zoom In cursor.

g. Attach a behavior to the Zoom Out button on the Stage that changes the cursor to the Zoom Out cursor.

h. Attach a behavior to the Fill Rectangle on the Stage that restores the cursor.

i. Play the movie, click the Zoom In button, click the filled rectangle, click the Zoom Out button, then click the filled rectangle again.

j. Save the movie, then exit Director.

3. You are the multimedia designer for Digital Magic, a sports game development company. Digital Magic is in final production for an upcoming sports game. You want to create a separate Director movie with the credits, so you can use it in more than one game. You use Director to create a movie with text animation to simulate rolling credits and a Return button, then create another movie with a Credits button to test the process of opening a separate movie.

To complete this independent challenge:

a. Start Director and save the movie as *Credits* in the drive and folder where your Project Files are located.

b. Create a text cast member with the text **Credits** and drag it to the top of the Stage.

c. Create a text cast member with 5 to 10 names, and drag it on the Stage.

d. Animate the text cast member with the names appearing from the bottom of the Stage, like rolling credits in a movie. (*Hint*: See the "Creating Animation Using Keyframes" lesson in Unit B.)

e. In the Paint window, create a button cast member with the text **Return**, add the cast member to the Stage, then attach a behavior to the Credits button on the Stage that jumps back.

f. Save the movie.

g. Create a new movie and save the movie as *Sports Game*.

h. In the Paint window, create a button cast member with the text **Credits**, add the cast member to the Stage, then attach a behavior to the Credits button on the Stage that opens the Credits movie.

i. Save and play the movie, click the Credits button, click the Return button, then exit Director.

4. You are the computer support person at Cornerstone Books, a small book-publishing company. You are the only computer support person for the company. You are responsible for helping employees get answers to computer-related problems. You don't have the time to answer every question, so you want to create a movie with hyperlinks to computer support Web sites, to help employees get answers. You use Director to create a movie with hyperlinks to several computer support Web sites.

To complete this independent challenge:

a. Connect to the Internet.

b. Search for three or four computer support Web sites on the Web, and write down their entire URLs.

c. Start Director and save the movie as *Computer Support* in the drive and folder where your Project Files are located.

d. Create a text cast member with the text **Favorite Computer Support Web sites**, then drag it to the top of the Stage.

e. Create text cast members with the name of each computer support Web site and the URL for each site, then drag each one on the Stage.

f. Open the Text Inspector.

g. Double-click a text sprite and select a URL, then enter the complete URL in the Hyperlink box and press Enter (Win) or Return (Mac). Repeat this step for each text sprite.

h. Open the Library palette and display the Text library.

i. Drag the Hyperlink – General behavior on the text sprites with the computer support Web sites.

j. Save the movie.

k. Play the movie, click a hyperlink, then click your Web browser.

l. Repeat Step k to access the hyperlinks, then exit Director.

▶ Visual Workshop

Recreate the screen shown in Figure K-20. Print the screen. (For Windows, use the Windows Paint program. Press the Print Screen key to make a copy of the screen, start the Paint program by clicking Start, pointing to Programs, pointing to Accessories, then clicking Paint; click Edit on the menu bar, click Paste to paste the screen into Paint, then click Yes to paste the large image if necessary. Click File on the menu bar, click Print, click Print or OK in the dialog box, then exit Paint. For the Macintosh, use the SimpleText program. Hold and press the Command, Shift, and 3 keys to make a copy of the screen, double-click the document Picture 1 located on your hard drive, click File on the menu bar, click Print, then click Print in the dialog box. *Note:* When you create a new document with a copy of the screen, and a document Picture 1 already exists, the Macintosh names the new document Picture 2.)

FIGURE K-20

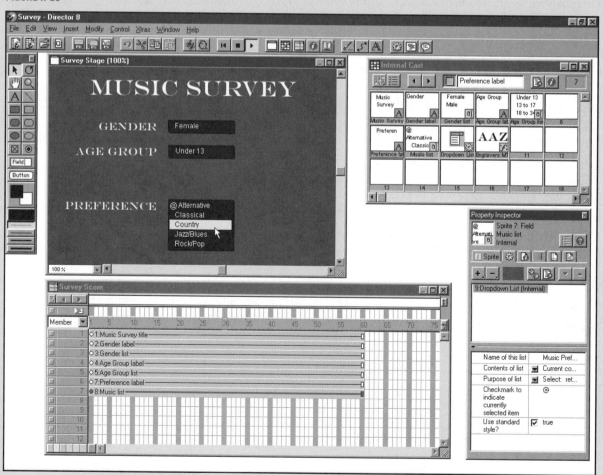

Writing

Scripts with Lingo

► **Understand scripts**
► **Understand handlers, messages, and events**
► **Examine Lingo elements**
► **Use the Message window**
► **Create cast member and frame scripts**
► **Use variables in a script**
► **Add functions to a script**
► **Debug a script**
► **Open a movie in a window**

Lingo, Director's scripting language, allows you to add functionality to a movie beyond what is normally possible when you only use the Score. First, you'll learn the basics behind scripting and Lingo. Then, you'll learn how scripting and Lingo work in Director. Finally, you'll learn how to create Lingo scripts to perform common tasks. ✐ Jean adds Lingo functionality to the SpaceWorks Online store.

Understanding Scripts

A Lingo script is a set of instructions that tell Director how to respond to specific events in a movie. An event is an action in a movie that generates messages for a script to perform specific actions. Events include mouse and keyboard input from an end user—such as clicking the mouse button, typing, or closing a window—or the frame position of the playback head. Director uses four types of scripts: behavior (sprite and frame), cast member, movie, and parent. The behavior, movie, and parent scripts appear as cast members in the Cast window, and a script icon appears in the lower-right corner of the Cast window thumbnail, as shown in Figure L-1. You attach a script to a sprite, a frame in the Behavior channel  (also known as the Script channel), a cast member, or the movie itself. See Table L-1 for instructions to create a script. The object or element to which you attach a script determines when and where its instructions are available for execution. You can view or change a script type on the Script tab in the Property Inspector, as shown in Figure L-2. ▬▬▬ Jean takes some time to familiarize herself with the types of scripts in Director.

Types of scripts:

Behavior scripts (sprite and frame) are Lingo scripts that make it easy to add interactivity to a movie. Director provides a Library palette with over 100 built-in behaviors that you can drag and drop onto sprites and frames in the Score window and on the Stage. You can use a prewritten script from a built-in behavior or create a script in the Behavior Inspector. You can attach multiple behavior scripts to one sprite, but you can attach only one script to a frame. Behavior scripts attached to sprites are helpful for mouse or keyboard input, while behavior scripts attached to frames are helpful for executing a command when the playback head is in a frame.

Cast member scripts are attached to a specific cast member and cannot be shared. These scripts are independent of the Score. When a cast member script is assigned to a sprite, the cast member's script becomes available for all sprites based on the cast member. A behavior, unlike a cast member script, may or may not be attached to a particular sprite. Cast member scripts are helpful for creating buttons that always produce the same response. You can only attach one script to a single cast member. When you attach a script to a cast member, a special script icon appears in the lower-left corner of the Cast window thumbnail, as shown in Figure L-1.

Movie scripts are available during playback of the entire movie; they are not attached to any object. The movie scripts are available regardless of which sprite or frame the movie is currently playing. Movie scripts are helpful for controlling events that determine when a movie starts, stops, or pauses. When a movie plays in a window or as a linked movie, a movie script is available only to its own movie. A movie can contain more than one movie script.

Parent scripts are special scripts that contain Lingo used to create child scripts, known as **child objects**. A parent script contains a set of rules that determine when and where to create a child object. When you attach a behavior to a sprite, it always executes in association with the sprite. When you create a parent script associated with a sprite, it only executes a child object when the conditions of a rule are met. Parent scripts provide a powerful way to customize a movie. Parent scripts are an advanced form of programming and are beyond the scope of this book.

FIGURE L-1: Cast window with different script types

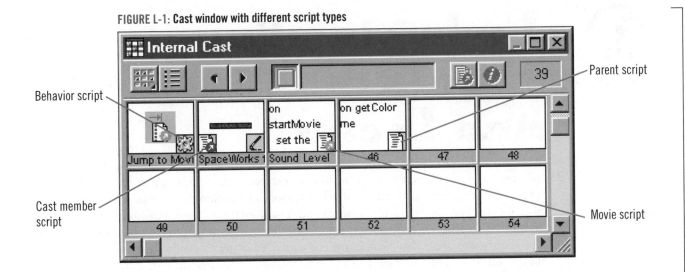

Behavior script

Parent script

Cast member script

Movie script

FIGURE L-2: Property Inspector with the Script tab

Script type for selected cast member

Script tab in the Property Inspector

Click arrow to change script type

TABLE L-1: Creating scripts in Director

script type	instructions
Behavior (sprite)	In the Score or on the Stage, select a sprite, click Window on the menu bar, point to Inspectors, click Behavior, click the Behavior pop-up menu, then click New Behavior.
Behavior (frame)	Double-click a frame in the Script channel.
Cast member	Select a cast member in the Cast window, then click the Cast Member Script button 🖹.
Movie	With no sprites or scripts selected in the Cast window, Score, or Stage, click Window on the menu bar, then click Script.
Parent	Create a script, select the script in the Cast window, click the Script tab in the Property Inspector, click the Type list arrow, then click Parent.

Understanding Handlers, Messages, and Events

The instructions in a Lingo script are organized into event handlers, which respond to messages triggered by a specific event during the movie's playback. An event is an occurrence, such as a key press, that Director detects, and to which it responds by sending a message. Each handler starts with the word **on** and ends with the word **end**. The word **on** is followed by a trigger message, such as **mouseUp**, which is a specific event to which the handler responds. The handler waits for the specific event to occur (for example, the end user releases the mouse button), and then carries out Lingo commands, one after another in the script, until it reaches the word **end**. Lingo scripts are written in a script window, as shown in Figure L-3. When a movie plays, Director continually checks for events that trigger messages associated with a handler. Because multiple handlers can respond to the same kind of event, Director uses a structured handler hierarchy in determining the order in which scripts can respond to a handler, as shown in Figure L-4. For example, when you click the mouse on a sprite, Director sends a **mouseUp** message and checks each handler (primary event, sprite, cast member, frame, or movie script) in the order shown in the Handler Hierarchy Flowchart in Figure L-4 until it finds a match. When it finds a match, the associated handler executes the Lingo commands in the script. For exceptions to this rule, refer to the "Choosing Event Handlers" lesson in the Appendix. If Director does not find an event handler, nothing happens.  Jean takes some time to familiarize herself with handlers, messages, and events in Director.

Working with events and handlers:

Director detects and responds to many types of events by sending a message. The most commonly used types are user feedback, playback, time, and window.

- **User feedback events** are related to mouse and keyboard actions performed by the end user. Examples include **keyDown**, **keyUp**, **mouseDown**, and **mouseUp**.

- **Playback events** are related to what happens when the playback head moves to another frame and when a movie is launched. Common playback events include **enterFrame**, **exitFrame**, **prepareMovie** and **startMovie**.

- **Time events** are related to the operating system and the end user when the system is inactive. There are only two time events: **idle** and **timeOut**.

- **Window events** are related to the running of multiple Director movies in multiple windows. Examples include: **activeWindow**, **openWindow**, and **moveWindow**.

Director has two types of event handlers: system handlers and custom handlers. System event handlers are built-in predefined handlers that recognize Director events. Table AP-10 identifies the system event handlers and the script types in which they will run. Custom event handlers are user-defined handlers that recognize actions defined by the developer.

The primary event handler is the first handler that Director checks when an event message is sent. The primary event handler is an important Lingo element, because you can define, or set up, the handler to meet your specific needs. The primary event handler uses an event handler property that corresponds to the message you want to handle, as shown in Figure L-3. For example, the event handler property **mouseupScript** in Figure L-3 is set to move the playback head to frame 1 when the end user clicks and releases the mouse button in the movie. The primary event handlers are a subset of Director's predefined system event handlers.

FIGURE L-3: Movie script window

startMovie handler

Lingo statement

Event

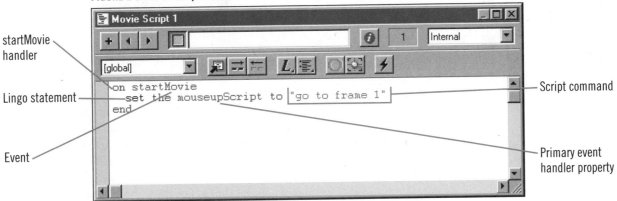

Script command

Primary event handler property

FIGURE L-4: Handler hierarchy flowchart

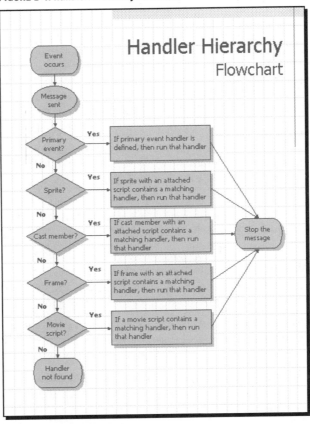

Setting up primary event handlers

Primary event handlers rank highest in the handler hierarchy; Director sends them messages first. To set up a primary event handler, click Window on the menu bar, click Script to open a movie script, create a handler (such as on startMovie), then type set the *property* to "command" in the middle of the handler before concluding with end. In this script, *property* is the primary event property that corresponds to the message you want to trap, and "command" is the script command that you want to execute, as shown in Figure L-3. In this case, the mouseupScript property is set to move the playback head to frame 1 whenever

an end user clicks the mouse button in the movie. Examples of an event handler property include mousedownScript, mouseupScript, keydownScript, and keyupScript. The Lingo Dictionary includes a complete list of primary event handler messages. To turn off a primary event handler, open the script window with the primary event handler, then type the statement set the property to EMPTY. For additional information on Lingo elements and commands, see "Examining Lingo Elements" in the next lesson.

Examining Lingo Elements

Director 8

Lingo scripts are composed of handlers. In the middle of a handler is a combination of Lingo elements, which form the statements (such as **go to frame 1**) that you want Director to execute when the handler is triggered, as shown in Figure L-5. Director executes a script starting with the first Lingo statement and continues in order until it reaches the last Lingo statement. The order in which statements are executed affects the order in which you place statements. For example, if you write a statement that requires a calculated value, you need to put in the statement that calculates the value first. Like most programming languages, Lingo has rules about how you can use Lingo elements to produce valid statements. See Table AP-11 for a list of some common Lingo rules. You don't have to remember all of the Lingo elements; Director provides a list of commands by category and by alphabetical order, in pop-up menus, as shown in Figure L-6. For help with Lingo commands, you can access the Lingo Dictionary on the Help menu. Jean takes some time to familiarize herself with Lingo elements in Director.

 Lingo elements:

- **Arguments** are placeholders that let you pass values to scripts. For example, the handler **on subtractThem a, b** subtracts the value it receives in argument **a** from the value it receives in argument **b**.

- **Commands** instruct a movie to do something while the movie plays. Examples include **go previous**, which moves the playback head to the previous marker, and **beep**, which produces a beep sound.

- **Comments** are information, such as notes or instructions, that you can add to a script to make it easier for you or someone else to use. Comments are preceded by double hyphens (--). You can place a comment on its own line or after any statement.

- **Constraints** are elements that never change. For example, **TRUE** and **FALSE** are constraints that always have the values 1 and 0, respectively, and the constraints **TAB, SPACE, EMPTY, RETURN**, and **ENTER** always have the same meaning.

- **Expressions** are parts of a Lingo statement that generate values. For example, **total = price * .0825** in a script creates a local variable named **total** and uses the expression **price * .0825** to generate the value.

- **Functions** return a value. Examples include **the date**, which returns the current date set in the computer, and **the number of words in**, which returns the number of words in a text cast member.

- **Keywords** are reserved words in Lingo that have special meaning. Examples include **the, of, cast, field, end**, and **me**.

- **Lists** are an effective way to store, track, and update a set of data, such as a series of names or numbers. Examples include **[1, 2, 3, 4]** and **["Bruno", "Thielen", "Teyler"]**.

- **Operators** are terms that change values using arithmetic operators, compare two values and determine whether the comparison is true or false, or combine text strings together. Examples include **+** (plus), **-** (minus), **<>** (not equal), **<** (less than), **"** (string), **&** (concatenation), **&&** (concatenation with space), and **not** (a logical operator).

- **Properties** are the various attributes of an object. Examples include **depth**, which retrieves the current color depth of a given graphic Cast member or image object, and **cursor**, which determines which cursor appears when the mouse pointer rolls over a given sprite.

- **Variables** are storage places in which you name and assign values. To assign values to variables or change the values, you use the equals (=) operator or the **set** command. For example, typing **price = 0** in a script creates a local variable named *price* and assigns the value 0 to it. Lingo supports both local and global variables.

FIGURE L-5: Lingo elements in a script

Event handler

Command

Function

Line by line execution of script

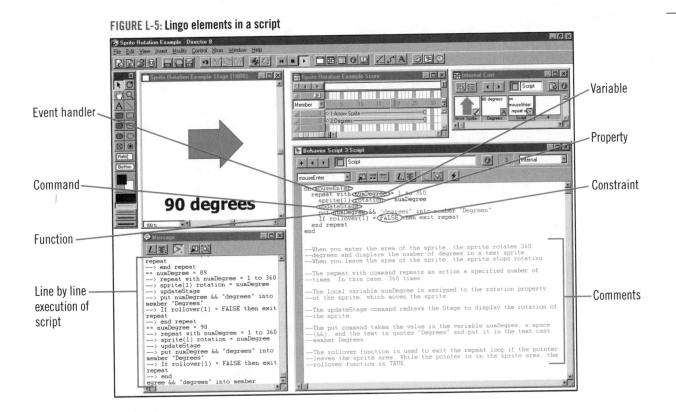

Variable

Property

Constraint

Comments

FIGURE L-6: Inserting Lingo commands

Click button to insert commands in alphabetical order

Click button to insert commands by category

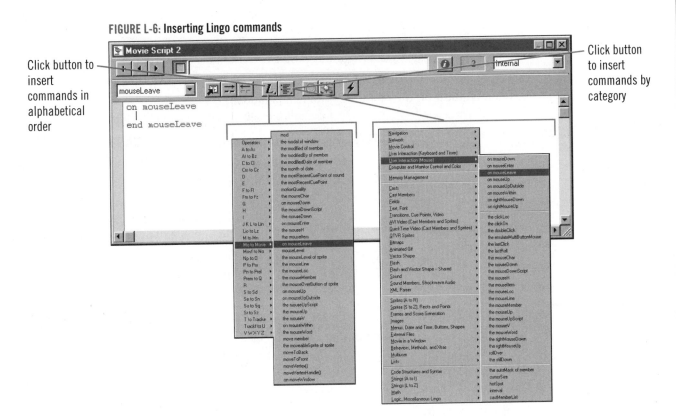

Using the Message Window

The Message window is a useful tool for executing and testing Lingo commands and scripts within Director. You can use the Message window to call handlers or to display messages activated by commands. The Message window shows you everything that goes on in the background, from event messages to Lingo commands. The Message window allows you to monitor, or trace, which handlers Director is currently executing. If a script is not working as expected, the Trace option can help you uncover the problem. When a movie is playing, the Trace option posts all script-related activities to the Message window, which also slows down the performance of the movie. Movie scripts are available during playback of the entire movie. The movie scripts are available regardless of which sprite or frame the movie is currently playing. Jean creates a custom handler in a movie script to display an alert message and executes it in the Message window.

Steps

1. Start **Director**, open the file **MD L-1** from the drive and folder where your Project Files are located, then save it as **SpaceWorks Online Final**
   Director opens, displaying the movie.

2. Click **Window** on the menu bar, then click **Script**
   The Movie Script window opens.

> **QuickTip**
>
> Director automatically colors different types of Lingo elements unless you turn off Auto Coloring in the Script Preferences dialog box.

3. Type the **script** shown in Figure L-7, then click the **Recompile All Modified Scripts button** ⚡ in the Movie Script window to activate the script
   After each line, press [Enter] (Win) or [Return] (Mac); after you type end, press [Enter] (Win) or [Return] (Mac) twice. Director will organize the script and indent commands automatically. When you type end, a new script cast member appears in the Cast window. Beep is a Lingo command that will sound the system beep; Put sends the text in quotes, known as a **string**, to the Message window. When you recompile all modified scripts, Director automatically checks a script for errors. If any problems exist, a dialog box appears, asking how you want to resolve the error. See the lesson "Debugging a Script" later in this unit for details.

4. Click **Window** on the menu bar, then click **Message**
   The Message window opens with a default message, "Welcome to Director".

> **QuickTip**
>
> Lingo commands are not case-sensitive. You can enter commands in the Message window in lowercase, uppercase, or any combination.

5. Type **doalert**, press [Enter] (Win) or [Return] (Mac), then click **OK** to close the alert dialog box
   The doAlert custom handler executes the beep, displays the error message text, time, and date, and opens an alert dialog box.

6. Click at the **end** of the script below the word "end" in the Movie Script window, type on **executeAlert**, press [Enter] (Win) or [Return] (Mac), type **doAlert**, press [Enter] (Win) or [Return] (Mac), type end, press [Enter] (Win) or [Return] (Mac) twice, then click the **Recompile All Modified Scripts button** ⚡ in the Movie Script window
   The executeAlert custom handler accesses the doAlert custom handler.

> **QuickTip**
>
> To trace all the handlers in a movie, click the Trace button ⊞ in the Message window to select it, then click the Play button ▶ on the toolbar.

7. Click the **bottom** of the Message window (if necessary), press [Enter] (Win) or [Return] (Mac), then click the **Trace button** ⊞ in the Message window to select it

8. Type **executealert**, press [Enter] (Win) or [Return] (Mac), then click **OK** to close the alert dialog box
   The Message window appears, as shown in Figure L-8. Each handler and Lingo statement Director executes is displayed, one after another.

9. Click the **Close button** in the Message window, then click the **Close button** in the Movie Script window

FIGURE L-7: Movie script with a custom handler

Custom handler

Executes a system beep

Displays an alert dialog box

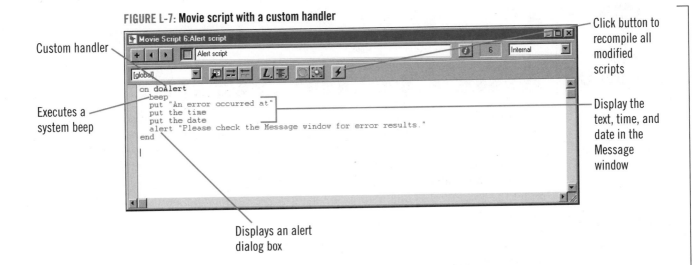

Click button to recompile all modified scripts

Display the text, time, and date in the Message window

FIGURE L-8: Executing Lingo in the Message window

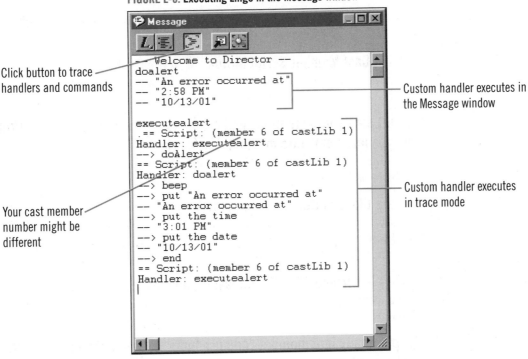

Click button to trace handlers and commands

Your cast member number might be different

Custom handler executes in the Message window

Custom handler executes in trace mode

CLUES TO USE

Finding Xtras using the Message window

Director can display a list of all the Xtras used in a movie, to help you ensure that you have bundled all the right Xtras internally with the movie, or that you have provided a separate folder containing the required Xtras. Type the put the movieXtraList command in the Message window, then press [Enter] (Win) or [Return] (Mac). This command returns a list of all the Xtras used in the current movie. Each of these Xtras will contain one of two possible properties displayed in the list: #name or #packagefiles. The #name property describes the name of the Xtras used on the current platform. If a #name description does not appear, it means that the Xtra is only available on the current platform. The #packagefiles property describes an Xtra marked for downloading. This property also contains a sublist of the #name and #version, which is useful when you want to gather all of the required Xtras and make sure that they are available for packaging and distribution.

Creating Cast Member and Frame Scripts

Cast member scripts are attached to a cast member, not to a behavior. A cast member script is useful when you want an action to occur whenever the cast member appears in the movie. When the cast member is assigned to a sprite, the cast member's script becomes available. A frame script is a behavior and is attached to a frame in the Script channel in the Score. Frame scripts are cast members and can be used in any frame. Jean wants to create a product calculator for the SpaceWorks Online store. She starts by creating simple scripts to initialize and reset field cast members.

Steps

1. **Click frame 25 in the Score**
   The playback head appears in frame 25 in the Score, and the Price scene appears on the Stage.

2. **Scroll down the Cast window, then click the Reset button cast member**
   The Reset button is selected in the Cast window.

3. **Click the Cast Member Script button 🖹 in the Cast window**
   The Script window of the Reset button cast member opens, displaying on mouseUp and end, the start and end statements of a handler, with a blinking insertion point in between.

4. **Type put empty into member "Add products", press [Enter] (Win) or [Return] (Mac), then type put empty into member "Total price"**
   These Lingo commands empty the contents of the Add products and Total price field cast members, as shown in Figure L-9.

5. **Click the Close button in the Script window**
   The cast member script icon appears in the Cast window in the lower-left corner of the Reset button cast member. When you play the movie and click the Reset button, Director erases the Add products field and the Total price field.

6. **Double-click frame 25 in the Behavior channel 🗐 in the Score**
   The Script window opens, displaying on exitFrame and end with a blinking insertion point in between.

7. **Type put empty into member "Add products", press [Enter] (Win) or [Return] (Mac), then type put empty into member "Total price"**

8. **Click the Cast Member Name text box, then type Clear calculation**
   The new name appears in the title bar.

9. **Click the Close button in the Script window, expand the Cast window to display all the cast members, drag the Clear calculation cast member to space 62 in the Cast window, then reduce the Cast window to its original size**
   The behavior frame script appears in the Cast window, as shown in Figure L-10. When you play the movie and click the Price button sprite, the Add products field and the Total price field are erased to start a new product list and price calculation. In the next two lessons, you'll add functionality to put products and prices in the Add products field, and to put the total price of the products in the Total price field.

FIGURE L-9: Cast member script

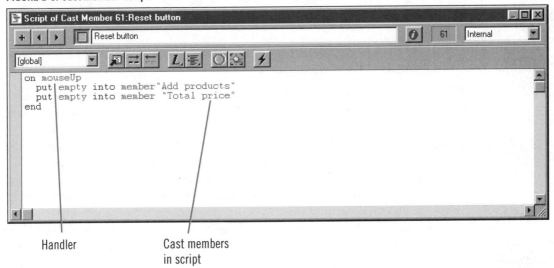

Handler

Cast members
in script

FIGURE L-10: Scripts in the Cast window

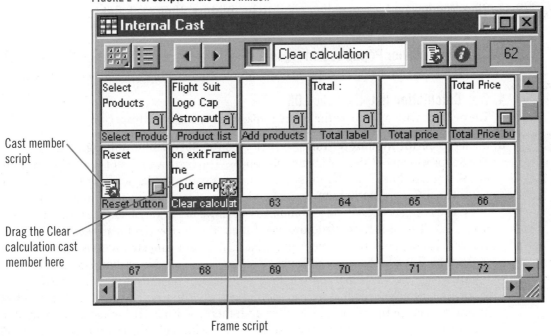

Cast member
script

Drag the Clear
calculation cast
member here

Frame script

Setting Script window preferences

You can change Script window preferences to customize the way you work with scripts in Director. You can change the default font type, size, and color in the Script window and the color of various Lingo elements. To set Script window preferences, click File on the menu bar, point to Preferences, click Script, then click the options and colors that you want to change. If you want to view all text in a script in the default color, click the Auto Coloring check box to clear it.

Using Variables in Scripts

Director 8

Lingo supports both local and global variables. A global variable can be used and set by all handlers in a movie. Before you can use a global variable, you need to declare it, or let Director know that the variable is global. To declare a global variable, you use the **global** keyword. For example, you can use the statement **global MyName**, where MyName is the global variable. Local variables exist only within a handler and are no longer available when the handler ends. You don't need to declare a local variable. You can give a local or global variable any name. Before you can use a local or global variable, you need to assign a value to it. To assign a value to a variable, you use the equals sign. For example, **Temp = 0**, where Temp is the variable. Lingo also comes with a special variable called **me**. **me** is a keyword that allows you to refer to an object without actually naming it, which comes in handy when you plan to use the same script many times. An **object** is any part of Lingo scripting that is designed both to receive input and produce a result. Every event handler is an object. ✎ Jean wants to add a script to create a product calculator.

1. Click the **Product list sprite** on the Stage to select it

QuickTip

Director will insert the new cast member in the next available space in the Cast window.

2. Click **Window** on the menu bar, point to **Inspectors**, then click **Behavior**
   The Behavior Inspector opens.

3. Click the **Behavior Popup button** ⊞ in the Behavior Inspector, then click **New Behavior**
   The New Behavior dialog box appears, asking you to enter a name for the new behavior.

4. Type **Calculation list**, then click **OK**
   The new behavior appears in the Behavior pane of the Behavior Inspector.

QuickTip

Director aligns the item after you press [Enter] (Win) or [Return] (Mac).

5. Click the **Script window button** 📄, then type the **script** shown in Figure L-11
   The Script window of the Calculation list opens. The first two lines of the script are comments. The next line is the **on mouseDown** handler with a **me** keyword. The **me** keyword is needed to define the **spritenum** property, which provides sprite channel numbers for variables. The next few lines of Lingo commands assign values to variables. The next set of commands is called an **If-then structure**. An **If-then** structure evaluates a statement and then branches to outcomes. If the statement is **TRUE**, the command after **then** is executed. If the statement is **FALSE**, the command after **else** is executed. The Lingo command uses the term **return**, which refers to [Enter] on Windows and [Return] on Macintosh. See Table AP-12 for the list of Lingo elements that refer to specific keys on Windows and Macintosh computers. The next set of commands is called a **case statement**, which is used to replace a chain of If-then structures. Lingo compares the case expression with the comparison in the lines below it. If it finds a match, Lingo performs the statement. Each line in the product list is associated with a price. The final command puts the product name and the price in the Add products cast member on the same line, separated by a (:) and ($). The variable **&** means to connect the strings in quotes ("), and **&&** means to connect the strings and add a space in between.

6. Click the **Close button** in the Script window and in the Behavior Inspector

7. Click the **Rewind button** ⏮ on the toolbar, click the **Play button** ▶ on the toolbar, then click the **Price button sprite** on the Stage to display the price

8. Click several items in the **Product list sprite** on the Stage
   The selected items appear in the Add products field cast member on the Stage, as shown in Figure L-12. The selected items are stored in the Product list cast member in the Cast window.

9. Click the **Reset button** on the Stage, then click the **Stop button** ■ on the toolbar
   The Reset button erases the contents of the Add products and Total price field cast members.

FIGURE L-11: Script with variables

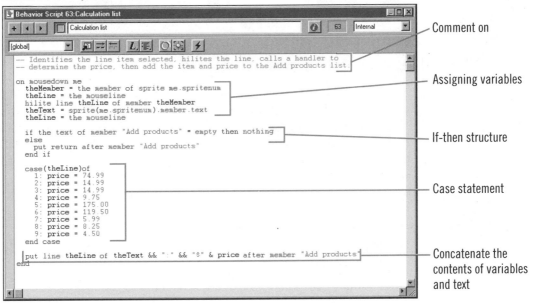

Comment on

Assigning variables

If-then structure

Case statement

Concatenate the contents of variables and text

```
-- Identifies the line item selected, hilites the line, calls a handler to
-- determine the price, then add the item and price to the Add products list

on mousedown me
  theMember = the member of sprite me.spritenum
  theLine = the mouseline
  hilite line theLine of member theMember
  theText = sprite(me.spritenum).member.text
  theLine = the mouseline

  if the text of member "Add products" = empty then nothing
  else
    put return after member "Add products"
  end if

  case(theLine)of
    1: price = 74.99
    2: price = 14.99
    3: price = 14.99
    4: price = 9.75
    5: price = 175.00
    6: price = 119.50
    7: price = 5.99
    8: price = 8.25
    9: price = 4.50
  end case

  put line theLine of theText && ":" && "$" & price after member "Add products"
end
```

FIGURE L-12: The Stage with script results

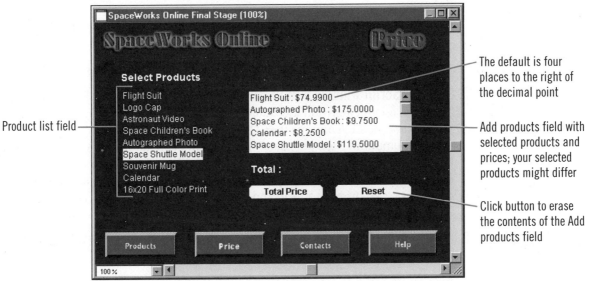

Product list field

The default is four places to the right of the decimal point

Add products field with selected products and prices; your selected products might differ

Click button to erase the contents of the Add products field

Writing Lingo statements in verbose or dot

When you write a Lingo statement, you can choose between two different styles: verbose and dot. The verbose writing style is similar to English, while the dot writing style is more concise, a shorter form. The verbose style is easier to read and understand, which makes it an excellent way to learn to use Lingo. However, the verbose style can become very long and hard to test. The dot style is harder to read and understand, but easier to manage and test. If you are just learning Lingo, it is a good idea to start with the verbose style and then start to use the dot style as you learn more about Lingo. You can use the verbose and dot styles in combination. Almost any Lingo statement can be written in the verbose or dot style. For example, the function for setting the window type can be written in the verbose style as the theMember = the member of the sprite me.spritenum or in the dot style as theMember = spritenum(me.spritenum). member.

Director 8

Adding Functions to a Script

A function is a Lingo element that returns a value on a particular state or condition. For example, the **date()** function will return the current date set in the computer, and the function **the number of lines in textParagraph** will return the number of lines in the Cast member textParagraph. Parentheses can occur at the end of a function, with a variable between them, to which the function is applied. Lingo provides a number of functions that can be invoked from any script. You can also design and program custom functions by writing handlers that return values. ✎ Jean uses functions to create a script to calculate the price of the selected products.

Steps

1. **Click an empty cast member space in the Cast window, then click the Total Price button sprite on the Stage**
   The Total Price button sprite is selected on the Stage.

2. **Click Window on the menu bar, point to Inspectors, then click Behavior**
   The Behavior Inspector opens.

3. **Click the Behavior Pop-up button ⊞ in the Behavior Inspector, then click New Behavior**
   The New Behavior dialog box appears, asking you to enter a name for the new behavior.

4. **Type Perform calculation, then click OK**
   The new behavior appears in the Behavior pane of the Behavior Inspector.

5. **Click the Script window button ▣, then type the script shown in Figure L-13**
   The script uses the function **the floatPrecision** to set the number of decimal places to display and the floating-point numbers (the values below the decimal point), and uses the function **the number of lines in** to determine the number of lines (defined as an Enter or Return keystroke) with text in the Add products cast member. The script also uses the **repeat with** statement to add up the prices for the products. A **repeat with** statement repeats the commands (between the **repeat with** and **end repeat** statements) a specified number of times. In this case, it reports the number of lines in the Add products cast member.

QuickTip

When you close the Script window, Director checks for any problems with the Lingo instructions. If it encounters a problem, an alert dialog box appears with troubleshooting options.

6. **Click the Close button in the Script window, then click the Close button in the Behavior Inspector**

7. **Click the Rewind button ◄ on the toolbar, click the Play button ► on the toolbar, then click the Price button sprite on the Stage**
   The price calculation scene appears on the Stage.

8. **Click several items in the Product list sprite on the Stage, then click the Total Price button sprite on the Stage**
   The total for the selected items appears in the Total price field cast member on the Stage, as shown in Figure L-14.

9. **Click the Reset button on the Stage, then click the Stop button ■ on the toolbar**
   The Reset button erases the contents of the Add products and Total price field cast members.

FIGURE L-13: Script with a repeating loop

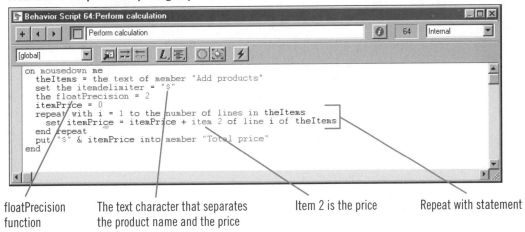

```
on mousedown me
    theItems = the text of member "Add products"
    set the itemdelimiter = "$"
    the floatPrecision = 2
    itemPrice = 0
    repeat with i = 1 to the number of lines in theItems
        set itemPrice = itemPrice + item 2 of line i of theItems
    end repeat
    put "$" & itemPrice into member "Total price"
end
```

floatPrecision
function

The text character that separates
the product name and the price

Item 2 is the price

Repeat with statement

FIGURE L-14: The Stage with script functionality

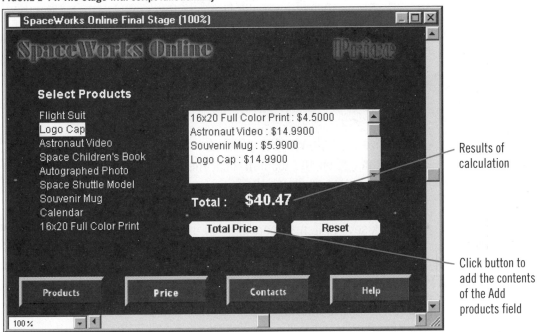

Results of
calculation

Click button to
add the contents
of the Add
products field

Finding handlers and text in scripts

When you are working with multiple scripts in a movie, it can be difficult to find the specific handler and text that you want. The Find command is useful for finding a handler or text in scripts and for replacing it with another handler or text, respectively. To find a handler in a script, click Edit on the menu bar, point to Find, click Handler, select the handler that you want to find, then click Find. To find text in a script, open the Script window that you want to search, click Edit on the menu bar, point to Find, click Text, type the text that you want to find in the Find box, then click Find. The handlers contain a description of their function and notes on how to use them. To replace text in a script, open the Find Text dialog box, type the text that you want to find in the Find box, type the text that you want to replace it with in the Replace box, then click Replace or Replace All.

Debugging a Script

When Director encounters a problem executing a part of a script, an alert dialog box appears and tells you what went wrong with the script. The alert dialog box allows you to click a button to debug the script, open the script, or ignore the problem. Using the Debugger, you can trace the execution of a script and locate errors as it progresses line by line or handler by handler. You can open the Debugger window from the Window menu or cause it to open by setting breakpoints in a script. A **breakpoint** is a location in a script where you want Director to stop executing Lingo commands, so you can look at the status of variables in the script. There are locations where you cannot set a breakpoint; lines beginning with keywords, such as **on** and **global**, don't allow you to set breakpoints. The Debugger helps you use basic troubleshooting techniques to quickly find and fix Lingo code that isn't doing what you want. If you are having problems getting a script to work correctly, you can access Director's support center on the Web. To access the Web site, click Help on the menu bar, click Web Links, click Troubleshooting Lingo, and follow the instructions. Jean sets a breakpoint in a script to find out the status of selected variables.

Steps

1. Click the **Perform calculation cast member** in the Cast window, then click the **Cast member Script button** 🖹 in the Cast window
   The Script window opens, displaying the Perform calculation script.

2. Click the beginning of the command **set itemPrice = itemPrice + item 2 of line i of theItems** in the script

3. Click the **Toggle Breakpoint button** 🔘 in the Script window
   A red circle appears to the left of the line, indicating that a breakpoint is set, as shown in Figure L-15.

   > **Trouble?**
   > If a gray circle appears instead of a red one, the Ignore Breakpoints button 🔲 is turned on in the Debugger window. Click the button to turn it off.

4. Resize the **Behavior Script window** so that you can see the Stage, click the **Rewind button** ◀ on the toolbar, click the **Play button** ▶ on the toolbar, then click the **Price button sprite** on the Stage
   The price calculation scene appears on the Stage.

5. Click several items (more than 3) in the **Product list sprite** on the Stage, then click the **Total Price button sprite** on the Stage
   The Debugger window opens, as shown in Figure L-16. See Table L-2 for a description of the buttons in the Debugger window.

6. Click the **Step Script button** 🔽 two times
   The Handler History pane shows the current handler and any handlers from which it may have been called. The Variable pane shows variables and property settings in the current handler as they existed when the breakpoint or problem occurred. It shows the current values of variables me, theItems, itemPrice, and i in the mouseDown handler. The Script pane shows the current handler, including the line of Lingo where the breakpoint or problem occurred. Each time you click the Step Script button, Director executes the next line of the script, which is identified by a green arrow. The script executes lines within the **repeat with** statement until it is complete.

7. Click the **red dot breakpoint** in the Script window
   The breakpoint is removed.

   > **QuickTip**
   > You can click the gray area to the left of a line in the Script window to set a breakpoint.

8. Click the **Close button** in the Debugger window and in the Script window
   The windows close.

9. Click the **Stop button** ■ on the toolbar
   The movie stops playing.

FIGURE L-15: Setting breakpoints in a script

Click button to set breakpoints

Click gray area to set breakpoints

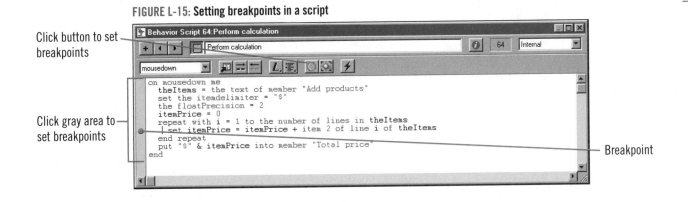

Breakpoint

FIGURE L-16: Debugging window

Handler History pane

Variable pane

Green arrow indicates current location in script

Script pane

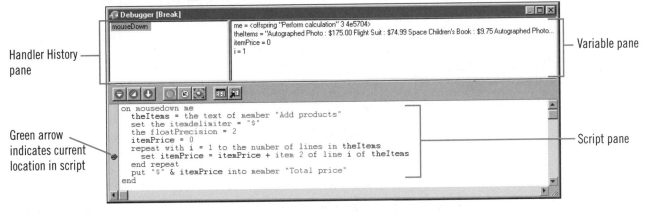

TABLE L-2: Debugger toolbar buttons

button	name	description
	Step Script	allows you to execute the next line of the script
	Step into Script	steps into and runs a handler, line by line
	Run Script	plays the movie without any control from the Debugger unless more breakpoints or errors are encountered
	Toggle Breakpoint	inserts or removes a breakpoint from the selected line of a script
	Ignore Breakpoints	passes by breakpoints in a script
	Watch Expression	adds the selected variable or expression to the Watcher window
	Watcher Window	opens the Watcher window
	Go to Handler	leaves the Debugger and opens the script window of the selected handler or line of Lingo

CLUES TO USE

Making troubleshooting easier

You can make troubleshooting easier by following some basic guidelines for writing Lingo code. There are four basic guidelines: include comments, use meaningful variable names, change one thing at a time, and work from a backup. The more comments you add to a script, the easier it will be later to decipher what the Lingo code is doing. Meaningful variable names that reflect their function make it easier to understand Lingo code. If you make one change at a time, you can isolate problems while avoiding new ones. Make a backup copy of a movie before you make significant changes to try to fix a problem.

Director 8

Opening a Movie in a Window

You can use a **Movie in a Window (MIAW)** script to open and play another movie in a separate window while the main movie plays on the Stage. Director allows you to open and play several movies at the same time. A MIAW is useful when you want to provide additional material in a movie, such as Help information, without having to permanently incorporate it in the main movie. The main movie and the MIAW can also communicate with each other to create interactive features, such as a status window. Before you create a MIAW, you need to realize that Shockwave does not support MIAWs, so only use them in movies that you intend to package as projectors. When you create a MIAW, you need to decide how you want to play it, whether the window will be able to move, and how the window will appear. See Table L-3 for a list of different MIAW window types. The easiest way to create a MIAW is to use the **open window** command, but if you want more control over the appearance of the window, you need to add Lingo commands to set specific window properties. The Lingo Dictionary located in the Help menu includes a complete list of Lingo commands for Movie in a Window. Jean opens a Help file movie in a window.

1. Click the **Help button sprite** on the Stage to select it

2. Click **Window** on the menu bar, point to **Inspectors**, then click **Behavior**
   The Behavior Inspector opens. The built-in behaviors currently attached to the Help button appear at the top. The events and actions associated with the selected behavior appear in the editing pane in the middle of the Behavior Inspector.

3. Click the **Behavior Popup button** in the Behavior Inspector, then click **New Behavior**
   The New Behavior dialog box appears, asking you to enter a name for the new behavior.

4. Type **Open Window Behavior**, then click **OK**
   The new behavior appears in the Behavior pane of the Behavior Inspector.

QuickTip

You can drag the lower-right corner to adjust the size of the Script window as necessary.

5. Click the **Script window button**, type the MIAW script shown in Figure L-17, then press **[Enter]** (Win) or **[Return]** (Mac) **twice** at the end
   The MIAW script appears in the Script window. The first line is the **on mouseUp** handler. The next line creates a global variable called **newWindow**. This will be used to create the MIAW. Next, you assign the variable **newWindow** to equal **window "New Window"**, the name on the title bar of the MIAW window. The next four lines add properties to the window: assign the name of the window to the movie filename you want to open, specify the movie filename (Online Help.dir) and path location (not specified, which means that the file needs to be located in the same folder as the main movie file), select a window type, turn on the modal type to prevent interaction with other elements while the window is open, and set the size of the window. The **stageLeft**, **stageTop**, **stageRight**, and **stageBottom** properties ensure that the new window is located in a specific place relative to the Stage of the main movie. The final command is to open the movie in a window.

6. Click the **Close button** in the Script window and in the Behavior Inspector

7. Click the **Rewind button** on the toolbar, click the **Play button** on the toolbar, then click the **Help button** on the Stage
   The Help movie opens in a window, as shown in Figure L-18.

8. Click the **Close button sprite** on the Stage
   The Help window closes. The Close button contains a script to close the window and purge it from memory.

FIGURE L-17: MIAW script in the verbose style

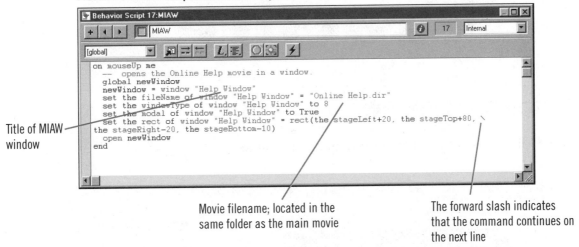

Title of MIAW window

Movie filename; located in the same folder as the main movie

The forward slash indicates that the command continues on the next line

FIGURE L-18: Movie in a window

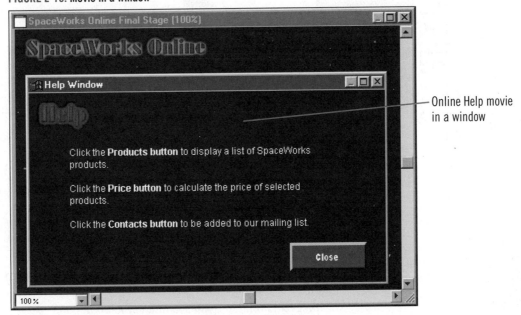

Online Help movie in a window

TABLE L-3: Common window types

type number	window type
0	moveable, sizable window without zoom box
1	alert box or modal dialog box; when you open a modal window, you cannot use another window until that window is closed
2	plain box, no title bar
3	plain box with shadow, no title bar
4	moveable window without size box or zoom box
5	moveable modal dialog box
8	zoomable, nonresizable window
16	rounded corner window

Practice

▶ Concepts Review

Label each of the elements of the screen shown in Figure L-19.

FIGURE L-19

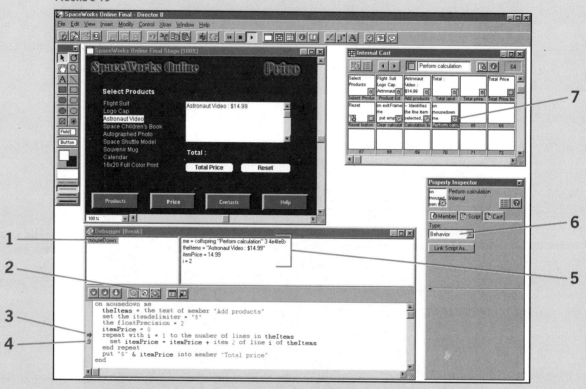

Match each of the terms with the statement that describes its function.

8. **Arguments**	a. Events related to mouse and keyboard actions
9. **User feedback**	b. Events related to the operating system and the end user
10. **Window**	c. Events related to multiple Director movies
11. **Variables**	d. Lingo elements that provide instructions to a movie
12. **Commands**	e. Lingo elements that store and assign values
13. **Properties**	f. Lingo elements that pass values to a script
14. **Time**	g. Lingo elements that control attributes of an object

Select the best answer from the following list of choices.

15. Which is **NOT** a script type?
   a. Sprite   **c.** Stage
   b. Frame   **d.** Movie

16. Which is **NOT** an event type?
   a. User feedback   **c.** Window
   b. System   **d.** Playback

17. **Which symbol is used for concatenation?**
    a. Hyphen (-)
    b. Double hyphen (--)
    c. Forward slash (/)
    d. Ampersand (&)
18. **Comments are preceded by:**
    a. Hyphen (-).
    b. Double hyphen (--).
    c. Forward slash (/).
    d. Ampersand (&).
19. **Which type of Lingo element is TRUE?**
    a. Keyword
    b. Constraint
    c. Command
    d. Argument
20. **Which type of Lingo element are the, of, and cast?**
    a. Keyword
    b. Variable
    c. Property
    d. Constant
21. **A case statement is a chain of:**
    a. Put statements.
    b. If-then statements.
    c. Expressions.
    d. Variables.

▶ Skills Review

1. **Understand scripts.**
   a. List and describe the four types of scripts.
   b. Describe how to create each type of script.
2. **Understand handlers, messages, and events.**
   a. List and describe the most commonly used types of events.
   b. Describe the structure of a handler.
3. **Examine Lingo elements.**
   a. List and give examples of the Lingo elements.
4. **Use the Message window.**
   a. Start Director, open the file **MD L-2** from the drive and folder where your Project Files are located.
   b. Save the file as *Nova Final* in the drive and folder where your Project Files are located.
   c. Open the Movie script window.
   d. Type a script with the handler on doAccept, sound a beep, display the alert "Your loan has been approved!", then end.
   e. Type a script with the handler doDecline, sound a beep, display the alert "Your loan has been declined!", then end.
   f. Recompile all modified scripts, then open the Message window.
   g. Test the doAccept handler and the doDecline handler in the Message window, then close the windows.
5. **Create cast member and frame scripts.**
   a. Select the Reset button in the Cast window.
   b. Create a cast member script like the one shown in Figure L-9 and close the Script window.
   c. Double-click frame 25 in the Behavior channel then create a script like the one shown in Figure L-9 and name it *Clear calculation*.
   d. Close the Script window.
6. **Use variables in a script.**
   a. Click the Product list on the Stage, then open the Behavior Inspector.
   b. Create a new behavior named *Calculation list*, then open the Script window.
   c. Type a script like the one shown in Figure L-11, but change the prices, then close the windows.
   d. Rewind and play the movie, then click the Calculator button on the Stage.
   e. Click several items in the Product list, click the Reset button, then stop the movie.

7. Add functions to a script.

    a. Click the Total Price button sprite on the Stage, then open the Behavior Inspector.

    b. Create a new behavior named *Perform calculation*, then open the Script window.

    c. Type a script like the one shown in Figure L-13, but delete the floatPrecision statement and change item 2 of line i of theItems to integer(item 2 of line i of theItems), then close the windows.

    d. Rewind and play the movie, then click the Calculator button on the Stage.

    e. Click several items in the Product list, click the Reset button, then stop the movie.

8. Debug a script.

    a. Open the script for the Perform calculation cast member.

    b. Set a breakpoint for the set itemPrice = itemPrice + integer(item 2 of line i of theItems) command.

    c. Rewind and play the movie, then click the Calculator button on the Stage.

    d. Click several items in the Product list on the Stage, then click the Total Price button sprite on the Stage.

    e. Step through the script.

    f. Remove the breakpoint, then close the windows and stop the movie.

9. Open a movie in a window.

    a. Create a script for the Guide button to open the Loan Guide movie in a window. (*Hint:* the Loan Guide movie needs to be located in the same folder as the main movie that opens it.)

    b. Type a MIAW script similar to the one shown in Figure L-17 without the set the rect of window.

    c. Rewind and play the movie.

    d. Click the Guide button to open the MIAW, then click the Return button to close the window.

    e. Save the movie and exit Director.

► Independent Challenges

1. You are an instructor at Silicon Valley College. You are preparing course materials to teach a class on Macromedia Director. You want to develop a presentation to show in class that outlines the basic concepts of Lingo. You use Director to create a movie presentation (like a slide show) that covers Lingo scripts, handlers, messages, and events.

    To complete this independent challenge:

    a. Start Director and save the movie as *Lingo Class* in the drive and folder where your Project Files are located.

    b. Create a text cast member with the text **Director Lingo Class** and drag it to the top of the Stage; drag the sprite across the entire presentation.

    c. Create a text cast member with text describing Lingo handlers, and drag it to the center of the Stage (frames 1 to 30).

    d. Create a text cast member with text describing Lingo messages, and drag it to the center of the Stage (frames 31 to 60).

    e. Create a text cast member with text describing Lingo events, and drag it to the center of the Stage (frames 61 to 90).

    f. Play the movie, save the movie, then exit Director.

2. You are a new developer for Casino Games, a small computer games company. You are prototyping a new casino game in Director. You are still learning Lingo, but you want to use the scripting language to become more familiar with its internal workings. To get started you want to create alerts for the winner and loser of the game. You use Director to create a script to display an alert dialog box and a beep for the winner and the loser, and use the Messenger window to test the script.

    To complete this independent challenge:

    a. Start Director and save the movie as *Casino Game* in the drive and folder where your Project Files are located.

    b. Create a text cast member with the text **Casino Game Prototype** and drag it to the top of the Stage.

    c. Open the Movie script window.

    d. Type a script with the handler on doWinner, sound a beep, display the alert "You have Won!", then end.

e. Type a script with the handler **on doLoser**, sound a beep, display the alert "You have Lost!", then **end**.

f. Recompile all modified scripts, then open the Message window.

g. Test the doWinner handler in the Message window.

h. Test the doLoser handler in the Message window.

i. Close the windows, save the movie, then exit Director.

3. You are the multimedia designer for Digital Magic, a sports game development company. Digital Magic is in final production for an upcoming sports game. You want to create a separate Director movie with the credits, so you can use it in more than one game. You use Director to create a movie with rolling credits and a Return button, then create another movie with a Credits button, to test the process of opening a movie in a window.

To complete this independent challenge:

a. Start Director and save the movie as *Credits* in the drive and folder where your Project Files are located.

b. Create a text cast member with the text **Credits** and drag it to the top of the Stage.

c. Create a text cast member with five to ten names, and drag it on the Stage.

d. Animate the text cast member, with the name to appear from the bottom of the Stage like rolling credits in a movie.

e. In the Paint window, create a button cast member with the text **Return**, add the cast member to the Stage, then attach a script to the Credits button on the Stage that returns to the previous movie. (*Hint*: Open the Online Help movie in the lesson, and open the Close button script.)

f. Save the movie.

g. Create a new movie and save it as *Sports Game*.

h. In the Paint window, create a button cast member with the text **Credits**, add the cast member to the Stage, then attach a script to the Credits button on the Stage that opens the Credits movie in a window.

i. Set the MIAW to open as a modal dialog box, and adjust the size of the window to display the Credits movie properly.

j. Save and play the movie, click the Credits button, click the Return button, then exit Director.

4. You are a new tester at Script It!, a multimedia development company that creates Xtras and behaviors for Macromedia Director. A developer at the company has created a behavior to drag a sprite on the Stage. The developer wants you to test the behavior script. You are new to testing behaviors and Lingo scripts, so you download the Troubleshooting guide by Macromedia and read the important details. You use Director's Debugger window to set breakpoints in the draggable behavior script and test it out.

To complete this independent challenge:

a. Connect to the Internet.

b. Start Director, choose Web Links on the Help menu, access the Troubleshooting Lingo link, download the troubleshooting file, then close the Web browser and Help window.

c. Decompress the file using WinZip (Win) or Stuffit (Mac). See your instructor for instructions or an uncompressed file.

d. Print and read the section on Using the Debugger window. (You need to have Acrobat Reader installed on your computer to open and print the Troubleshooting document.)

e. Save the movie as *Debugging* in the drive and folder where your Project Files are located.

f. Create a text cast member with the text **Debugging a Script**, then drag it to the top of the Stage.

g. Create bitmap cast members, then drag each one on the Stage.

h. Open the Library Palette, then display the Interactive behaviors.

i. Drag the draggable behavior onto the bitmap sprite.

j. Open the script for the draggable behavior, and set a breakpoint when the draggable bitmap tries to go outside the Stage. The Lingo statements are located in the **mDragSprite** handler.

k. Play the movie and drag the bitmap off the Stage to display the Debugger window.

l. Check to make sure the correct breakpoint stopped the script, then close the Debugger window.

m. Save the movie, then exit Director.

Visual Workshop

Recreate the screen shown in Figure L-20. Print the screen. (For Windows, use the Windows Paint program. Press the Print Screen key to make a copy of the screen, start the Paint program by clicking Start, pointing to Programs, pointing to Accessories, then clicking Paint; click Edit on the menu bar, click Paste to paste the screen into Paint, then click Yes to paste the large image if necessary. Click File on the menu bar, click Print, click Print or OK in the dialog box, then exit Paint. For the Macintosh, use the SimpleText program. Hold and press the Command, Shift, and 3 keys to make a copy of the screen, double-click the document Picture 1 located on your hard drive, click File on the menu bar, click Print, then click Print in the dialog box. *Note*: When you create a new document with a copy of the screen, and a document Picture 1 already exists, the Macintosh names the new document Picture 2.)

FIGURE L-20

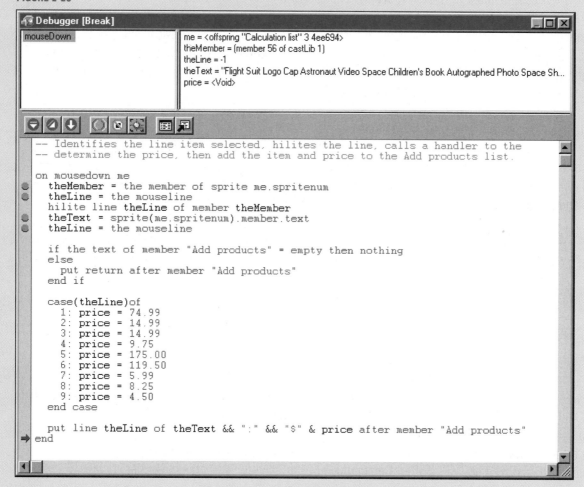

Getting
Started with Shockwave 8

Objectives

► **Understand Shockwave**
► **Install Shockwave Player**
► **Install Shockmachine**
► **Play Shockwave Content**
► **Set Shockwave Playback Options**
► **Set Shockwave Publishing Options**
► **Set Shockwave Compression Options**
► **Create and Play a Shockwave Movie**

You can create and fine-tune a movie in Macromedia Director, and then prepare and deliver it as Shockwave content on the Web. This unit introduces you to basic skills for preparing and delivering a Shockwave movie for playback on the Web, using a Web browser and Shockwave Player. First, you'll learn about Shockwave and Shockwave Player, and how to install the required software. Then, you'll learn how to set Shockwave options in Director. Finally, you'll learn how to create and play a shockwave movie in a Web browser. After completing a promotional movie in Director for SpaceWorks Interactive, an educational software company, Jean Young, an instructional designer, wants to install the necessary Shockwave software and create a Shockwave movie for the Web.

Understanding Shockwave

Shockwave is multimedia Web content you can view within Web browsers, such as Microsoft Internet Explorer, Netscape Navigator, and America Online (AOL). Web sites use Shockwave content for interactive product training and demonstrations, e-commerce programs, music, multiuser games, and communication. Statistics by King, Brown & Partners Inc. (a market research company) have shown that offering Shockwave Web content increases both traffic and user retention. Shockwave content is created with Director as a compressed movie and viewed on the Web with Shockwave Player. Shockwave Player is free, easily accessible, and widely distributed over the Web, in addition to being bundled with the Director program. Jean takes some time to familiarize herself with some of the particulars about Shockwave and Shockwave Player.

Details

Facts about Shockwave and Shockwave Player:

 Shockwave Player is one of the most widely distributed software components on the Internet. Over 120 million users have Shockwave Player installed, and approximately 200,000 users install Shockwave Player daily.

 Shockwave Player is downloadable free from www.macromedia.com and www.shockwave.com, as shown in Figure A-1. Macromedia also offers Web publishers free licensing to distribute Shockwave Player on the Internet, corporate Intranets, and CD/DVD-ROMS. Shockwave Player installs as a shared system component and includes an automatic updating feature. Shockwave Player also installs the Macromedia Flash Player, another popular Web content player.

 Shockwave Player supports multiple platforms and multiple Web browsers. Shockwave Player comes preinstalled on all Macintosh computers with System 8 or higher and PCs with Microsoft Windows 95/98/Me and Windows 2000 or later. The player also comes with every AOL 5.0 or later browser CD-ROM, Microsoft Internet Explorer 4 and 5 or later CD-ROM, and Netscape Navigator 4 or later Personal Edition and Netscape Communicator 4 or CD-ROM.

 Director, the industry's leading multimedia development program, creates the Shockwave Web content. Director allows developers to create an interactive multimedia experience that includes graphics, sound, video, animation, and text. The latest version of Director (Macromedia Director 8 Shockwave Studio) allows developers to incorporate Macromedia Flash 4, Apple QuickTime 4, and Moving Pictures Experts Group (MPEG) Audio Layer 3 (MP3) media to create streaming, multiuser, interactive content you can distribute on the Web or on CD/DVD-ROM. Shockwave Player is backwards compatible with Web content created in earlier versions of Director.

 Director 8 Shockwave Studio includes Shockwave Multiuser Server 2, which enables the development of multiuser collaboration on the Web. When Shockwave Multiuser Server 2 software is installed on a Web server, you can develop a variety of interactive Web content, such as real-time messaging, chat rooms, whiteboard discussions, auctions, and multiplayer games supporting up to 1000 simultaneous users.

 Shockwave content examples are available on the Web. These examples can give you ideas on how you can create Shockwave Web content. You can visit the Shockwave Web site at www.shockwave.com or the Macromedia Gallery Web site on the Macromedia Web site at www.macromedia.com to see some of these examples in action, as shown in Figure A-2.

FIGURE A-1: Macromedia's Shockwave Player Web page

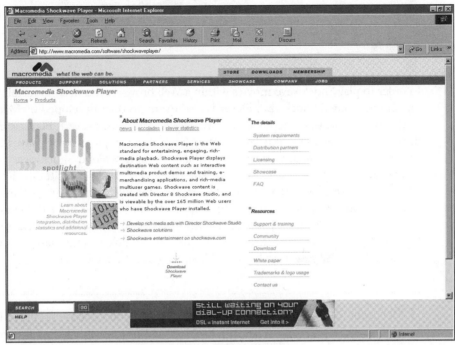

FIGURE A-2: Macromedia's Shockwave Showcase Web page

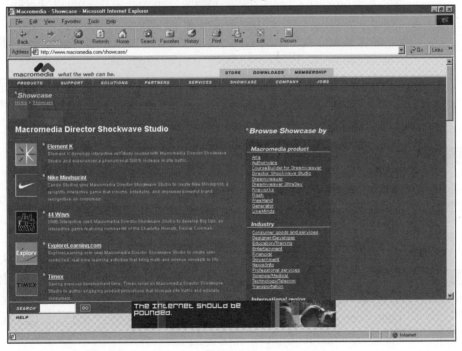

Understanding the difference between Shockwave and Flash Players

Shockwave and Flash Players are free Web players from Macromedia; both players display rich multimedia content on the Web, and each player has a distinct purpose. Shockwave Player displays multimedia Web content, such as interactive product training and demonstrations, e-commerce programs, music, multiuser games, and communication, developed in Macromedia Director. Flash Player displays fast-loading high-impact Web animation, such as advertising and promotion, developed in Macromedia Flash. By installing both players, you can ensure that you can display the widest variety of animated and interactive Web content.

Installing Shockwave Player

In order to play Shockwave movies within a Web browser, you need to install Shockwave Player on your computer. Shockwave Player is a software product developed by Macromedia, Inc. for Web browsers on the Macintosh and Windows. The Shockwave 8 Player can play Shockwave movies back to version 5. You can download the latest version of Shockwave Player free from the Macromedia Web site at www.macromedia.com. To download Shockwave Player on the Web, you need a connection to the Internet. The Director 8 Shockwave Studio CD-ROM also comes with Shockwave Player. If you already completed a full installation of Director 8 Shockwave Studio on your computer, you automatically installed the Shockwave Player and you don't need to perform the installation procedure. Once you install Shockwave Player, you can set the Auto Updates option in the Shockwave Properties dialog box to automatically receive Shockwave Player updates. Jean begins by installing Shockwave Player.

Steps

1. **Open your Web browser, connect to the Internet, and go to www.course.com. Navigate to the page for this book, click the link for the Student Online Companion, then click the link for this unit**

   The Web browser appears, displaying the Web page to download Shockwave Player. The location and look of the Web page for Shockwave might vary.

2. **Point to Products on the Web site menu bar, then click Shockwave Player**

   The Macromedia Shockwave Player Web page appears.

3. **Click the System requirements link**

   The computer system requirements for Windows and Macintosh appear. Check to make sure your computer meets the system requirements. If you are not sure, ask your instructor or technical support person.

   ### Trouble?
   Before you modify preferences on a computer that does not belong to you, check the policies or guidelines of the institution or company that owns the computer.

4. **Click the Back button on the Web browser toolbar**

   The Macromedia Shockwave Player Web page appears.

5. **Click the Download Shockwave Player graphical link at the bottom of the page (your link might be different), or click the Download link and then click the Download Shockwave Player link**

   The Macromedia Shockwave Player Web page appears, as shown in Figure A-3.

   ### Trouble?
   If the downloaded file is a compressed file with the extension .sea.hqx, you need to get Stuffit Expander to decompress the file (Mac). See your instructor or technical support person for assistance.

6. **Click the AutoInstall Now! button (Windows Internet Explorer) or Download Now button, save the installer file to your local hard drive, quit your browser, double-click the installer icon, then follow the instructions and your browser reopens (Windows Netscape or Macintosh Internet Explorer or Netscape)**

   For some computer systems, a dialog box appears, asking for additional settings.

7. **Follow the instructions for any dialog boxes that appear, if necessary**

   When both the Shockwave Player and Flash Player movies begin to play without comment, the Shockwave Player installation is successful, as shown in Figure A-4.

   ### QuickTip
   To turn on Shockwave Player Auto Updates, right-click (Win) or Control-click (Mac) a Shockwave movie, click Properties, then click the Auto Updates check box to select it.

8. **Close your Web browser**

   The Web browser program closes.

FIGURE A-3: Download Shockwave Player Web page

Click link to test Shockwave and Flash Players

Click button to install Shockwave Player

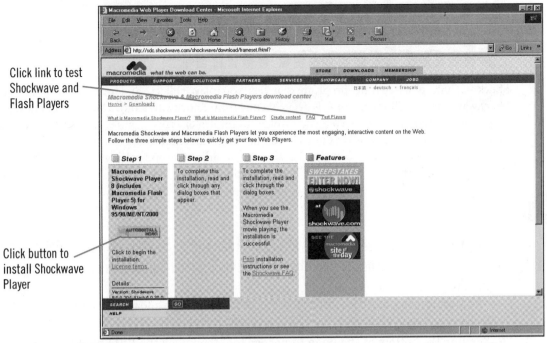

FIGURE A-4: Successful Shockwave Player installation

Shockwave movie appears when installation is successful

Testing the Shockwave and Flash Players

If you are not sure whether Shockwave and Flash Players are installed correctly on your computer, you can test them by using a link on Macromedia's Web site. The test determines if you have Shockwave Player and Flash Player installed on your computer and, if you do, which version. If you have any version of Shockwave Player and Flash Player, two movies appear on the test Web site. To access the test Web site, open your Web browser, go to www.macromedia.com, point to Products on the Web site menu bar, click Shockwave Player, click the Download Shockwave Player graphical link, then click the Test Players link.

Installing Shockmachine

Shockmachine is a separate program that lets you play, collect, and manage your favorite Shockwave movies. Shockmachine is available free from Shockwave.com, a Web site operated by Macromedia. The Shockwave Web site displays examples of music, games, and MP3 audio. To download the Shockmachine on the Web, you need a connection to the Internet. Once you have downloaded Shockmachine, you can use Director to adjust several settings to customize playback features of a Shockwave movie in Shockmachine. ➤ Jean installs Shockmachine.

Steps 1 2 3 4

1. **Open your Web browser, connect to the Internet and go to www.course.com. Navigate to the page for this book, click the link for the Student Online Companion, then click the link for this unit**
   The Web browser appears, displaying the Web page to download Shockwave Player. The location and look of the Web page for Shockmachine might vary.

2. **Scroll to the bottom of the page (if necessary), then click the Get Shockmachine link or the Get Shockmachine Free! link**
   The Shockmachine installation Web page appears, as shown in Figure A-5.

QuickTip

You might need to wait several seconds for the introduction to finish loading.

3. **Click the Go button (Basic)**
   The File Download dialog box appears.

4. **Click the Save this program to disk option button (if necessary), then click OK**
   The Save As dialog box appears.

Trouble?

If the Download dialog box closes upon completion, use Windows Explorer (Win) or Finder (Mac) to locate the installation program (InstallShockmachine), then double-click it.

5. **Click Save, then click Open when the download is complete**
   The Welcome to Shockmachine! dialog box appears.

6. **Click Next, click Accept for the End User License Agreement, then click Next to choose the default installation location for Shockmachine**
   The Start Installation dialog box appears.

7. **Click Next to start the installation, then click Finish upon completion**
   The Shockmachine installation is successfully completed, and the Shockmachine window appears, as shown in Figure A-6.

8. **Click OK to restart your computer (if necessary), then close your Web browser**
   The Web browser program closes.

9. **Open Windows Explorer (Win) or switch to Finder (Mac), then delete the Shockmachine installation file**

FIGURE A-5: Shockmachine download Web page

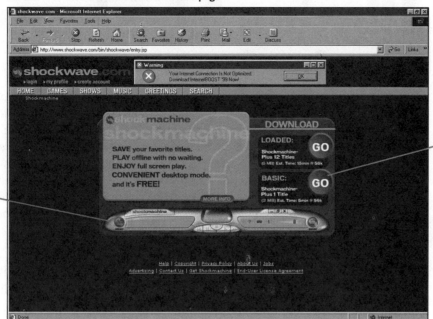

Click button to install Shockmachine and one movie

Sample of Shockmachine

FIGURE A-6: Shockmachine installation

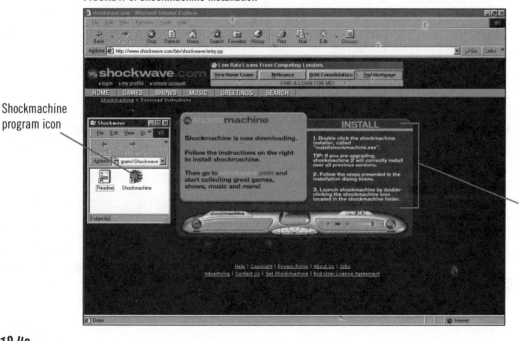

Shockmachine program icon

Shockmachine installation instructions

Uninstalling Shockmachine

If you no longer use Shockmachine, you can uninstall the program using the Add/Remove Programs utility in the Control Panel (Win) or drag the program icon into the Trashcan and empty it (Mac). To uninstall Shockmachine (Win), click the Start button, point to Settings, then click Control Panel to open the Control Panel window. Double-click the Add/Remove Programs icon, click the Install/Uninstall tab if necessary, click Shockmachine in the list of installed programs, click Add/Remove, then follow the uninstall program instructions.

Unit A

Shockwave 8

Playing Shockwave Content

The best way to learn about Shockwave is to view examples of Shockwave content on the Web. Macromedia provides two Web sites that show off Shockwave's many multimedia multiuser features: the Showcase Web site and the Shockwave Web site. The Showcase Web site displays descriptions and links to Web sites with Shockwave content. The Shockwave Web site displays Shockwave examples of music, games, and MP3 audio. Shockmachine allows you to play and organize Shockwave movies, also known as **cartridges**. You can save your Shockwave movies in Shockmachine for easy access and playback. Shockmachine plays Shockwave movies in full-screen format or offline with no waiting. Jean views examples of Shockwave content on the Web in Shockmachine.

QuickTip

To start Shockmachine (Win), you can also click the Start button, point to Programs, point to Shockwave, then click Shockmachine.

1. Double-click the **Shockmachine icon** in the Shockwave window, then click the **Next button** in Shockmachine Help until you reach the end, as shown in Figure A-7, and click the **Close Help button** if available

   Your Web browser opens and displays the Shockmachine. The Help screen in Figure A-7 shows the navigational features in Shockmachine.

2. Click the **Spin Carousel buttons** on the Shockmachine to display the cartridge you want to play, then click the cartridge in the carousel

   The Shockwave movie opens.

3. Follow directions to play the Shockwave movie

4. Click the **Eject button** on the Shockmachine

   The Shockwave movie closes.

5. Click the **Menu button**, then click **Shockwave.com**

   The Shockwave.com Web page appears.

6. Click the **Games button** GAMES on the Web page, click a **game category**, then click a **game title**

   The Shockwave game appears in the Shockmachine.

7. Click the **Download button** or **Save button**

   The Save to Shockmachine dialog box appears, as shown in Figure A-8.

8. Click **OK**, then close your Web browser

   The Shockwave game on the Shockwave.com Web site is downloaded to Shockmachine. When you close your Web browser, the Shockwave game appears in the carousel.

QuickTip

To save a Shockwave movie on a Web site to Shockmachine, right-click (Win) or Control-click (Mac) the movie, then click Save.

9. Click the **Quit button** in Shockmachine

FIGURE A-7: Shockmachine with Help screen

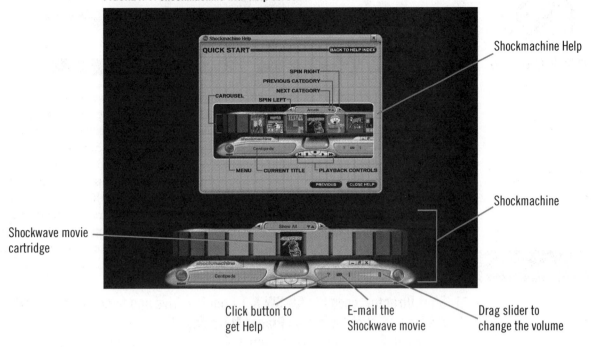

Shockmachine Help

Shockmachine

Shockwave movie cartridge

Click button to get Help

E-mail the Shockwave movie

Drag slider to change the volume

FIGURE A-8: Saving a Shockwave movie to Shockmachine

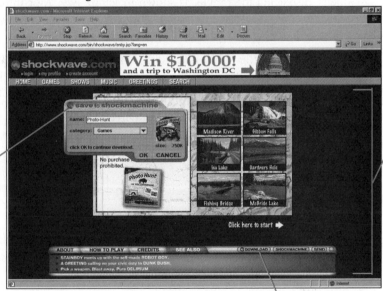

Shockwave movie

Save to Shockmachine dialog box

Click button to download movie

CLUES TO USE

Managing and organizing Shockwave cartridges

Once you save a Shockwave movie in Shockmachine, you can manage and organize Shockwave cartridges. You can delete, rename, and get information about cartridges. When you save a Shockwave movie in Shockmachine, you can select a category to help you organize your cartridges. You can change the category at any time. To choose the Delete, Rename, Change Category, Info, or Visit Web Site commands, right-click (Win) or Control-click (Mac) on a cartridge in the carousel to display a pop-up menu, then click a command. If you want to move a cartridge in the carousel, you can drag the cartridge to a different location in the carousel.

Setting Shockwave Playback Options

Streaming is the process that allows you to view a Shockwave movie in your browser while it continues to download from the Web. You don't have to wait for the entire movie to download before it starts to play. Streaming does not decrease the total time needed to download a movie, but it does reduce the time it takes to start viewing the movie. You can use the Movie Playback Properties dialog box to set Streaming playback options for the movie. In the Streaming area, you can set the movie to stream, and then specify the number of frames downloaded before the movie begins to play. If you have an introductory scene that plays while other media are downloading, you need to set the download value so that all of the required media for the introductory scene are loaded before the movie begins to play. The playback option can be set or changed at any time before you create the Shockwave movie. ✐━━ Jean sets movie playback options for a Shockwave movie.

1. Start **Director**, open the file **SW A-1** from the drive and folder where your Project Files are located, then save it as **Planet Matching**

   For Windows, click the Start button, point to Programs, point to Macromedia Director 8, then click Director 8. For Macintosh, double-click the hard drive icon, double-click the Macromedia Director 8 folder icon, then double-click the Director 8 program icon. Director opens, displaying the movie, as shown in Figure A-9. Your initial settings in Director can vary, depending on previous usage. Director remembers the previous user's window and preference settings.

2. Click **Modify** on the menu bar, point to **Movie**, then click **Playback**

   The Move Playback Properties dialog box appears, as shown in Figure A-10.

   > **QuickTip**
   >
   > If the Play While Downloading Movie check box is clear, Director downloads all cast members before the movie starts to play.

3. Click the **Play While Downloading Movie check box** to select it, if necessary

   This option turns on streaming for the Director movie.

4. Double-click the **Download box** to select the current value

   The Download box allows you to specify the number of frames downloaded before the movie begins to play.

   > **QuickTip**
   >
   > Setting a higher download value is useful for streaming movies that were not created for streaming.

5. Type **30**, if necessary

   The download value is set to 30 frames.

6. Click the **Show Placeholder check box** to select it, if necessary

   This option displays placeholders for media elements that did not completely download in time to be displayed in the movie.

7. Click **OK**

   The Play While Downloading Movie dialog box closes. The options you set in the Movie Playback Properties dialog box take effect when you create a Shockwave movie, or preview the movie in a Web browser.

FIGURE A-9: Director movie

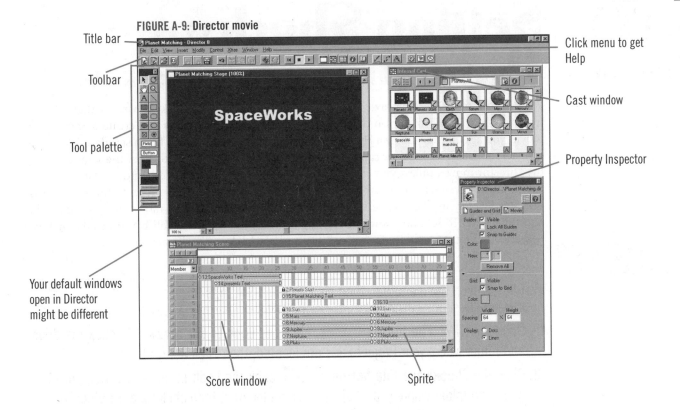

Title bar

Toolbar

Tool palette

Click menu to get Help

Cast window

Property Inspector

Your default windows open in Director might be different

Score window

Sprite

FIGURE A-10: Movie Playback Properties dialog box

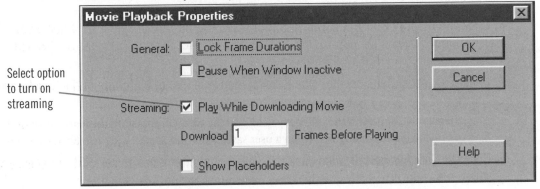

Select option to turn on streaming

Streaming Shockwave movies in Director

A streaming movie starts to play as soon as Director downloads the Score information and the cast members for the first frame. After the movie starts to play, Director continues to download cast members and any linked media in the background as they appear in the Score. When you create a movie to stream, you need to make sure all cast members have been downloaded by the time the movie needs them—otherwise the cast members will not appear in the frame.

Setting Shockwave Publishing Options

You can convert a Director movie and its entire linked media to a Shockwave movie that you can play back in a Web browser on the Internet or on an Intranet. When you create a Shockwave movie, you also need to create a Hypertext Markup Language (HTML) file (a standard Web page format) so that a Web browser can play it. The Shockwave and HTML files use the same name as the Director movie, unless you change it. The Shockwave movie's width and height are set to match the dimensions of the Director movie, and the background color is set to the one used as the Stage color in the movie. You can also set the Shockwave movie to play back in Shockmachine. To set Shockwave publishing options, you use the Publish Settings dialog box. Jean sets Shockwave format settings and playback in Shockmachine.

Steps

1. Click **File** on the menu bar, then click **Publish Settings**
   The Publish Settings dialog box appears, displaying the Formats tab, as shown in Figure A-11.

2. Click the **HTML File button** [....], click the **Look in list arrow** [▼], click the drive and folder where your Project Files are located, then click **Select Folder**

3. Click the **Shockwave File button** [....], click the **Look in list arrow** [▼], click the drive and folder where your Project Files are located, then click **Select Folder**

4. Click the **HTML Template list arrow** [▼], then click **Center Shockwave**
   This option centers the Shockwave movie in the Web browser window. Table A-1 describes the HTML Template options.

5. Ensure that the View in Browser check box is selected, then click the **Shockwave Save tab**
   The Shockwave Save tab appears, as shown in Figure A-12.

6. Click the **Display Context Menu in Shockwave check box** to select it, if necessary
   This option displays the pop-up menu when you right-click (Win) or Control-click (Mac) the Shockwave movie in a Web browser.

7. In the Suggested Category box, type **Games**, then type **Planet Matching** in the Shockwave Title box
   This category will appear in the Category field, and the title will appear in the Name field of the Save to Shockmachine dialog box when a user saves your Shockwave movie to Shockmachine.

8. Click the **Shockwave tab**, then click the **Save Local check box** to select it, if necessary
   This option allows users to save the Shockwave movie to Shockmachine.

9. Click **OK**
   The file locations for the HTML and Shockwave files are set to the folder where your Project Files are located and set to play back in Shockmachine.

FIGURE A-11: Formats tab in the Publish Setting dialog box

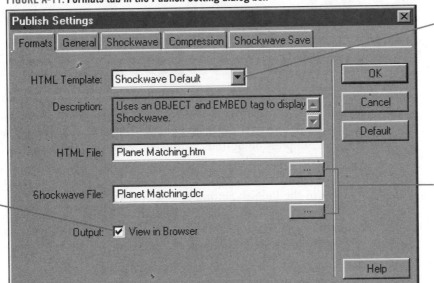

Click arrow to select an HTML template

Select option to view movie in a Web browser after you publish it

Click button to select a folder destination for the file

FIGURE A-12: Shockwave Save tab in the Publish Setting dialog box

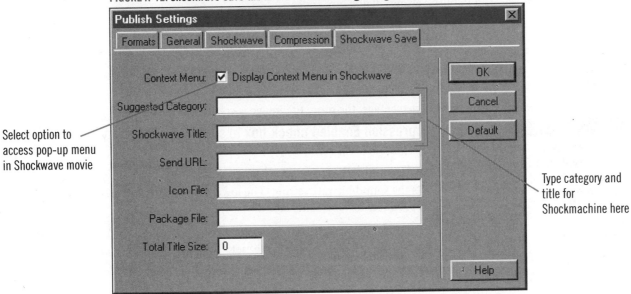

Select option to access pop-up menu in Shockwave movie

Type category and title for Shockmachine here

TABLE A-1: HTML Template options

HTML template	description
No HTML Template	Creates only the Shockwave file, without the HTML file
Shockwave Default	Creates an HTML file that runs a Shockwave movie in a Web browser
Detect Shockwave	Detects whether users have the correct version of Shockwave Player installed
Fill Browser Window	Expands the Shockwave movie to fill the entire Web browser window
Loader Game	Displays a game with a progress bar while the Shockwave movie loads
Progress Bar with Image	Displays a progress bar and an image while the Shockwave movie loads; the Image tab of the Publish Settings dialog box appears
Shockwave with Image	Automatically installs the Windows version of the Shockwave Player, if not installed
Simple Progress Bar	Displays a progress bar while the Shockwave movie loads
Center Shockwave	Centers the movie in the Web browser window

Setting Shockwave Compression Options

The Compression tab in the Publish Settings dialog box allows you to compress all bitmap cast members and sounds when you create a Shockwave movie. When you compress graphics and sound in a Shockwave movie, it downloads faster from the Web. The Compression tab allows you to set general compression options for the entire movie. If you want to set individual compression options for a selected graphic, you can use the Compression pop-up menu on the Bitmap tab in the Property Inspector. This setting overrides the general settings on the Compression tab in the Publish Setting dialog box. You can use Shockwave Audio (SWA) to compress all internal sound cast members. Shockwave Audio makes sounds much smaller in a Shockwave movie, by a ratio of as much as 12 to 1, without noticeable loss in sound quality. Jean sets compression options for the entire movie.

Steps

1. Click **File** on the menu bar, then click **Publish Settings**
   The Publish Settings dialog box appears.

2. Click the **Compression tab**
   The Compression tab appears, as shown in Figure A-13.

3. Click the **JPEG option button**, if necessary

4. Drag the Image Compression Slider to **70**
   The lower the percentage, the more the image is compressed.

5. Click the **Compression Enabled check box** to select it, if necessary
   This option compresses sounds in the movie.

6. Click the **kBits/second list arrow** ▼, then click **56**
   This option sets the sound bit-rate setting. The lower the value, the more the sound is compressed, which produces lower-quality sound.

7. Click **OK**
   The Shockwave compression options are set. You are ready to create and play a Shockwave movie.

Trouble?

If you use Shockwave Audio compression and distribute the movie, you need to include the SWA decompression Xtra. Click Modify on the menu bar, point to Movie, click Xtras, click the SWA decompression Xtra, then click Add.

FIGURE A-13: Compression tab in the Publish Settings dialog box

Drag slider to adjust compression quality

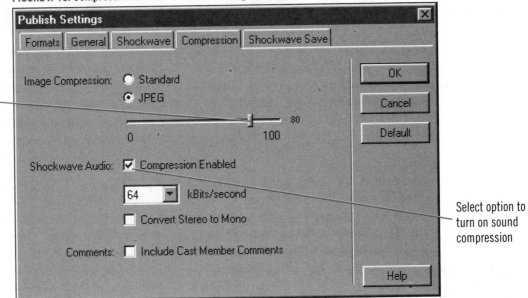

Select option to turn on sound compression

CLUES TO USE

Creating multiple movies to Shockwave files

You can use the Convert to Shockwave Movie option in the Update Movies dialog box to create compressed Shockwave movies. Once a movie is compressed into the Shockwave format, you cannot edit the file. You need to change the original Director movie and then convert the movie to Shockwave again. The conversion creates a movie file with the .dcr extension and a cast with the .cxt extension, which the end user cannot modify. If you have multiple Director movies and casts, you can convert them to Shockwave files all at once, instead of converting each one individually. You can convert the files while preserving the original files, or convert the files and delete the original files. To convert multiple movies to Shockwave files, click Xtras on the menu bar, click Update Movies, click the Convert to Shockwave Movie option button, click the Backup into Folder option button, click Browse, select the folder where you want to put the original files, click Open, click OK, select the movie(s) you want to convert, click Add for each individual file or Add All, then click Proceed. Director does not automatically save linked External Casts. You need to add each External Cast that you want to convert.

Creating and Playing a Shockwave Movie

Before you create a Shockwave movie, you can preview and test it in your Web browser. When you preview or create a Shockwave movie, Director checks to make sure all of the required Xtras are available and downloaded on the computer where the Shockwave movie appears. An Xtra is software module you can add to Director, which extends the capabilities in Director. If an Xtra is needed and is not included in the Plug-in folder, you can set an option in the Movie Xtras dialog box to have Director inform the end user that the Xtra is needed, and then download it. Xtras are generally implemented as plug-ins in Director. Director can also incorporate plug-ins written to other standards, such as Photoshop standards. When you create a Shockwave movie, you also need to create an HTML file, so that a Web browser can play it. After you create the HTML file, you can use other Web page editing programs, such as Macromedia Dreamweaver, to further customize the HTML file. Once you create a Shockwave movie, you cannot modify it; you need to change the original movie in Director, and then create a new Shockwave file. ✒ Jean previews the Planet Matching movie in a Web browser, then creates a Shockwave movie.

Steps

1. **Click File on the menu bar, then click Save and Compact**
   Director saves and compacts the movie.

2. **Click File on the menu bar, then click Preview in Browser**
   Your Web browser appears, loads the movie, and plays it. Director creates a temporary Shockwave and HTML file to preview the movie in the Web browser. Because the Shockwave file is only temporary, it is not centered and the background doesn't match.

3. **Play the matching game in the Web browser by dragging the planets from the bottom to their original positions**
   The movie plays in the Web browser.

4. **Close your Web browser**
   The Web browser closes. Now you are ready to save your Director movie as a Shockwave movie.

5. **Click File on the menu bar, click Publish, then click Yes, if necessary, to save the movie**
   Director publishes the Shockwave file with the .dcr extension (Win) and the HTML file with the .htm extension (Win) in the folder where your Project Files are located, and then the movie plays in a Web browser, as shown in Figure A-14.

6. **Close your Web browser**
   The Web browser closes.

7. **Click File on the menu bar, then click Exit (Win) or Quit (Mac)**
   Director closes.

Trouble?

If a warning dialog box about missing an Xtra appears, write down the missing Xtra, then click OK. Click Modify on the menu bar, point to Movie, click Xtras to open the Movie Xtras dialog box, click the missing Xtra, then click Add.

QuickTip

To play a Shockwave movie, you can also open your Web browser, click File on the menu bar, click Open File, select the HTML file (.htm extension on Windows) that plays the Shockwave movie, then click Open.

FIGURE A-14: Shockwave movie in a Web browser

Shockwave movie
centered

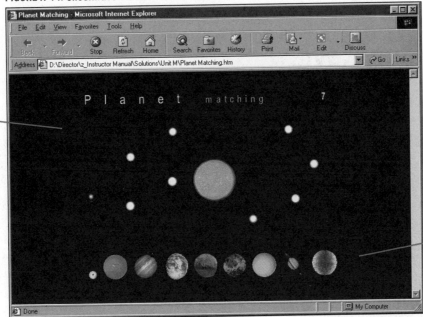

Browser background
color matches the
Director movie

CLUES TO USE

Specifying a Web browser for previewing a movie

You can specify the Web browser you want to use when Director previews a Shockwave movie. To specify a Web browser, click File on the menu, point to Preferences, then click Network to display the Network Preferences dialog box, as shown in Figure A-15. Click Browse, choose the browser program file you want Director to use for previewing a movie, then click Open.

FIGURE A-15: Network Preferences dialog box

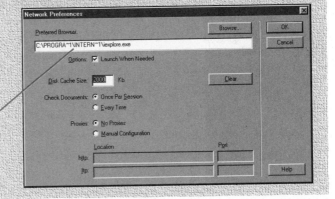

Microsoft Internet Explorer; your
browser might be different

Practice

► Concepts Review

Label each of the elements of the screen shown in Figure A-16.

FIGURE A-16

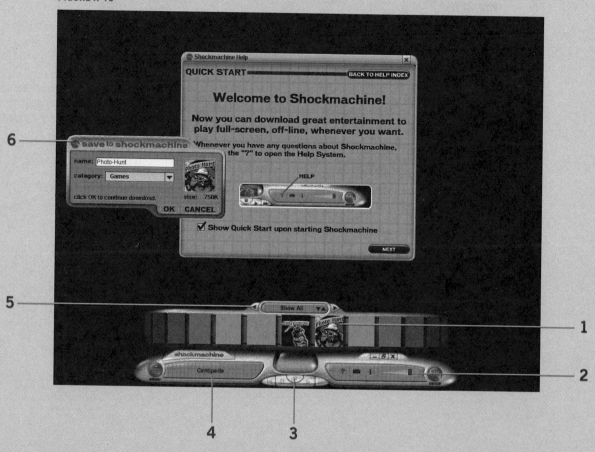

Match each of the terms with the statement that describes its function.

7. Shockwave
8. Shockmachine
9. Cartridge
10. Shockwave Player
11. Streaming

a. The process that allows you to continuously view Shockwave movies in a browser
b. The Web content that allows you to view Shockwave movies in a browser
c. A Shockwave movie in Shockmachine
d. A program that organizes and manages Shockwave movies
e. A program that displays Shockwave movies

Select the best answer from the following list of choices.

12. Shockwave content is created with:
a. Director.
b. Shockmachine.
c. Flash.
d. Shockwave Player.

13. What player is also installed with Shockwave Player?
a. Shockmachine
b. Director
c. Flash
d. Fireworks

14. A movie in Shockmachine is called a:
a. File.
b. Document.
c. Cartridge.
d. Movie.

15. What is created along with a Shockwave movie?
a. HTML file
b. Movie file
c. Cartridge file
d. Document file

16. Which is NOT a Publish Settings dialog box tab?
a. Formats
b. Shockwave Save
c. Compression
d. Movie

17. Which is NOT an HTML Template option?
a. Shockwave Default
b. No HTML Template
c. Progress Bar without Image
d. Loader Game

18. Which HTML Template option installs Shockwave Player (Win)?
a. Shockwave Default
b. Detect Shockwave
c. Shockwave with Image
d. Center Shockwave

19. **Shockwave Audio compresses sound by a ratio of as much as:**
    a. 4 to 1.
    b. 8 to 1.
    c. 12 to 1.
    d. 16 to 1.

20. **Which program allows you to edit a Shockwave file?**
    a. No program
    b. Dreamweaver
    c. Director
    d. Flash

21. **Which program allows you to edit an HTML file?**
    a. Shockmachine
    b. Dreamweaver
    c. Director
    d. Flash

 # Skills Review

1. **Understand Shockwave.**
    a. List and describe the main facts about Shockwave and Shockwave Player.

2. **Install Shockwave Player.**
    a. Open your Web browser.
    b. Display the Shockwave Player Web page.
    c. Display the Download Shockwave Player Web page.
    d. Describe the steps to install Shockwave Player (instead of reinstalling it).
    e. Close your Web browser.

3. **Install Shockmachine.**
    a. Open your Web browser.
    b. Display the Shockmachine installation Web page.
    c. Describe the steps to install Shockmachine (instead of reinstalling it).
    d. Close your Web browser.

4. **Play Shockwave content.**
    a. Start Shockmachine.
    b. Close Shockmachine Help, if necessary.
    c. Click the Menu button, then click Shockwave.com.
    d. Open a Shockwave movie.
    e. Download or save the Shockwave movie to Shockmachine.
    f. Play the Shockwave movie in Shockmachine.
    g. Close your Web browser and quit Shockmachine.

5. **Set Shockwave playback options.**
   a. Start Director, then open the file **SW A-2** from the drive and folder where your Project Files are located.
   b. Save the file as *State Matching* in the drive and folder where your Project Files are located.
   c. Open the Movie Playback Properties dialog box.
   d. Turn on the streaming option.
   e. Set the Download value to 15.
   f. Close the Movie Playback Properties dialog box.

6. **Set Shockwave publish options.**
   a. Open the Publish Settings dialog box.
   b. Select the drive and folder where your Project Files are located for the HTML file.
   c. Select the drive and folder where your Project Files are located for the Shockwave file.
   d. Set the HTML Template to Progress Bar with Image.
   e. Click the Shockwave Save tab.
   f. Select the Display Context Menu in Shockwave check box.
   g. Type **State Matching** in the Shockwave Title box.
   h. Type **Games** in the Suggested Category box.
   i. Click the Shockwave tab.
   j. Select the Save Local check box, if necessary.
   k. Close the Publish Settings dialog box.

7. **Set Shockwave compression options.**
   a. Open the Publish Settings dialog box.
   b. Click the Compression tab.
   c. Set the JPEG option.
   d. Select the Compression Enabled check box.
   e. Set the sound bit-rate setting to 48.
   f. Close the Publish Settings dialog box.

8. **Create and play a Shockwave movie.**
   a. Save and compact the movie.
   b. Preview the movie in a browser.
   c. Close your browser.
   d. Publish the Shockwave movie.
   e. Close your browser.
   f. Exit Director.

▶ Independent Challenges

1. You have bought a new computer and want to surf the Web. Many Web pages contain Shockwave content, so you want to make sure your computer contains the latest version of Shockwave Player. You use a Web browser to test the version of Shockwave Player on your computer and install Shockwave Player and Shockmachine.

To complete this independent challenge:

a. Open your Web browser.
b. Display the Shockwave Player Web site.
c. Test the version of Shockwave Player on your computer.

d. Print the Web page with the test results.

e. Install Shockwave Player. (*Hint*: Use the Macromedia Web site.)

f. Install Shockmachine; remember where you store the installation program. (*Hint*: Use the Shockwave.com Web site.)

g. Delete the Shockmachine installation program. (*Hint*: Use Windows Explorer or Finder.)

h. Close your Web browser.

2. You are a multimedia instructor at a local college. You are teaching a class on Macromedia Director Shockwave Studio and want to show real-world examples of Shockwave content on the Web. You use a Web browser to access Macromedia's Showcase Web site and show trendy examples of Shockwave content, including Shockwave Multiuser server.

To complete this independent challenge:

a. Open your Web browser.

b. Display the Macromedia Web site.

c. Display the Macromedia Showcase Web site.

d. Browse the showcase by Director Shockwave Studio.

e. Display four Showcase Web sites with Shockwave content.

f. Print the Web page for each Showcase Web site.

g. Close your Web browser.

3. You are a teacher at an elementary school and want to create learning material that students at the school can view through a Web browser. You are learning how to use Director to create Shockwave content for the Web and want to test out the process. You use Director to open a movie and save the file as a Shockwave movie and HTML to view in a Web browser.

To complete this independent challenge:

a. Start Director, open the file **SW A-3** from the drive and folder where your Project Files are located, then save the movie as *Shuttle Landing*.

b. Open the Publish Settings dialog box, then click the Formats tab.

c. Select the drive and folder where your Project Files are located for the HTML file.

d. Select the drive and folder where your Project Files are located for the Shockwave file.

e. Set the HTML Template to Center Shockwave.

f. Click the Shockwave Save tab and select the Display Context Menu in Shockwave check box.

g. Type **Demo** in the Suggested Category box.

h. Type **Shuttle Landing** in the Shockwave Title box.

i. Click the Compression tab, set the JPEG option, then drag the compression slider to 50.

j. Select the Compression Enabled check box, then set the sound bit-rate setting to 48.

k. Close the Publish Settings dialog box.

l. Save and compact the movie.

m. Publish the Shockwave movie and view it in a Web browser.

n. Close your Web browser.

o. Save the movie, then exit Director.

4. You are a software reviewer for *GamingX* magazine. You are writing a review of games developed with Macromedia Director and delivered over the Web using Shockwave. As part of your review, you want to access and play the games on the Shockwave.com Web site, a popular gaming site for Shockwave content. You use a Web browser to run Shockwave games on the Shockwave.com Web site and add them to Shockmachine.

To complete this independent challenge:

a. Start Shockmachine.

b. Click the Menu button, then click Shockwave.com.

c. Display the games on the Shockwave Web site.

d. Open and play several games on the Shockwave Web site.

e. Print the Web page for one of the games.

f. Download or save two Shockwave games to Shockmachine.

g. Play the Shockwave movies in Shockmachine.

h. Delete the Shockwave movie cartridges.

i. Close your Web browser and quit Shockmachine.

▶ Visual Workshop

Recreate the screen shown in Figure A-17. Print the screen. (For Windows, use the Windows Paint program. Press the Print Screen key to make a copy of the screen, start the Paint program by clicking Start, pointing to Programs, pointing to Accessories, then clicking Paint; click Edit on the menu bar, click Paste to paste the screen into Paint, then click Yes to paste the large image if necessary. Click File on the menu bar, click Print, click Print or OK in the dialog box, then exit Paint. For the Macintosh, use the SimpleText program. Hold and press the Command, Shift, and 3 keys to make a copy of the screen, double-click the document Picture 1 located on your hard drive, click File on the menu bar, click Print, then click Print in the dialog box. *Note*: When you create a new document with a copy of the screen and a document Picture 1 already exists, the Macintosh names the new document Picture 2.)

FIGURE A-17

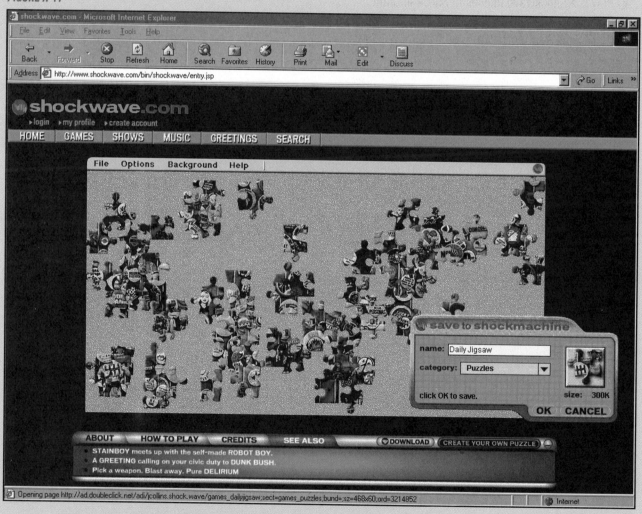

Unit B

Making
Web Content with Shockwave 8

Objectives

► **Design Shockwave movies**
► **Install Shockwave Multiuser Server**
► **Start the Shockwave Multiuser Server**
► **Add streaming behaviors to a movie**
► **Add Multiuser behaviors to a movie**
► **Make a Shockwave movie resizable**
► **Create a Shockwave movie for the Multiuser Server**
► **Connect to a Multiuser Server**

Director 8 Shockwave Studio comes with the functionality and built-in additional software to create multiuser applications for the Web, such as games or chat rooms, which allow more than one user to interact or communicate with each other in real time. This unit introduces you to basic skills for preparing and delivering a multiuser Shockwave movie for playback on the Web, using a Web browser and Shockwave Multiuser Server. First, you'll learn about designing Shockwave movies for the Web and how to install and start the required software. Then, you'll learn how to add Internet behaviors, which control how a movie functions on the Web. Finally, you'll learn how to set Shockwave publishing options, create and open a Shockwave movie, and connect to a Multiuser Server.

Jean wants to create a chat room movie, using Director, Shockwave, and Shockwave Multiuser Server.

Designing Shockwave Movies

Designing a Shockwave movie for the Web is slightly different from designing a Director movie for a local computer or CD-ROM. Web technology has limitations that prevent some of Director's features from being functional in a Shockwave movie. When you create a Shockwave movie, you should take into account some important design considerations. The main design consideration is to keep the size of the Shockwave movie as small as possible so that you can minimize the download time from the Web. For example, if you have a 70K Director movie file and save it as a Shockwave movie, the file reduces to 25K. If your Internet connection downloads files at 2K per second, it will take 12 seconds to download the file, which can be a long time to wait, for today's Web user.  Jean takes some time to familiarize herself with some design considerations for developing Shockwave movies.

Design considerations for Shockwave movies

 Keep the movie size small; smaller movies will download, display, and play faster.

 Keep graphic files as small as possible; use **JPEG (Joint Photographic Experts Group)** and **GIF (Graphics Interchange Format)** files. JPEG file format supports millions of colors (24-bit color depth), but loses image quality by discarding image data. GIF file format, which Director considers as standard, uses only 256 colors, but it doesn't lose any image quality in the compression. Use the Image Compression feature for JPEG to reduce file size, as shown in Figure B-1.

 Minimize the number of cast members; delete any unused cast members.

 Do not select the Loop Continuously feature; a movie with a continuous loop ties up computer memory while the Web page is open.

 Use low color depth (8-bit or less); color depth is a measure of the number of colors that an image can contain.

 Use the Compression Enabled feature for Shockwave audio and choose a low setting, as shown in Figure B-1.

 Avoid palette issues such as inadvertent color flashes; use the Web Index Color Palette (Web 216), as shown in Figure B-2.

 Keep imported sounds as small as possible; use the lowest possible sampling rate.

 Loop small audio files for long background tracks.

 Use short film loops, such as a cast member produced from a sequence of other cast members.

 Use the Tiling feature in the Paint window to create backgrounds.

 Use the Paint window to create objects; objects you create in Director have smaller file sizes than imported graphics.

 Use Ink Effects to produce different effects using the same cast member.

 Use field cast members instead of text cast members; field cast members require less space.

FIGURE B-1: Shockwave compression settings

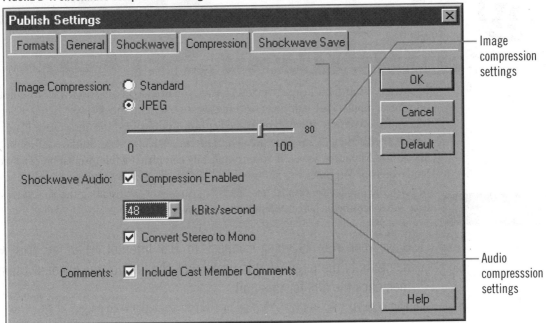

Image compression settings

Audio compresssion settings

FIGURE B-2: Web Index Color Palette

Director color palette for Web browsers

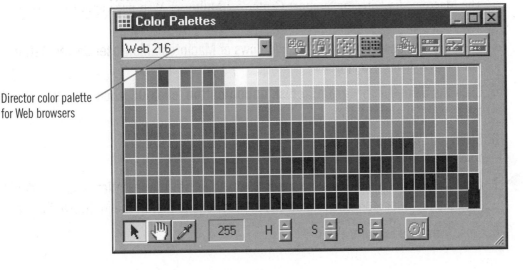

Features not available for a Shockwave movie

Director is a full-featured multimedia program, but Web technology is not full-featured, so not all Director features are available when you create a Shockwave movie. The following list identifies common features that Shockwave does not support.

- Movie in a Window (MIAW), a Director movie running in a window of its own, separate from the Stage of the main movie

- External files that are not within the support folder
- **Lingo** commands that change system settings such as Restart or Shutdown or run external files
- FileIO Xtra or other Xtras that open external files
- Printing
- Transition effects

Installing Shockwave Multiuser Server

In order to use the Shockwave Multiuser Server, you need to install Shockwave Multiuser Server software on your computer. You can download the latest version of Shockwave Multiuser Server free from the Macromedia Web site at www.macromedia.com. To download the Shockwave Player on the Web, you need a connection to the Internet. The Director 8 Shockwave Studio CD-ROM also comes with Shockwave Multiuser Server. If you have already completed a full installation of Director 8 Shockwave Studio on your computer, you automatically installed Shockwave Multiuser Server, and you don't need to perform the installation procedure. Jean begins by installing the Shockwave Multiuser Server from the Macromedia Director Support Center Web site.

Steps

1. Open your Web browser, connect to the Internet, then go to www.course.com. Navigate to the page for this book, click the link for the Student Online Companion, then click the link for this unit
   The Web browser appears, displaying the Macromedia Web page.

2. Click **Support** on the Web site menu bar, then click **Director**
   The Macromedia Director Support Center Web page appears.

QuickTip

The location and look of the Web page for Shockwave might vary.

3. Click the **Multiuser** link in the list on the left side of the page
   The Macromedia Director Support Center for Multiuser Web page appears, as shown in Figure B-3.

4. Click the link associated with the Windows or Macintosh Multiuser Server installer
   The Save As dialog box appears.

5. Click the **Save this program to disk option button**, click **OK**, then save the installer file to your local hard drive

6. Close your Web browser
   Your Web browser program closes.

Trouble?

If the downloaded file is a compressed file with the extension .sea.hqx, you need to install Stuffit Expander to decompress the file (Mac).

7. Use Windows Explorer (Win) or Finder (Mac) to locate the installer program, double-click the installer icon, then follow the instructions to install the Multiuser Server

8. Close Windows Explorer (Win)

FIGURE B-3: Macromedia Director Support Center for Multiuser Web page

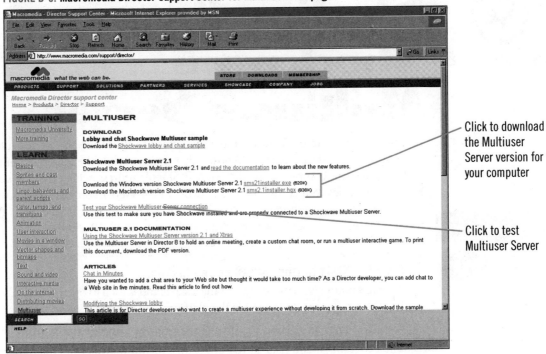

Click to download the Multiuser Server version for your computer

Click to test Multiuser Server

Testing the Shockwave Multiuser Server connection

If you are not sure whether Shockwave Multiuser Server is installed correctly on your computer, you can test it by using a link on Macromedia's Web site. The test determines if you have Shockwave Multiuser Server installed on your computer and, if you do, which version. If you have any version of Shockwave Multiuser Server, a movie appears on the test Web site, as shown in Figure B-4. To access the test Web site, connect to the Internet, open your Web browser, go to www.macromedia.com, click Support on the Web site menu bar, click Director, click Multiuser, then click the Test your Shockwave Multiuser Server connection link.

FIGURE B-4: Testing the Shockwave Multiuser Server Connection

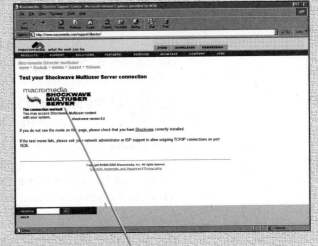

If you see a short movie and then this message, the Shockwave Multiuser Server connection is working

Starting the Shockwave Multiuser Server

Before you can set up the Director movie, you need to start the Shockwave Multiuser Server program. You need to start the server to host a chat session. While the server is running, you can use it to determine your computer's **IP (Internet Protocol)** address, which is a unique set of four numbers that identifies your computer on a network or the Web. In order to connect to the server from a Director or Shockwave movie, you need to know your computer's IP address. Jean starts the Shockwave Multiuser Server and displays the computer's IP address.

WIN

1. **Click the Start button** 🏁Start **on the taskbar**
   The Start button is on the left side of the taskbar and is used to open programs on your computer. Use the set of steps designed for the platform you are using.

2. **Point to Programs, then point to Macromedia Shockwave Multiuser Server 2.1**
   The Programs menu lists all the programs, including Macromedia Shockwave Server, that are installed on your computer.

3. **Click MultiuserServer**
   The MultiuserServer program opens, displaying server configuration information, as shown in Figure B-5.

4. **Click Status on the menu bar, then click Server**
   Server status information appears, as shown in Figure B-6. The server IP address is the location where the Shockwave Multiuser Server is running. The **server port** is the communications port number where the server communicates with the Director movie.

5. **Write down the IP address for use later in this lesson, then click the Minimize button on the MultiuserServer window**
   In this instance, the IP address is 24.15.86.108. Shockwave Multiuser Server continues to run minimized.

MAC

1. **Double-click the hard drive icon**
   The contents of your hard drive is displayed on your desktop.
   Use the set of steps designed for the platform you are using.

2. **Double-click the Macromedia Shockwave Multiuser Server 2.1 folder**
   The Macromedia Shockwave Multiuser Server 2.1 folder opens, displaying the program icon and associated files that come with the product.

3. **Double-click the MultiuserServer program icon**
   The MultiuserServer program opens, displaying the server configuration information.

4. **Click Status on the menu bar, then click Server**
   Server status information appears. The server IP address is the location where the Shockwave Multiuser Server is running. The server port is the communications port number where the server communicates with the Director movie.

5. **Write down the IP address for use later in this lesson, then click the Finder menu, then click Hide MultiuserServer**
   In this instance, the IP address is 24.15.86.108. Shockwave Multiuser Server continues to run in the background.

FIGURE B-5: MultiuserServer window

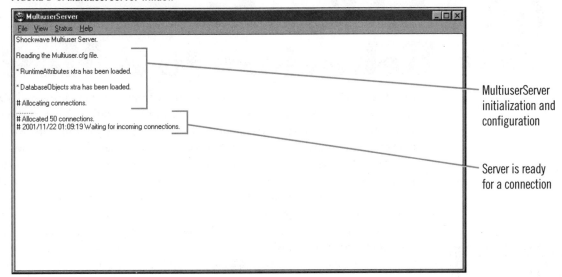

MultiuserServer
initialization and
configuration

Server is ready
for a connection

FIGURE B-6: MultiuserServer window with status information

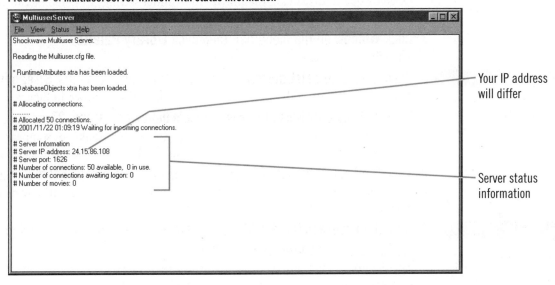

Your IP address
will differ

Server status
information

Getting Shockwave Developer's Guide

For more information about developing Shockwave movies with the Multiuser Server, you can visit the Shockwave Multiuser Support Center on Macromedia's Web site. The Shockwave Multiuser Support Center contains the latest technotes and troubleshooting information for using Shockwave. It also provides articles with tips and techniques, printable documentation, quick-reference cards, and other information. The support center contains full documentation on how to create Multiuser programs

with Director and details on running the Shockwave Multiuser Server. This information is not included in Director's printed documentation. To access the Shockwave Multiuser Support Center on the Web, open the Shockwave Multiuser Server 2.1 README file. To open the README file, double-click the Macromedia Shockwave Server 2.1 folder, then double-click the README file icon, or click the Start button, point to Programs, point to Macromedia Shockwave Server 2.1, then click README (Win).

Adding Streaming Behaviors to a Movie

Internet bandwidth is the amount of data that can be transmitted in one second. Bandwidth is still limited for Web users, which can affect the ease with which you download or stream files. Shockwave movies are often too big to stream without hiccups. One strategy you can employ to make streaming more effective is to loop a sequence of your movie while cast member media download in the background. Director comes with built-in streaming behaviors (prewritten Lingo scripts) that allow you to control how a movie plays while Shockwave media are downloading from a Web server. There are two types of streaming behaviors: Jump and Loop. Both behaviors wait for streaming media to become available and then move the playback head to the next frame, a specified frame, or a specified marker. The two behaviors differ slightly: the Jump behaviors loop the playback head on only a single frame while the media are loading, while the Loop behaviors can loop the playback head over a range of frames while the media are loading.  Jean adds streaming behaviors to a Shockwave movie.

Steps

1. Start **Director**, open the file **SW B-1** from the drive and folder where your Project Files are located, then save it as **Chatroom**

   Director opens, displaying the movie. Your initial settings in Director can vary, depending on previous usage.

2. Click **Window** on the menu bar, then click **Library Palette**

   The Library Palette appears.

3. Click the **Library List button** 🔲, point to **Internet**, then click **Streaming**

   The Library Palette with Streaming behaviors appears, as shown in Figure B-7.

   > **QuickTip**
   > If the behavior you want is not visible, use the arrows to scroll the Library list or resize the Library Palette.

4. Drag the **Loop Until Next Frame is Available behavior** to **frame 27** in the Behavior channel

   The Parameters for "Loop Until Next Frame is Available" dialog box appears. This behavior loops the playback head until media in the subsequent frame are available for use.

5. Click the **Loop Type list arrow** 🔽, click **Loop To Specified Frame**, then click **OK**

   The behavior is set to loop through the introductory animation until the media in frame 28 are available for use.

   > **QuickTip**
   > You might find it less confusing to open only those Director windows shown in Figure B-8.

6. Drag the **Progress Bar for Streaming Movies behavior** onto the **Progress bar sprite** on the Stage, as shown in Figure B-8

   The Parameters for "Progress Bar for Streaming Movies" dialog box appears. This behavior creates an animated progress bar for a streaming movie.

7. Click the **Enable Display of Percentage Loaded check box** to select it

   The option displays the percentage of the completed download of the streaming movie in a specified text or field cast member.

8. Click the **Display Percent Loaded in Member list arrow** 🔽, click **Progress percentage**, then click **OK**

   The Parameters for "Progress Bar for Streaming Movies" dialog box closes. The behavior is set to display the percent loaded in the Progress percentage field cast member.

9. Click the **Rewind button** ⏮ on the toolbar, if necessary, click the **Play button** ▶ on the toolbar, then click the **Stop button** ⏹ on the toolbar, if necessary, when the movie reaches the end

   The progress percentage changed from 0% to 100% very quickly. Since the Shockwave movie is not downloaded from the Web, where slow connections and high traffic can affect the time it takes to download the movie, the streaming behavior is executed too fast to see the complete process. In this instance, the media elements load from local drives, which simply occurs too quickly to trigger a loop through the introductory animation. You cannot adjust the load time in Director.

FIGURE B-7: Library Palette with Streaming behaviors

Click button to access Library Palette behavior categories

Streaming behaviors

FIGURE B-8: Attaching a streaming behavior to a sprite

Loop Until Next Frame is Available behavior

Progress Bar for Streaming Movies behavior

Drag the Progress Bar behavior to the Director object

Drag the Loop Until Next Frame is Available behavior to the Behavior channel

Creating a progress bar

Director comes with built-in streaming behaviors to create an animated progress bar for streaming movie or URL-linked content. A **URL (Uniform Resource Locator)** is a Web address. You can use the Progress Bar for Streaming Movie and Progress Bar for URL Linked Assets behaviors to turn a sprite into a progress bar, indicating the progress of the movie stream or linked URL. You can attach either of these behaviors to any sprite that you draw with Director's built-in drawing tools. To use either behavior, attach it to a bitmap or to a rectangular sprite. The sprite is displayed with an increasing width as the object downloads. You can also use a text or field cast member to display the progress percentage of the streaming media download.

Adding Multiuser Behaviors to a Movie

You can add functionality to a Shockwave movie that allows multiple users to interact and communicate with each other simultaneously. Director comes with eight Multiuser behaviors that you can use to create a chat room for real-time conversation, for an online meeting with a shared whiteboard or paint canvas on which each participant can write, and for a meeting place or lobby for a multiplayer game. The Multiuser behaviors allow you to connect to and disconnect from the Shockwave Multiuser Server; input, send, and display chat room messages; display group list and group member names; and use a shared whiteboard. Before end users can participate in a Multiuser movie, they need to be able to connect to a Multiuser Server. Jean adds Multiuser behaviors to the Chatroom movie.

Steps

QuickTip

You can change behavior settings in the Property Inspector. Click the sprite with the attached behavior, click the Behavior tab, click the behavior, then change parameter settings at the bottom.

1. Click **frame 28** in the Frame channel
   The playback head appears in frame 28.

2. Click the **Library List button** 🏢, point to **Internet**, then click **Multiuser**
   The Library Palette with Multiuser behaviors appears, as shown in Figure B-9.

3. Drag the **Connect to Server behavior icon** onto the **Connect up sprite** (Connect button) on the Stage
   The Parameters for "Connect to Server" dialog box appears.

4. Click the **server address text box**, then enter the **server IP address** that you wrote down earlier from the Multiuser Server window, as shown in Figure B-10
   In this instance, the IP address is 24.15.86.108. These options allow you to connect to the Macromedia Shockwave Multiuser Server. If you have access to the Internet, you can use the default IP address (trialserver.macromedia.com) that appears in the dialog box. This is a trial Multiuser Server IP address available on the Internet at the Macromedia Web site.

5. Click **OK**
   The Connect to Server settings are attached to the Connect button.

6. Drag the **Disconnect from Server behavior icon** onto the **Disconnect up sprite** (Disconnect button) on the Stage
   The Disconnect from Server setting is attached to the Disconnect button.

7. Drag the **Chat Input behavior icon** onto the **enter chat here text box** on the Stage
   The Parameters for "Chat Input" dialog box appears, as shown in Figure B-11. In the Chat group name box, you can assign a group name to all users who enter text in this box. The Use Return Key to Send Message? option is turned on by default, which allows you to send chat room messages quickly by pressing [Enter] (Win) or [Return] (Mac).

8. Click **OK** to accept the default settings

9. Drag the **Chat Output behavior icon** onto the **chat appears here text box** on the Stage, then click **OK** to accept the default settings
   The Group name box contains the same group name as in the Chat group name box in the Chat Output Parameters dialog box. The group name is preceded by the @ symbol.

FIGURE B-9: Library Palette with Multiuser behaviors

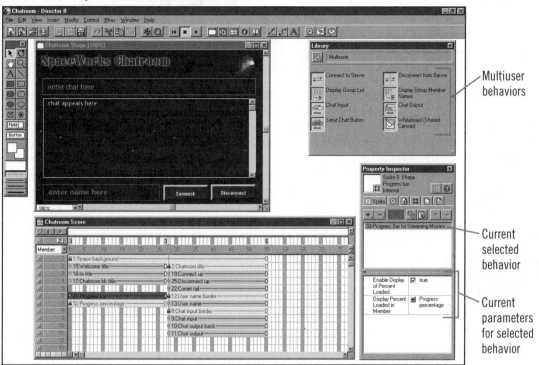

Multiuser behaviors

Current selected behavior

Current parameters for selected behavior

FIGURE B-10: Parameters for "Connect to Server" dialog box

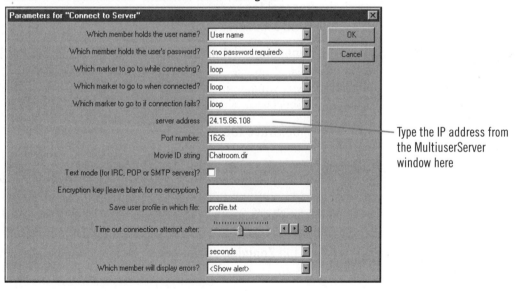

Type the IP address from the MultiuserServer window here

FIGURE B-11: Parameters for "Chat Input" dialog box

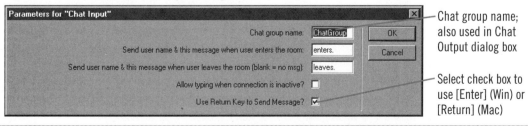

Chat group name; also used in Chat Output dialog box

Select check box to use [Enter] (Win) or [Return] (Mac)

Making a Shockwave Movie Resizable

You can control how your Shockwave movie behaves when an end user resizes a Web browser window. You can set the Shockwave movie to stretch with the Web browser window, or not to stretch, so that it remains the same size. To make a Shockwave movie stretchable, you need to set options in the Publish Settings dialog box. In the Publish Settings dialog box, you need to set the Dimensions value to Percentage of Browser Window in the General tab, and select the Zooming check box and a Stretch Style in the Shockwave tab. All three options work together to make a Shockwave movie resizable in a Web browser. The three Publish Settings options and the size of the Web browser window determine the size of the Shockwave movie. When you are developing a resizable Shockwave movie, you need to be aware that fonts and bitmaps, which are made up of individual pixels or dots, do not stretch well and might become difficult to read or appear skewed. ✍ Jean sets the Director publish settings to make the Shockwave Chatroom movie resizable.

1. Click **File** on the menu bar, then click **Publish Settings**
   The Publish Settings dialog box appears.

2. Click **Default**
   The default settings for the Publish Settings dialog box appear.

3. Click the **HTML Template list arrow** ▼, then click **Center Shockwave**
   This option positions the Shockwave movie in the center of the Web browser.

4. Click the **General tab**
   The General tab appears, as shown in Figure B-12.

> **Trouble?**
> If you use Netscape as your Web browser, click Match Movie instead of Percentage of Browser Window. The Match Movie and Pixels options set the movie to a fixed size.

5. Click the **Dimensions list arrow** ▼, then click **Percentage of Browser Window**
   The Percentage of Browser Window option allows you to resize the Shockwave movie along with the browser window. If you select this option, you also need to select the Stretch Style list arrow in the Shockwave tab, then select Preserve Proportions, Stretch to Fill, or Expand Stage.

6. Click the **Shockwave tab**
   The Shockwave tab appears, as shown in Figure B-13.

7. Click the **Stretch Style list arrow** ▼, then click **Preserve Proportions**
   The Preserve Proportions option allows you to retain the same aspect ratio of your movie, regardless of the size of the Web browser window. Only the Stage changes size; sprites remain the same size. See Table B-1 for a description of the Stretch Style options.

> **QuickTip**
> To automatically set the Dimensions and Stretch Style option, click the Formats tab in the Publish Settings dialog box, click HTML Template, then click Fill Browser Window.

8. Ensure that the **Zooming check box** is selected, then click **OK** twice, if necessary
   The Publish Settings dialog box closes.

FIGURE B-12: Publish Settings dialog box with the General tab

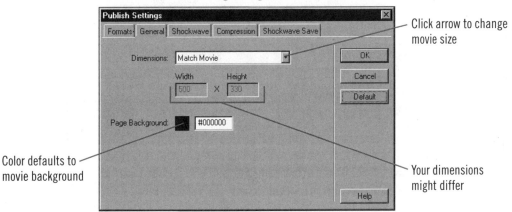

Click arrow to change movie size

Your dimensions might differ

Color defaults to movie background

FIGURE B-13: Publish Settings dialog box with the Shockwave tab

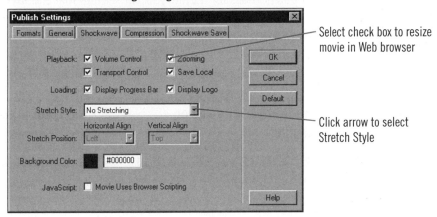

Select check box to resize movie in Web browser

Click arrow to select Stretch Style

TABLE B-1: Stretch Style options

dimensions options	description
No Stretching	Makes the movie play at the size specified in the General tab's Dimensions pop-up menu. Resizing the browser crops your movie if it doesn't fit.
Preserve Proportions	Retains the same aspect ratio of your movie, regardless of the size of the Web browser window. The movie is aligned with respect to the Horizontal Align and Vertical Align settings.
Stretch to Fill	Stretches the movie to fill the Web browser window. The aspect ratio of your movie might change, which will distort the appearance.
Expand Stage Size	Expands the stage size to equal the height and width dimensions in the HTML file. Only the Stage changes size; sprites remain the same size.

Using linked media with Shockwave

If your Shockwave movie uses any linked media or External Casts and you want to preview the movie locally in your Web browser, you need to place the external files in the dswmedia folder inside the Shockwave Player folder, along with the Shockwave movie (with the .DCR extension) and the HTML file. For Windows, the dswmedia folder is located in the path C:\Windows\System\Macromed\Shockwave 8; for the Macintosh it is located in the path Hard drive:System:Macromedia:Shockwave 8. You only need to place the files once on your local computer; end users will not have to place them on their computers in order to view the movie from a Web site. The dswmedia folder is part of Director's security scheme, which prevents the movie from accessing your local drive and your personal data.

Creating a Shockwave Movie for the Multiuser Server

You can convert a Director movie and all of its linked media to a Shockwave movie that you can play back in a Web browser on the Internet or on an intranet. End users need to have the Shockwave player installed on their computer in order to play the Shockwave movie. Before you release your movie, it's important to test the final product on a variety of computer systems, to make sure it plays properly under different conditions. During the testing process, check to make sure all linked media and fonts appear correctly on the screen, and that the movie plays properly on all computers and color monitor display settings that end users are likely to use. You also need to check to make sure the movie plays fast enough over a slow Internet connection. ✒️ Jean creates a Shockwave chatroom movie for use with the Multiuser Server.

Steps 1 2 3 4

1. Click **File** on the menu bar, then click **Publish Settings**

   The Publish Settings dialog box appears, displaying the Formats tab, as shown in Figure B-14.

2. Click the **HTML File button** `...`, click the **Look in list arrow** ▼, click the drive and folder where your Project Files are located, if necessary, then click **Select Folder**

3. Click the **Shockwave File button** `...`, click the **Look in list arrow** ▼, click the drive and folder where your Project Files are located, if necessary, then click **Select Folder**

4. Click **OK**

   The file locations for the HTML and Shockwave files are set to the folder where your Project Files are located.

5. Click **File** on the menu bar, then click **Save and Compact**

   Director saves and compacts the movie.

QuickTip

To specify an alternate location or Shockwave name and any External Casts, hold down [Alt] (Win) or [Option] (Mac) while you click File on the menu bar, then click Publish.

6. Click **File** on the menu bar, then click **Publish**

   Director publishes the Shockwave file with the .dcr extension (Win) and the HTML file with the .htm extension (Win) in the folder where your Project Files are located, and then the movie plays in your Web browser, as shown in Figure B-15.

7. Switch to Director, then click **Director** on the taskbar (Win) or click the **Finder** menu, then click **Director** (Mac)

   The Director window appears. Your Web browser is still open.

8. Click the **Save button** 💾 on the toolbar, if necessary

   Director saves the movie.

9. Click **File** on the menu bar, then click **Exit** (Win) or **Quit** (Mac)

   Director closes and your Web browser appears.

FIGURE B-14: Publish Settings dialog box with the Format tab

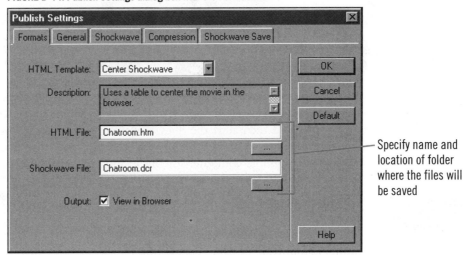

Specify name and
location of folder
where the files will
be saved

FIGURE B-15: Stretchable Shockwave movie in a Web browser

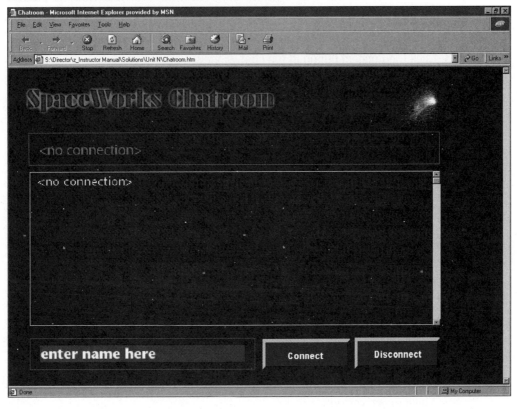

CLUES TO USE

Preparing a Shockwave movie for Web distribution

After you create a Shockwave movie in Director, you need to move the Shockwave movie and its related files to a Web server before end users can access the Shockwave movie over the Web. To prepare a Shockwave movie for Web distribution, group the Shockwave movie and its related files in the same folder, with media files in a subfolder, then download the folder to a Web server with an **FTP (File Transfer Protocol)** program. A Shockwave movie's data is compressed to help reduce download times. Shockwave movies are protected, which means that you cannot edit them directly; you can only edit the Director movie and then create a new Shockwave movie.

Connecting to a Multiuser Server

Once you publish a Director movie, you can view it as a Shockwave movie in your Web browser. In order to play a Shockwave movie and connect to a Multiuser Server, you need to start the server and then start the Shockwave movie in a Web browser. If the server is not running, the Shockwave movie will not be able to connect. Although the server and Web browser are on the same computer for this lesson, the server and the Shockwave movie chat room can be anywhere on the Internet. While you are connected to a Multiuser Server, you can open the Multiuser Server window and display status information. ✐ Jean starts a chat room by connecting to the Multiuser Server.

Steps

1. **Switch to your Web browser, if necessary**
   Your Web browser appears, displaying the chat room.

2. **Select the enter name here text in the chat window in your Web browser (if necessary), then type your name**
   Your name appears in the chat room discussion.

3. **Click the Connect button in the chat window**
   A connection message appears in the chat output box.

4. **Click the empty green text box in the chat window in your Web browser as indicated in Figure B-16, type Where can I get help with your interactive games?, then press [Enter] (Win) or [Return] (Mac)**
   The message appears in the chat output box, as shown in Figure B-16.

5. **Switch to MultiuserServer, click Status on the menu bar, then click Users**
   The MultiuserServer window appears, displaying user status information, as shown in Figure B-17.

6. **Switch to your Web browser**
   Your Web browser appears.

7. **Click the Disconnect button in the chat window**
   A disconnect message appears in the chat output box.

8. **Close your Web browser, then switch to the MultiuserServer window, if necessary**
   Your Web browser closes, and the MultiuserServer window appears.

9. **Click File on the menu bar, then click Exit (Win) or Quit (Mac)**
   MultiuserServer closes.

FIGURE B-16: Connecting to the MultiuserServer

Enter chat messages here

Welcome to server message

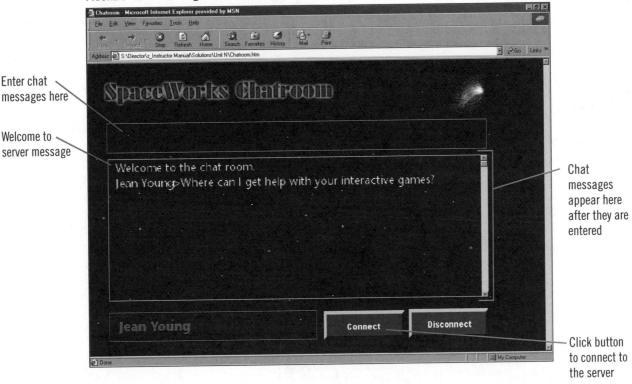

Chat messages appear here after they are entered

Click button to connect to the server

FIGURE B-17: MultiuserServer window with connection status information

Click Status, then click Users to display connection information

Your server status will differ

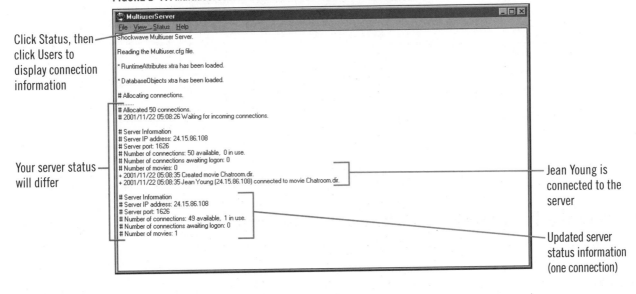

Jean Young is connected to the server

Updated server status information (one connection)

CLUES TO USE

Setting up another chat participant

You can open another Web browser and open the chatroom.htm Web page again to add another chat participant. The same Web page is open in two Web browsers. In the Web browser, click the enter name here text and type a different name, click the Connect button to connect to the server, then type

a chat message in the chat text box. Your message appears in the chat window in both Web browsers. Switch between the two Web browsers to chat. If you want more chat room participants, you can open additional instances of the chatroom.htm Web page.

Practice

▶ Concepts Review

Label each of the elements of the screen shown in Figure B-18.

FIGURE B-18

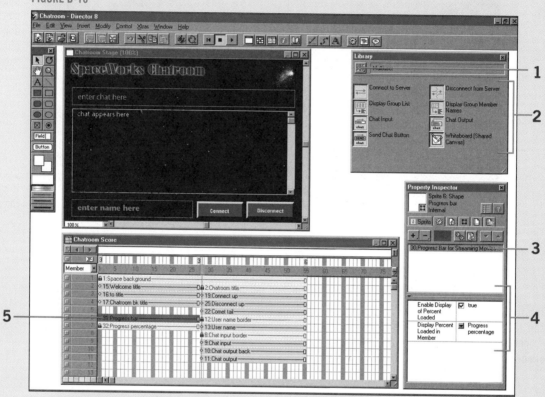

Match each of the terms with the statement that describes its function.

6. JPEG   **a.** A movie running in a window of its own

7. GIF   **b.** A file format that supports millions of colors

8. MIAW   **c.** A file format that uses only 256 colors

9. Behavior   **d.** A compressed movie that end users play in a Web browser

10. Shockwave movie   **e.** A prewritten Lingo script

Select the best answer from the following list of choices.

11. Which feature is NOT available for a Shockwave movie?
   a. Ink effects
   b. Behaviors
   c. Movie in a Window
   d. Film loops

12. After MultiuserServer starts, the program displays:
   a. Setup information.
   b. Configuration information.
   c. A Help screen.
   d. An introduction screen.

13. Which menu command in the MultiuserServer window displays the number of connections?
   a. Server
   b. Movies
   c. Users
   d. Groups

14. IP stands for:
   a. Internet Port.
   b. Internet Protocol.
   c. Internet Player.
   d. Internet Provider.

15. An IP address is a set of:
   a. Two numbers.
   b. Three numbers.
   c. Four numbers.
   d. Five numbers.

16. What does a Shockwave movie need to connect to a Multiuser Server?
   a. Server name
   b. Server IP address
   c. Computer name
   d. Computer IP address

17. Which option is NOT required to create a resizable Shockwave movie?
   a. Dimensions
   b. Compression Enabled
   c. Zooming
   d. Stretch Style

18. **Which is NOT a streaming behavior?**
    a. Loop Until Next Frame is Available
    b. Loop Until Media in Frame is Available
    c. Progress Bar for Movie
    d. Progress Bar for URL Linked Assets

19. **Which Stretch Style option retains the same aspect ratio of a movie regardless of the size of the Web browser window?**
    a. No Stretching
    b. Preserve Proportions
    c. Stretch to Fill
    d. Expand Stage Size

20. **Which tab in the Publish Settings dialog box contains the Dimension option?**
    a. Formats
    b. Shockwave Save
    c. General
    d. Movie

21. **Which tab in the Publish Settings dialog box contains the Stretch Style option?**
    a. Formats
    b. Shockwave Save
    c. General
    d. Movie

Skills Review

1. **Design Shockwave movies.**
    a. List and describe the five ways to reduce the size of a Shockwave movie.
    b. List five Director features not available for Shockwave movies.

2. **Install Shockwave Multiuser Server.**
    a. Open your Web browser.
    b. Display the Macromedia Director Support Center Web page.
    c. Display the Multiuser Director Support Center Web page.
    d. Describe the steps to install Shockwave Multiuser Server (instead of reinstalling it).
    e. Use the online test feature and test the Shockwave Multiuser Server connection.
    f. Close your Web browser.

3. **Start the Multiuser Server.**
    a. Use the Start menu (Win) or Finder (Mac) to start MultiuserServer.
    b. Display server status information.
    c. Write down the IP address for use later in the Skills Review.
    d. Minimize (Win) or hide (Mac) the MultiuserServer window.

4. Add streaming behaviors to a movie.
   a. Start Director, then open the file **SW B-2** from the drive and folder where your Project Files are located.
   b. Save the file as *MyChat* in the drive and folder where your Project Files are located.
   c. Open the Library Palette, if necessary, and display the Streaming behaviors.
   d. Drag the Progress Bar for Streaming Movies behavior onto the Progress Bar sprite on the Stage.
   e. Select the Enable Display of Percentage Loaded check box.
   f. Change the Display Percent Loaded in Member to Progress percentage.
   g. Review and play the movie. (*Note*: The media elements load from local drives too fast to trigger a loop through the introductory animation.)
   h. Stop the movie.

5. Add Multiuser behaviors to a movie.
   a. Open the Library Palette and display the Multiuser behaviors.
   b. Drag the Connect to Server behavior onto the Connection button on the Stage.
   c. Change Which member holds the user name? to the User name sprite.
   d. Type the IP address that you wrote down from the MultiuserServer window.
   e. Drag the Disconnect to Server behavior onto the Disconnection button on the Stage.
   f. Drag the Chat Input behavior onto the enter chat *here* text box (Chat input sprite) on the Stage, then accept the default settings.
   g. Drag the Chat Output behavior onto the chat appears here text box (Chat output sprite) on the Stage, then accept the default settings.

6. Make a Shockwave movie resizable.
   a. Open the Publish Settings dialog box and set the default settings.
   b. Change HTML Template to Center Shockwave.
   c. Change Dimensions to Percentage of Browser Window in the General tab.
   d. Change Stretch Style to Preserve Proportions in the Shockwave tab.
   e. Select the Zooming check box if necessary in the Shockwave tab, then close the Publish Settings dialog box.

7. Create a Shockwave movie for the Multiuser Server.
   a. Open the Publish Settings dialog box.
   b. Select the folder location for the HTML and Shockwave files to the drive and folder where your Project Files are located, then close the Publish Settings dialog box.
   c. Save and compact the movie.
   d. Publish the Director movie as Shockwave movie.
   e. Switch to Director, save the movie if necessary, then exit Director.

8. Connect to a Multiuser Server.
   a. Switch to your Web browser if necessary.
   b. Select the enter name here text in the chat window in your Web browser (if necessary), then type **your name**.
   c. Click the Connect button to establish a connection with the Multiuser Server.
   d. Click the enter chat here text in the chat window in your Web browser, type **What are you doing tonight?**, then press [Enter] (Win) or [Return] (Mac).
   e. Switch to MultiuserServer, then display the user status information.
   f. Switch to your Web browser.
   g. Click the Disconnect button to discontinue the connection with the Multiuser Server.
   h. Close your Web browser, switch to MultiuserServer, then exit the program.

▶ Independent Challenges

1. You are a computer technician at InsideOut Gaming. The company wants to create multiuser games using Macromedia Director for use on the Web. In order to play multiuser games, you need to install the Shockwave Multiuser Server on a computer or Web server. Your boss asks you to make sure all the computers in the company contain the latest version of Macromedia Shockwave Multiuser Server. You use a Web browser to test the version of Shockwave Multiuser Server on your computer and install the software from the Web, if necessary.

To complete this independent challenge:

a. Open your Web browser.

b. Display the Macromedia Director Support Center Web page.

c. Display the Multiuser Director Support Center Web page.

d. Use the online test feature and test the Shockwave Multiuser Server connection.

e. Print the Web page with the test results.

f. If the Shockwave Multiuser Server is not installed, download the installation program, then install the program. (*Hint*: Use the Macromedia Web site.)

g. Close your Web browser.

2. You are an entrepreneur who wants to start a Web business called Xpress Yourself. Web technology makes it easy to communicate with others, so you decide to create an online chat room for simultaneous communication. You use Director to create a chat room and add the Multiuser behaviors to interact with the Shockwave Multiuser Server.

To complete this independent challenge:

a. Start Director and save the movie as *Xpressions* in the drive and folder where your Project Files are located.

b. Create a text cast member with the text **enter chat here** and drag it on the Stage.

c. Create a text cast member with the text **chat appears here** and drag it on the Stage.

d. Create a text cast member with the text **enter name here** and drag it on the Stage.

e. Create Connect and Disconnect buttons as Paint cast members, and drag them on the Stage.

f. Resize and move the Stage elements to create a chatroom design.

g. Open the Library Palette and display the Multiuser behaviors.

h. Drag the Connect to Server behavior onto the Connect button on the Stage, then accept the default settings.

i. Drag the Disconnect from Server behavior onto the Disconnect button on the Stage.

j. Drag the Chat Input behavior onto the "enter chat here" text box on the Stage, then accept the default settings.

k. Drag the Chat Output behavior onto the "chat appears here" text box on the Stage, then accept the default settings.

l. Save the movie, then exit Director.

3. You are now the owner of Xpress Yourself, an online chat room for simultaneous communication. You have completed the development of a chat room in Director, and now you want to test it out. You start the Shockwave Multiuser Server and determine the IP address, then you use Director to open the chat room movie *Xpressions* you created in Independent Challenge 2, add the IP address to the Connect button, and publish and test the movie.

To complete this independent challenge:

a. Start Shockwave Multiuser Server, display the IP address, write it down, then minimize or hide the program.

b. Start Director, open the file **Xpressions** (the file you created in Independent Challenge 2) from the drive and folder where your Project Files are located, then save the movie as *Xpressions Test*.

c. Display the Connect to Server behavior in the Behavior tab of the Property Inspector, then replace the IP address with the one you wrote down.

d. Open the Publish Settings dialog box, set the default settings, then display the Formats tab, if necessary.

e. Select the drive and folder where your Project Files are located for the HTML file.

f. Select the drive and folder where your Project Files are located for the Shockwave file.

g. Set the HTML Template to Center Shockwave.

h. Display the Compression tab, set the JPEG option, then drag the compression slider to 50.

i. Close the Publish Settings dialog box, then save and compact the movie.

j. Publish the Shockwave movie and view it in a Web browser.

k. Enter your name, connect to the server, then enter several chat messages in the text boxes provided.

l. Disconnect from the server, close your Web browser, then exit Director and MultiuserServer.

4. You are the dean at Weatherby Art College, a place for painters, photographers, and other visual artists. The college is sponsoring a digital art contest. When the students submit their entries, you want to create a slide show in Director to display the submissions over the Web. You use Director to create a slide show of different paintings, drawings, or photographs and create a resizable Shockwave movie. To complete this independent challenge:

a. Connect to the Internet and go to www.course.com. Navigate to the page for this book, click the link for the Student Online Companion, then click the link for this unit.

b. Browse the Web site for paintings, drawings, or photographs and download four to six different images in the drive and folder where your Project Files are located.

c. Start Director and save the movie as *Art Contest* in the drive and folder where your Project Files are located.

d. Create a text cast member with the text **Weatherby Art Contest Submissions** and drag it to the top of the Stage.

e. Import the images you downloaded and drag them sequentially in the same channel in the Score.

f. Open the Publish Settings dialog box, set the default settings, then click the Formats tab.

g. Select the drive and folder where your Project Files are located for the HTML file.

h. Select the drive and folder where your Project Files are located for the Shockwave file.

i. Change Dimensions to Percentage of Browser Window in the General tab.

j. Change Stretch Style to Stretch Fill and select the Zooming check box, if necessary, in the Shockwave tab, then click OK.

k. Save and compact the movie, then publish it to make a Shockwave movie.

l. Print the first page, then close your Web browser.

► Visual Workshop

Recreate the screen shown in Figure B-19. Use a completed file from either the unit or the Skills Review, copy and modify a button, then apply the Send Chat Button behavior to the button. Print the screen. (For Windows, use the Windows Paint program. Press the Print Screen key to make a copy of the screen, start the Paint program by clicking Start, pointing to Programs, pointing to Accessories, then clicking Paint; click Edit on the menu bar, click Paste to paste the screen into Paint, then click Yes to paste the large image if necessary. Click File on the menu bar, click Print, click Print or OK in the dialog box, then exit Paint. For the Macintosh, use the SimpleText program. Hold and press the Command, Shift, and 3 keys to make a copy of the screen, double-click the document Picture 1 located on your hard drive, click File on the menu bar, click Print, then click Print in the dialog box. *Note*: When you create a new document with a copy of the screen and a document Picture 1 already exists, the Macintosh names the new document Picture 2.)

FIGURE B-19

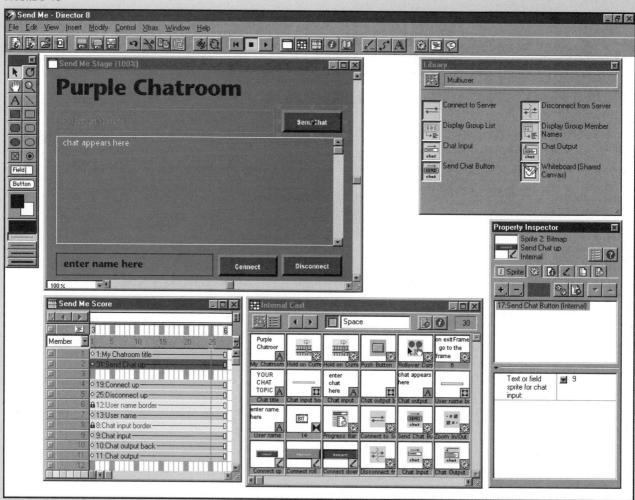

Unit A

Getting
Started with Fireworks 4

Objectives

- ▶ **Define Web graphics software**
- ▶ **Start Fireworks 4 and create a document**
- ▶ **View the Fireworks window**
- ▶ **Import an image**
- ▶ **Create and modify objects**
- ▶ **Organize objects**
- ▶ **Add and edit text**
- ▶ **View and print a document**
- ▶ **Close a document and exit Fireworks**

Macromedia Fireworks 4 is a professional Web graphics design and production program that lets you easily create images and animations for use on the Internet. Fireworks integrates easily with other Macromedia products, such as Shockwave and Director. In this unit, you'll learn basic Fireworks concepts and skills, such as identifying elements within the Fireworks window, creating a new document, drawing objects within a document, and saving documents and exiting the program. ✐ Jean Young, the instructional designer at SpaceWorks Interactive, wants to create a graphic image that the company will use as a logo. This image will also be turned into a patch and will be sent to customers as a promotion. She begins by becoming acquainted with Fireworks.

Defining Web Graphics Software

Fireworks 4 is a software program that lets you create dynamic Web graphics and animations. You can create your own unique graphics, use scanned artwork, use images from a digital camera, or import existing files from other programs to enhance documents and Web pages. Fireworks contains the tools you need to create buttons and animations—all in an editable format. Its automation features help you keep your documents and Web pages up to date. When you finish creating your graphics, Fireworks makes it easy to export them into other programs. Jean has never used Fireworks before, and wants to learn what it can do.

Details

Create and edit graphics

Fireworks contains both bitmap and vector editing tools. A **bitmap image** is composed of tiny dots, or pixels. As a bitmapped image becomes larger, it has a tendency to lose its crispness. A **vector image** is composed of paths and points, rather than pixels. As a vector image is resized, it retains its crispness. Images created in Fireworks have vector paths that you can modify, and pixels that you can edit without losing image quality. These features make Fireworks a powerful graphic images program—it has the ability to use the best features of both bitmap and vector editing tools.

Optimize graphic images

Web graphics should be dynamic, exciting, and vibrant. Unfortunately, these qualities often go hand-in-hand with large file sizes. Because the Web is about speed and performance, graphic images should be as small as possible. Fireworks lets you optimize graphic images so your images will look great and download efficiently. Using the Preview, 2-Up, or 4-Up tab in the document window, you can experiment with various settings to see how your images will look. The document window is shown in Figure A-1.

Add interactivity to graphic images

To make your Web pages more interesting, add interactive features such as rollover buttons, animated banners, and image maps. Using these techniques, as well as adding behaviors, makes your Web pages spring to life. A behavior is the result of mouse movement within a page. It is caused by a series of JavaScript code that triggers an action to occur.

Export graphic images into other programs

After you create graphic images in Fireworks, you can export them in common Web and print formats for use in other programs, such as Macromedia Director, Macromedia Flash, Macromedia Dreamweaver, and Adobe Illustrator. Fireworks gives you several ways to export an image: Export Special, Export Preview, and Export Wizard. With Export Special, you can export an image in a specific format or for a program. With Export Preview, you can optimize and export an image and preview the results. If you prefer to use a wizard, you can use the Export Wizard to guide you through the export process and suggest settings. If you want to import Fireworks graphic images in Director, you can install and use a custom Fireworks Import Xtra in Director to retain the attributes of the graphic images.

FIGURE A-1: Graphic image

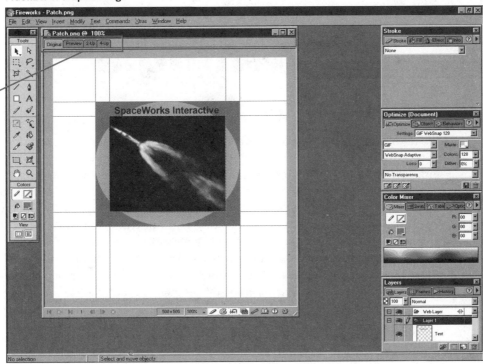

Optimization tabs

Importing Fireworks files into Director

If you create files in Fireworks 3 or 4 to import into Macromedia Director 7 or 8, you can install and use the Fireworks Import Xtra for Director to optimize the process. The Fireworks Import Xtra for Director allows you to export layers, rollovers, and slices from Fireworks into Director as fully functional cast members. Before you can export files from Fireworks and import them into Director, you need to install the Fireworks 4 Import Xtra for Director (located on the Fireworks installation CD-ROM or Macromedia Web site), which installs files for both programs. For complete instructions, see "Installing an Xtra" in the Appendix. You can export layered graphics or sliced graphics by using the Setup for Director commands on the Commands menu, or by using one of the

export commands on the File menu in Fireworks. To insert the Fireworks objects into Director, start Director, click Insert on the menu bar, point to Fireworks, then click Images from Fireworks HTML. Select the HTML document exported with the Fireworks objects, then select insert settings: Color, which defines the color depth; Registration, which defines how registration points function; Import to Score, which inserts images to both Score and Cast; and Import Rollover Behaviors, which retains slices and rollover behaviors as Director behaviors. When inserted into Director, these behaviors are attached to sprites in the Score (version 8) or saved as separate cast members (version 7).

Fireworks 4

GETTING STARTED WITH FIREWORKS 4   FIREWORKS A-3

Starting Fireworks 4 and Creating a Document

If Fireworks is not installed on your computer, you must first install it according to the instructions that accompany the program. Depending on the platform you are using, after Fireworks is installed, you can start the program in several ways. When you start Fireworks, the computer displays a splash screen, and then the Fireworks workspace opens. The **workspace** is the entire Fireworks screen, including the document window and all the tools you need for your creations. Fireworks displays a blank window in which you can create and edit images. In Fireworks, a graphic image is called a **document**. By default, Fireworks uses its own file format, which has the .PNG file extension. However, you can open files created by many other graphics programs. Although Fireworks operates similarly on Windows and Macintosh computers, Jean reviews the differences between opening the program on each platform.

Steps

WIN

1. Click the Start button 🎀 Start **on the taskbar**
The Start button is on the left side of the taskbar and is used to open programs on your computer. Use the set of steps designed for the platform you are using.

2. Point to Programs, then point to Macromedia Fireworks 4
The Programs menu lists all the programs, including Macromedia Fireworks, that are installed on your computer, as shown in Figure A-2. Your Programs menu may look different, depending on the programs installed and the operating system in use.

3. Click Fireworks 4
The Fireworks program opens, displaying the workspace where you can create a new document.

Trouble?

If necessary, change the resolution to 72 and the canvas color to white.

4. Click File on the Menu bar, then click New
The New Document dialog box opens, displaying the default settings for size (in pixels), resolution (72), and canvas color (white).

5. Type 500, press Tab, type 500, then click OK
When you click OK, you accept these default settings.

MAC

1. Double-click the hard drive icon
The contents of your hard drive is displayed on your desktop.
Use the set of steps designed for the platform you are using.

2. Double-click the Macromedia Fireworks folder
The Macromedia Fireworks folder opens, displaying the program icon and associated files that come with the product, as shown in Figure A-3.

3. Double-click the Fireworks 4 program icon
The Fireworks program opens, displaying the workspace for a new document.

Trouble?

If necessary, change the resolution to 72 and the canvas color to white.

4. Click File on the menu bar, then click New
The New Document dialog box opens, displaying the default settings for size (in pixels), resolution (72), and canvas color (white).

5. Type 500, press Tab, type 500, then click OK
When you click OK, you accept these default settings.

FIGURE A-2: Starting Fireworks 4 (Windows)

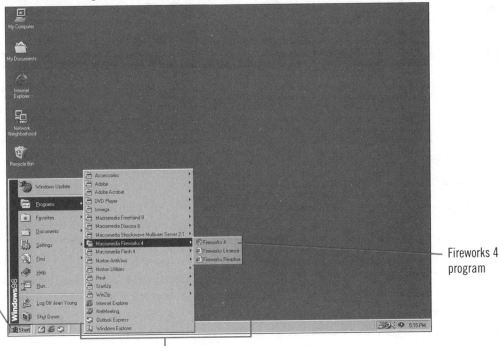

Click here to open Start Menu

Fireworks 4 program

Your list of programs might differ

FIGURE A-3: Starting Fireworks 4 (Macintosh)

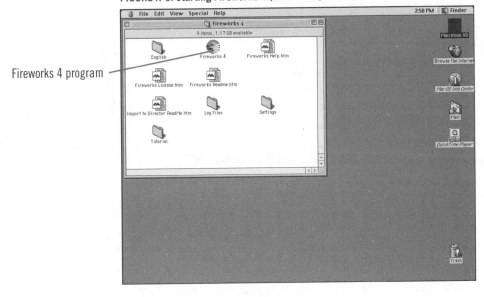

Fireworks 4 program

Opening an existing document

If you already have an existing document with a graphic image, you can open the document and modify it in the same way you create a new document. With Fireworks, you can open or import several file formats, including Macromedia FreeHand, Adobe Photoshop, Adobe Illustrator, uncompressed CorelDRAW, and animated GIF files. To open an existing document, click File on the menu bar, then click Open. If necessary, select the file format specific options you want, then click OK. When you open a file with a format other than PNG (the default Fireworks file format), Fireworks creates a new document. Although the new document is a PNG file, the original file remains unchanged.

Viewing the Fireworks Window

When you open Fireworks, the screen contains a variety of components designed to assist you in creating graphic images. Some elements in the workspace will change, depending on your current task or operation. For example, if you click a particular button, a new panel (on the right edge of the workspace) may appear. Jean reviews the common elements found in the Fireworks workspace. Refer to your screen and to Figure A-4 for Windows and Figure A-5 for the Macintosh, as you locate the elements of the Fireworks workspace.

Details

Trouble?
The size and location of your windows might differ.

 The program window **title bar** displays the name of the open document (in this case, Untitled-1, because the document has not yet been named) and the program name, Fireworks. The title bar also contains a Control Menu box, a Close button, and resizing buttons.

 A **menu** is a list of commands that you use to accomplish certain tasks. You've already used the Start menu to open Fireworks. A **command** is a directive that accesses a program feature. Fireworks has its own set of menus, which are located on the menu bar along the top of the program window.

 The **menu bar** organizes commands into groups of related operations. Each group is listed under the name of the menu, such as "File" or "Help." You can choose a menu command by clicking it. Some commands display shortcut keys in the right-hand column of the menu. Commands may also appear dimmed, which means they are not currently available. Commands with a triangle have a submenu from which you can select additional commands. Commands with an ellipsis indicate that you must use a **dialog box** to enter or select information.

QuickTip
Each docked toolbar can be repositioned by dragging it to a new location.

 The **toolbar** contains buttons for the most frequently used commands (Windows only). Toolbars in Fireworks do not appear by default; you need to display them. To display a toolbar, click the Window menu, point to Toolbars, then click a toolbar name. The Main and Modify toolbars appear in Figure A-4. Clicking a button on a toolbar is often faster than clicking a menu and then clicking a command. When you position the mouse pointer over a button, a **ScreenTip** appears. Use the ScreenTip feature to display the name of a button on the toolbar.

 The **Tool panel** contains a set of tools you can use to make selections, draw objects, edit shapes, magnify, create clickable areas, and add color and outlines to objects.

 The **document window** is the area in which you create and modify images. By default, this window contains four tabs: the Original tab and three preview tabs. The preview tabs are used to **optimize**, or fine-tune, the appearance of the document.

QuickTip
Each floating panel or inspector can be docked by dragging it to the edge of the workspace.

The Fireworks workspace contains a variety of panels and inspectors. A **panel** is used to control options on a document or tool, and an **inspector** is used to control the characteristics of selected objects. Each panel or inspector is docked on the right edge of the workspace, although their title bars are visible. Examples of panels and inspectors are listed below.

- The History panel lets you see recent commands, and can be used to undo and redo actions.
- Use the Layers and Frames panels to organize the structure within a document. The Frames panel is used to modify animations.
- The Color Mixer, Swatches panel, and Color Table panel you can use to make modifications to a document's color palette.
- The Library panel contains an array of graphic symbols that you can drag onto your document and use as buttons.
- You can use the Object, Stroke, Fill, and Effect inspectors to control characteristics of objects.
- The Behaviors inspector manages the way areas within a document react to mouse movement.

 The **status bar** appears at the bottom of the program window (Win) or document window (Mac). It contains information about any selected objects and a description of a selected tool. The bottom of the document window contains VCR buttons that you use to run animations, window view size controls, and a mini-launcher that you use to open and close commonly used panels.

FIGURE A-4: Fireworks elements (Windows)

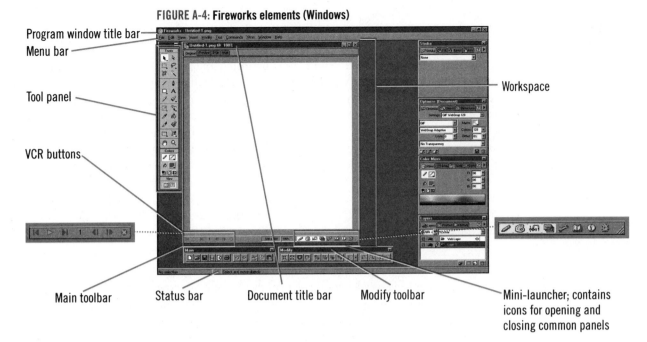

Program window title bar
Menu bar

Tool panel

VCR buttons

Main toolbar

Status bar

Document title bar

Modify toolbar

Workspace

Mini-launcher; contains icons for opening and closing common panels

FIGURE A-5: Fireworks elements (Macintosh)

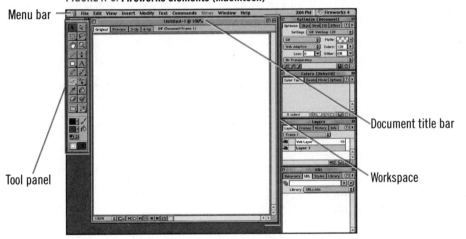

Menu bar

Tool panel

Document title bar

Workspace

Getting Help

Fireworks Help includes an extensive manual that is displayed in your Web browser. You can open Help at any time by pressing [F1] or by clicking Help on the menu bar, then clicking Using Fireworks. Once the Help window opens you can use the scroll bars to access information. Figure A-6 shows the Displaying and choosing tools Help window. You can also access a tutorial by clicking Help on the menu bar, then clicking Tutorial. You can search for an individual topic by clicking Search, then entering one or more keywords. To access online Fireworks support, connect to the Internet, click Help on the menu bar, then click Fireworks Support Center.

FIGURE A-6: Help window

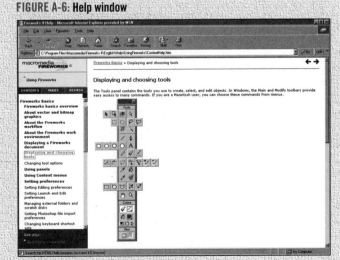

Importing an Image

With Fireworks, you can save time and effort by importing an existing image. You can import several file formats, including Macromedia FreeHand, Adobe Photoshop, Illustrator, uncompressed CorelDRAW, and animated GIF files. Later, you can enhance the existing image by surrounding it with additional objects. Rather than having to approximate where to position objects, Fireworks lets you view **rulers** in the document window that you can use to determine an object's precise position. You can also create **guides**, nonprinting green lines that help you position and align objects. Guides make it easy to position objects, because objects automatically snap to them. A **grid**, which looks similar to graph paper but does not print, can also be displayed in the entire document window to make positioning objects easier. ✎ Jean begins creating the promotional image for SpaceWorks Interactive. Before she can create guides, she displays the rulers.

Steps 1234

1. **Click View on the menu bar, then click Rulers**
   A horizontal and a vertical ruler display on the top and left edges of the document window. As you move your mouse pointer, a line appears in both rulers indicating your exact position. While rulers let you determine an exact position in the window, guides let you position an object more accurately. You can use the rulers to create guides.

2. **Position the arrow pointer anywhere along the horizontal ruler, click and drag ⬍ to the 120 V mark, then release the mouse button**
   A horizontal guide appears in the document. When you place the mouse pointer over a horizontal guide, it changes to ⬍. A vertical guide is created in the same manner.

3. **Position the arrow pointer anywhere within the vertical ruler, click and drag ⬌ to 120 H, then release the mouse button**
   Vertical and horizontal guides now appear in the document window.

4. **Add an additional horizontal guide at 320 V and an additional vertical guide at 370 H**
   There are now four guides in the document window, as shown in Figure A-7.

5. **Click File on the menu bar, then click Import**
   The Import dialog box opens.

6. **Click the Look in list arrow, click the drive and folder where your Project Files are located, click the file Rocket.gif as shown in Figure A-8, then click Open**
   The pointer changes to ⌐. You can use this pointer to define where you want to place the image.

7. **Drag ⌐ from 120 H/120 V to 370 H/320 V, using the guides to locate the dimensions, then release the mouse button**
   The rocket image appears in the area you outlined with the pointer. Saving your document ensures that your work will be preserved so you can use it later or allow others to access it.

8. **Click File on the menu bar, then click Save**
   The Save As dialog box opens. You use this dialog box to give your document a unique name, and to determine where Fireworks will save it.

9. **Click the Save in list arrow, click the drive and folder where your Project Files are located, type Patch in the File name text box, then click Save**
   The Fireworks document is saved in the designated location in the PNG format, and the new document name is displayed in the document window's title bar. Compare your document to Figure A-9.

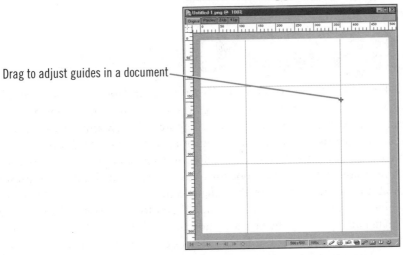

Drag to adjust guides in a document

FIGURE A-8: **Import dialog box**

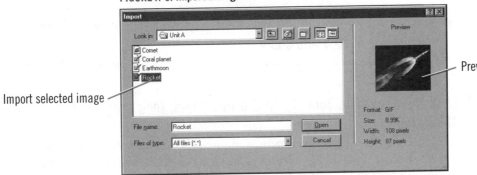

Import selected image

Preview of selected image

FIGURE A-9: **Image in document**

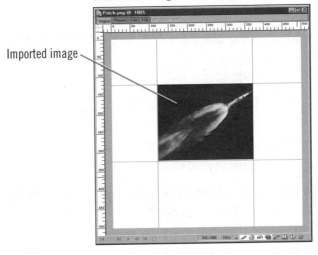

Imported image

Using the grid

You can further customize your document window by displaying a grid, which is measured in pixels. When you turn on the grid, a nonprintable series of black horizontal and vertical lines appears on the document. You can turn the grid on by clicking View on the menu bar, pointing to Grid, then clicking Show Grid. You can also modify the grid color and the size of the grid boxes by clicking View on the menu bar, pointing to Grid, then clicking Edit Grid. You can turn the grid off by clicking View on the menu bar, then clicking Grid.

Fireworks 4

Creating and Modifying Objects

By default, a new Fireworks document opens in Object mode. In **Object mode**, each object is composed of pixels, or tiny dots, that form paths and points. This is important because path objects (vector images) will not lose their definition as they are resized. Many objects can be drawn using buttons in the toolbox. Shapes, such as rectangles or ellipses, can be filled with colors or patterns to make them more attractive. Colors can be applied using a palette in the toolbox, or by picking up an existing color from within the document itself. To edit an object, you must select it. You can select objects by clicking them or by dragging selection marquees around them using the Pointer, Select Behind, or Subselection tool. When a selection tool is active and the mouse rolls over an object, a highlight appears on the object to indicate that it is selectable. When an object is selected, it is surrounded by a thin, blue border. Small dots, or **handles**, are displayed around the perimeter of a selected object. Jean wants to draw additional objects in the document.

Steps

1. Add the following guides in the document: a horizontal guide at **90 H** and **400 H**, and a vertical guide at **90 V** and **350 V**

   Compare your document to Figure A-10. You can use these guides to place objects in the document.

2. Click the **Rectangle Tool** in the Tool panel, then drag $+$ from **90 H/90 V** to **400 H/350 V**

   A rectangle appears in the document, and the rocket image is no longer visible. In fact, the imported image is still in the document, but it is *behind* the rectangle. You can apply a color to the object, using a palette in the Tool panel.

3. Click the **Fill Color Box list arrow** in the Tool panel

   The color palette is displayed, as shown in Figure A-11.

4. Click the **lavender color box** (#9966FF) in the third column of the last row of the color palette

   The rectangle is filled with the new color, lavender.

5. Click and hold , then select the **Ellipse Tool**

   The Ellipse Tool is now displayed in the Tool panel.

6. Drag $+$ from **90 H/90 V** to **400 H/350 V**

   You can fill the ellipse using the Fill Color Box.

7. Click the **Fill Color Box list arrow** in the Tool panel, then click the **yellow color box** (#FFFF00) at the end of the seventh row of the color palette

   The ellipse turns yellow, as shown in Figure A-12.

8. Click **File** on the menu bar, then click **Save**

   Fireworks saves the document with the new shape and color changes.

FIGURE A-10: Guides added to document

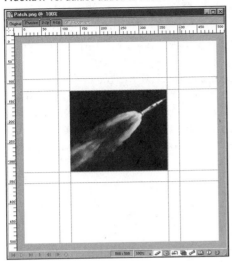

FIGURE A-11: Fill Color Box palette

Current color is displayed in the Fill color box

Click arrow in the Fill Color Box to display color palette

#33CCFF

FIGURE A-12: Filled drawn objects

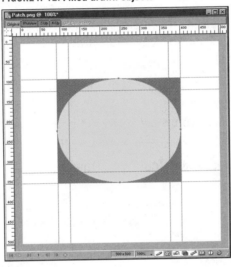

Using styles

Fireworks comes with a set of predefined styles from which you can apply to an object. A style consists of a predefined fill, stroke, effect, or text attribute. Styles are more like paint mixes on an artist's palette than styles in a word processor. You can use the Styles panel to apply, add, change, and remove styles. To apply a style to an object, select the object, then click a style in the Styles panel, as shown in Figure A-13. To add a new style, select an object or text with the stroke, fill, effect, or text settings you want, click the New Style button ⊞ in the Styles panel, select the properties you want for the style, then click OK. To change a style, double-click the style in the Styles panel, then change settings in the Edit Style dialog box. To remove a style, select the style in the Styles panel, then click the Delete Style button 🗑 in the Styles panel.

FIGURE A-13: Styles panel

Organizing Objects

You have just learned how to apply colors from the Fill Color Box. Another color technique is to pick up colors that exist within one object and apply them to another object. While color is one way of distinguishing objects, the order in which objects are visible can give the illusion of depth or order. Using the commands on the Arrange submenu on the Modify menu or buttons on the Modify toolbar (Win), you can rearrange objects so that they obscure or overlap one another. You can turn multiple objects into single objects using a process called **grouping**. Grouped objects can be separated into their original components by **ungrouping** them. Jean can further modify the colors used and can change the order in which the objects appear.

Steps

1. Click the **Pointer Tool** in the Tool panel, position the **arrow pointer** anywhere on the visible portion of the rectangle, then click the **rectangle**
Blue handles surround the rectangle. You can change the order of objects on the screen using toolbar buttons.

2. Click **Modify** on the menu bar, point to **Arrange**, then click **Send to Back**
The rectangle is moved behind the other existing objects (the yellow ellipse and the rocket image), revealing the corners of the rocket image, as shown in Figure A-14.

QuickTip

You can also click the Send to Back button on the Modify toolbar (Win).

3. Click anywhere within the ellipse, click **Modify** on the menu bar, point to **Arrange**, then click **Send Backward**
The ellipse is moved behind the rocket image, which is now visible. You can apply a color that is part of an object, using the Eyedropper tool.

4. Click the **Eyedropper Tool** in the Tool panel, then click the portion of the rocket located at **260 H/180 V**
The color of the ellipse changes to the color you sampled. Compare your document to Figure A-15. In addition to changing the colors of objects and rearranging them, you can also group multiple objects so they turn into a single object.

5. Click the **Pointer Tool** in the Tool panel, click anywhere in the visible portion of the ellipse, press and hold **[Shift]**, click anywhere in the visible portion of the rectangle, then release **[Shift]**
Blue handles surround both the ellipse and the rectangle.

QuickTip

You can click Modify on the menu bar, then click Ungroup to separate a grouped object into its components.

6. Click **Modify** on the menu bar, then click **Group**
The outline of the ellipse is no longer visible. The two individual objects (the rectangle and the ellipse) have been grouped to form a single object. You can flip the rocket to change its appearance.

7. Click anywhere within the rocket image, then click **Modify** on the menu bar, point to **Transform**, then click **Flip Horizontal**
The rocket image is flipped.

8. Click **File** on the menu bar, then click **Save**

FIGURE A-14: **Rectangle sent to back**

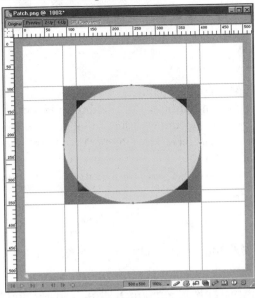

FIGURE A-15: **Ellipse color changed**

Sampled color

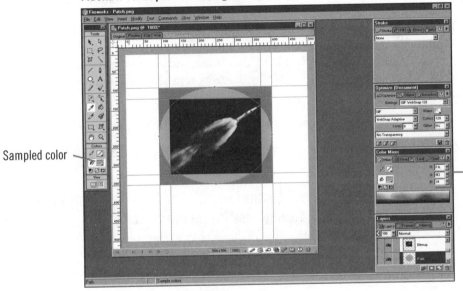

Your RGB values might vary

CLUES TO USE

Setting preferences

Fireworks settings can be changed as needed, or you can modify program settings on a more permanent basis. Preferences are divided into four categories: General, Editing, Folders, and Import. You can open the Preferences dialog box, shown in Figure A-16, by clicking Edit on the menu bar, then clicking Preferences. By clicking each tab, you can modify the behavior of the program to suit your work habits.

FIGURE A-16: **Preferences dialog box**

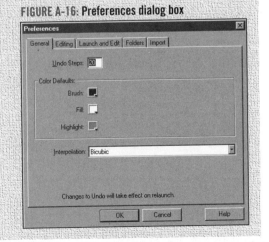

Adding and Editing Text

In Web pages, text is used to supplement an image or idea. Text is generally used in small quantities, especially in comparison to the amounts of text used in word-processing programs. Text can be created within a document, using a tool in the tool panel. When you create text, you can control the font, font size, color, and alignment of the characters. You can modify existing text by double-clicking the text box. Like other drawn objects, a text box is an object. When selected, it is surrounded by handles. ◆━━ Jean wants to add text that identifies the company.

Steps 1234

1. Click the **Text Tool** A in the Tool panel, then click I at **150 H/110 V**
   The Text Editor dialog box opens, as shown in Figure A-17.

2. Verify that the **Left Alignment button** and the **Bold button** are selected, and that **Arial 20 pt** is the active font and font size, then type **SpaceWorks** in the text box, as shown in Figure A-17

3. Click **OK**
   The text box appears at the top of the rocket image, and is shown as an individual object. You can move a selected text box by dragging it to a new location.

4. Double-click the **text box**
   The Text Editor dialog box opens. You can edit the text in the text box.

5. Click I to the right of SpaceWorks in the text box, press **[Spacebar]**, type **Interactive**, then click **OK**

6. Position the **arrow pointer** over the text box, click and drag the **text box** so the **top-left edge** is at **130 H/100 V**, then release the **mouse button**
   The text box is centered above the rocket image, as shown in Figure A-18.

7. Click **File** on the menu bar, then click **Save**

FIGURE A-17: Text Editor dialog box

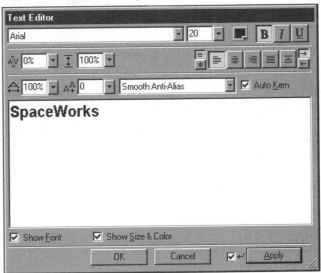

FIGURE A-18: Text in document

CLUES TO USE

Attaching text to a path

Instead of creating simple text boxes, you can draw a path and attach text to it. The text flows along the shape of the path and remains editable. To attach text to a path, select a text box and a path, click Text on the menu bar, then click Attach to Path. Once you attach text to a path, any changes you make to the combined object are applied to the text, not the path, and the path temporarily loses its stroke, fill, and effects attributes until the text is detached from the path. To edit

the text attached to a path, double-click the combined object to open the Text Editor, click the Text Tool, then modify the text. To edit the shape of the path, click the combined object, click Text on the menu bar, click Detach from Path, edit the path, then attach the text to the path again. You can also change the orientation (vertical) of the text box by clicking Text on the menu bar, pointing to Orientation, then clicking an option.

Viewing and Printing a Document

Although your Fireworks document will probably be posted on a Web page or be duplicated by a professional printer, there may be times when you want to print a hard copy. In addition to the ability to reproduce your image on a printer, you can also magnify parts of a document, to look more closely at specific areas. You can enlarge areas of a document using a button in the tool panel. ✐ Jean wants to view various portions of the document and then print a hard copy.

Steps 1 2 3 4

1. Click the **Zoom Tool** 🔍 in the Tool panel

The pointer changes to ⊕, which you can use to click an area of the document to enlarge it.

> **QuickTip**
>
> Once an area is enlarged, you can view the remainder of the document by using the horizontal and vertical scroll bars.

2. Click ⊕ at **190 H/180 V**

Compare your screen with Figure A-19.

3. Press and hold **[Alt]** (Win) or **[Option]** (Mac)

The pointer changes to ⊖.

> **QuickTip**
>
> To reduce an image to fit the window, right-click the image, then click Fit All.

4. Click **190 H/180 V**

The document returns to its original size. You can print your document.

5. Click **File** on the menu bar, then click **Print**

The Print dialog box opens, as shown in Figure A-20 (Win). The Print dialog box will differ on the Macintosh.

6. Verify that the name of your printer is shown in the Name list box, and that the number of copies is 1, then click **OK**

Fireworks prints the document.

FIGURE A-19: Document magnified

FIGURE A-20: Print dialog box

Your default printer might be different

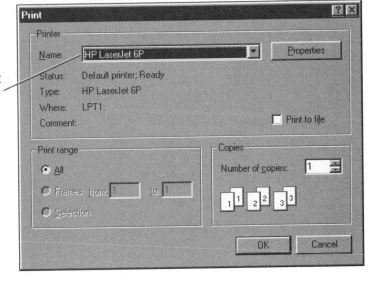

Setting up the page format

When you print a document, you can use the Page Setup dialog box to control the way text and graphics are printed on a page. The Page Setup dialog box specifies the printer properties for page size, paper source (location of the paper), orientation, and margins (the extra space around the dotted rectangle); in most cases, you won't want to change them. To change the page setup, click File on the menu bar, then click Page Setup.

Fireworks 4

Closing a Document and Exiting Fireworks

After you work on an image, you can close the document by saving it or by exiting Fireworks. Unless you don't want to use the changes you made to the document, you should save it. Closing the current document leaves the Fireworks program open. Exiting Fireworks closes the current document as well as the program. You can use the Exit (Win) or Quit (Mac) command on the File menu to close a document and exit Fireworks. ✐ Jean is finished using Fireworks, so she closes the Patch document and exits the program. As a courtesy to the next Fireworks user, she turns off the rulers before she exits the program.

Steps

1. Click **View** on the menu bar, then click **Rulers**

The rulers are no longer visible.

2. Click **File** on the menu bar

The File menu opens, as shown in Figure A-21.

3. Click **Close**

If asked if you want to save your work, click Yes (Win) or Save (Mac). The Patch document closes, although the Fireworks program is still open.

4. Click **File** on the menu bar, then click **Exit** (Win) or **Quit** (Mac)

The Fireworks program closes, returning you to the desktop.

FIGURE A-21: Closing a document using the File menu

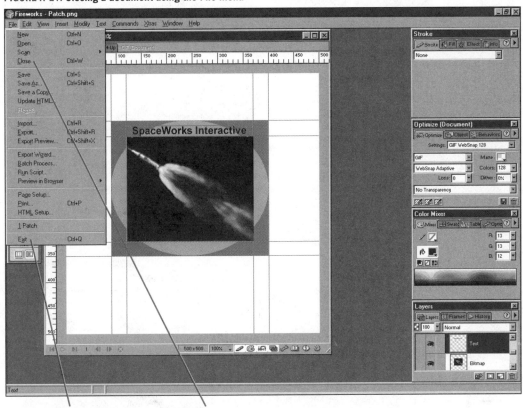

Click Exit (Win) or Quit (Mac) to close a document and exit Fireworks

Click Close to close a document

Using the Fireworks Support Center on the Web

The Fireworks Support Center Web site contains the latest information on Fireworks, plus additional topics, examples, tips, and updates, to allow you to get the most out of the program. Click Help on the menu bar, then click Fireworks Support Center. Figure A-22 shows the Fireworks Support Center Web site. Because this site is continually updated, your screen might look different. You can also get general information about Fireworks at the Fireworks Product Web site. Click Help on the menu bar, then click Fireworks Product Web Site. To find additional sites on the Web with Fireworks information, you can use a search engine.

FIGURE A-22: Fireworks Support Center Web site

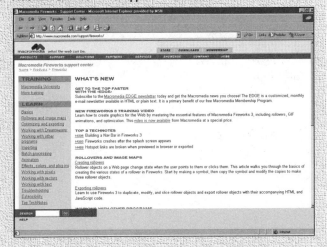

Practice

▶ Concepts Review

Label each of the elements of the screen shown in Figure A-23.

FIGURE A-23

Match each of the terms with the statement that describes its function.

7. Eyedropper Tool
8. Guide size pointer
9. Text Tool
10. Rectangle Tool
11. Image placement pointer
12. Selection pointer

a. ☐
b. A
c. ▶
d. ⌐
e. ⥮
f. ⤓

Select the best answer from the following list of choices.

13. **What kind of documents can you create with Fireworks?**
    a. Spreadsheets
    b. Databases
    c. Web graphics and animations
    d. Newsletters and informative brochures

14. **A file created in Fireworks is called a:**
    a. Presentation.
    b. Document.
    c. Graphicana.
    d. Slipstream.

15. **Which button is used to sample an existing color?**
    a. [icon]
    b. [icon]
    c. [icon]
    d. [icon]

16. **Which of the following is the default Fireworks file extension?**
    a. .GIF
    b. .PNG
    c. .PSD
    d. .BMP

17. **The collection of buttons to the left of the document window is called the:**
    a. Accessory toolbar.
    b. Main toolbar.
    c. Modify toolbar.
    d. Tool panel.

18. **Tiny dots surrounding a selected object are called:**
    a. Ingots.
    b. Serifs.
    c. Handles.
    d. Implants.

19. **Which key can you press to see Help?**
    a. [F1]
    b. [F3]
    c. [F5]
    d. [F6]

20. **Which menu is used to turn rulers on/off ?**
    a. Edit
    b. View
    c. Modify
    d. Window

21. **Which menu is used to turn individual objects into a single object?**
    a. Edit
    b. View
    c. Modify
    d. Window

▶ Skills Review

1. **Define Web graphics software.**
   a. Write down the basic features of the Fireworks program.
   b. What are the key features of the program?

2. **Start Fireworks 4 and create a document.**
   a. Click the Start button, point to Programs, point to Macromedia Fireworks 4, then click Fireworks 4 (Win), or double-click the hard drive icon, double-click the Macromedia Fireworks folder, then double-click the Fireworks 4 program icon (Mac).
   b. Click the New button, accept the default settings (W: 500, H: 500, R: 72; C: White), then click OK.

3. **View the Fireworks window.**
   a. Identify and list elements in the Fireworks workspace without referring to the unit material.
   b. Compare your results with Figure A-4 (Win) or Figure A-5 (Mac).

4. Import an image.

a. Click View on the menu bar, then click Rulers.

b. Create a vertical guide at 100 H and 350 H.

c. Create horizontal guides at 150 V and 400 V.

d. Import **Coral planet.gif** to the dimensions formed by the guides, from the drive and folder where your Project Files are located.

e. Save the document as *Vacation* (in PNG format) in the drive and folder where your Project Files are located.

5. Create and modify objects.

a. Add horizontal guides at 120 V and 430 V.

b. Add vertical guides at 70 H and 380 H.

c. Create a rectangle from 70 H/120 V to 380 H/430 V.

d. Use the Fill Color Box to apply the last color box in the second row of the color palette.

e. Save your work.

6. Organize objects.

a. Send the rectangle behind the imported image.

b. Make sure the rectangle is selected.

c. Use the Eyedropper Tool to sample 310 H/300 V.

d. Group the rectangle and the imported image.

e. Save your work.

7. Add and edit text.

a. Create a text box at 100 H/70 V.

b. Use the following settings: Arial 20 pt, bold, black, and center aligned.

c. Type **Need a vacation?**, then close the Text Editor dialog box.

d. Reposition the text box so the lower-left edge aligns at 140 H/150 V.

e. Save your work.

8. View and print a document.

a. Use the Zoom Tool to zoom in to the center of the planet.

b. Zoom out to the original image size.

c. Create a text box in the lower-left corner that contains your name.

d. Save the document.

e. Print the document.

9. Close a document and exit Fireworks.

a. Close the Vacation document.

b. Exit Fireworks.

▶ Independent Challenges

1. You are new to Fireworks and want to learn how to use the product. Fireworks 4 has an extensive Help system. At any time, you can get the assistance you need from the Help menu. Use the Help system to learn about the topics listed below.
To complete this independent challenge:

a. Locate and read the Help information on optimizing settings.

b. Locate and read the Help information on using panels and inspectors.

c. Locate and read the Help information on selecting objects.

d. Locate and read the Help information on displaying the Tool panel.

e. Locate and read the Help information on grouping objects.

f. Print one or more of the Help topics you located.

g. Close the Help window.

2. You are new to Fireworks and need to learn how to use the product. Your boss sends you to a class in which the instructor asks you to open a sample file that comes with the program. The sample and instructional documents that are installed with the Fireworks program are typically located in subfolders inside the Fireworks 4 folder.

To complete this independent challenge:

a. Click the Open button on the Main toolbar.

b. Locate the Samples folder. In the typical Fireworks 4 installation, the folder is located in the Programs Files folder, Macromedia folder, Fireworks 4 folder, and Samples folder (Win) or Fireworks 4 and Samples folder (Mac).

c. Open the Numbers file.

d. Identify as many familiar elements as you can in the Fireworks workspace without looking back in the lessons.

e. Play the animation. (*Hint*: Use the Play button ▷ at the bottom of the document window.)

f. Print the document.

g. Exit Fireworks without saving any changes you may have made.

3. The class you took on Fireworks 4 is about to pay off. RocketScience, a store in a local mall, is looking for someone to design its Web page. You have an appointment for an interview, at which you will have to use Fireworks to come up with a preliminary design.

To complete this independent challenge:

a. Start Fireworks and open a new document, using the default settings (W: 500, H: 500, R: 72; C: White).

b. Create some preliminary horizontal and vertical guides within the document.

c. Import the Rocket.gif image into the document.

d. Save the file as *RocketScience logo* in the drive and folder where your Project Files are located.

e. Add two drawn objects to the document.

f. Add colors to each of the shapes.

g. Group the two shapes.

h. Add a text box containing your name.

i. Save the document and print the screen.

j. Exit Fireworks.

4. You want to find out more about Fireworks—in particular, what online support is available. The Macromedia Web site provides extensive information about their products.

To complete this independent challenge:

a. Connect to the Internet.

b. Use the Fireworks Help menu to open the Fireworks Support Center on the Macromedia Web site.

c. Go to the information on Basics.

d. Print the page.

e. Close the Web browser and disconnect from the Internet, if necessary.

▶ Visual Workshop

Recreate the screen shown in Figure A-24. Create a document using the default settings, then save it in the designated location as *Visit planets*. Use the images Comet.jpg and Earthmoon.gif in the drive and folder where your Project Files are located. The color of the SpaceWorks text (in the lower-right corner) should come from a sample of the document at 400 H/130 V and it should be in an Arial 14 pt bold font. The title text should be in an Arial 20 pt bold font in black. The background rectangle color should come from a sample of the document at 380 H/140 V. Add text in the lower-left corner containing your name, then save and print the document.

FIGURE A-24

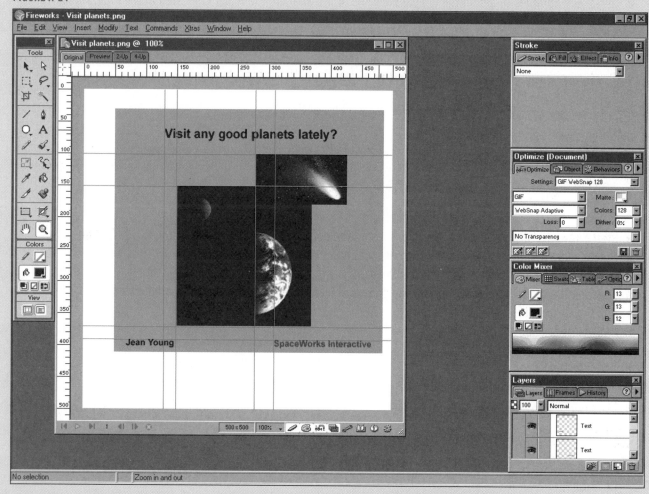

Enhancing
Documents with Fireworks 4

Objectives

▶ **Understand Web documents**
▶ **Optimize a graphic image**
▶ **Create and edit a hotspot**
▶ **Create a button**
▶ **Copy a button and apply an effect**
▶ **Export a graphic image**
▶ **Plan an animation**
▶ **Manage frames**
▶ **Customize an animation**

Once you create a Web page, you can use Fireworks to enhance it. You can optimize images so they are easier to download, create clickable areas within images, and create buttons and special effects that occur when the end user places the mouse over text. You can also create effects that make individual images appear to move. Jean Young continues her work on SpaceWorks Interactive pages. She has created a Web page that she wants to augment using features in Fireworks.

Understanding Web Documents

Certain areas within Web pages are used to perform specific tasks. You can design areas that open a new Web page when the end user clicks them. Because Web pages depend on visual elements, Fireworks makes it easy to create intuitive features that look attractive, improve performance, and are enjoyable to use. Before proceeding further, Jean reviews possible Fireworks enhancements.

Details

Optimize images
To make your Web pages appear more quickly when opened, you can optimize them. Optimizing images makes them as small as possible *without* sacrificing quality.

Hotspots and slices
A hotspot is a specific area in an image that initiates an event from a mouse activation (such as when the end user positions or clicks the mouse on it), as shown in Figure B-1. It is drawn on a special layer within the document, called the Web Layer. A slice is an area within a document that can be manipulated separately from the main document. Because both hotspots and slices can have URLs attached to them, the difference between the two elements is subtle.

Rollovers
A rollover is an effect that causes a change elsewhere on the Web page. This change could be triggered by a mouse pointer. For example, the rollover could cause text to change color or an image to appear. Figure B-2 shows a button rollover. When the pointer is moved over the Earth button, the background and text colors change.

Animation
By using multiple images in frames within a layer, you can make images appear to move. You can use VCR buttons on the document window to play, pause, and stop the animation, as shown in Figure B-2.

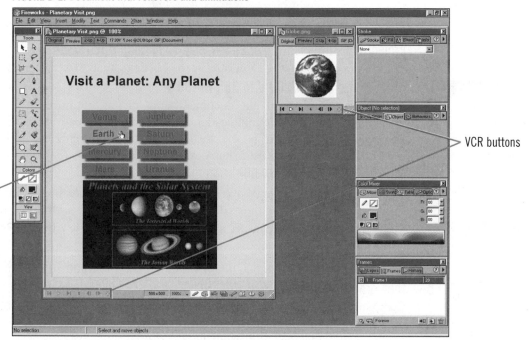

Rollover button

VCR buttons

Changing and repeating a document's history

The History panel lists the most recent actions you have performed in Fireworks. With the History panel, you can undo and redo commands, repeat commands, and save commands for reuse. To open the History panel, click Window on the menu bar, then click History. Using the History panel Undo Marker, you can quickly undo and redo recent commands. The History panel lists the most recent commands up to the number you can specify in the Undo Steps box in the General tab of the Preferences dialog box. You can also select a command in the History panel and click the Replay button to repeat the command. If you perform the same set of steps over and over again, you can save the commands as a group. To save a group of commands, select the commands you want to save, click the Save button at the bottom of the History panel, type the command name, then click OK. To use the saved group of commands, click the Command menu, then click the command name.

Optimizing a Graphic Image

Modifying the properties of an image, or **optimizing,** reduces the size of the file and makes it easy for end users to download the page. You can optimize image files that you've created in Fireworks, or you can optimize images that you have imported into an existing Fireworks document, even if the image has a different graphic file type from other graphics in the document. For example, you can open a JPEG file in Fireworks and optimize it as a Fireworks PNG file. You optimize an image from within a Fireworks document using a slice. A **slice** is a smaller section within a document that allows you to modify the properties of that area. Each slice is drawn on the Web Layer and appears as a green, translucent object. Jean wants to optimize an image once it is inserted into the Web page.

1. Start **Fireworks**, click **File** on the menu bar, click **Open**, then open the file **FW B-1** from the drive and folder where your Project Files are located

   The Open dialog box opens, and the document appears in the Fireworks window. Fireworks remembers your previous settings, such as open panels.

2. Click **View** on the menu bar, then click **Rulers**, if necessary

   You can insert an existing image in any graphics format.

3. Click **File** on the menu bar, click **Import**, navigate to the drive and folder where your Project Files are located, click **FW B-2**, then click **Open**

   The pointer changes to ⌐. You can use the existing guides to easily insert the image.

4. Drag ⌐ from **70 H/280 V** to **385 H/480 V**

   The image is displayed in the document, and you can optimize the image from within Fireworks. Notice that the middle-right panel in the workspace is Optimize (Document). The Optimize (Document) panel is displayed because no specific area within the document is selected. You can create a slice based on the selected object—the imported image.

5. Click **Insert** on the menu bar, then click **Slice**

   A translucent green rectangle overlays the imported image, as shown in Figure B-3. Notice that the panel displayed in the middle-right of the workspace is Optimize (Slice).

6. Click the **Settings list arrow** ▼ in the Optimize tab, then click **JPEG – Smaller File**

   The settings change to JPEG – Smaller File.

7. Click the **2-Up tab** in the document window, click the **Hand Tool** 🖐 in the Tool panel, then drag the imported image in the left panel so the planets are centered in the panel

   Compare your screen to Figure B-4. When you display the 2-Up tab or 4-Up tab in the document window, the view on the left or in the upper-left corner is the view of the original graphic. Notice that the optimized panel (on the right) has a file size of approximately 7.48K (your size might be different), while the size of the original image is approximately 42.16K. A smaller file size decreases the time required to download the file. The optimized panel also displays 2 sec @ 28.8bps, which indicates how long the image will take to download in a Web browser using a 28.8 bytes per second (bps) modem.

8. Click the **Original tab** in the document window, click **File** on the menu bar, then click **Save As**

   The Save As dialog box appears.

9. Click the **Save in list arrow**, navigate to the drive and folder where your Project Files are located, type **Planetary Visits** in the File name text box (Win) or Name text box (Mac), then click **Save**

   Fireworks saves the initial document with the new name, and the imported image is saved with its newly optimized settings (the settings in the original document remain unchanged).

Trouble?

If the Optimize panel is not visible, click Window on the menu bar, click Optimize, then click the Optimize tab (if necessary).

QuickTip

To save optimization settings as a preset, click the Save button in the Optimize panel, type a name for the optimization preset, then click OK.

QuickTip

To preview an image based on the current optimization settings, click the Preview tab in the document window. The Preview window displays the total file size and the estimated download time.

FIGURE B-3: Inserted slice

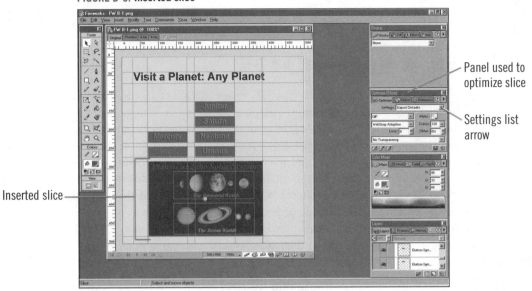

Panel used to optimize slice

Settings list arrow

Inserted slice

FIGURE B-4: Optimized image

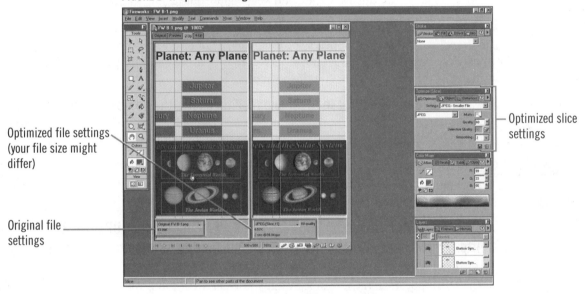

Optimized file settings (your file size might differ)

Original file settings

Optimized slice settings

CLUES TO USE

Selecting the appropriate file format

GIF, JPEG, and PNG are common graphic file formats used on Web pages. These graphic formats are compressible, which means the file size is smaller and transfers faster over the Internet. Each file format uses a different compression method, which produces different results. When you compress a graphic file, the appearance of the graphic can vary from one format to another. The file format Graphics Interchange Format, or GIF, uses only 256 colors, but it doesn't lose any image quality in the compression. This format is best for compressing images with repetitive areas of solid colors, cartoon-like graphics, logos, graphics with transparent areas, and animations. JPEG is a file format developed by the Joint Photographic Experts Group that supports millions of colors (24-bit color depth), but loses some image quality by discarding image data. Portable Network Graphics, or PNG, is a file format developed for Web graphics, yet not all Web browsers fully support its capabilities without using plug-ins. This format is best for compressing images with high color (32-bit color depth), transparent areas, and low color (best quality).

Creating and Editing a Hotspot

A **hotspot** is a clickable area within an image that takes an end user to a specific Web site. Each hotspot image triggers a response to mouse movement. A hotspot is created using a special tool located in the Tool panel. You can create hotspots that are circles, rectangles, or polygons; they are displayed as blue translucent objects. You draw hotspots on the Web Layer of a document. The **Web Layer** appears as the top layer in each new document and contains the interactive elements. Every Fireworks document contains a Web Layer. Regardless of the number of layers in the document, the Web Layer contains hotspot objects and slice objects. You can hide the Web Layer while in the Original tab or Preview tab, enabling you to get a better look at the document. You can move the Web Layer in the Layers panel, but you cannot delete it. ✎ Jean wants to add a hotspot to the earth in the Planetary Visits image.

Steps 1 2 3 4

QuickTip

To change the shape of a hotspot you've already created, select the hotspot, click the Object tab in the Optimize panel, click the Shape list arrow ▾, then click a different shape.

1. Click and hold the **Rectangle Hotspot Tool** ▣ in the Tool panel, then click the **Circle Hotspot Tool** ◉

You can draw a circular hotspot over the image of the earth (the planet directly under the word "Solar"). You can also create odd-shaped hotspots using the Polygon Hotspot Tool.

2. Drag + from **240 H/310 V** to **280 H/360 V**

A translucent blue circle appears encompassing most of the earth image, but not within the image's exact dimensions, as shown in Figure B-5. If the blue circle is not exactly over the image of the earth, you can edit the hotspot.

3. Click the **Pointer Tool** ▚ in the Tool panel, then click the **hotspot circle**, if necessary

Blue drag points appear around the hotspot. You can drag any of the drag points to change the size of the hotspot, or drag the object (not the drag points) to move the hotspot.

QuickTip

You can use the arrow keys to nudge the hotspot up, down, left, or right.

4. Drag any of the **drag points** and move the hotspot to cover the earth image

The edited translucent blue circle appears over the image of the earth. You can apply a URL to the hotspot, which is the target Web page after an end user clicks the earth.

5. Click the **Object tab** on the Optimize panel, click the **Current URL text box** ✎, type **http://www.spaceworksinteractive.com/earth.html**, then press **[Enter]** (Win) or **[Return]** (Mac)

The URL appears in the text box. When you enter a URL to a Web page, it is important to enter the complete URL that includes the server protocol, which is usually *http://* for Web pages. You can test the hotspot and see the cursor change.

QuickTip

To lock a layer in place so you can't accidentally move it, click the blank box in the column next to the layer in the Layers panel.

6. Click the **Preview tab** in the document window, then place the pointer over the earth

The pointer changes to 🖑 when it is placed over the hotspot, as shown in Figure B-6. Under the Preview tab, you can also view style and effects changes you make to buttons.

7. Click the **Layers tab** in the Layers panel (if necessary) and scroll to the top, then click the **Eye icon** 👁 to the left of the Web Layer

The Web Layer is hidden while in the Preview tab, enabling you to get a better look at the document.

8. Click the **Original tab** in the document window, then click the **blank box** in the column to the left of the Web Layer

The document is returned to the Original tab, and the Web Layer is displayed.

9. Click **File** on the menu bar, then click **Save**

Fireworks saves the document.

FIGURE B-5: Inserted hotspot

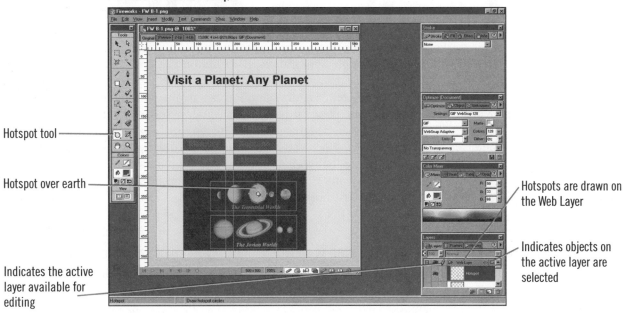

Hotspot tool

Hotspot over earth

Indicates the active layer available for editing

Hotspots are drawn on the Web Layer

Indicates objects on the active layer are selected

FIGURE B-6: Pointer over hotspot

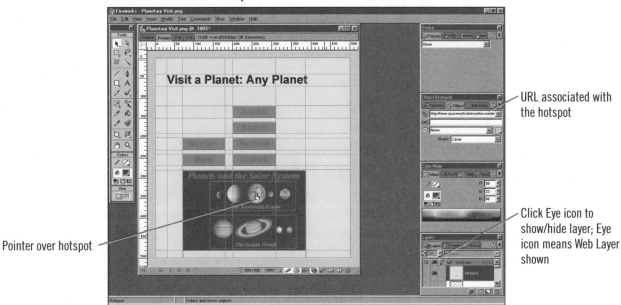

URL associated with the hotspot

Click Eye icon to show/hide layer; Eye icon means Web Layer shown

Pointer over hotspot

CLUES TO USE

Creating and using a URL library

If you use the same URLs frequently in your Fireworks document, you can create URL libraries to store and manage them for future use. To create a URL library, click Window on the menu bar, click URL, click New URL Library from the URL panel Options pop-up menu, type a library name, then click OK. The library filename appears in the Library pop-up menu in the URL panel. To add a URL to a URL library, click the Library pop-up menu, click a library, type a URL in the Link text box, then click the Add Current URL to Library button ➕. To assign a URL in the URL library to a selected hotspot, click the Library pop-up menu, click a library, then click a URL from the list in the URL panel.

Creating a Button

In Fireworks, a button is an object that contains a slice and different states. These states determine all of a button's possible appearances. Each button can have up to four appearances, depending on its response to the mouse pointer, although most buttons only have two appearances. Table B-1 lists the different button states. You can use the Button Editor to assemble all of the different button states and place the button in the Fireworks document. A button is a special type of symbol. A **symbol** is a designated object (the original), which gets copied into other **instances** of the same object. When you change the symbol object, the instances (copies) automatically change to resemble the symbol. When you move a button, all the components and states associated with it also move. Jean wants to create a new button. Later, she will copy the button and change its appearance.

Steps 1 2 3 4

QuickTip

The Layers panel displays each layer and its associated graphics. You can click ▬ (Win) or ▼ (Mac) to collapse or ⊞ (Win) or ▶ (Mac) to expand the layers display.

1. Ensure that the Layers tab is selected, click ▬ (Win) or ▼ (Mac) next to each layer to collapse it, click **Layer 1** on the Layers panel, click the **Rectangle Tool** ▢ in the Tool panel, then drag + from **70 H/120 V** to **180 H/150 V**

   A rectangle appears in the window. You can select a color from the Fill Color Box.

2. Click the **Fill Color Box list arrow** ▣ in the Tool panel, then click the **magenta color box** (#CC0099) in the seventh color box in the tenth row of the color palette

   The rectangle color changes to magenta. You can convert the rectangle into a button using a command on the Insert menu.

3. Click **Insert** on the menu bar, then click **Convert to Symbol**

   The Symbol Properties dialog box opens. You can use this dialog box to determine the type of symbol you're converting.

4. Select the **text in the Name box**, if necessary, type **Button**, click the **Button option button**, then click **OK**

   The Symbol Properties dialog box closes. You can modify the text and color of the button.

Trouble?

If the mouse is positioned on a guide when you double-click the button, and the Move Guide dialog box opens, click Cancel.

5. Click the **Pointer Tool** ▶ in the Tool panel, then double-click the newly created **button**

   The Button dialog box opens. You can use this dialog box to create the text that will be displayed on the button face.

6. Click the **Text Tool** Ⓐ in the Tool panel, then click Ɪ at **0 H/0 V**

   The Text Editor dialog opens, as shown in Figure B-7. You create the text and determine its attributes.

7. Change the **Font** to **Arial**, change the **Font Size** to **20**, click the **Fill Color Box list arrow** ▣, click the **blue color box** (#3300FF) in the seventh color box in the sixth row of the color palette, click the **Bold button** Ⓑ if necessary, type **Venus**, then click **OK**

   The text appears over the magenta button, but it is not aligned within the button. You can align the objects vertically using a command on the Modify menu.

QuickTip

To remove guides, click View on the menu bar, point to Guides, then click Show Guides. To remove slice guides, click View on the menu bar, then click Slice Guides.

8. Press [Shift], ensure that the Venus text box is selected, click the **magenta button**, click **Modify** on the menu bar, point to **Align**, then click **Center Vertical**

   The text box is centered between the left and right edges of the button. You can also align the objects horizontally.

9. Click **Modify** on the menu bar, point to **Align**, click **Center Horizontal**

   The text box is centered between the top and bottom edges of the button, as shown in Figure B-8. In the next lesson, Jean copies and changes the appearance of the button.

FIGURE B-7: **Text Editor dialog box**

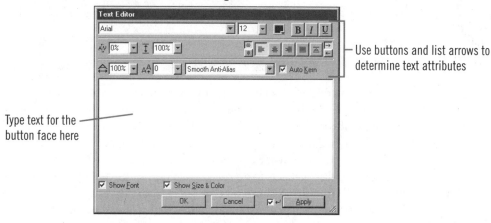

Use buttons and list arrows to determine text attributes

Type text for the button face here

FIGURE B-8: **Up tab in Button dialog box**

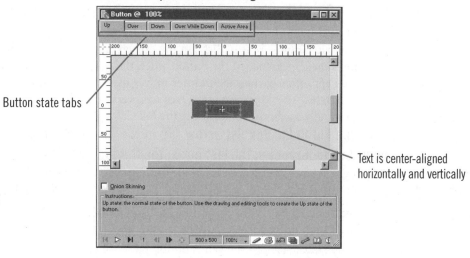

Button state tabs

Text is center-aligned horizontally and vertically

TABLE B-1: **Button states**

state	description
Up	When the pointer is away from the button: the normal, default appearance
Over	When the pointer moves over the button
Down	When the button has been clicked
Over While Down	When the pointer is over the button while it is in the Down state

Inserting ready-made buttons

Fireworks has a library of ready-made button styles you can insert into your document. To insert a ready-made button, click Insert on the menu bar, point to Libraries, click Button, click a button style, then click OK. The button is placed into the document. If you create a button in another Fireworks document, you can insert that button into the current document. To insert a button from another Fireworks document or an external button library, click Insert on the menu bar, point to Libraries, then click Other. Click the Look in list arrow and navigate to the Fireworks document or button library. For a typical Fireworks installation, the Libraries folder is located in the Program Files folder, Macromedia folder, Fireworks 4 folder, Settings folder, and Libraries folder (Win) or Fireworks 4 folder and Libraries folder (Mac). Open the document or button library, select a button, then click Import.

Copying a Button and Applying an Effect

Sometimes your Web design may require that all the buttons look exactly alike, or you may wish to add an effect to buttons. In Fireworks, you can copy a button exactly, or change the original and apply those changes to all the buttons. Fireworks includes special effects, such as bevels, drop shadows, glows, and embossing, that you can apply to buttons and other objects. You use the Effect panel to apply the effects live, which means the effect takes effect immediately. You can also apply multiple effects to an object. Each time you add an effect, it is added to the list in the Effect panel. You can also turn an effect on and off by using the check box next to each effect in the list. ![scissors icon] Jean wants to copy the recently created button, modify the text on the button face, then add a live drop shadow effect. She begins by modifying the Over button state.

1. Click the **Over tab**, click the **Copy Up Graphic button**, then click the **magenta button** (not the text box)

   The Copy Up Graphic button displays the objects from the Up state to the Over state. The Up state is the appearance of the button when the pointer is off the button, while the Over state is its appearance when the pointer moves over it. Many buttons on the Web only use these two states. After you create the Over state version of the button, you need to modify it. You can modify the button color using the Fill Color Box.

2. Click the **Fill Color Box list arrow** ![icon] in the Tool panel, then click the **light green color box** (#66FF66) in the last box in the third row of the color palette

   A light green background appears in the button. You can also modify the text color.

3. Click the **text box**, click the **Fill Color Box list arrow** ![icon], click the **blue color box** (#000099) in the first box in the fourth row, compare your screen to Figure B-9, then click the **Close button** in the Button dialog box

   The Up and Over states of the Venus button have been modified. Since all the properties for the button have been defined, you can copy this button and place it in a new location.

4. Position ![pointer] over the new button, press **[Alt]** (Win) or **[Option]** (Mac), then drag the **button** so that the bottom-left corner aligns at **70 H/190 V**

   A copy of the button has been created. Now you can modify the text on the button face.

5. Double-click the **Button Text text box** in the Object (Button Symbol) panel, type **Earth**, press **[Enter]**, then click **Current**

   Compare your Object panel to Figure B-10. The button text has been modified. Now you can select all of the buttons in the page.

6. Press and hold **[Shift]**, then click all the **planet buttons** (Venus, Earth, Mercury, Mars, Jupiter, Saturn, Neptune, and Uranus) to select them

   All the planet buttons are selected.

7. Click the **Effect tab** on the Stroke panel, click the **Add effects or choose a preset list arrow** on the Effect tab, point to **Shadow and Glow**, then click **Drop Shadow**

   The live drop shadow effect is applied to each button, and a pop-up edit window appears in the Effects tab. You can change the live effect settings.

8. Click the **Distance list arrow** ![icon] on the pop-up edit window, drag the **slider** to **10**, then click an empty area in the document window to deselect the buttons

   The distance of the drop shadow is increased. Compare your document to Figure B-11.

9. Click **File** on the menu bar, then click **Save**

   Fireworks saves the document.

QuickTip

You can use the arrow keys to precisely position the button on the Web page.

QuickTip

To remove a live effect, click the effect in the Effect panel, then click the Delete button ![icon] in the Effect panel.

QuickTip

To edit a live effect, click the Info button ![icon] in the Effect panel.

FIGURE B-9: Over tab in Button dialog box

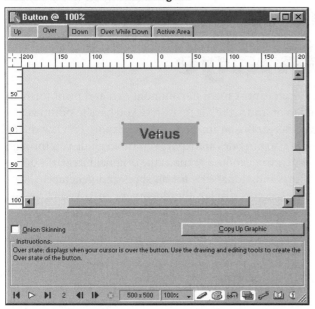

FIGURE B-10: Object panel

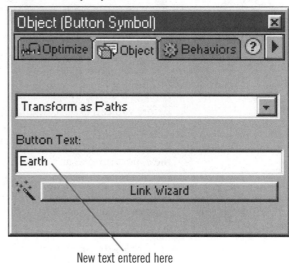

New text entered here

FIGURE B-11: Completed buttons

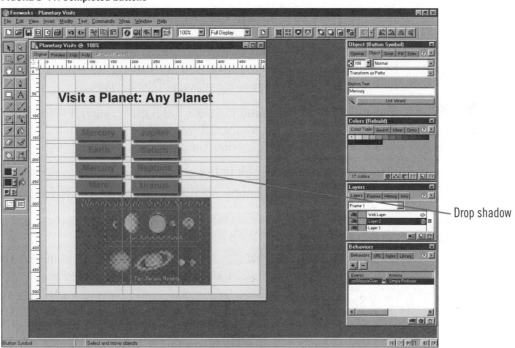

Drop shadow

Using Photoshop plug-ins as live effects

You can install Photoshop plug-ins in Fireworks to extend the capabilities of the program and take advantage of Photoshop tools already available. To install Photoshop plug-ins, click the Options pop-up menu list arrow ▶ in the Effect panel, click Locate Plug-ins, select the folder where the Photoshop Plug-ins are located, click OK, then restart Fireworks to load the plug-ins. To apply a Photoshop plug-in to a selected object as a live effect, click the Effect pop-up menu list arrow ▼ in the Effect panel, then click a plug-in.

Exporting a Graphic Image

After you create images in Fireworks, you can export them in common Web and print formats. Before you can export an image, you need to optimize the file first. Since you have to optimize the image, Fireworks allows you to optimize and export an image using the Export Preview dialog box. If you prefer to use a wizard, Fireworks also provides an Export Wizard to guide you through the export process and suggest settings. When you export a graphic, the original Fireworks document remains unchanged. Fireworks exports individual files for all slices and generates all the required HTML and JavaScript code necessary to display the document in a Web browser. ✒️ Jean creates a new multiframe document and imports images into the frames.

1. Click **File** on the menu bar, then click **Export Wizard**

The Export Wizard dialog box appears, as shown in Figure B-12. The Wizard helps you select a file format, minimize the file size, and maximize the quality of the image.

2. Click **Continue**

The next Export Wizard dialog box appears, asking you to choose a destination for the image.

3. Click **The Web option button**, if necessary, then click **Continue**

The Analysis Results dialog box appears, recommending GIF and JPEG file formats.

4. Click **Exit**

The Export Preview dialog box appears, as shown in Figure B-13. The Export Preview dialog box provides a preview of the image in the GIF and JPEG formats. The preview information for the JPEG version of the image appears in the left pane.

QuickTip

You can select up to four previews of the exported image.

5. Click the **top preview pane** to select the JPEG version, if necessary

The preview information for the GIF version of the image appears in the left pane, and the file format is selected for exporting the image.

6. Click **Export**, click the **Look in list arrow** ▼, navigate to the drive and folder where your Project Files are located, create a new folder as **FW Export**, then double-click the **FW Export folder**

The Export dialog box appears, as shown in Figure B-14.

7. Click the **Slices list arrow** ▼, then click **Export Slices**, if necessary

Fireworks exports the individual slices, using the GIF file format.

8. Click **Save**

Fireworks exports the files and creates an HTML file you can use in Director or in the selected HTML program.

9. Create a new text box, place it in the lower-right corner of the document, type **your name**, save and print the document, then click the **Close button** in the document window

The document closes, leaving the Fireworks program open.

FIGURE B-12: Export Wizard dialog box

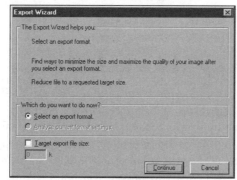

FIGURE B-13: Export Preview dialog box

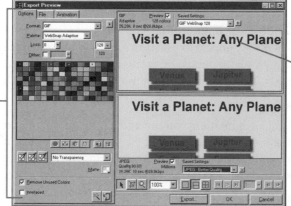

Current file format options for the selected export type

Currently selected file format for exporting

FIGURE B-14: Export dialog box

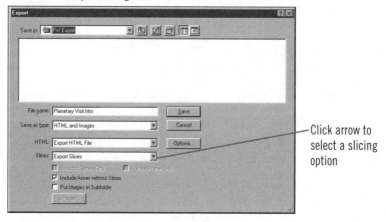

Click arrow to select a slicing option

CLUES TO USE

Importing or opening Photoshop files

You can import or open Photoshop files in Fireworks and select the options from the Photoshop files you want to adjust or keep the same. Fireworks can import native Photoshop (PSD) files and retain much of the structure of the PSD file, including layers and editable text. To import or open a Photoshop file, click Edit on the menu bar, click Import or Open, select the PSD Photoshop file, click Open, select the Photoshop file options you want, then click OK. The Photoshop file options include:

Maintain Layers and Make Shared Layers or Convert to Frames in the Layers area, and Editable or Maintain Appearance in the Text area. You can also use the Use Flat Composite Image option to ignore all objects and import the file as a flat image. You can set the defaults for the Photoshop file options dialog box. To set the defaults, click File on the menu bar, click Preferences, click the Import tab, then click the Photoshop File Conversion options you want to appear by default.

Unit B

Fireworks 4

Planning an Animation

An object appears **animated** by displaying a series of still images in rapid succession. Creating an animated series of images requires careful planning and attention to detail. Without planning, an animation can look choppy and unprofessional, or may not function correctly. In an animation, a single layer contains many frames, and each frame contains a unique image. Once the images are placed in the frames and the speed at which each frame is displayed has been set, the animation can be played. Jean wants to animate several images of the earth. Later, she can include them in a Web page or multimedia program.

Details

Create objects for animation
You can obtain the images to use in an animation from several sources. You can purchase them, take your own photographs, or create graphic images. Figure B-15 shows the frames in the Frames panel. This document contains 2 frames in Layer 1.

Plan frames
As you build an animation, you can add, delete, move, or copy frames. You can also change the order of the frames within the layer. Fireworks lists frame information in the Frames panel, and you can see individual frame images by clicking the Frames list arrow in the Layers panel. Figure B-16 shows the first four frames in an animation of the earth rotating.

Set the animation speed
In the animation process, each image is displayed at a specific speed. The rate at which each frame is displayed is called the **frame delay**. If the frame delay is too short, the image may appear blurred or unrecognizable; if the frame delay is too long, the animation will appear choppy.

CLUES TO USE

Opening multiple files as an animation

Once you gather the images you want to use in an animation, you can open all the files at once. When you select and open the files, each one is placed on a separate frame in the same document. To open multiple files as an animation, click File on the menu bar, click Open, navigate to the file folder, press and hold [Shift], and click each file you want to add to the animation, click the Open as Animation check box to select it, then click Open. Fireworks creates a document and places each file in a separate frame, in the order in which you selected them in the Open dialog box.

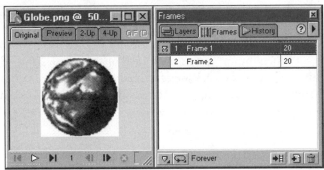

FIGURE B-15: Document with multiple frames

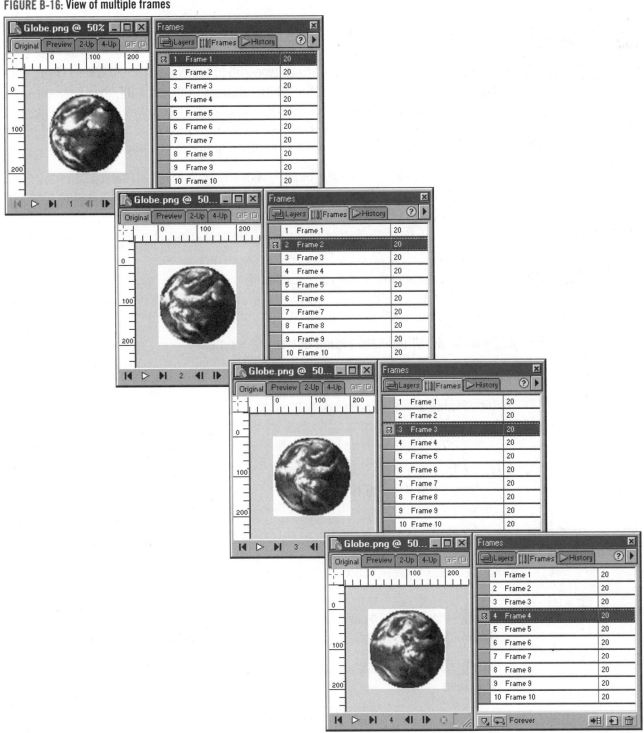

FIGURE B-16: View of multiple frames

Managing Frames

Fireworks makes it easy to create an animation. Once you have created a document, you can add frames, and then import images into each of the frames. You add, create, remove, and arrange frames in the Frames panel. When the images are in place, you can play the animation using the VCR buttons in the document window. ✏️ Jean creates a new multiframe document and imports images into the frames.

Steps 1 2 3 4

1. Click **File** on the menu bar, click **New**, type **200** in the Width text box, press **[Tab]**, type **200** in the Height text box, click the **White option button**, click **OK**, then save the document as **Animated Earth** in the drive and folder where your Project Files are located
The newly named document is displayed in the workspace. You can import the initial graphic image into the document. This image will be placed in frame 1 in Layer 1.

2. Click **File** on the menu bar, click **Import**, click the **Look in list arrow** ▼, click the drive and folder where your Project Files are located, double-click the **Media folder**, click the file **Earth01**, click **Open**, then drag ⌐ from **0 H/0 V** to **200 H/200 V**
Compare your screen to Figure B-17. Notice the two layers in the Layers panel: the Web Layer and Layer 1.

3. Click the **Frames tab** in the Layers panel
In order to create the animation, each image must be placed in its own frame. Since there are 10 images of the earth, you must create 10 frames (9 additional frames).

4. Click the **New/Duplicate Frame button** 🔲 **9 times**
Layer 1 contains 9 empty frames and 1 frame that contains the Earth01.gif graphic. You can change active frames using the Frame list arrow in the Layers tab.

5. Click **Frame 2** in the Frames panel
Frame 2, which is empty, is active and appears in the document window. Compare your Frames panel to Figure B-18. You can import an image to a frame once that frame is active.

6. Click **File** on the menu bar, click **Import**, click the file **Earth02**, click **Open**, then drag ⌐ from **0 H/0 V** to **200 H/200 V**
The second image of the earth is placed in frame 2 in Layer 1.

7. Repeat **Steps 5** and **6** until each of the 10 earth images is placed in its own frame
Compare frame 10 of your document to Figure B-19. All 10 frames of Layer 1 contain a unique image. You can play the animation using the frame controls in the status bar (Win) or document window (Mac).

8. Click the **Play button** ▷ on the document window
The animation plays, displaying the frame numbers in the document window.

9. Click the **Stop button** ■ on the document window, click **File** on the menu bar, then click **Save**

FIGURE B-17: **Image in Frame 1**

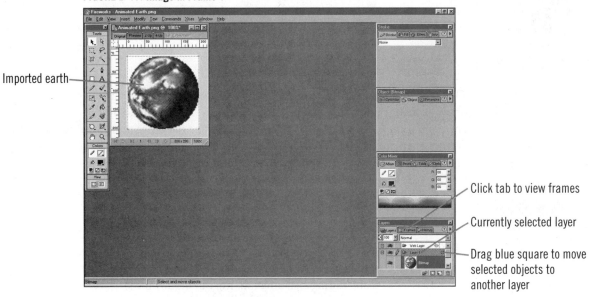

Imported earth ⎯

Click tab to view frames

Currently selected layer

Drag blue square to move selected objects to another layer

FIGURE B-18: **Frames panel**

Active frame ⎯

Click button to copy a layer in a frame

Click button to delete layer in a frame

FIGURE B-19: **Frame 10 in document**

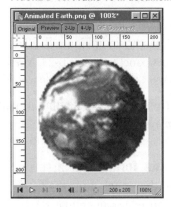

Changing the order of frames

You can change the order of frames by clicking and dragging a frame to a new location in the frames list. Figure B-20 shows frame 7 being dragged to a new position in the list: between frames 5 and 6. Once the frames are moved to their new location, Fireworks automatically renumbers them.

FIGURE B-20: **Moving a frame**

Customizing an Animation

Once the animation images are in place, you can adjust the properties of the frames. You can show or hide frames, and change the frame delay. In addition, you can set the number of times the animation plays. After you create and optimize the animation, you can export the series of frames as an animated GIF. Jean wants to change the properties of some frames.

Steps

1. Click **Frame 1** in the Frames tab

   Each frame in the panel is followed by the number 7, indicating that each frame is visible for 7/100th of a second during an animation. You can modify the length of time each frame is shown.

2. Double-click the **number 7** in **Frame 1** in the Frames panel

   Compare your Frames panel with Figure B-21. A pop-up box window is displayed, allowing you to change the time each frame is visible. You want the image in frame 1 to be displayed for half a second.

3. Type **50** in the /100 second text box, then press **[Enter]** (Win) or **[Return]** (Mac)

   When the animation is played, frame 1 will be displayed for 50/100th of a second. You can select multiple frames and make modifications to them simultaneously.

4. Click **Frame 3**, press and hold **[Shift]**, click **Frame 4**, then release **[Shift]**

   Frames 3 and 4 are selected. Holding [Shift] makes it possible to make multiple selections. Frames can be hidden during an animation by changing their properties.

5. Click the **Frames panel list arrow** ▶, click **Properties**, deselect the **Include when Exporting check box** shown in Figure B-22, then press **[Enter]** (Win) or **[Return]** (Mac)

   Compare your Frames panel to Figure B-23. A red X displays to the right of the frame delay in each hidden frame. You can clear the Include when Exporting check box to show hidden frames.

6. Click the **Play button** ▷ on the document window, then click the **Stop button** ■

   As the animation plays, frame 1 is displayed for a longer amount of time than each of the other frames. As the animation cycles, it skips frames 3 and 4.

7. Click the **Export file format list arrow** ▼ in the Optimize tab of the Optimize (Document) panel, then click **Animated GIF**

   The frames are optimized for an animated GIF.

8. Click **File** on the menu bar, click **Export**, navigate to the drive and folder where your Project Files are located, then click **Save**

   The frames are exported as an animated GIF file, which can be imported into a Web development or multimedia program.

9. Create a **new text box**, type **your name** in **18pt Arial Bold**, place the text box in the lower-right corner of the document, save and print the document, then exit Fireworks

FIGURE B-21: **Frame properties**

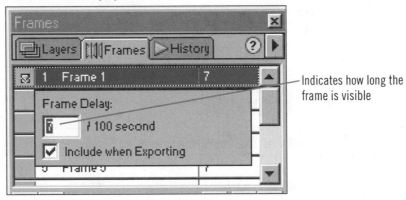

Indicates how long the frame is visible

FIGURE B-22: Deselected check box

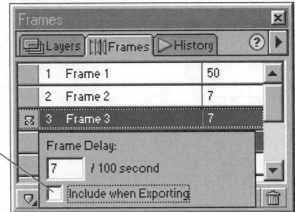

Deselecting hides a frame during animation

FIGURE B-23: Hidden frames

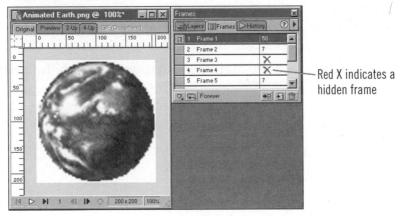

Red X indicates a hidden frame

CLUES TO USE

Sharing layers across frames

When you create an animation, you can use layers to include objects that you want to appear throughout the animation, such as a background. You can place background objects on a layer and use the Layers panel to share the layer across all the frames. The Web Layer is always shared across all frames. To share a layer across frames, double-click the layer, then click the Share Across Frames check box to select it. Fireworks adds the objects on the shared layer to all frames with the content of that layer. When you edit objects on a frame of shared layers, the changes are reflected on all frames.

Practice

► Concepts Review

Label each of the elements of the screen shown in Figure B-24.

FIGURE B-24

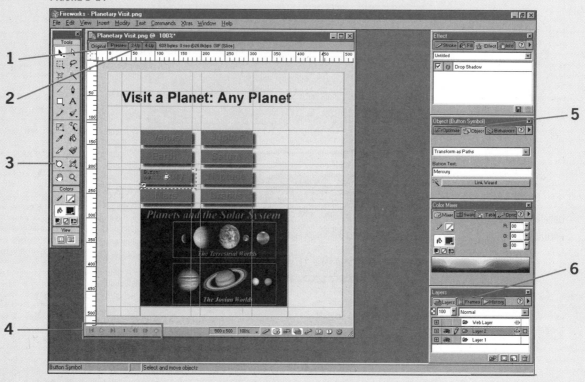

Match each of the terms with the statement that describes its function.

7. Delete button
8. Info button
9. Rectangle Hotspot Tool
10. Hide Hotspots and Slices button
11. New/Duplicate Frame button
12. Play button

a.
b.
c.
d.
e.
f.

Select the best answer from the following list of choices.

13. A clickable area that takes an end user to a new Web location is called a:
   a. Rollover.
   b. Hotspot.
   c. Animation.
   d. Optimizer.

14. An animation is controlled using:
   a. VCR buttons.
   b. Menu commands.
   c. Buttons on the Animation Tool panel.
   d. None of the above

15. An effect that causes a change elsewhere on a Web page is called a(n):
   a. Animation.
   b. Hotspot.
   c. Slice.
   d. Rollover.

16. **A smaller section within a document that can be manipulated is called a:**
    a. Slice.
    c. Hotspot.
    b. Rollover.
    d. Tool panel.

17. **Which of the following image types can be optimized using Fireworks?**
    a. A JPEG image in a PNG file
    c. A GIF image in a JPEG file
    b. A GIF image in a PNG file
    d. All of the above

18. **On which layer are slices and hotspots displayed?**
    a. Layer 1
    c. Layer 3
    b. Layer 2
    d. None of the above

19. **Which button state occurs when the pointer is away from the button?**
    a. Up
    c. Down
    b. Over
    d. Over While Down

20. **Which button state occurs when the pointer moves over the button?**
    a. Up
    c. Down
    b. Over
    d. Over While Down

21. **The amount of time each image in an animation is visible is called the:**
    a. Animation delay.
    c. Frame delay.
    b. Frame speed.
    d. Go time.

▶ Skills Review

1. **Understand Web documents.**
   a. Start Fireworks, then list methods you can use to enhance Web pages using Fireworks.

2. **Optimize a graphic image.**
   a. Open the file **FW B-3** from the drive and folder where your Project Files are located, then save it as *Good Planets*.
   b. Import the image **FW B-4** from the drive and folder where your Project Files are located in the area 100 H/250 V to 200 H/325 V.
   c. Insert a slice based on the selected object.
   d. Change the Settings list arrow to JPEG – Better Quality.
   e. View the optimized image in the 2-Up tab, and then in the Original tab.

3. **Create and edit a hotspot.**
   a. Select the Rectangle Hotspot Tool.
   b. Draw a hotspot over each of the four graphic images in the document.
   c. Enter the following URL for the image you imported and optimized:
      http://www.spaceworksinteractive.com/orangerings.html.
   d. View the document using the Preview tab, then test the hotspot by placing your pointer over the optimized image.
   e. Hide the Web layer, then return to the Original tab.
   f. Show the Web layer and save the document.

4. **Create a button.**
   a. Make Layer 1 active.
   b. Use the Rectangle Tool to create a box from 100 H/150 V to 200 H/190 V.
   c. Change the color of the rectangle to blue. (*Hint*: Use color #3300FF, the seventh color box in the sixth row.)
   d. Convert the rectangle to a symbol, using the Name box with the text button and choosing the Button option button.
   e. Double-click the button, select the Text Tool, click the button, adjust the font to 25 pt bold, Arial text in red, then type **Yes**. (*Hint*: Use color #FF3366, the fourteenth color box in the fourth row from the bottom.)
   f. Center-align the text box and rectangle horizontally and vertically. Do not close the Button dialog box.

5. Copying a button.

   a. Click the Over tab in the Button dialog box.

   b. Copy the graphic in the Up tab to the Over tab.

   c. Change the color of the rectangle to lavender. (*Hint*: Use color #FFCCFF, the second to last color box in the bottom row.)

   d. Change the text color to orchid. (*Hint*: Use color #9966FF, the third color box in the bottom row.)

   e. Close the Button dialog box, then use the arrow keys to reposition the button within the guides, if necessary.

   f. Copy the Yes button so the upper-left corner aligns at 250 H/150 V.

   g. Change the button text in the copied button to **No**.

   h. Select the Yes and No buttons.

   i. Apply the Inner Bevel live effect to the buttons. (*Hint:* Use the Effect tab in the Stroke panel.)

   j. Change the width of the Inner Bevel to 5.

6. Export a graphic image.

   a. Start the Export Wizard and use the Web option.

   b. In the Export Preview dialog box, select the JPEG image.

   c. Export the image into a new folder, *FW Export SR* then save the image.

   d. Create a text box, type **your name**, then place it in the lower-right corner of the image.

   e. Save, print, and close the document.

7. Plan an animation.

   a. List and discuss the main areas you need to consider when planning an animation.

8. Manage frames.

   a. Open a new Fireworks document having a height and width of 200 pixels, with a white canvas color, then save the document as *Reverse Earth*.

   b. Import Earth10 from 0 H/0 V to 200 H/200 V in frame 1, Layer 1.

   c. Create nine additional frames in Layer 1.

   d. Import images Earth 02 through Earth09 in the new frames in reverse order (the images should be placed Earth10, Earth09, Earth08, and so on).

   e. Play the animation, stop the animation, then save the document.

9. Customize an animation.

   a. Change the frame delays for frames 3 and 5 to 20.

   b. Hide frame 2 and frame 7.

   c. Play the animation and then stop it.

   d. Show all the frames and change the frame delays to 40 for all the frames.

   e. Optimize the frames for an animated GIF and export the animation with the default filename.

   f. Create a text box, type **your initials**, then place it in the lower-right corner of the first frame of the image.

   g. Save the document, play the animation, then stop the animation.

   h. Print the document and exit Fireworks.

▶ Independent Challenges

1. You were the only employee from your company to attend a one-day course in Fireworks. Now everyone in your office wants to know about the program's capabilities. Your boss asks you to summarize the key points by creating a Fireworks document.

  To complete this independent challenge:

   a. Start Fireworks; in the drive and folder where your Project Files are located, open a new document called *Fireworks Summary*, with 400 height × 600 width and a black background.

   b. Import the file Mwm_Logo into the document from the Media folder where your Project Files are located, and resize the image to be displayed 10 H/150 V to 120 H/250 V.

c. Create a text box and list the different ways you can use Fireworks to enhance Web documents.
d. Resize and move the text boxes around to fit on the page. (*Hint*: Modify the font size if necessary.)
e. Change the color of the text and background to complement the black background.
f. Include your name in the document.
g. Save and print the document, then exit Fireworks.

2. You are interviewing for a position at WebPC It, a Web development company. As part of your interview, you want to create a simple Fireworks document. Your page will be for the PC Parts division, and should include buttons for a variety of merchandise.
To complete this independent challenge:

a. Start Fireworks and open a new 400 height × 400 width document called *WebPC It* in the drive and folder where your Project Files are located.
b. Create a text box that contains the company name, **WebPC It PC Parts**, and use Arial 44 pt Bold.
c. Add a rectangle, using any color you choose.
d. Convert the rectangle to a symbol, then add the text **CPUs** in any contrasting color.
e. Copy up the graphic, then change the color of the copied rectangle and text.
f. Copy the new button five times, using any arrangement on the page you choose.
g. Change the text and point size of the five new buttons to **Monitors**, **Keyboards**, **Books**, **Printers**, and **Boards**.
h. Test the rollovers in the Preview tab.
i. Add a text box that includes your name.
j. Save and print the document, then exit Fireworks.

3. You are an experienced Web developer at Space Exploration Laboratories, a space mapping company. You want to show a new colleague how to import an image and use hotspots in a Fireworks document.
To complete this independent challenge:

a. Start Fireworks and open a new document called *Hotspots*, using the settings 400 height × 400 width, and a black background in the drive and folder where your Project Files are located.
b. Import file FW B-5 into the document from the drive and folder where your Project Files are located.
c. Create hotspots over each of the planets in the document, then create fictitious URLs for each of the hotspots.
d. Add a text box containing your name.
e. Save the document, print the screen, then exit Fireworks.

4. You want to find out more about how other products work with Fireworks. The Macromedia Web site provides information about their own and other manufacturers' products that work with Fireworks. Find out more about these other products, using the Showcase.
To complete this independent challenge:

a. Connect to the Internet, start Fireworks, then open a new document called *Fireworks Info*, using the settings 400 height × 400 width.
b. Choose the Fireworks Support Center command on the Help menu.
c. Locate the Showcase page for Fireworks and the Support page for Fireworks. Write down the URLs associated with these Web pages.
d. Close the Web browser, and disconnect from the Internet, if necessary.
e. Create two buttons with the text **Showcase** and **Support**, respectively.
f. Add a glow live effect to each button. (*Hint*: Click link in the Link Wizard.)
g. Enter the URLs for each button.
h. Add a text box containing your name.
i. Save the document, print the screen, then exit Fireworks.

▶ Visual Workshop

Recreate the screen shown in Figure B-25. Open the Project File FW B-6, then save it as *Getaway* in the drive and folder where your Project Files are located. Figure B-26 shows the completed document with the Web Layer turned off. Create hotspots over the four largest planets, and use the following colors in the buttons.

TABLE B-2: Button colors

position	background	text
Up	#00FF00	#2F00FF
Over	#9767FF	#FF2F67

If necessary, add text in the lower-left corner containing your name, then save and print the document.

FIGURE B-25

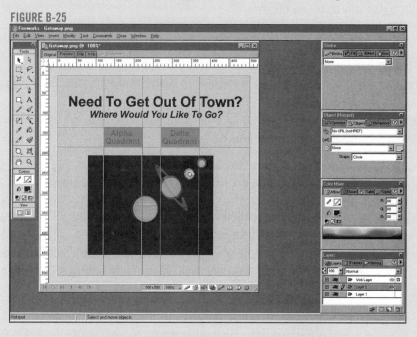

FIGURE B-26

Appendix

Objectives

► **Import file types**
► **Identify cast members**
► **Use the Paint window tools**
► **Choose a Paint ink effect**
► **Use sprite keyboard shortcuts**
► **Choose a sprite ink effect**
► **Install the QuickTime player**
► **Install an Xtra**
► **Choose behavior events and actions**
► **Choose event handlers**
► **Use Lingo rules and elements**

This appendix provides a quick reference for using Director more effectively. You can quickly find out options and descriptions for import file types, cast member types, paint window tools, paint ink effects, sprite keyboard shortcuts, and sprite ink effects. Director uses other external programs to help you extend the functionality and capabilities of your movies. Before you can use the external programs, such as QuickTime and Xtras, you need to install them. You can find common commands and descriptions for choosing behavior events and actions. When you work with scripts, you can determine which event handlers work with which Director script types, and find out common Lingo rules and elements for cross-platform keys.

Director 8

Importing File Types

If you already have developed animations and multimedia content, images, sounds, video, or text in other programs, you can import these media elements into the active Cast window. Importing media elements is an important part of creating a movie with Director. Before you can import a media element into Director, you need to know the different types, or formats, Director can import, as shown in Figure AP-1. Table AP-1 summarizes formats you can import into Director. If you have a media element in a format not included in the supported list of formats, you need to convert the media element to one of the supported formats, or use an Xtra to insert the media element. Director comes with built-in Xtras, on the Media Element submenu on the Insert menu, as shown in Figure AP-2, or you can install third-party Xtras developed by other companies. For more information on installing a third-party Xtra, see the topic "Installing an Xtra" in this appendix.

TABLE AP-1: **Import file types**

type of file	supported formats
Animation and multimedia	Animated GIF, Flash movies, PowerPoint 4.0 presentations, Director movies, Director External Cast files
Image	BMP, GIF, JPEG, LRG (xRes), Photoshop 3.0 (or later), MacPaint, PNG, TIFF, PICT, Targa
Multiple-image file	FLC, FLI (Win); PICS, Scrapbook (Mac)
Sound	AIFF, WAV, MP3 audio, Shockwave Audio, Sun AU uncompressed, IMA compressed (Win); System 7 sounds (Mac)
Video	QuickTime 2, 3, 4; AVI (Win)
Text	RTF, HTML, ASCII (often called Text Only), Lingo scripts
Palette	PAL, Photoshop CLUT

FIGURE AP-1: Import Files into "Internal" dialog box

Click arrow to select import file type

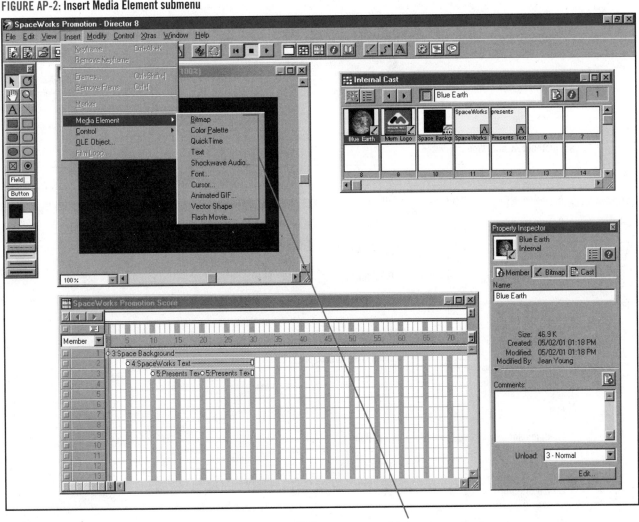

FIGURE AP-2: Insert Media Element submenu

Click menu command to insert a media element

Identifying Cast Members

When you create cast members in Director or import media elements created in other programs, a small icon in the lower-right corner of each cast member identifies its type, as shown in Figure AP-3. Table AP-2 summarizes formats and objects you can import into Director. You can turn off or on the display of cast member icons in Thumbnail view and change the Cast window display. To change the Cast window display preferences, click Choose File on the menu bar, point to Preferences, then click Cast. To specify whether Director displays an icon in the lower-right corner of each cast member, indicating the cast member's type, click the Media Type Icons list arrow, then click All Types, All but Text and Bitmap, or None, as shown in Figure AP-4. To display a script indicator icon in the lower-left corner of each cast member that has a script attached, click the Script check box to select it.

TABLE AP-2: Cast member symbol type

symbol	type	symbol	type
	Animated GIF		Palette
	Behavior		PICT
	Bitmap		QuickTime video
	Button		Radio button
	Check box		Script
	Custom cursor		Shape
	Digital video		Shockwave Audio
	Field		Sound
	Film loop		Text
	Flash movie		Transition
	Font		Vector shape
	Linked bitmap		Xtra
	OLE		

FIGURE AP-3: Internal Cast window

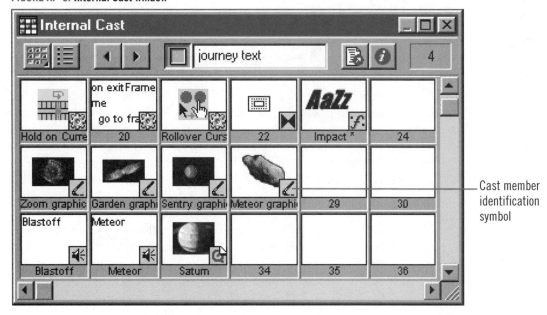

Cast member identification symbol

FIGURE AP-4: Cast Window Preferences for "Internal" dialog box

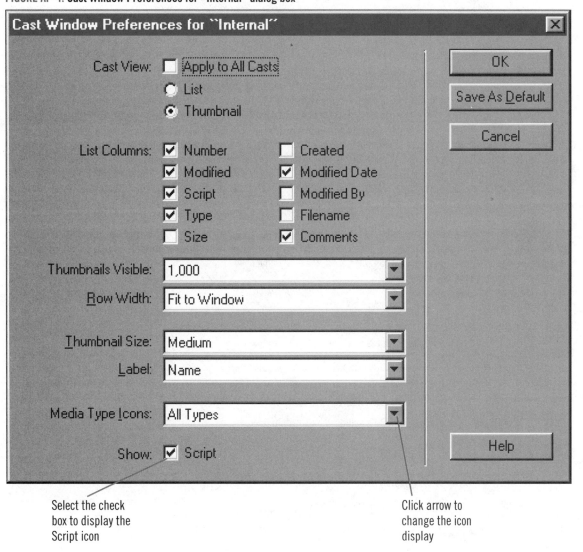

Select the check box to display the Script icon

Click arrow to change the icon display

Director 8

Using the Paint Window Tools

Director includes a simple paint program to make it easier for you to create and edit bitmapped cast members without having to open another program, such as Adobe Photoshop. You create and modify a bitmapped cast member by using the tools on the Tool Palette. Table AP-3 describes the paint tools. A small arrow in the lower-right corner of a tool indicates that pop-up menu options are available for that tool. To display the pop-up menu, click a tool, then press and hold the mouse button. The toolbar at the top of the Paint window contains buttons you can use to apply effects to bitmapped cast members. Table AP-4 describes the buttons on the Paint toolbar. Before you can apply an effect, you need to select all or part of the bitmap with the Lasso or Marquee tool. Effects that change the shape of the selection, such as flip, rotate, skew, warp, and perspective, work only when you make the selection with the Marquee tool. Effects that change colors within the selection work with both the Marquee and the Lasso tools.

TABLE AP-3: Paint tool palette

tool	name	function
	Lasso	Selects an irregular area
	Marquee	Selects a rectangular area
	Registration Point	Changes the location of the registration point
	Eraser	Erases pixels or cast member
	Hand	Moves the view of the Paint window
	Magnifying Glass	Zooms in or out on an area
	Eyedropper	Selects a color in a cast member
	Paint Bucket	Fills all adjacent pixels of the same color with the foreground color
	Text	Enters bitmap text
	Pencil	Draws a 1-pixel line in the current foreground
	Air Brush	Sprays variable dots of the foreground color
	Brush	Brushes strokes of the foreground color
	Arc	Paints an arc shape
	Line	Paints a line
	Filled Rectangle	Paints a filled rectangle shape with the foreground or gradient color
	Rectangle	Paints a rectangle shape
	Filled Ellipse	Paints a filled ellipse shape with the foreground or gradient color
	Ellipse	Paints an ellipse shape
	Filled Polygon	Paints a filled polygon shape with the foreground or gradient color
	Polygon	Paints a polygon shape
	Gradient Colors	Blends from one color to another color

TABLE AP-3: Paint tool palette (continued)

tool	name	function
	Foreground Color	Default color in single color shapes and primary color in multicolor patterns (top color box)
	Background Color	Secondary color in multicolor patterns (lower color box)
	Pattern	Fills a shape with a pattern or tile
4 pixels	**Other Line Width**	Selects thickness of a line
16 bits	**Color Depth**	The number of colors a graphic can display

TABLE AP-4: Paint toolbar buttons

button	name	function
	Flip Horizontal	Flips artwork along the horizontal axis; left to right
	Flip Vertical	Flips artwork along the vertical axis; top to bottom
	Rotate Left	Rotates artwork 90 degrees to the left
	Rotate Right	Rotates artwork 90 degrees to the right
	Free Rotate	Rotates artwork freely in one-degree increments
	Skew	Slants the artwork while maintaining a parallelogram shape
	Warp	Bends and stretches artwork
	Perspective	Makes one part of the artwork appear closer than the other
	Smooth	Softens the edges of artwork
	Trace Edges	Creates an outline around the edges of the artwork
	Invert	Flips the color palette and reassigns all the colors
	Lighten	Increases brightness
	Darken	Decreases brightness
	Fill	Fills the selected area with the foreground color and pattern
	Switch Colors	Switches between the current foreground color and destination color

Choosing a Paint Ink Effect

You can use Paint window inks to create color effects for bitmap cast members. You can select an ink effect from the Ink list arrow at the bottom of the Paint window, as shown in Figure AP-5. The result of the ink you choose depends on whether you are working in color or black and white. Also, some inks work better when you paint with patterns, and others work better when you paint with solid colors. Table AP-5 describes the different ink effects. To apply a Paint ink effect, select the bitmap in the Paint window, click the Ink pop-up menu, then click an ink effect.

TABLE AP-5: Paint ink effects

Paint ink effect	works with	description
Normal	Solids and patterns; B&W and Color	Uses the current foreground color and any selected patterns
Transparent	Patterns; B&W and Color	Makes the background color in patterns transparent; you can see any artwork behind the pattern
Reverse	Solids and patterns; B&W	Changes any color to its mirror color at the opposite end of the color palette; a color 10 spaces from the top of the palette changes to the color 10 spaces from the bottom of the palette
Ghost	Solids (B&W) and patterns (Color)	Paints with the current background color
Gradient	Brush, Bucket, shape tools; B&W and Color	Paints a blend of colors, starting with the foreground color and ending with the destination color
Reveal	Brush, shape tools; B&W and Color	Reveals a previous cast member in its original foreground color
Cycle	Solids and patterns; Color	Cycles through all the colors in the color palette between the foreground color and the destination color
Switch	Brush; Color	Changes any pixels in the foreground color to the destination color
Blend	Solids and patterns; Color	Blends with the background color to create transparent artwork
Darkest	Patterns; Color	Replaces pixels with the artwork color anywhere the foreground color is darker than the pixels of the artwork
Lightest	Patterns; Color	Replaces the pixels with the foreground color anywhere the foreground color is lighter than the pixels of the artwork
Darken	Brush; Color	Reduces the brightness of artwork
Lighten	Brush; Color	Increases the brightness of artwork
Smooth	Brush; Color	Blurs artwork; useful for smoothing out jagged edges
Smear	Brush; Color	Causes the paint of your artwork to spread or smear in the direction you drag
Smudge	Brush; Color	Causes the paint of your artwork to spread; like smear, except that the colors fade faster
Spread	Brush; B&W and Color	Uses the artwork under the brush as the shape for the paintbrush
Clipboard	Brush; B&W and Color	Uses the contents of the clipboard as the pattern for the paintbrush

FIGURE AP-5: Applying Paint ink effects

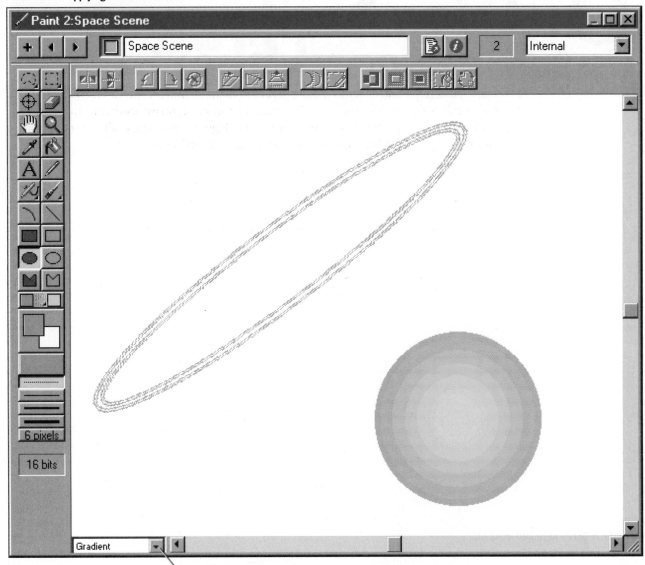

Click arrow to
change ink effects

Director 8

Using Sprite Keyboard Shortcuts

Sometimes, it is easier and faster to use the keyboard than the mouse. You can use key combinations, also called keyboard shortcuts. The most common keyboard shortcuts appear on the right side of menus, as shown in Figure AP-6 and Figure AP-7, while all others appear in Director Help. Table AP-6 lists commonly used sprite keyboard shortcuts.

TABLE AP-6: Sprite keyboard shortcuts

shortcut	Windows	Macintosh
Move 1 pixel in a direction	Arrow keys	Arrow keys
Move 10 pixels in a direction	[Shift][Arrow key]	[Shift][Arrow key]
Open the source cast member	Double-click a sprite	Double-click a sprite
Access the Inks pop-up menu	[Ctrl][Click a sprite]	[Command][Click a sprite]
Display a pop-up menu	Right-click a sprite	[Control][Click a sprite]
Exchange cast members in the Score	[Ctrl][E]	[Command][E]
Delete a sprite	[Backspace]	[Delete]
Find selected cast member in the Score	[Ctrl][H]	[Command][H]
Apply Extend Sprite	[Ctrl][B]	[Command][B]
Join sprites	[Ctrl][J]	[Command][J]
Move playback head to beginning of Score	[Shift][Tab]	[Shift][Tab]
Jump to next marker comment	[Ctrl][Right arrow]	[Command][Right arrow]
Jump to previous marker comment	[Ctrl][Left arrow]	[Command][Left arrow]

FIGURE AP-6: Sprite keyboard shortcuts on the Edit menu

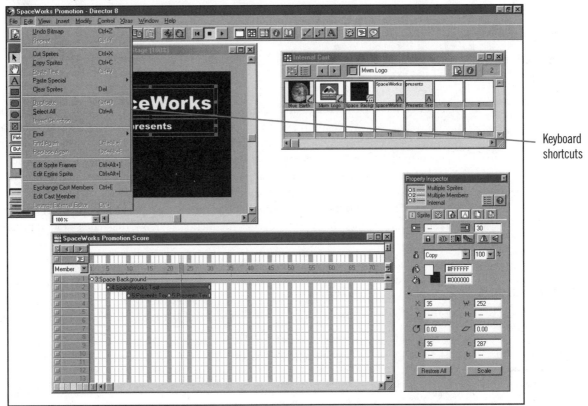

Keyboard shortcuts

FIGURE AP-7: Sprite Keyboard shortcuts on the Modify menu

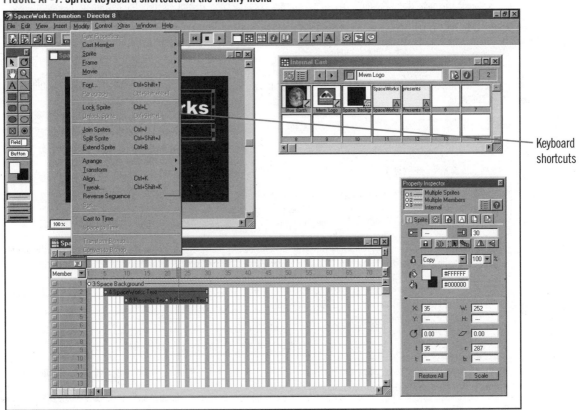

Keyboard shortcuts

Director 8

App

Director 8

Choosing a Sprite Ink Effect

Sprite inks change the display of a sprite's colors. Inks are most useful to hide white backgrounds, but they can also create useful and dramatic color effects. Inks can reverse and alter colors, make sprites change colors depending on the background, and create masks that obscure or reveal portions of a background. Unlike Paint ink effects, which are applied in the Paint window and are permanent, sprite ink effects are applied in the Score and can be changed at any time. Table AP-7 describes the different sprite ink effects. To apply a sprite ink effect, select the sprite in the Score window, click the Ink list arrow in the Sprite tab of the Property Inspector, then click an ink effect, as shown in Figure AP-8. For many ink effects, you can also apply a blend percentage to lighten or darken an ink effect. To apply a blend, click the Blend list arrow, then click a blend percentage.

TABLE AP-7: Sprite ink effects

sprite ink effect	description
Copy	Displays all the original colors in a sprite with a white background; copy is the default ink and animates faster than sprites with any other ink
Matte	Removes the white bounding box around a sprite; artwork within the boundaries is opaque
Background Transparent	Makes the background color of a sprite transparent; you can see the background color on the Stage behind it
Transparent	Makes all light colors of a sprite transparent; you can see any lighter colors behind it
Reverse	Reverses overlapping colors; changes any color to its mirror color at the opposite end of the color palette; a color 10 spaces from the top of the palette changes to the color 10 spaces from the bottom of the palette
Ghost	Reverses overlapping colors; nonoverlapping colors are transparent
Not Copy	Reverses all colors to create a negative of the original
Not Transparent, Not Reverse, Not Ghost	Reverses the foreground color of a sprite, then applies the Not Transparent, Not Reverse, or Not Ghost ink
Mask	Defines the transparent or opaque parts of a sprite
Blend	Blends with the background color to create transparent artwork
Darkest	Compares RGB colors in the foreground and background and uses whichever color is darkest
Lightest	Compares RGB colors in the foreground and background and uses whichever color is lightest
Add	Creates a new color by adding the RGB color values of the foreground and background colors; if the value of the two colors exceeds the maximum RGB color value, Director determines the new color from the color palette
Add Pin	Creates a new color by adding the RGB color values of the foreground and background colors, but the new color value cannot exceed the maximum RGB color value
Subtract	Creates a new color by subtracting the RGB foreground color value from the background color value; if the value of the two colors is less than zero, Director determines the new color from the color palette
Subtract Pin	Creates a new color by subtracting the RGB foreground color value from the background color value, but the new color value cannot be less than zero
Darken	Changes the foreground and background properties of a sprite to darken and tint it on the Stage
Lighten	Changes the foreground and background properties of a sprite to lighten it on the Stage

FIGURE AP-8: Applying a sprite ink effect

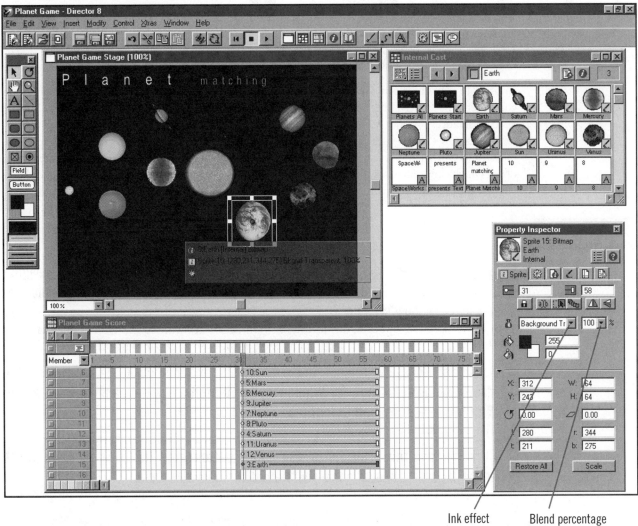

Ink effect   Blend percentage

Director 8

Installing the QuickTime Player

In order to play QuickTime movies in Director, you need to install the QuickTime player on your computer. The QuickTime player is a software product developed by Apple Computer, Inc. for Macintosh and Windows computers. Director 8 supports QuickTime version 3 or later, but recommends version 4. The QuickTime software comes in two versions: QuickTime player, a basic movie player, and QuickTime Pro, a movie creator, editor, and player. You can download the latest version of the QuickTime player for free and QuickTime Pro for a price, from the Apple Computer Web site at www.apple.com. To download the QuickTime player, you need a connection to the Internet.

Steps

1. Start your **Web browser**, connect to the Internet, and go to www.course.com. Navigate to the page for this book, click the link for the Student Online Companion, then click the link for the Appendix

   The Web browser appears, displaying the Web page to download the QuickTime player, as shown in Figure AP-9. The location and look of the Web page for QuickTime may vary.

2. Scroll as necessary, fill out the required information, click the **QuickTime for Macintosh** or **QuickTime for Window option button**, click the **Language list arrow** ▼, then click **Download QuickTime**

   The Download dialog box opens.

3. Click the **Save this program to disk option button**, click **OK**, click the **Look in list arrow** ▼, select a location on your hard disk, then click **Save**

   The QuickTime software is downloaded to the location on your hard disk.

4. Close your Web browser, start **Windows Explorer** (Win) or open **Finder** (Mac), then open the folder with the downloaded QuickTime software

   The QuickTime installation program appears in the window.

5. Double-click the **QuickTimeinstaller icon**, then follow the instructions to download the Minimum QuickTime installation, view the QuickTime README file, and view the Sample Movie

   A window opens with the QuickTime software, the QuickTime README file, and the Sample Movie, as shown in Figure AP-10.

6. Close the QuickTime movie window, QuickTime window, Windows Explorer (Win), and the README file

FIGURE AP-9: Apple Computer's QuickTime Web page

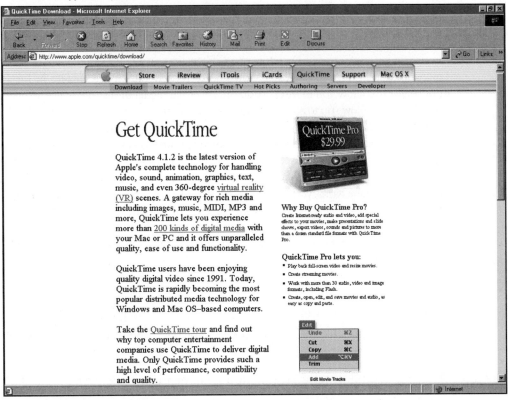

FIGURE AP-10: QuickTime player installation

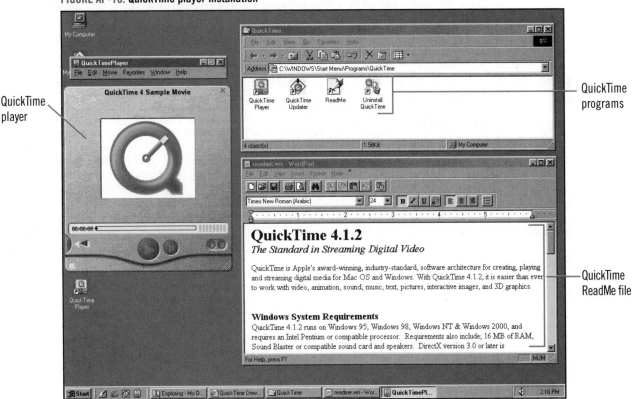

QuickTime player

QuickTime programs

QuickTime ReadMe file

Director 8

Installing an Xtra

An Xtra is a software module you can add to Director, which extends the capabilities of Director. You can use six types of Xtras in Director: image filters, importing, transition, cast member, scripting or Lingo, and tool. Image filters Xtras allow you to modify bitmapped images in the Paint window; importing Xtras allow you to insert additional external media into a movie not standard to Director; transition Xtras allow you to add transition effects not built into Director; cast member Xtras allow you to add new media types, such as a spreadsheet or database, to a movie; scripting Xtras allow you to add new Lingo language elements to Lingo; and tool Xtras allow you to add external authoring aids. Director comes with a set of third-party Xtras on the Director installation CD. You can incorporate these and many other Xtras, which you can find on the Macromedia Web site (www.macromedia.com), into your movies. To use these Xtras, you need to install them first. Xtras are used in Director in different ways. The transition Xtras appear in the Transition dialog box, and the cast member Xtras appear in the Cast window, while other Xtras appear as a menu command on the Xtras menu or the Media Element submenu on the Insert menu. For this example, you install the Fireworks Import Xtra for Director, which imports Fireworks layers, rollovers, and slices, or the DirectMedia Xtra (Win), which plays MPEG movies, by Tabuleiro da Baiana Prod. e Ed Ltda.

Steps

1. Start your Web browser, connect to the Internet, and go to www.course.com. Navigate to the page for this book, click the link for the Student Online Companion, then click the link for the Appendix

QuickTip

You can insert a CD or floppy disk with the third-party Xtra folder.

2. Locate the third-party Xtra, read installation instructions, and download the third-party Xtra from the Internet to a location on your hard disk, as shown in Figure AP-11

For this example, you don't have to download a third-party Xtra. Xtras are included where your Project Files are located.

3. Start **Windows Explorer** (Win) or open **Finder** (Mac), then open the folder with the third-party Xtra

The third-party Xtra folder appears. For this example, you can find the DirectMedia Xtra in the Xtras folder where your Project Files are located.

QuickTip

You can place the Xtra in a folder nested inside the Xtras folder no more than five folder levels.

4. Double-click the installation program and follow the instructions, or drag the third-party Xtra folder in the Xtras folder in the Director program folder, as instructed on the Web site

For example, you can double-click the installation programs (fw4_import_xtra.exe for Windows; fw_import_xtra_for_director for Macintosh) to install a Fireworks import Xtra or (DirectMediaXtra150.exe for Windows) to install the DirectMedia Xtra.

5. Start Director

Trouble?

The menu location of the third-party Xtra command might vary. Read installation information for more details.

6. Click **Insert** on the menu bar, point to **Media Element** or a command related to the Xtra's product name, then click the Xtra command

The Xtra dialog box appears with options.

7. Select the options or files related to the Xtra

In most cases, the Xtra appears in the Cast window, as shown in Figure AP-12.

8. Drag the **Xtra** on the Stage or in the Score

The Xtra works just like any other cast member.

FIGURE AP-11: **File Download dialog box**

Downloading Xtra from the Internet

Click option button to save Xtra to local hard disk or network

FIGURE AP-12: **Director window with a DirectMedia Xtra**

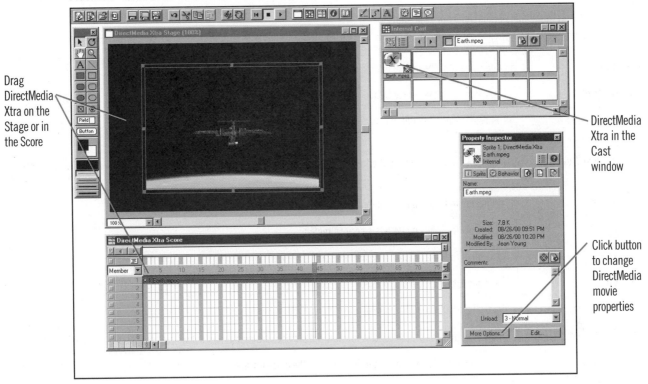

Drag DirectMedia Xtra on the Stage or in the Score

DirectMedia Xtra in the Cast window

Click button to change DirectMedia movie properties

Inserting an ActiveX control

In Director for Windows, you can insert ActiveX controls that let you take advantage of the technology, and adapt ActiveX controls to make them function as sprites in Director. The range of uses for ActiveX in Director is as limitless as the variety of ActiveX controls available. Before you can insert an ActiveX control, you need to use the manufacturer's installation utility to install the ActiveX control in Director on your computer. To insert an ActiveX control on the Stage, click Insert on the menu bar, point to Control, click ActiveX, select the ActiveX control you want to insert, then click OK.

The ActiveX Control Properties dialog box appears, which lets you edit the ActiveX control and view information related to its properties, functionality, and support. Set the values for each property in the ActiveX control, then click OK. The ActiveX control appears in the Cast window. Drag the ActiveX control from the Cast on the Stage, and then it can be repositioned and resized just like any other sprite Xtra. When you pause the movie, the ActiveX control stays in authoring mode and does not react to mouse or keyboard events. When you play the movie, the control responds to user input.

Director 8

App

Director 8

Choosing Behavior Events and Actions

All behaviors detect an event and then perform one or more actions in response. The events and actions included with Director are basic building blocks you can use to create simple or complex behaviors. A behavior performs two main functions. The first function is to detect a specified event, such as a Mouse Up or End Frame, associated with a sprite or frame, and the second one is to perform one or more actions, such as Go to Frame or Wait on Current Frame, in response, as shown in Figure AP-13. The Behavior Inspector lists the most common events and actions used in behaviors. Table AP-8 describes events in the Behavior Inspector, and Table AP-8 describes actions in the Behavior Inspector.

TABLE AP-8: Event Commands in the Behavior Inspector

events and actions	description
Mouse Up	Indicates that the mouse button was released
Mouse Down	Indicates that the mouse button was clicked
Right Mouse Up	Indicates that the right mouse button was released (Win) or that Control was pressed and the mouse button was released (Mac)
Right Mouse Down	Indicates that the right mouse button was clicked (Win) or that Control was pressed and the mouse button was clicked (Mac)
Mouse Enter	Indicates that the pointer entered a sprite's region
Mouse Leave	Indicates that the pointer left a sprite's region
Mouse Within	Indicates that the pointer is within the sprite's region
Key Up	Indicates that a key was released
Key Down	Indicates that a key was pressed
Prepare Frame	Indicates that the playback head has left the previous frame but has not yet entered the next frame
Enter Frame	Indicates that the playback head has entered the current frame
Exit Frame	Indicates that the playback head has exited the current frame
New Event	Indicates that a specified message was received from a script or behavior; you need to supply a name for this event

TABLE AP-9: Action Commands in the Behavior Inspector

events and actions	description
Go to Frame	Moves the playback head to the specified frame
Go to Movie	Opens and plays the specified movie
Go to Marker	Moves the playback head to the specified marker
Go to Net Page	Goes to the specified URL
Wait on Current Frame	Waits at the current frame until another behavior or script advances to the next frame
Wait until Click	Waits at the current frame until the mouse button is clicked
Wait until Key Press	Waits at the current frame until a key is pressed

TABLE AP-9: Action Commands in the Behavior Inspector (continued)

events and actions	description
Wait for Time Duration	Waits at the current frame for the specified time
Play Cast Member	Plays the specified sound cast member
Play External File	Plays the specified external sound file
Beep	Plays the current system beep
Set Volume	Sets the system volume level to the specified setting
Change Tempo	Changes the movie's tempo to the specified setting
Perform Transition	Performs the specified transition
Change Palette	Changes to the specified palette
Change Location	Moves the current sprite to the specified coordinates
Change Cast Member	Switches the sprite's cast member to the specified cast member
Change Ink	Switches to the specified ink
Change Cursor	Changes the pointer to a shape you choose from the pop-up menu
Restore Cursor	Restores the current system pointer
New Action	Executes any Lingo function or sends a message to a handler; you specify the new handler's name

FIGURE AP-13 Behavior Inspector

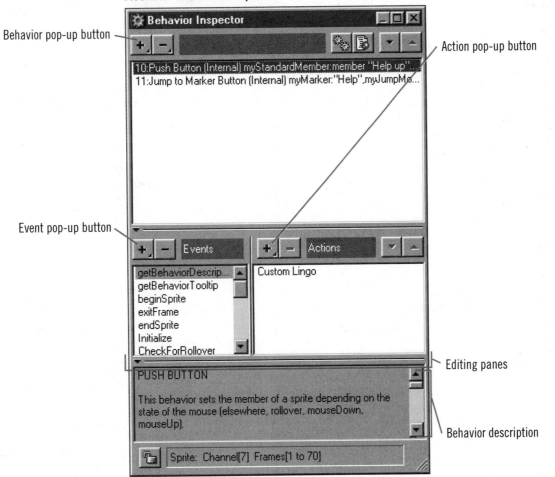

Behavior pop-up button

Action pop-up button

Event pop-up button

Editing panes

Behavior description

Director 8

App

Director 8

Choosing Event Handlers

An event is an action, such as a mouse click, that is performed during the playback of a movie. Each time an event occurs, Director sends a message to execute a handler corresponding to that event. Event handlers are Lingo commands grouped together to perform one or more procedures. There are two types of event handlers: predefined system handlers and user-defined handlers. Predefined system event handlers are built-in handlers that recognize Director events. Table AP-10 identifies the predefined system event handlers and the script types in which they will run. User-defined event handlers are custom handlers that recognize actions defined by the developer. Because multiple handlers can respond to the same kind of event, Director uses a structured handler hierarchy in determining the order in which scripts respond to a handler, as shown in Figure AP-14.

TABLE AP-10: Predefined system event handlers

events	primary event handler	sprite script	cast member script	frame script	movie script
prepareMovie					✓
prepareFrame		✓	✓	✓	✓
startMovie					✓
stopMovie					✓
beginSprite		✓		✓	
enterFrame		✓		✓	✓
exitFrame		✓		✓	✓
endSprite		✓		✓	
mouseDown	✓	✓	✓	✓	✓
mouseUp	✓	✓	✓	✓	✓
mouseEnter		✓	✓		
mouseLeave		✓	✓		
mouseUpOutside		✓	✓		
mouseWithin		✓	✓		
rightMouseDown	✓	✓	✓	✓	✓
keyDown	✓	✓	✓	✓	✓
keyUp	✓	✓	✓	✓	✓
timeout	✓				
idle				✓	✓

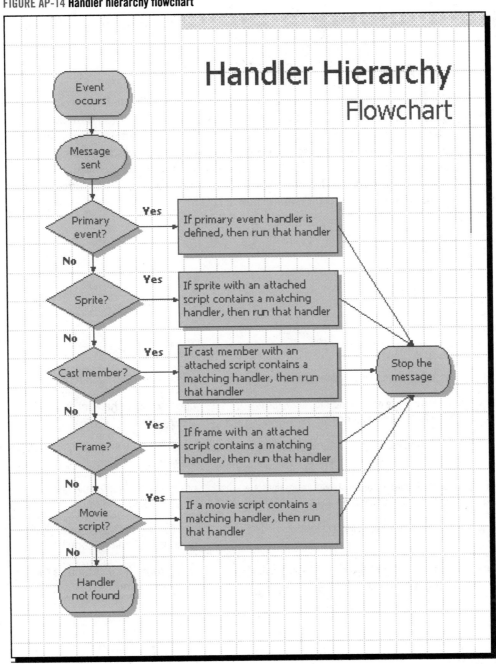

Handler Hierarchy
Flowchart

Event occurs

Message sent

Primary event? — **Yes** → If primary event handler is defined, then run that handler

No

Sprite? — **Yes** → If sprite with an attached script contains a matching handler, then run that handler

No

Cast member? — **Yes** → If cast member with an attached script contains a matching handler, then run that handler

No

Frame? — **Yes** → If frame with an attached script contains a matching handler, then run that handler

No

Movie script? — **Yes** → If a movie script contains a matching handler, then run that handler

No

Handler not found

Stop the message

Message handler exceptions

When Director finds a matching handler for a message, the handler executes the Lingo commands, and the message does not continue to the next level in the hierarchy. One exception occurs when a sprite has multiple behaviors attached to it with the same handler. If a sprite has both a cast member script and a behavior script, the behavior script takes precedence in trapping events. This is important to keep in mind when you decide which type of script to use. If a movie contains two movie scripts that respond to the same event, only the first one that Director finds is executed. Director ignores the other movie script. If the event associated with a handler doesn't occur in the duration of a sprite or frame, Director continues to play the movie.

Using Lingo Rules and Elements

Lingo scripts are composed of handlers. In the middle of a handler is a combination of Lingo elements, which form the statements, such as **go to frame 1**, that you want the script to execute when the handler is triggered, as shown in Figure AP-15. Like most programming languages, Lingo has rules about how you can use Lingo elements to produce valid statements. See Table AP-11 for a list of some common Lingo rules. If you work on Windows and Macintosh platforms, note that there are some important differences in how Lingo interprets keyboard commands. See Table AP-12 for a list of Lingo elements for cross-platform keys.

TABLE AP-11: **Lingo rules**

category	rule	example
Parentheses	You need to use parentheses to define a function.	sprite(whichSpriteNumber).color
	You can use parentheses after keywords to refer to the sprite or cast member object.	open window (the application Path & "theMovie")
	You can use parentheses to establish precedence in math operations.	The expression 10 * 6 - 4 will yield 56, while 10 * (6 - 4) will yield 20
Character spaces	Words within statements and expressions are separated by spaces. Lingo ignores extra spaces.	play movie "Help" is the same as play movie "Help"
Uppercase and lowercase letters	You can use uppercase and lowercase letters.	Go To Frame "Main Menu" is the same as go to frame "main menu"
Abbreviated commands	You can abbreviate some Lingo commands to make them easier to enter.	go to frame "Main Menu" is the same as go "Main Menu"

TABLE AP-12: **Lingo elements for cross-platform keys**

Lingo element	Windows key	Macintosh key
Return	Enter	Return
commandDown	Ctrl	Command
optionDown	Alt	Option
controlDown	Ctrl	Control
Enter	Enter key on the numeric keypad	Enter key on the numeric keypad
Backspace	Backspace	Delete

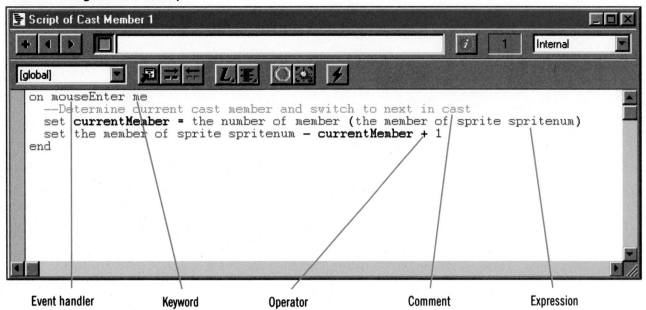

Event handler   Keyword   Operator   Comment   Expression

Director 8

Project Files List

To complete many of the lessons and practice exercises in this book, students need to use a Project File that is supplied by Course Technology. Once obtained, students select where to store the files, such as to the hard disk drive, network server, or Zip disk. Depending on where students store the files, you might need to relink any external files, such as a QuickTime (.mov) or AVI (.avi) video file, associated with a Director project file. When you open a project file, Director will ask you the location of the external file. Below is a list of the files that are supplied, and the unit or practice exercise to which the files correspond. For information on how to obtain Project Files, please see the inside cover of this book. The following list only includes Project Files that are supplied; it does not include the files students create from scratch or the files students create by revising the supplied files. Note that Unit G contains files that are Macintosh-specific.

Unit	File or Folder supplied	Folder File supplied	Location file is used in unit
Director Unit A	MD A-1.dir		Lessons/Skills Review
Director Unit B	MD B-1		Lessons/Skills Review
	Media folder	Space Background.gif Blue Earth.jpg Mwm Logo.tif	
Director Unit C	MD C-1.dir		Lessons/Skills Review
Director Unit D	MD D-1.dir		Lessons
	Media folder	Colorful Star.gif Jupiter.gif Space Background.gif 4 Planets.jpg 9 Planets.jpg Blue Earth.jpg Mostly Space.jpg Saturn.jpg Space Planet.jpg Uranus.jpg	Lessons/Skills Review
Director Unit E	MD E-1.dir		Lessons
	MD E-2.dir		Skills Review
Director Unit F	MD F-1.dir		Lessons
	MD F-2.dir		Skills Review

Unit	File or Folder supplied	Folder File supplied	Location file is used in unit
Director Unit G	MD G-1.dir MD G-2.ppt MD G-2m.ppt (Mac)		Lessons
	Media folder	Blastoff.mov Blastoff.wav Blastoffm.swa (Mac) Earthvenus.avi Meteor.wav	
	MD G-3.dir MD G-4.ppt MD G-4m.ppt (Mac)		Skills Review
	Media SR folder	Birds.wav Birdsm.swa (Mac) Dog.aiff Dog.mov Eagle.wav Lion.au Monkey.au Monkey.mov Tiger.au Tiger.avi Wolf.au Wolf.mov	
	MD G-5.ppt MD G-5m.ppt (Mac)		Independent Challenge 3
Director Unit H	MD H-1.dir Saturn.mov		Lessons
	MD H-2.dir Monkey.mov Tiger.mov Wolf.mov		Skills Review
	Earth.mpeg		Independent Challenge 4
Director Unit I	MD I-1.dir		Lessons
	Media	Orange Storm.gif Light Blue Storm.gif Color Table.act (Win) Color Tablem (Mac) Color Storm.gif	
	MD I-2		Skills Review
	Media SR	Color Meter Table.act (Win) Color Meter Tablem (Mac) Color Meter.gif	
Director Unit J	MD J-1		Lessons
	MD J-2		Skills Review
	Shuttle.jpg		Visual Workshop
Director Unit K	MD K-1.dir Help.dir		Lessons
	MD K-2.dir Guide.dir		Skills Review

Unit	File or Folder supplied	Folder File supplied	Location file is used in unit
Director Unit L	MD L-1 Online Help.dir		Lessons
	MD L-2 Loan Guide.dir		Skills Review
Director Appendix	Xtras	DirectMediaXtra150 fw3_import_xtra (Win) FW3 Import Xtra for Director (Mac)	Lessons
Shockwave Unit A	SW A-1.dir		Lessons
	SW A-2.dir		Skills Review
	SW A-3.dir		Independent Challenge 3
Shockwave Unit B	SW B-1.dir		Lessons
	SW B-2.dir		Skills Review
Fireworks Unit A	Rocket.gif Coral planet.gif		Lessons
	Comet.jpg Earthmoon.gif		Visual Workshop
Fireworks Unit B	FW B-1.png FW B-2.png		Lessons
	FW B-3.png FW B-4.png		Skills Review
	FW B-5.png		Independent Challenge 3
	FW B-6.png		Visual Workshop
	Media folder	Earth01.gif Earth02.gif Earth03.gif Earth04.gif Earth05.gif Earth06.gif Earth07.gif Earth08.gif Earth09.gif Earth10.gif	Lessons/Skills Review
		Mwm Logo.tif Orange rings.gif	Independent Challenge 1

Glossary

& A variable that connects the strings in quotes (").

&& A variable that connects the strings and adds a space in between.

Active A window with a blue title bar, indicating any actions you perform will take place in this window.

Actual tempo Documents the real speed of playback.

Align window Moves sprites not to a specific location on the Stage, but to positions relative to one another.

Animated Apparent movement that appears by displaying a series of still images in rapid succession.

Animation library Behaviors that make sprites move in sophisticated ways. Consists of three categories: Automatic, Interactive, and Sprite Transitions.

Anti-aliasing Blends the bitmap's colors with background colors around the edges to make the edge appear smooth instead of jagged.

Arguments Placeholders that pass values to scripts.

Authoring tool A software program, also known as a development platform, that allows you to create your own software.

Background color The secondary color in multicolored patterns.

Behavior channel A place to write frame scripts, also known as the script channel.

Behavior scripts (sprite and frame) Lingo scripts that add interactivity to a movie using over 100 built-in library behaviors.

Bézier curve A type of vector shape curve.

Bit depth A measure of how much data space is available to store a given moment of sound. The higher the bit depth, the higher the sound quality.

Bitmap A pixel-by-pixel representation of a graphic.

Bitmap image An image composed of tiny dots, or pixels.

Blend The transparency level of a sprite.

Blend list arrow Selects a blending percentage.

Blend value Makes a sprite more or less transparent. A blend value of 100% makes a sprite completely opaque and a blend value of 0% makes a sprite completely transparent.

Breakpoint A location in a script where you want Director to stop executing Lingo commands.

Brightness A measure of how much black is mixed with the color.

Bullet mark An identifying feature indicating that an option is enabled.

Button Editor Docked on the right edge of the Fireworks workspace, used to create rollover buttons and navigation bars using JavaScript.

Cartridges Shockwave movies played in Shockmachine.

Case statement Commands used to replace a chain of If-then statements.

Cast Library A special type of unlinked External Cast. Libraries are useful for storing any type of commonly used cast members, especially behaviors.

Cast member scripts Scripts attached to a specific cast member that cannot be shared.

Cast members Media elements in the Cast window.

Cast window The storage area that contains media elements, such as graphics, images, digital videos, sounds, animations, text, color palettes, film loops, and scripts.

Channels Rows in the Score window.

Chat room An interactive discussion on a specific topic.

Check mark An identifying mark indicating that a feature is currently selected.

Child objects A child script that is executed only when a rule is met for its parent script.

Closed shape A shape in which the points do connect.

Color cycling A special color palette effect that changes the appearance of a display by rapidly showing each color from a range of colors in a sequence.

Color mode Director specifies color in RGB (Red, Green, Blue) and palette index modes. The RGB color mode identifies a color by a set of hexadecimal numbers that specify the amounts of red, green, and blue needed to create the color. The palette index color mode identifies a color by the number (0 through 255) of its position in a color palette.

Color palette A set of colors used by a movie or cast members.

Command A directive that accesses a program's feature.

Comments Information, such as notes or instructions, that you can add to a script.

Compression Reduces the size of a file. The higher the compression ratio, the smaller the file size.

Constraints Elements that never change, such as TRUE and FALSE constants.

Context-sensitive help A help function that specifically relates to what you are doing.

Control handles Vector shape components that determine the degree of curvature between the vertices.

Control Panel A way to control the playback of a movie using VCR-type controls, including rewind, stop, and play buttons.

Controls library Behaviors that create and control user interface elements, such as push, toggle, and radio buttons, check boxes, pop-up menus, and tooltips.

Cue point A marker in a sound or video that you can use to trigger an event in Director.

Destination color The ending color of gradient blends that start with the foreground color.

Development platform A software program, also known as an authoring tool, that allows you to create your own software.

Dialog box An onscreen display, indicated by an ellipsis, used to enter or select information.

Dithering Blends the colors in the new palette to approximate the original colors in the bitmap.

Document A graphic image in Fireworks.

Document window The area in Fireworks in which you create and modify images.

Dynamic color management The use of a changeable color palette in Windows that lets the program define all but 16 colors, which Windows reserves for its interface elements, in the 256-color palette.

Editable button Sets a text sprite's editable property.

Editable property Allows users to enter text on the Stage while the movie is playing.

Editable sprites Allows end users to enter text (in a field or text sprite) on the Stage while the movie is playing.

Effects channels The upper channels in the Score window.

End frame The last frame in a sprite, denoted in a sprite by a small bar.

Expressions Parts of a Lingo statement that generate values.

External Cast A cast that is saved in a separate file outside of the movie.

Film loop Combines many sprites and effects over a range of frames into a single cast member.

Field text The text created using the field tool or field window.

Director 8

File A collection of information stored together as an individual unit.

File extension A three-letter extension at the end of a file-name that identifies the file type for the operating system.

First line indent marker Sets the indent for only the first line of the text in a paragraph.

Flip Flips a sprite horizontally or vertically.

Flip horizontal button Flips a sprite horizontally.

Flip vertical button Flips a sprite vertically.

Floppy disk Removable media that you insert into the disk drive of your computer.

Foreground and Background color The color or tint of a sprite.

Foreground color The default color used with the painting tools, the fill color for solid patterns, and the primary color in multicolored patterns.

Foreground or Background color box Used to select a color from the color palette.

Frame channel The shaded channel, also known as the timeline, which contains the numbers that identify the frame number.

Frame delay The rate at which each frame is displayed in Fireworks.

Frame-by-frame animation A series of cast members placed in the Score one frame at a time. The process involves altering cast members slightly from frame to frame to build an animated sequence.

Frame scripts One way to add interactivity and extended functionality to a movie.

Frames Columns in the Score window.

Frames per second (fps) A measurement of a movie's tempo in frames per second.

FTP File Transfer Protocol – a method used to transfer files over a network or the Internet.

Functions Operations that return a value.

GIF Graphics Interchange Format file format uses only 256 colors, but doesn't lose any image quality in the compression.

Gradient blend Shading from one color to another color.

Grid A set of rows and columns of a specified height and width that are used to help place sprites on the Stage (Director), or objects in the document window (Fireworks).

Grouping The process used to turn multiple objects into single objects.

Guides Horizontal or vertical lines you can either drag around the Stage or lock in place to help you align sprites in a straight line (Director), or non-printing green lines that help you position and align objects because objects automatically snap to them (Fireworks).

Handles Small dots that display around the perimeter of a selected object in Fireworks.

Handlers Respond to messages triggered by a specific event during the movie's playback. A handler starts in the Behavior Script window with the word *on* followed by the name of a trigger message.

Hanging indent Indent where the first line left margin starts at 0" while the margin for the remaining lines starts at 1".

Hard disk The storage media that is built into the computer.

Highlight White text on a black background indicating that the text has been selected.

Hotspot A specific area in an image that initiates an event from a mouse activation.

HTML Hypertext Markup Language

Hue The color created by mixing primary colors (Red, Blue, and Yellow).

If-then A structure that evaluates a statement and then branches to outcomes. If the statement is TRUE, the command after *then* is executed. If the statement is FALSE, the command after *else* is executed.

Indent markers Displayed on the ruler, they show the indent settings for the paragraph that contains the insertion point in the text window.

Ink effect Changes the display of a sprite's colors.

Ink list arrow Sets an ink effect for a sprite.

Inspector Docked on the right edge of the Fireworks workspace, used to control the characteristics of selected objects.

Instances Copies of the same Fireworks symbol that update automatically when the original is modified.

Interactive multimedia Software produced with Director that combines the elements of interactivity and multimedia.

Interactivity A software program that includes user feedback and navigation.

Internal Cast An internal storage area for cast members that is saved as part of the movie.

Internet bandwidth The amount of data that can be transmitted over the Internet in one second.

Internet library Behaviors that control activities on the Web. Consists of three categories: Forms, Multiuser, and Streaming.

IP Internet Protocol address, which is a unique set of four numbers that identifies your computer on a network or the Web.

Irregular shape A freeform object.

JPEG Joint Photographic Experts Group file format supports millions of colors (24-bit color depth), but loses image quality by discarding image data in the compression.

Java applet A movie converted to Java, a programming language. Java applets created in Director provide extended functionality to play simple movies in a Web browser where plug-ins, such as the Shockwave player, are not allowed.

Kerning A specialized form of spacing between certain parts of characters, kerning improves the appearance of text in large sizes but does very little to improve small text.

Keyboard shortcuts Keyboard combinations that you use to perform commands and functions instead of clicking the mouse. The most common keyboard shortcuts appear on the right side of menus.

Keyframe The first frame in a sprite, denoted in a sprite by a circle.

Keywords Reserved words in Lingo that have special meaning.

Lasso tool Tool in the Paint window that selects anything that is surrounded with it.

Left indent marker Sets the indent for entire text in a paragraph.

Library behaviors Adds navigation controls and interaction to a movie using a built-in behavior from the Library palette with a prewritten Lingo script.

Linear gradient Shading from one color on one side to another color on the other side.

Lingo Director's programming language.

Lingo script Creates simple scripts that can be attached to sprites or frames to navigate to a specific location in a movie. You can create a script by double-clicking a frame in the Behavior channel, and then typing one or more Lingo instructions.

Lock button Used to set a sprite's locking property.

Locking property Locks a sprite on the Stage to prevent any changes made to the sprite.

Luminosity A measure of how much black is mixed with the color.

Marker A number or a distinctive icon at the beginning of each channel.

Marquee tool Tool in the Paint window that selects everything within its rectangle bounds.

me A keyword in a Lingo command that refers to an object without actually naming it.

Media library   Behaviors that control Flash, QuickTime, and Sound media.

Menu   A list of commands that you use to accomplish certain tasks.

Menu bar   Organizes commands into groups of related operations. You can choose a menu command by clicking it or by pressing [Alt] plus the underlined letter in the menu name (Win), or by pressing [Command] plus the designated letter (Mac).

MIAW   A Movie in a Window script that opens and plays another movie in a separate window while the main movie plays on the Stage.

Moveable button   Sets a sprite's moveable property in the Sprite tab of the Property Inspector.

Moveable property   Allows users to drag a sprite on the Stage while the movie is playing.

Movie   A Director file.

Movie scripts   Scripts that are available during playback of the entire movie; they are not attached to any object.

MP3   Moving Pictures Experts Group (MPEG) Audio Layer 3 – an audio compression technology.

Multimedia   A combination of graphics, images, digital video, sound, text, and animation.

Navigation library   Behaviors that control the movement and location of the playback head.

Object   Any part of Lingo scripting that is designed to both receive input and produce a result.

Object mode   The default mode into which a document opens in Fireworks, where each object is composed of pixels, or tiny dots, that form paths and points.

Open shape   A shape in which the starting point and the ending point do not connect.

Optimize   A process that fine-tunes or reduces the appearance of the document without losing image quality.

Paintbox library   Behaviors that create and modify bitmap images using Director's built-in drawing tools.

Palette channel   Sets the available colors for the movie.

Panel   Docked on the right edge of the Fireworks workspace, used to control options on a document or tool.

Parent scripts   An advanced form of programming that contain Lingo statements used to create child scripts.

Path name   The full name that includes specific information about the file's location on a floppy disk, CD-ROM, hard disk, or network.

Pixel   An individual point in a graphic with a distinct color.

Playback events   Events related to what happens when the playback head moves to another frame and when a movie is launched.

Playback head   The object in the frame channel that moves through the Score, indicating the frame that is currently displayed on the Stage.

Postscript   A common graphics format.

Preload value   Determines when cast members are loaded into memory as the movie plays.

Projector movie   A stand-alone program that end users can play on their computers without having Director installed.

Property Inspector   A way to view and change attributes of any selected object or multiple objects in a movie.

Protected movie   An uncompressed movie that end users cannot open and modify in Director. Protected movies do not include any player software to play the movie.

QuickDraw graphics   Shapes created with the tool palette.

Radial gradient   Shading from one color in the center to another color on the outside.

RAM (random access memory)   A temporary storage space that is erased when the computer is turned off.

Real-time recording Records the movement of a cast member on the Stage. The process involves setting up the recording attributes and manually dragging a cast member around the Stage.

Registration point Adjusts the location of a sprite on the Stage by entering a horizontal (X) and vertical (Y) value measured from the top left corner of the Stage.

Regular shape An oval, rectangle, or rounded rectangle.

Regular text The text created using the text tool or text window.

Remapping Replaces the original colors in the bitmap with the most similar solid colors in the new palette, which is often the preferred option.

Removable media Portable media that you insert into the disk drive of your computer.

Resize Adjusts the size of a sprite by dragging a resize handle on the Stage or by entering width (W:) and height (H:) dimensions in the Sprite tab of the Property Inspector.

Restore Re-establishes the height and width to the cast member by using the Restore All button.

Right indent marker Sets the indent for the text from the right margin in a paragraph.

Rollover An effect that causes a change elsewhere on the Web page, such as that triggered by a mouse pointer.

Rotate Rotates a sprite by entering a number of degrees; a positive number rotates the sprite clockwise in degrees and a negative number rotates it counterclockwise.

Rulers Horizontal and vertical rulers in Fireworks that display in the document window that you can use to determine an object's precise position.

Sampling rate The frequency with which samples are taken per second, measured in kilohertz, or kHz.

Saturation A measure of how much white is mixed in with the color. A fully saturated color is vivid; a less saturated color is washed-out pastel.

Scale button Proportionately resizes a sprite.

Score window The window that organizes and controls media elements over a linear timeline.

ScreenTip A feature that displays the name of a button on the toolbar, or additional information when you position the mouse pointer over a button (Fireworks).

Script channel A place to write frame scripts, also known as the behavior channel.

Seconds per frame (spf) Seconds per frame, a more accurate measure of a movie's tempo.

Select Text that has been highlighted.

Server A computer on a network.

Server port The communications port number where the server communicates with the Director movie.

Shockwave A separate program that lets you play, collect, and manage Shockwave movies, especially games, offline.

Shockwave movie A compressed movie that does not include the standard player. A Shockwave movie is intended for play over the Internet in a Web browser.

Shockwave projector movie A compressed movie that end users can play on their computers independent of a Web browser.

Skew Tilts a sprite. Entering a positive value skews the sprite to the right; entering a negative value skews it to the left.

Slice An area within a document that can be manipulated separately from the main document.

Sound channels Used to add music, sound effects, and voice-overs.

Span duration A default duration of 28 frames that each new sprite contains.

Spread value Controls whether the gradient is weighted more toward the start color or end color. Values greater than 100 weight the gradient toward the starting color, and vice versa.

Sprite A representation of a cast member that has been placed on the Stage or in the Score.

Sprite bar The line that connects the circle and the small bar.

Sprite channels The numbered channels at the bottom of the Score window used to assemble and synchronize all the cast members in the Cast window.

Sprite label The text that identifies the sprite in the Score window.

Sprite Overlay Panel Displays important sprite properties directly on the Stage.

Sprite span The range of frames in which the sprite appears.

Stage window Serves as the viewing area for the visual elements of a Director movie.

Standard player A self-contained Director movie player that the projector uses to play the Director movie.

Start frame The first frame in a sprite.

Status bar Appears at the bottom of the Fireworks application window (Windows) or the bottom of the document window (Mac). It contains information about any selected objects, a description of a selected tool, and contains VCR buttons that can be used to run animations.

Step recording A process of real-time recording of one frame at a time that involves setting up the recording attributes, moving the playback head forward one frame, changing the sprites' attributes, and moving the playback head forward again one frame.

Stereo or mono encoding Two types of sound quality. Stereo encoding produces high-quality sound, but the file size associated with a stereo file is twice the size of a mono sound.

Streaming The process that allows you to view a Shockwave movie in your browser while it continues to download from the Web.

String The part of a Lingo statement that is in quotes.

Stroke width Determines the thickness of lines and outlines.

SWA Shockwave Audio – Shockwave's audio compression tool.

Symbol An original designated object inserted into a Fireworks document.

Tab Used to position text at a specific location in the text window.

Tab stop A predefined position in the text to which you can align tabbed text. By default, tab stops are located every ½" from the left margin.

Tempo The speed of a movie.

Tempo channel Used to adjust the speed or time of the movie as it plays.

Tempo mode Displays the playback rate that Director is currently attempting to achieve.

Tempo settings Sets the speed of the movie and pauses the movie at a specific frame.

Text library Behaviors that format numbers, force upper or lowercase characters, and create hypertext.

Tile A graphic used to repeat in a pattern to create backgrounds, textures, or fillers.

Time events Events related to the operating system and the end user when nothing is happening.

Timeline The shaded channel, also known as the frame channel, which contains the numbers that identify the frame number.

Title bar Displays the filename of the open file.

Title bar Displays the name of the open Fireworks document, the program name, a Control Menu box, a Close button, and resizing buttons.

Tool palette Contains a set of tools used to create shapes, such as lines, rectangles, rounded rectangles, and ellipses.

Toolbar Contains buttons for the most frequently used commands.

Toolbox Contains a set of Fireworks tools you can use to make selections, draw objects, edit shapes, magnify, create clickable areas, and add color and outlines to objects.

Trail property Leaves a trail of images on the Stage.

Trails button Sets a sprite's trail property in the Sprite tab of the Property Inspector.

Transition channel Sets screen transitions, such as fades, wipes, dissolves, and zooms.

Transition setting Sets a transition effect used to move smoothly from one scene to another, and also sets the duration and smoothness of a transition.

Tweening A way to make a sprite move from one position to another.

Ungrouping The process used to separate grouped objects into their original components.

Unload value Determines which cast members stay in memory and which ones are removed when the movie plays.

URL Uniform Resource Locator is a Web address.

User feedback events Events related to mouse and keyboard action performed by the end user.

Vector image An image composed of paths and points, rather than pixels.

Vector shape A mathematical description of a geometric form.

Vertices Fixed points of a vector shape.

Web Layer Appears in every Fireworks document as the top layer in each new document and contains the interactive elements.

White board A method for online participants to simultaneously view multiple participants' input.

Windoid A window that can be moved but not resized.

Window events Events related to the times when multiple Director movies are running in multiple windows.

Workspace The entire Fireworks screen.

Xtra A software module you can add to Director, which extends the capabilities of Director.

Index

Index

Index

Index

Index

Index

Index